D0930040

Advance Praise for
Empower Your Investing: Adopting Best Practices from
John Templeton, Peter Lynch, and Warren Buffett

"If you only read one book about investing, make it this one! Scott Chapman is absolutely brilliant at bringing together in one book the lessons of three legendary investing masters: Sir John Templeton, Peter Lynch, and Warren Buffett. You will learn fascinating stories about their background, their investment approach, philosophy, and timeless nuggets of wisdom, as well as case studies for each investor."

—THOMAS M. ARRINGTON, CFA, Investment Professional
with over thirty years of experience in the financial services industry

"Scott has unveiled methods of determining investment values that have resulted in his own track record of consistently outperforming the market and other fund managers. Enjoy reading this timeless book that will also enhance your understanding and appreciation of the successful methods used by the icons of stock investing."

—GEOFFREY HEATHCOCK, Director of Corporate Development at Fortune 500
companies and Professor of Finance and Accounting for over thirty years

"Scott Chapman's book is a clear read for any investor who wants to learn how to invest better. Scott is a successful long-term investor and educator who is someone all investors can learn from. He shares some of the best investment advice and actual experiences of three of the best investors in history—Peter Lynch, Warren Buffett, and Sir John Templeton. This book will help every person improve their investment skill from the beginning investor to professionally trained CFA analysts."

—CRAIG BRAEMER, CFA, Blossom Wealth portfolio manager
and founder of Braemer Asset Management, LLC

"Just as athletes might study Michael Jordan, Mohammed Ali, and Babe Ruth, every investor should know and understand John Templeton, Peter Lynch, and Warren Buffett. Scott Chapman brilliantly showcases the investment world's Greatest of All Time (G.O.A.T.) so every stock market participant, from novice to seasoned professional, can learn the lessons of those who have reached the pinnacle of success. With a comprehensive step-by-step approach, Chapman provides a deep understanding of what it takes to be the best."

—ROBERT P. MILES, Author, *The Warren Buffett CEO*;
Executive in Residence, University of Nebraska at Omaha

EMPOWER YOUR
INVESTING

ADOPTING
BEST PRACTICES FROM

JOHN TEMPLETON, PETER LYNCH,
AND WARREN BUFFETT

SCOTT A. CHAPMAN, CFA

A POST HILL PRESS BOOK

Empower Your Investing:
Adopting Best Practices from John Templeton, Peter Lynch, and Warren Buffett
© 2019 by Scott A. Chapman, CFA
All Rights Reserved

ISBN: 978-1-64293-238-6
ISBN (eBook): 978-1-64293-239-3

Cover design by Howry Design Associates
Author Photo by Gina Logan Photography

Excerpt(s) from THE SNOWBALL: WARREN BUFFETT AND THE BUSINESS OF LIFE by Alice Schroeder, copyright © 2008 by Alice Schroeder. Used by permission of Bantam Books, an imprint of Random House, a division of Penguin Random House LLC. All rights reserved.

From BEATING THE STREET by Peter Lynch. Copyright © 1993, 1994 by Peter Lynch. Reprinted with the permission of Simon & Schuster, Inc. All rights reserved.

From ONE UP ON WALL STREET: How to Use What You Already Know to Make Money in the Market by Peter Lynch. Copyright © 1989 by Peter Lynch. Introduction copyright 2000 by Peter Lynch. Reprinted with the permission of Simon & Schuster, Inc. All rights reserved.

Excerpt(s) from INVESTMENT GURUS: A ROAD MAP TO WEALTH FROM THE WORLD'S BEST MONEY MANAGERS by Peter J. Tanous, copyright © 1997 by Peter J. Tanous. Used by permission of Berkley, an imprint of Penguin Publishing Group, a division of Penguin Random House LLC. All rights reserved.

The information and advice herein is not intended to replace the services of financial professionals, with knowledge of your personal financial situation. The advice and strategies contained herein may not be suitable for your situation. You should consult with a professional where appropriate. Neither the publisher nor author shall be liable for any loss of any profit or any other commercial damages, including, but not limited to special, incidental, consequential, or other damages. All investments are subject to risk, which should be considered prior to making any financial decisions.

No part of this book may be reproduced, stored in a retrieval system, or transmitted by any means without the written permission of the author and publisher.

PRESS
Post Hill Press
New York • Nashville
posthillpress.com

Published in the United States of America

To my family and friends who believed in me, especially Celeste.

To entrepreneurs whose ingenuity and growth mindset enhance our standard of living and make investing rewarding.

To you, dear reader, with gratitude and best wishes that with these investment best practices, you can empower your financial future.

Table of Contents

List of Figures

Introduction

I think the best investment most people can make is in themselves.

—WARREN BUFFETT[1]

The market, like the Lord, helps those who help themselves. But, unlike the Lord, the market does not forgive those who know not what they do.

—WARREN BUFFETT[2]

If you want to learn how to complete the grueling Ironman Triathlon, would you prepare for it by reading about the theory of calorie consumption and hydration authored by professors, or would you prefer to read about it by those who have successfully completed the event—or better yet, won it convincingly? Most of us will never attempt the Ironman Triathlon, but we all have an interest in preparing ourselves as investors for the challenging journey of funding a home, an education, or a retirement. Professional investors have a duty to arm themselves with wisdom born from the experience and best practices of great investors, yet the industry offers little to no practical training. Many seasoned investors hold their cards close to the vest and ask young professionals to sink or swim on their own. What is needed is a proven investment model based on best practices of master investors in one convenient book.

On my first day on the job as a professional investor in 1989, I was given a desk and a phone. The managing partner said, "You don't need anything fancy like a computer, do you?" A few years later I was working as a securities analyst for another west coast investment firm, supporting a number of portfolio managers. I expressed interest, in particular, in the firm's growth stock mutual fund. In 1993 the firm reassigned two successive portfolio managers due to poor performance as the fund was ranked one star—the lowest performing category—by the mutual fund rating agency Morningstar Inc. There were serious discussions by senior management of discarding the mutual fund. Fortunately, the Chief Investment Officer believed the firm needed to complement its flagship value-based mutual fund, and he defended the growth mutual fund. With his ringing endorsement, he looked at me and said, "Well, I guess you're it."

I couldn't have been more excited. I had the energy, enthusiasm, passion, and credentials for the job but still felt naked in my new responsibility as a portfolio manager. I had a bachelor's degree in Accounting, an MBA in Finance, earned my Chartered Financial Analyst (CFA) designation, taught several years of evening review classes for CFA candidates, had thirteen years of experience as a financial and securities analyst, and yet I still felt unprepared because I lacked the wisdom of experience and the knowledge of best practices.

When I was a young boy, I admired the San Francisco Giants center fielder, Willie Mays. I studied his batting stance, how he positioned himself in centerfield to anticipate the ball differently for each hitter and in different game situations. I studied how he warmed up and how he interacted with his teammates, opposing players, and umpires. I admired his love for the game and, in my own way, tried to emulate his best traits in my Little League games. In later years, I attempted to play basketball in the style of Larry Bird, while my close friend and work colleague looked and played like Magic Johnson. We played endless games at lunch and on weekends borrowing from the style of our basketball heroes. We loved how Bird and Magic elevated their teams, and we tried to model that on the court as well as in the office. Today I see adolescents wearing the team jersey of their favorite players and copying the style of their heroes in their play.

What seems so instinctively natural for youngsters—the study of habits and skill sets of their athletic heroes—somehow is lost in the formal preparation for investing. In almost every career endeavor, including athletics, art, literature, music, and many trade professions, the traditional method to improve is to study from those who have already demonstrated success in their field.

The CFA is analogous to the Certified Public Accountant designation for accountants. The CFA is the highest professional designation for investment professionals. It requires a minimum of three years of study covering financial statement analysis, fixed income, economics, ethics, and portfolio management. Despite over 1,000 pages of assigned reading each year, the study of successful money managers is woefully missing. Instead, the readings are extremely theoretical and are predominately written by academics. Among the worst offenders is the Financial Analysts Journal which is a publication of the CFA Institute. The CFA Institute is a global association of investment professionals that offers the CFA designation. A recent article written by four professors included this formula to measure the relative mispricing of a stock: $r_{iT} = \text{Alpha} + {}_1\text{MKT}_T + {}_2\text{SMB}_T + {}_3\text{HML}_T + {}_4\text{UMD}_T + \Sigma_T$. Contrast this with the common sense advice that a stock is cheap if it is priced below its intrinsic value, where "intrinsic value" is the present value of its future cash flows.

What is largely missing is a practical course of study of the most successful investors to arm investors with the proper mental framework, discipline, and tools to secure their financial future. Usually, these valuable lessons are learned the expensive way; with one's own portfolio.

Warren Buffett, quoting from Isaac Newton, said, "If I have seen further than others, it is because I have stood on the shoulders of giants." Those successful investor giants were Benjamin Graham, Philip Fisher, Philip Carret, and Charlie Munger. Buffett acknowledged, "I have been lucky in life by having the right heroes. Tell me who your heroes are and I'll tell you how you'll turn out to be."

In my search for best practice-based wisdom to help resurrect the mutual fund, I chose three master investors who demonstrated success over many market cycles: John Templeton, Peter Lynch, and Warren Buffett. I studied their investment process with a special emphasis on case studies of their winning stocks. After I earned my MBA, my wife embarked on her MBA at the same San Francisco university. While I waited in the library for her to finish her evening classes, I downloaded and printed old news articles using microfiche (this was long before Google) about the companies in which the three investors made their successful investments. I recreated the news context that existed at the time of their investments to better understand the investment opportunities. I then formed case studies which blended the prevailing news and popular opinion at the time with their rationale for buying stocks as they explained in subsequent interviews. After studying dozens of case studies, I discovered lasting insights and common threads of investment principles. These common threads became the fabric for my own investment process, which resurrected the bottom-ranked mutual fund in four years to earn the highest mutual fund rating of five-stars as ranked by Morningstar. Using the same process, I repeated this five-star rating with a different mutual fund years later with a team of two other portfolio managers at another investment firm.

These investing principles are not elusive concepts laden with complex mathematical formulas. They are grounded in practical, common-sense business principles. This book presents the personal backgrounds of each investor to better understand the motives and reasoning behind their investment process. *Empower Your Investing* also explores the research filters that each master investor used to select stocks, how they managed their portfolios, why they sold stocks, and how they thought about risk and prevailing academic theories. The similarities and differences between the three master investors are presented with a synthesis of their best practices. This investment process can serve as a guide to manage your own investments.

Accumulating enough wealth to fund a college education, a dream home, or comfortable retirement can be challenging without the right guide. Entitlements such as generous pensions are relics of the past. Social Security may be rationed in the future. We are responsible for our own financial future but face a myriad of choices in 401(k)s, IRAs, Keogh plans, mutual funds, Exchange-traded funds, as well as direct investments in stocks and bonds. All too often, many delegate these important decisions to a "trusted" advisor with disastrous results.

The first step toward setting a course for a prosperous future is to understand how prosperous investors achieved their own success. *Empower Your Investing* uniquely profiles three master investors—Sir John Templeton, Peter Lynch, and Warren Buffett—into one convenient and very readable book and blends their best practices into one proven investment process. This book fills a void for serious investors that want to improve their skills by studying from proven practitioners rather than from abstract theorists, and for amateur investors who want to arm themselves with a life skill for securing their own financial independence.

The Ironman Triathlon and a lifetime of investing can both be grueling. The journey is much more satisfying and rewarding with the right preparation. The ex-UCLA basketball Hall-of-Fame coach and Hall-of-Fame player, John Wooden, said, "Failing to prepare, is preparing to fail." Coach Wooden was legendary for his wisdom on the basketball court and in life. His wisdom is just as applicable for a lifetime of investing. *Empower Your Investing—Adopting the Best Practices of John Templeton, Peter Lynch, and Warren Buffett* will help you set a course for a prosperous future by understanding how others got there. The journey is well worth it.

SIR JOHN M. TEMPLETON

"The Capitalist Missionary"

If we look to the lives of the famous as the unsung heroes of the past and present...we will find many models for useful, happy living. And, when we examine their words and deeds, we will discover the principles that inspired and sustained their benefits to future generations.

—JOHN TEMPLETON[1]

CHAPTER 1

Personal Background

God gave every one of us some talents. And I believe the parable of the talents teaches us it's our duty to use them as long as He allows. So, I intend to work as long as God allows trying to help people not only financially but also spiritually.

—JOHN TEMPLETON[2]

John Templeton's childhood and young adult experiences shaped his personal values and heavily influenced his investment philosophy. Templeton's moral compass was grounded in self-reliance, thrift, bargain hunting, positive thinking, stewardship, humble graciousness, worldliness, and spirituality. These guideposts helped him navigate from the small rural town of Winchester, Tennessee, in the Depression era, to become a Rhodes Scholar, a CFA charter-holder[3], and one of the most revered investors of the twentieth century. As a naturalized British citizen living in the Bahamas, he was knighted in 1987 by Queen Elizabeth II for his many philanthropic accomplishments. He was a pioneer in global investing who amassed a fortune and gave away hundreds of millions of dollars through the Templeton Foundation, which he established to foster progress in religion.

Sir John Marks Templeton was born on November 29, 1912, the second son to Harvey and Vella Templeton. (Note that where I refer to Sir John as either John or Templeton, it is purely to fit the context or to be consistent with references to the other master investors. However, in whatever manner Sir John is referenced herein, it is meant with the utmost respect.) John Templeton's parents naturally influenced his habits and insights. Harvey was an attorney even though he had never attended college. In a town of less than 2,000 people, he had to supplement his law profession with ventures that included operating a cotton gin and cotton storage facilities, trading cotton on the New York and New Orleans cotton exchanges, retailing fertilizer, selling insurance, as well as being a farm speculator and a landlord. Harvey's law office overlooked the county courthouse on the town square, and he knew when farms came up for auction in the 1920s after they were foreclosed for failure to pay real estate taxes. If the auction failed to produce a bid, he would opportunistically bid on farms for pennies on the dollar. By the mid-1920s, he'd accumulated six properties upon which he built twenty-four homes as rental property.

John observed that it was his father's opportunistic resourcefulness and entrepreneurial ambition that allowed the Templeton family to live comfortably; they were only the second family in the county to own a telephone and an automobile. John's aversion to debt was rooted in his early years, as he saw firsthand how many farmers lost their land in the auctions; he vowed to never become a borrower. By the time he was forty, he had still never owned a credit card or store charge card. John also observed that his father prospered at the auctions because he opportunistically bid on properties where there were no other bidders, and he was able to buy well below the farm's inherent value.

Not all of Harvey's ventures were successful. He made large investments in cotton futures on the cotton exchanges, and one day he delivered the news to the family that they were ruined. The roller coaster ride from despair to paper wealth to despair without an adequate safety net of savings left John scarred and a with deep reverence for savings and thrift.

John's mother, Vella, was equally influential but in a different manner. She was exceptionally well educated, which was a rarity for a woman in Winchester, Tennessee, in the early 1900s. She studied mathematics, Greek, and Latin for more than seven years at Winchester Normal College. After graduating, her brother, Father John Marks—a Roman Catholic convert and Paulist priest— found her a job tutoring children at a ranch in Texas that was spread over one million acres. She would later travel alone from Winchester to Texas to tutor when John was a young boy. She also tended their two-acre garden of vegetables and flowers as well as another three acres where she raised chickens, cattle, ducks, and pigs, and grew fruit and nut trees. His mother influenced John's thirst for knowledge and his enterprising work ethic.

John's appreciation of geographic and cultural diversity was also influenced by his mother. When John was twelve, Vella took him and his brother, Harvey Jr., on a two-month summer trip throughout the Northeast. Vella and her sons shared equally in planning the travel logistics. They traveled one hundred miles per day, stayed in campsites, and toured all the museums in Washington, New York, and Philadelphia. Four years later, Vella repeated the two-month car camping adventure with John, Harvey Jr., and a classmate, visiting the national parks, monuments, and historic sites from just west of the Mississippi to the Pacific Ocean.

Vella gave John much more than an appetite for cultural diversity and a zeal for learning. She also gave John the wisdom that money, once earned, was further enriched by what it could do for others. She was an active church elder of the Cumberland Presbyterian congregation. Vella and her sister, Leila Singleton, raised money to pay the salary for the congregation's part-time minister. She also earned money and continually raised funds to provide more than one half of the expenses for a Christian missionary in China named Gam Sin Qua. Her generosity gave John a sense of charity that knew no cultural or geographic boundaries.

As John later recalled, "She relied on love and continual prayers and providing books and magazines of the 'how-to-do-it' type."[4] When John was eleven, he read about spirituality in a magazine called *Weekly Unity*. "It was from reading that magazine that I learned that spirituality is more important than money."[5]

Years later, John began his annual meetings with prayers to calm and clear the minds of shareholders. He also later served as a Presbyterian elder and served on the board of the American Bible Society. Vella raised John and his brother in a laissez-faire manner, believing—as a Unity thinker—that divine guidance would direct her sons in the proper way. Harvey and Vella, in John's recollection, never spanked their boys, and their method of answering their sons' questions was to give them one-half of the answer and then provide library books for them to discover the rest. This instilled in John a sense of self-confidence and empowerment to satisfy his endless curiosity. The only real boundary that was strictly enforced was not allowing tobacco or alcohol in their home for any reason.

Harvey and Vella's constructive permissiveness gave John the freedom to pursue his early enterprising ambitions.

At age four, John grew his own beans from seeds in his mother's garden and sold them to a local country store for a profit.

After John's first test in first grade, he discovered that another classmate scored higher. He surmised that he must not have tried hard enough, so he promised to get the highest grade in the class from then on. After the first semester, he had all As. Upon seeing how well John did, his father made him a deal—each time John got all As, Harvey would give John a bale of cotton. If John received any grade less than an A on a report card, John would have to give his father a bale of cotton. For the next eleven years, John earned all As, and Harvey owed John twenty-two bales of cotton.

In second grade, at age eight, John ordered fireworks from the Brazil Novelty Company's mail-order catalog in Cincinnati, Ohio, about one month in advance of Christmas and July 4th. Just before the holidays, he would sell his fireworks to other children at five times his cost.

In eighth grade, John discovered an old broken Ford while he was playing with some friends in a hay barn. He bought the car from the owner for $10. He then searched the entire county and found another Ford that could be used for parts and, even though it was in worse condition, bought it for $10. After six months of work after school and on weekends, and many trips to the local Ford dealer to read car manuals, John and his friends got one of the cars to run, and they used it all through their high school years.

John's goals were challenged in high school when he learned that Yale College required four years of mathematics. Even before high school, John had his heart set on attending Yale when he heard of its renowned excellence from other adult conversations. The problem was that Winchester High School offered only three years of math. John devised a plan with his high school principal, Fred Knight, for the school to offer a fourth year of math and that John would be its teacher and student along with the required minimum of at least eight other students, whom John recruited. The principal devised and graded the final exam. All of the students passed. John learned early that Yale also required special entrance exams to qualify. He sent away for copies of several years of previous exams and studied them four hours daily for one month prior to his tests. John took the subject tests in stages at the end of each year in high school. His diligence and preparation were rewarded in 1930 when he was admitted into Yale.

In the summer before John attended Yale, he sold *Good Housekeeping* magazines door-to-door in rural Tennessee. He hated high-pressure cold-calling, especially during the Depression era, but he persevered because he needed the money for school. John earned a base commission of one dollar on each two-dollar subscription, and he earned a bonus of $200 for lasting through the summer and selling at least two hundred subscriptions. John characteristically committed himself totally to the challenge, made the sacrifices to succeed, and saw the task through to completion.

In his freshman year at Yale, John learned that his GPA was among the top ten of his class. His joy was short-lived after his father told John, in the heart of the Depression in 1931, that he simply couldn't afford even one more dollar to send John to college. John helped his father by returning the twenty-two bales of cotton he had earned as a reward during his grade school and high school years. John prayed and sought advice from others. His uncle Watson Templeton loaned John $200 to return to Yale if John promised to work his way through school. Yale offered John a partial scholarship and employment on campus due to his excellent academic record. John later said that the bad news from his father was one of the best things that ever happened to him, as it taught him the meaning of hard work and thrift. "Seeming tragedy can be God's way of educating his children."[6]

John worked on Yale's yearbook, the *Yale Banner and Pot Pourri,* and sold ad space for the *Yale Record* but found that they simply didn't generate sufficient income to afford tuition, room, and board. John resorted to supplementing his income by playing poker, which funded 25 percent of his college expenses. Poker was a calculated risk for John because he had played for small stakes since he was eight years old and had learned to count cards to increase his odds of winning. He also prudently safeguarded his winnings above $100 by allocating it strictly for his school expenses. John played poker with rich guys who were playing for fun while he played to win. He listened to them discussing investments and learned that none of them invested outside the U.S. "That seemed to me to be short-sighted. So, I decided as a sophomore at Yale that I would focus on being an adviser for people to invest worldwide."[7] John always believed that the greatest opportunities were the places where others weren't looking. The notion of searching beyond the shores of the U.S. was hatched before he even earned his Yale diploma.

After turning twenty-four, John never played poker again and even insisted in his professional investment career to never invest in shares of gambling businesses because of his distaste for the ugly addictive effects it had on others.

Upon graduating from Yale, John accomplished his goals:

- He earned a degree in economics, graduated near the top of his class, and served as president of Yale's chapter of Phi Beta Kappa fraternity.

- He committed himself to become an investment counselor, and he funded his first brokerage account with $300 from his poker winnings.

- He was awarded a Rhodes Scholarship to study law at Balliol College in Oxford where he earned a Master of Arts in Law in 1936. John chose to study law to understand the various tax and legal issues of investment counseling. With the extra money from his Rhodes Scholarship, John traveled extensively to satisfy his thirst for adventure and cultural education. In his first year, he traveled with his Rhodes Scholar friends to Spain during their Christmas break and to Italy during their Easter break. The trips were always thoroughly researched and bargain purchased with rail passes and thrifty hotels.

After graduating from Oxford, John and a close friend, James Inksetter, visited twenty-seven countries in seven months on a frugal £200 budget, nearly half of which came from poker winnings left over after paying for his school expenses. Every aspect of the trip was planned in advance. They averaged $0.25 per night in lodging expenses for two hundred nights and protected themselves from overspending and theft by mailing equal parts of their money to five different locations. Their travel included Germany during the 1936 Olympics, as well as India, China, and Japan. By then, John accumulated a wealth of knowledge about political systems, lifestyles, customs, and opportunities, which cemented his conviction to search for investment bargains worldwide. This was in contrast to the conventional bias that the only relevant stocks were those based in the United States.

Before departing on his seven-month travel adventure, John wrote letters to one hundred investment counseling firms where he thought he could learn the most about the investment business. In his letters, John detailed his background and goals, and asked for interviews after his expected date of return. Upon returning, he had twelve appointments waiting, five of which resulted in offers.

John took the lower paying of the two job offers for $150/month at Fenner & Beane, a stock brokerage firm in New York, which had just recently established an investment counseling division that would eventually become part of

Merrill Lynch. John believed that he could learn the most at this firm despite the lower pay. At this time, he studied at night school under Benjamin Graham who, according to Templeton, "did more than any man I know of to make security analysis a science."[8] Templeton later recalled that in 1937 there were only seventeen people who called themselves "security analysts," compared to over 296,000 "financial analysts" in 2016.

John married Judith Dudley Folk, a graduate of Wellesley College, in April 1937. She found a job as an advertising copywriter for the same salary that John was making, and they committed to put aside 50 percent of their income to save for their future.

After just three months, John left Fenner & Beane to join National Geophysical Company (NGC)—a seismograph exploration company in Dallas—as secretary-treasurer based on a referral from his Rhodes Scholar friend George McGhee who worked there. After discussing the $350/month offer with the owners at Fenner & Beane, they agreed that the NGC offer was too good to pass up and supported John with the move. John never lost sight of his goal to start his own investment counseling business. His sense of opportunity, his resources at NGC, and his contacts at Fenner & Beane would later converge to make his dream a reality.

In September 1939, two years after joining NGC, John concluded that the United States would inevitably come to the aid of its allies in Europe where the war had just begun. Pessimism was pervasive. The stock market had fallen almost 50 percent in the prior year, as the consensus feared the impact of the Nazi's power grab in Europe and that the U.S. would relapse into another depression. John reasoned that U.S. participation would resurrect many companies that were still suffering lingering effects from the Depression. He acted on his conviction by uncharacteristically borrowing $10,000 from his former manager, Dick Platt of Fenner & Beane, to invest $100 in every stock in the U.S. stock exchange that was selling for no more than $1/share. Even though John loathed borrowing money for buying personal items of declining value, he rationalized borrowing money to make money. This was the only instance where John borrowed money for any purpose.

John believed that the risk in this business venture was manageable for several reasons. For two years, he had researched how businesses and stock prices reacted in previous calls to war, when companies supplied the government with war provisions, industrial commodities, food, and logistics. He concluded that he was unlikely to lose money and that the companies with the most to gain in earnings growth and stock price were those that were among the least efficient and had low expectations. He also learned that governments tended to tax incremental wartime boom earnings at confiscatory high rates. Companies with a history of losses, however, had tax-loss carry-forwards that could shield their earnings from such high rates. Thus, in this scenario, there was less upside in owning well-run companies.

Second, John managed his risk by diversifying among many stocks, as he reasoned that probabilistically most but not every company would prosper. Third, the value of his personal investment portfolio had accumulated to over $30,000, which provided a cushion to cover his debt if his theory proved incorrect.

He placed the order with Fenner & Beane, who purchased stock in over one hundred companies, thirty-seven of which were bankrupt, and only four of which turned out to be worthless. Within one year, John paid back his entire loan, and after holding the stocks for an average of four years, sold them for $40,000, quadrupling his original investment.

Rather than paralyzing himself with fear by siding with the conventional pessimism, John gained conviction to act through clear-headed, thorough research and an opportunistic mindset for bargains. With financial resources in hand, John was ready to realize his dream of becoming an investment advisor and execute his lifelong motto: "To buy when others are despondently selling and to sell when others are avidly buying requires the greatest fortitude and pays the greatest ultimate reward."[9]

Motivations for Becoming a Professional Investor

John Templeton decided to become a professional investor for several reasons. First, he believed that he had a keen sense of judgment. He had developed an exceptional ability to discern the relevant strengths and weaknesses of an investment and had the courage and conviction to act on his judgment. His conviction to assess the tradeoff between risk and reward was the result of his thorough research process, which we will cover shortly.

Second, John believed that he could make more money in the investment field than in any other. John studied the biographies of Benjamin Franklin and John D. Rockefeller, and he was intrigued by Rockefeller's observation that the path to wealth through wages was dwarfed by creating wealth through astute investments and the power of compound interest. A wise investor colleague once told me that he knew of no other field of business where the simple recognition of a great investment idea—and the conviction to act on it—could have such enormous potential for prosperity. John also felt that a byproduct of his research was accumulating a large enough body of knowledge that would serve him well if he had to change professions.

The third, and perhaps most important, reason why John chose to become a professional investor was to help people become financially independent. He viewed himself as God's servant, who used his gifts and developed skills to benefit those who could not financially help themselves. John was proud of his service orientation and later said, "I always tried to please everyone who I came in contact with including all clients and employees...I have never been sued by anyone, nor have I ever sued anyone."[10]

Approach to Investing

Several admirable qualities were already evident in John's development that would shape his approach to investing and life, such as his kindness, humility, positive attitude, discipline, and fierce commitment to accomplish his goals. Four of his perspectives are worth exploring further as they served as cornerstones for his approach to investing: setting goals, extra effort, thrift, and avoiding consumer debt.

John was a goal-setter. Whether he was determined to earn bales of cotton by getting all As, get accepted into Yale, or fund his tuition, he lived his own credo to not just set goals, but to act on them. John offered this timeless wisdom: "The way to make conscious change, achieve new goals, and perfect our skills is through diligent practice, to study on a constant basis. This means making the commitment to develop our self-discipline and to persist and endure until the goal is met. Don't give up easily.... Focus on where you want to go, instead of where you have been. Much valuable time can be wasted in getting bogged down in past experiences or mistakes. After learning from past experiences, continue forward optimistically toward your goals."[11]

John observed early that people of average means did almost as much as those who were dramatically more successful and wealthy. The difference in effort between the two wasn't even the proverbial "extra mile," but only an "extra ounce." He coined this principle the "Doctrine of the Extra Ounce" and believed it applied universally to a variety of endeavors. John applied this throughout his life but especially in his early professional career when he moved the research division of his money management firm close to his home in Englewood, New Jersey, so he could conveniently go back to the office in the evenings and on weekends to work the "extra ounce" that would make a difference in performance. He typically worked twelve hours a day, Monday through Saturday, and often worked on Sunday after church.

John was legendary with his thrift. The Depression and boom–bust cycle of his childhood experiences motivated John to become self-reliant. Financial security demanded a discipline of savings. As we mentioned earlier, John and his wife, in their early years of marriage in the 1930s, committed to saving 50 percent of their income. They never paid more than $100/month for rent, and John's goal was to limit rent to less than 16 percent of income after taxes and savings. They once outfitted their five-room apartment for $25, as they were the sole bidders at a second-hand furniture auction. John instructed his secretary in 1940 to buy only used typewriters—usually at 40 percent below retail price—since new typewriters declined 30–40 percent in value right after their purchase. The goal of his thrift was to free up as much investable income as possible to allow money to make money.

John also planned for his financial security by avoiding consumer debt. He resolved to never borrow for personal purposes. He witnessed all too often in his childhood years the enslaving effect of debt from undisciplined spending. In 1944, he bought his first home in New Jersey—which was twenty-five years old and had an estimated replacement value of $25,000—for a bargain price of $5,000 in cash. He sold it five years later for $17,000 and used the proceeds to upgrade to a larger home in a better neighborhood without needing a mortgage. John later advised others to limit their mortgages to one-half of annual income. He also purchased his first five cars for less than $200 each, in contrast to his contemporaries, who spent five to twenty-five times as much. He traveled coach when he flew and often used subways and buses rather than taxis. John believed that the benefit of peace-of-mind from having a fortress balance sheet with little to no mortgage debt outweighed the tax advantages of a mortgage.

CHAPTER 2

Investment Performance

Sir John Marks Templeton's investment objective was "to be much better on average than the stock market or the average results of similar funds."[1]

In 1940, Templeton bought a small investment firm for $5,000 located in midtown Manhattan that was to become a predecessor to his firm, Templeton, Dubbrow & Vance.

He entered the mutual fund industry in November 1954 when he established the Templeton Growth Fund in Canada to minimize the taxes of its shareholders, since at that time Canada had no capital gains tax. Investors' gains were taxed at a 25 percent rate only when shares in the mutual fund were sold. Templeton also wanted to showcase the global reach of his investment strategy, so the Templeton Growth Fund was one of the first mutual funds to offer U.S. investors an avenue to invest in a diversified portfolio of international stocks.

Templeton raised $6.6 million to start the Templeton Growth Fund in November 1954 and then underperformed the S&P 500 his first three years. The fund ranked 115th out of 133 funds in a Weisenberger study of relative investment performance, and the fund ended 1957 with just $2.9 million in it. The fund did not get back to $7 million until 1969—fifteen years after its founding. Templeton's investments had appreciated five-fold since the mutual fund initially launched, but more than 80 percent of the originally issued shares were redeemed, which is why the fund's net assets remained frustratingly low.

His firm did grow to $300 million in managed assets including eight mutual funds. He eventually sold the firm to Piedmont Management in the early 1960s and kept only the Templeton Growth Fund. Piedmont declined to take it because the fund was based in Canada, and a decision by the U.S. Treasury to tax purchases of foreign securities by U.S. citizens, and a new Canadian ruling required withholding taxes on non-dividend income, made it unattractive to distribute in the U.S.

Templeton's move to the Bahamas in 1969 allowed him to think more independently and act more boldly, as evidenced by his prescient move into Japanese stocks before they became wildly popular. By 1974, the Templeton Growth fund had just $13 million in net assets, which meant it had merely treaded water for twenty years when adjusted for inflation. The hidden gem underlying the stagnant net assets afflicted by constant redemptions was Templeton's record of generating 12 percent compound returns. Templeton was convinced more than ever of the importance of effective distribution and marketing in order to leverage his stock-picking ability and to allow more investors to benefit.

Templeton partnered with Jack Galbraith who marketed the fund full-time. Galbraith ran a full-court press with a PR campaign that included many regular appearances by Templeton on Louis Rukeyser's *Wall Street Week* promoting Templeton's exemplary track record. The combination of investment success and intelligent marketing resulted in explosive growth in net assets. The Templeton Growth Fund in 1980 reached $420 million in net assets, and by 1986, it climbed another six-fold to $2.4 billion.

By 1992, the Templeton Growth Fund had reported a 14.5 percent average annual return. A $10,000 initial investment in 1954, with dividends reinvested, would have appreciated to $1.74 million by 1992. By comparison, the S&P 500 index had a 10.9 percent average annual return over the same thirty-eight-year period and would have grown to $529,900.[2] The Templeton Growth Fund had the best twenty-five-year record through 1981 of any mutual fund and had only eight negative return years out of thirty-nine years under Templeton's management.

Interestingly, this stellar record was achieved despite underperforming the S&P 500 by over twenty-five percentage points in his first year and underperforming in six of his first ten years. The average annual return for the first ten years (1955–1964) of the Templeton Growth Fund was 9.5 percent compared to 12.8 percent for the S&P 500. One wonders how patient modern day mutual

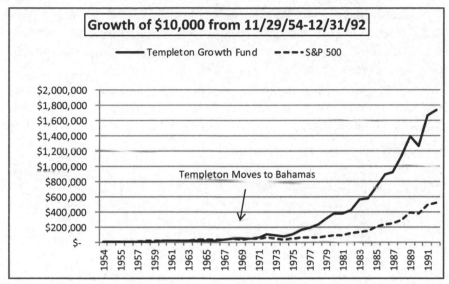

Growth of $10,000 from 11/29/54-12/31/92

— Templeton Growth Fund   – – – S&P 500

Source. Templeton Growth Fund performance data from Franklin Templeton Investments

fund investment boards would be with a contemporary investor posting a similar performance for the first ten years. The Templeton Growth Fund, over thirty-eight years, never lost money over any five-year period, which is a tribute to Sir John Templeton's valuation and stock selection discipline.

By October 1992, Templeton's partnership, Templeton, Galbraith & Hansberger Ltd., had amassed $21.3 billion of assets under management, including $13 billion in mutual funds, and the company was sold to Franklin Resources Inc. for $913 million, of which John Templeton's stake was valued at $440 million.

Franklin controlled $66.5 billion of assets primarily in U.S. fixed-income securities, and the combined company would become the fourth largest mutual fund company behind Fidelity, Merrill Lynch, and Vanguard. Templeton had purchased 126,000 shares of Franklin stock ten years prior at an average cost of $0.30/share compared to the price in 1992 of about $30/share. He originally bought Franklin stock after meeting one of Franklin's employees and, "as with everybody I meet, I asked him a hundred questions."[3] He was impressed by the cheapness of the stock and by the company's marketing prowess. The experience of following Franklin Resources for ten years and benefitting from the stock's impressive rise "gave me the impression that the company was well managed."[4]

After the merger with Franklin Resources, Sir John retired from professional investment management to spend more time devoted to philanthropy. He drove his own car, never flew first-class, and said that, apart from spiritual programs, he never watched more than eighty-four hours of television in his life.

In 1999 *Money Magazine* called Sir John Templeton "arguably the greatest global stock picker of the century."[5] Succumbing to pneumonia, Sir John passed away July 8, 2008 at age 95 in Nassau, Bahamas, where he had lived for decades.

CHAPTER 3

The Templeton Mental Model

We don't ever ask ourselves, 'Shall we buy big companies or little ones?' or, 'Shall we buy American companies or Japanese?' We just search every day by keeping in mind the simple question, 'Where is something selling for a tiny price in relation to its true value?'

—JOHN TEMPLETON[1]

The core of John Templeton's approach to investing is to look for the most attractive bargains worldwide. This may appear deceptively simple and obvious, but it is a conclusion that recognizes that the wider we scan for unbiased investment values, the more likely we will find opportunities to increase our investments many-fold.

Many professional investors today are constrained by an institutional mandate that limits their investment horizon by size of company (small, mid, or large), by a particular industry (software, retail), by sector (consumer durables, utilities), by style (value, growth, blend), or by geography (U.S., China). Many intermediaries that control asset allocation for large pension funds and endowment funds limit professional investor horizons based on the belief that the intermediary can select best-of-breed managers who can fill a style box. The result can be a Noah's Ark of investment managers that often results in overall mediocre performance since the outperformance of one style that may be timely is offset by the underperformance of another style that is overpriced but still recommended to fill the style box. Individual investors have an advantage by not being so constrained.

John Templeton was opportunistic in his search. He simply advocated buying the best bargains, which are found in areas where others are selling. He said, "Looking for a good investment is nothing more than looking for a good bargain." Exactly how does he do this?

There are ten pillars to John Templeton's mental model that comprise his perspective toward investing:

1. Be a Bargain Hunter

The first pillar in his mental model is to adopt a bargain-hunting mindset. Templeton said, "If you buy the same stocks that other people buy, you'll have the same record as other people. The only way you can hope to have a record superior to other people is to buy what the other people are not buying."[2]

Templeton famously advised to buy at the point of maximum pessimism and sell at the point of maximum optimism:

> People are always asking me where the outlook is good, but that's the wrong question. The right question is: Where is the outlook the most miserable? You're trying to buy a share at the lowest price possible in relation to what that corporation is worth. And there's only one reason a share goes to a bargain price: because other people are selling. There is no other reason. To get a bargain price, you've got to look for where the public is most frightened and pessimistic. The time to buy is when everyone is scared and you are a bit scared yourself.[3]

He warned against becoming too immersed into mathematical formulas and digging too deeply into the details of every corporation, especially those stocks that have been popular. Fisherman avoid overfished holes; so should investors. Templeton also believed that an investor should be able to clearly and succinctly state the strengths and weaknesses of a purchase candidate. A long-winded answer likely means that one needs to do more analysis to better understand the investment rationale.

Sir John said, "No matter what the conditions are, (the investor) wants to have his money in those things that have the lowest price relative to long-term value. Put your investments in markets that have already gone down. Buy things that have the lowest market price relative to value."

The following examples indicate the success of this approach, as Sir John invested in South Korean stocks, airlines, and short-sale tech stocks.

South Korean Stock Fund

Sir John, at 85 years of age, invested in a number of Korean stock funds in late 1997, one of which was the Matthews Korea Fund, whose 65 percent decline ranked it as one of 1997's worst-performing U.S.-based mutual funds, following a 32 percent decline in 1996. The poor performance was linked to a period of overdevelopment and a chain reaction of selling that began with Thailand's currency devaluation in July 1997 and spread to Malaysia, the Philippines, Singapore, and South Korea.

Sir John was impressed with South Korea's high domestic savings rate of over 30 percent, which encouraged project investments, high single-digit GDP growth, and the country's strong exports. Like Japan, South Korea also had restricted foreign investment, but in 1992 they changed this to allow foreign investments in the country. South Korean price-earnings ratios (P/E ratios) were cut in half from over 20x to 10x. Lastly, Sir John was impressed that fund manager Paul Matthews' investment strategy paralleled his own. Sir John's investment accounted for more than 25 percent of the Korea fund's $25 million in assets. Sir John said that Korean stocks were cheaper relative to earnings than stocks in other hard-hit Asian nations such as Thailand and Malaysia. The Matthews Korea Fund soared 96 percent in 1998 and, in 1999, was the best performing mutual fund with another leap of 108 percent.

Airline Investments

The tragic attacks of September 11, 2001, are seared in our memories forever. Immediately following the attacks, the U.S. and other countries were placed on high alert against potential follow-on attacks. Civilian air travel across the country was, for the first time ever, almost completely suspended for three days. To prevent panic selling, the NYSE and Nasdaq closed stock markets for trading from September 11th until September 17th. Many vowed to never fly again. Sir John, on the other hand, sensed an opportunity to capitalize on "maximum pessimism." He developed a list of eight airline stocks that already had low P/Es, and he entered orders to buy any of these that dropped 50 percent or more once the markets reopened. He reasoned that the government would not allow the airlines to fail after the attacks. He bought three: American Airlines owner AMR, US Airways Group, and Continental Airlines. In a

November 12, 2001 interview with *Forbes*, Sir John said that he would likely hold on to the three stocks until "gloom around the stocks lets up and investors return to them. Six months." Even though each of the three stocks made new lows after the crisis decline, six months later, AMR gained 61 percent, Continental Airlines rose 74 percent, and US Airways climbed 24 percent.

Technology Shorts

In March 2000, Cisco Systems was the most valuable company in the world with a market capitalization of over $500 billion and was priced at 29x *sales*. The Nasdaq index was priced at over 150x earnings, and even the more conservative S&P 500 index at 30x earnings was priced at double its long-term average. Many technology company valuations were justified by new-era metrics, such as market capitalization to "reach" measured in eyeballs, rather than such mundane metrics like earnings or cash flow. Market euphoria was rampant. Sir John sensed an opportunity to capitalize on "maximum optimism." He arranged with his broker in January 2000 to short eighty-four technology stocks eleven days before company executives were allowed to sell their stock, which was typically six months after an initial public offering (IPO). He focused on technology companies whose stock price had at least tripled from their IPO price, and where it was likely that insiders would cash out of their overpriced stock. Each investment averaged $2.2 million. "This is the only time in my 88 years when I saw technology stocks go to 100 times earnings or when there were no earnings, 20 times sales. It was insane, and I took advantage of the temporary insanity."[4] In nearly one-half of his shorts, he waited until the stock dropped 95 percent from what he paid before covering his short. In other cases, he covered when the stock dropped to 30x trailing earnings. Sir John described the frothy speculative bubble of the Nasdaq as a "once-in-a-lifetime" opportunity. The Nasdaq index peaked at 5408 on March 10, 2000, and plunged 79 percent to 1139 by late 2002. Sir John made $90 million on his short positions.

Assessing Value

An investment is a bargain only if its market price is below the company's intrinsic value. We will explore specific case studies of Sir John's investments in Chapter 6. For now, it is important to recognize that while determining "intrinsic value" is critical, the process of estimating a company's worth eludes a simple formula. A company's value is determined after considering a number of factors, such as the value of its assets, the impact of economic, political, and demographic forces on the company, and the future normalized earnings power of the company's product or service.

Sir John also assessed the stability and competence of the company's management and the threats that the company faced from competition. He believed the most reliable information on any company often came from competitors rather than the company itself. His approach relied on exhaustive research and sound judgment. Different companies had their own requirements for reaching an appropriate level of due diligence. He evaluated depletion rates for mining companies, cash flow for oil and gas companies, and demographics for retailers. Traditional financial metrics, such as low price/earnings ratio, price/replacement value, and price/book values, were evaluated in the context of other favorable indicators, such as a high number of corporate takeovers, high levels of corporate share buybacks, and high levels of cash available for investment by institutional investors such as pension funds, foreign investors, and insurance companies.

2. Diversify Investments

The second pillar in Templeton's mental model is to diversify investments. Templeton observed that few investors, himself included, are ever right more than two-thirds of the time. To protect against the risk of making mistakes at least one-third of the time, he recommended that individual investors diversify with at least ten stocks in a portfolio with exposure to different industries and different nations. An unrealized loss arising from a bear market in one country may be offset by a bull market in another country.

Templeton believed that all assets are risky. He said that people can fool themselves by thinking that they will play it safe by holding cash. Cash continues to lose its purchasing power in every nation. He believed that the best approach to safety is to widely diversify by holding stocks in more than three dozen corporations in more than a dozen nations. He also believed that "income producing assets maintain their value in the long run better than cash, gold, or collectibles, or any other asset."[5]

3. Invest Overseas Only in Free Enterprise Countries

The third pillar is to focus overseas investments in countries that encourage human freedom and free enterprise without undue restraints. He avoided socialistic countries heavily dominated by a command and control structure where the few regulate the many. He observed that Hong Kong, for example, was transformed from poverty to prosperity because it adopted free enterprise, while Calcutta remained mired in destitute poverty. Templeton explained:

> ...the major difference is the difference between free enterprise and socialism. The government of India regulates nearly everything, so there's very little progress; whereas in Hong Kong the government keeps its hands off. There are all kinds of enterprises flourishing. The standard of living in Hong Kong has multiplied more than tenfold in forty years, while the standard of living in Calcutta has improved hardly at all.[6]

Templeton also avoided foreign companies that are subject to confiscation by sovereignties and domestic companies subject to price controls.

4. Keep an Open Mind

The fourth pillar is to remain flexible and avoid a fixed mindset that is anchored in investing in stocks that are comfortable because they have already done well in recent years. This is the proverbial rear-view mirror approach to investing rather than looking through the windshield at more attractively priced opportunities. Templeton recommended, "Those things (companies) that helped you so much in the last two or three years can't be the bargains they were when you first bought them. So instead of staying in those things that have treated you well in the past, you should be looking for those things that performed worst in the past—and consider buying those now."[7]

Prospecting for stocks that have performed worst in the past may uncover bargains where the stock was unfairly punished for a temporary, non-structural reason. It is human nature to invest in what is popular, but that popularity is due to its recent outperformance. These investments will not likely be a source of depressed prices offering bargain opportunities today. Templeton did not advocate being contrarian just for the sake of being different, but he always advocated thoroughly researching before investing. Templeton's discipline and consistent research efforts were an integral part of his success. He acknowledged that you won't be right all the time and that success requires a time horizon of two to five years.

Templeton also warned against fixating on only one specialized niche of the market, such as only Chinese stocks, small cap stocks, or biotech stocks.

When Templeton was asked to identify the single, most important strategy that he could identify for long-term investment success, he replied, "The key to long-term success is to keep an open mind. And by that, I mean the willingness to adapt any approach, any technique suitable for the investment. And to explore any type of investment in any place in the world."[8]

In 1991 Templeton paid $1 million for DAIS Group Inc., Drexel Burnham Lambert's former quantitative and research division that traded baskets of stocks using computer models. "They invest without reference to basic value. Some of these quant methods do work. We've always thought we should develop any new method as long as its works." Templeton wasn't so much as abandoning his strategy of bargain hunting worldwide, but the acquisition was another prescient bet that other money managers, especially large pension funds, would rely more on computer aided quantitative research.

5. Be Patient

The fifth pillar of John Templeton's mental model is to have a differentiated long-range perspective, which requires patience. Templeton emphasized that patience was a critical factor for investment success, especially when buying "at the point of maximum pessimism." Templeton didn't have a set time period to hold a stock, but in retrospect, he found that his average holding period was about five years. "We don't intend to hold them (stocks) five years, but we find if you buy things when they're terribly unpopular and depressed, they don't suddenly come back. You have to be patient."[9]

The former professional ice hockey Hall of Famer and all-time leading scorer, Wayne Gretzky, famously advised hockey players to "skate to where the puck is going, not where it has been." In the same way, Templeton anticipated prospects for companies well beyond the conventional crowd's short-term fixation on recent winners. Templeton explained, "…we try to have a longer-range viewpoint—and the patience that goes along with that. So we try to buy those things that others have not yet thought about. Then we *wait* until the short-term prospects become good and other people start coming in and buying the stock and pushing the price up."[10]

He was asked what was it going to take for investors to recognize what Templeton believed to be impressive value. Templeton responded, "Just patience. If you buy something for as little as one quarter of what you think it's worth, you may have to keep it a year or five years but in the long run, most of the things do go up to what they are really worth."[11]

After the stock market crash of 1987, Templeton's advice to investors was:

Patience. Be a long-term investor. Be prepared financially and psychologically to live through a series of bull markets and bear markets because in the long-run, common stocks will pay off enormously. The next bull market will carry prices far higher than this one because the whole nation is growing more rapidly. Gross National Product for the nation will double in at least the next ten years. We think the Gross National Product in the nation forty years from now will be sixty-four times as high as it is now. That will be reflected in sales volume and profits in share prices.[12]

Templeton advised his clients to prepare for bear markets. "We know that there will be at least two bear markets every twelve years."[13] He advised them not to have too much debt so they wouldn't be forced to sell at the wrong time and not to get frightened at the wrong time.

In an interview one year after he sold his company to Franklin, he was asked for his best advice for investors. "Don't try to outguess the market, and don't move in and out of the market often…It takes patience. If you are diversified and hold shares of well-managed, established companies, the rewards will be there."[14]

6. Research Thoroughly

The sixth pillar is to thoroughly research each investment opportunity. Today a trade to buy or sell a security can be executed with a few keystrokes, in a fraction of a second. While the barriers to execute a stock purchase are low, Templeton would say the barriers to decide to purchase are quite high. Templeton made informed decisions after many hours of reading and research. As in any endeavor, there is no substitute for hard work and building a foundation through preparation, observation, and in-depth analysis. Sir John worked seven days a week and came into work after church on Sundays. Templeton advised,

Prepare yourself by study and observation—by watching other people, by reading, and by practice that will enable you to become a real expert…if you aren't willing to lay that foundation—then you are likely to be one of those people who goes through life frustrated and upset and beset by feelings of inferiority. You don't have to go through that. All you have to do is be

24

willing to do the work. Be willing to spend the hours and the concentration to build those foundation bricks on the bottom. Then the wall of your life will stand up and be a protection and a support for you until you die.[15]

The barriers to overseas investing—including different accounting and reporting standards, withholding taxes, foreign currency risks, political risks, and foreign investor restrictions—were opportunities to be objectively evaluated with an open, inquisitive, and opportunistic mindset, not dismissed categorically for inconvenience.

What exactly constitutes thorough and disciplined research? Templeton was one of the first security analysts to use quantitative analysis to compare one company's productivity and profitability against another. He was interested in measuring the strength of management with quantitative yardsticks, such as a company's growth in market share, its return on invested capital, and its profit margins. He would then combine the quantitative metrics with his estimate of the future earnings power of the company to arrive at an estimate of value.

I've made a career of quantitative analysis. We built our list of clients by showing them the advantages of quantitative analysis and explaining it to them. We showed them what we were doing that was different from other investment counselors who were using qualitative analysis. Our quantitative analysis turned out to be a good way to attract clients, and it was also a good way to produce a superior record.[16]

The publications that Templeton used included *Value Line*, Standard & Poor's *Stock Reports, The Wall Street Journal,* and research published by the more than one hundred brokerage firms that he did business with. *Value Line* was one of his favorite resources "because *Value Line* pack(s) into that page the largest amount of relevant figures and facts. Also, they arrange the information in a way that makes it easy to compare one corporation with another." Templeton would typically scan *The Wall Street Journal* and other newspapers for the four or five stories worth his serious attention and avoided getting bogged down in articles of less importance.

Templeton also interviewed top management extensively, particularly early in his career. He was more interested in their strategic long-range plans than reviewing past records. His favorite interview question was, "If you were going to buy shares, and you couldn't buy shares in your own company, which one of your competitors, suppliers, or customers would you buy shares in—and why?" The answers proved invaluable. He would quickly learn the relative strengths and weaknesses of individual companies, which he could validate through similar questions of other executives. A clearer picture of the competitive landscape emerged, and his conviction increased for his purchase decisions.

7. Consult Your Network

The seventh pillar of Templeton's mental model was to stay connected to his network of colleagues and friends. Templeton was on a first-name basis with hundreds of people due to his genuine amiable personality. He didn't hesitate to contact them for help regarding an investment decision if they had extensive knowledge about a particular industry.

8. Think and Act Productively

The eighth pillar is thought control. Templeton explained, "If you fill up the entire capacity of your mind with thoughts that you think are good and productive, you won't have room for the others. The ones you want to crowd out are feelings of envy, hatred, covetousness, self-centeredness, criticism, revenge— and also any time-wasting thoughts that are unproductive for your ultimate goals in life."[17] Templeton focused his energies on investments and his religious commitments. He avoided television and movies and said that he didn't have time to read novels because he prioritized more important things in his life.

He was so punctual that he would set his watch ten to fifteen minutes ahead of time and arrived at meetings early. His punctuality was a reflection of his respect and courtesy for the schedules of others as well as his own efficiency. He always brought along reading material to review during his "dead time," such as waiting for others to arrive or during plane or subway rides.

On the television program *Wall Street Week,* Frank Cappiello once asked John Templeton what qualities a young professional should look for to be successful in the investment business. His answer was, "Frank, diligent work; simple-minded common sense; thrift and prayer."[18]

9. Think Positively and Be an Optimist

The ninth pillar is to think positively, be an optimist, and expect success. Not everything Templeton did was a success. He admitted that he counted more than a dozen business ventures that he started that were never successful. He viewed these as opportunities to learn rather than as defeats. He said, "I do believe that positive thinking is a great help—not only in spiritual growth and human relations, but a help in financial matters and every other activity in life."[19] He looked for the good in people rather than dwelling on their flaws. In almost every guest appearance on *Wall Street Week with Louis Rukeyser*, John Templeton's optimism and gratefulness were refreshing antidotes to popular pessimism and worries.

The crash on October 19, 1987, is referred to as Black Monday, when the Dow Jones Industrial Average sank 22.6 percent. A few days after that Monday, Templeton was a voice of calm reason on *Wall Street Week with Louis Rukeyser*. Rukeyser asked Templeton, "Have you changed that (optimistic) attitude a little?"

Templeton responded,

No, Louis. The outlook is so wonderful that none of us really understands. All the world is progressing more and more rapidly. Half of all that's been discovered in science was in the last fifty years, half of all discovered in medicines were in the last twenty years, there are ten times as many shareholders now as there were forty years ago. The pension funds, the individual retirement accounts, are all growing so rapidly and the quantity of shares available to buy is shrinking so that in the long run, shares prices are likely to be much higher than they ever been before. There has never been a time in the last forty years when you could have invested in common stocks that you wouldn't have made money over a five-year period. We are already now well into a bear market, but it's possible the bear market has already ended.[20]

The bear market retested its low in early December, but one year after the crash, the S&P 500 was 23 percent higher. Templeton presciently observed that, unlike the 1929 crash, the bear market in stocks in 1987 would not spill over into a general business decline because there were economic buffers, such as unemployment insurance, guarantees of bank deposits, insurance on broker's accounts, and social security.

In nearly every interview, his unflinching optimism was clear, consistent, and backed with evidence.

From a long-range viewpoint, I believe the rate of progress is going to be greater in the next twenty years than in any previous twenty years in history. Because the two greatest worries of our lifetime have been largely removed.

One was the fear of nuclear war. Up until four years ago, that was a major factor for everybody. The other one was the fear that the communists were right when they said they were going to dominate the earth. They had captured twenty-three nations. None had ever become free again up until four years ago. Those two great threats had a depressing influence. Now that they are gone, there's going to be more investing across international boundaries, more foreign trade, less money wasted on armaments, more spread of brotherhood and religion. The whole world is coming into a peaceful, glorious, rapid growth period.

I would go as far to say I believe the standard of living in America will double within twenty-five years, which is an enormous rate.... There are so many good things that are not publicized. For example, the number of people attending universities in America is ten times as great as it was a hundred years ago. The number of people getting doctor's degrees in America now is ten times as great as it was just sixty years ago. ...In 1800, 85 percent of the people had to live on the farms just to produce enough food. Now, with a little over 3 percent of Americans on the farms, we worry about surpluses, not shortages of food. This could go on and on."[21]

I had the pleasure of meeting Sir John Templeton at a dinner in 1998 when he was honored by the Independent Institute for outstanding global contributions in advancing business excellence, free market entrepreneurship, education, and moral principles, as well as for his role as a champion of freedom and free competition to allow people to pursue their God-given talents in every nation. His genuine optimism and humility were fully evident that evening:

We need to recognize that we are living in the most glorious period of world history. In almost every area of life, you can see how much has been accomplished by free competition... The amount of knowledge on Earth took a thousand years to double, but now some experts in knowledge say that knowledge is doubling every three years; some say faster than that. But suppose knowledge continues to double every three years—I predict it will accelerate—but even if it just continues to double every three years, a little arithmetic will show you that, in only thirty years, you'll have a thousand times as much information as you have today. And in sixty years, you'll have a million times as much information as we have now.

What has been said tonight is extremely heartwarming, of course. But it also makes me feel very, very humble. I do not deserve the wonderful things that you have said. You deserve them. It is the people here who have been tremendous leaders and innovators in bringing blessings to the world. All over this room are people who are doing things far more wonderful than I have been able to do. I do believe that you are the heroes. I believe that you are the benefactors of humanity—and I believe you are carrying out God's purposes.... So finally, my friends, I love you, every one of you. I love you to an unlimited extent and without exception. I try my best to love every human being without any exception, and I think you share that viewpoint with me. And if you do that, all other things seem to fall in place: success comes to you, happiness comes to you, wealth comes to you, and much more, if you genuinely try your level best to love every human being to an unlimited extent without any exception.

And so tonight, dear friends, I look forward to living enough longer after my current age of eighty-five that I can attend a great banquet to toast the wonderful things that you, all of you, will have done to help freedom and religion.[22]

10. Mental Preparation

These pillars of Templeton's mental model of investing are fastened together with three stages of mental preparation. They are prayer, retreat, and generous giving.

Prayer

Templeton attributes prayer as the most instrumental factor in his success as an investor, giving him clarity of mind and insights he otherwise wouldn't have had. He prayed throughout the day, often simply saying, "Thy will be done." Templeton believed that prayer should be an appeal that "God will use you as a clear channel for His wisdom and His love."[23] With particularly difficult decisions, after Templeton gathered all the information he needed, he would petition God before going to sleep, "God, I have done the best I can—now guide me in my decision." The next morning, very often he would have an answer that was better than he could have thought by himself the day before.

We start all of our meetings—including our shareholders' meetings and our directors' meetings—with prayer. If you start meetings with prayer, the meetings are more fruitful and more productive; you reach decisions that are more likely to help everybody concerned. There is less controversy if you begin a meeting with prayer. Or, as I like to say, 'Prayer helps you to think more clearly.' And in selecting investments, that is the most important thing—to be able to think more clearly.[24]

Templeton's emphasis on prayer, which was absent during the first twenty years of his career, coincided with his greatest performance success of the Templeton Growth Fund. Templeton became a self-styled capitalist missionary. He observed that "the people who have become professionals in most religions are relatively ignorant about the workaday world…they become caught up in the concept that if someone becomes rich, it's because he stepped on someone else. That's not true. You become rich by helping people."[25] He even advocated that the American government should make every American a shareholder. He believed it would help the sick and poor, help people understand business, and give people self-respect.

Retreat

The retreat principle also coincided with Sir John's greatest performance success of the Templeton Growth Fund. In 1951, Templeton's wife Judith died tragically when they were touring Bermuda on motorbikes. With three young children, Templeton married his neighbor Irene Reynolds Butler in December 1958, who had two children of her own. As the 1960s progressed, Templeton realized that he "had spent my early career helping people with their personal finances, but helping them to grow spiritually began to seem so much more important."

He and Irene chose the Bahamas as their permanent home in 1968 where they could find time for reflection in a beautiful setting. It was conducive to religious study and work, and was detached from Wall Street's excessive fear and enthusiasm. While New York provided access to investment information and an opportunity to build a client base early in his career, he felt it was now time to leave the hectic, high-pressure environment of Wall Street for the tranquility of the Bahamas where he could think more clearly and more creatively.

I find it's (the shade of a beach) an excellent place to work. You can work with greater concentration there than you can in an office or in a home. I spend, at most, an hour a day at the beach thinking and doing my work…I do it almost every day I'm not traveling, and that turns out to be about one hundred and fifty days a year. To be able to work with the sand and the ocean surrounding me seems to help me think in worldwide terms.[26]

Sir John later added another benefit of a regular retreat from daily distractions: "Once we got 1,000 miles away, it was easier to do the opposite of everybody else."[27] He devoted thirty hours a week to managing his family's investments and the Templeton Growth Fund, and another thirty hours to his religious and philanthropic work. The Bahamian location allowed him to devote more time for value-added research in his search for bargains. It limited distractions, the heavy time demands of administration and client meetings, and allowed Templeton more time to practice his strength of securities analysis.

He built a Southern plantation-style house in the exclusive Lyford Cay Club on the main island of New Providence and became a British citizen to more fully help his adopted country. The Lyford Cay Club had about 1,000 members who were successful industrialists from more than two dozen countries. This provided Templeton with access to firsthand information from a valuable network of contacts in a relaxed setting.

As mentioned in Chapter 2, the performance record of the Templeton Fund dramatically improved after Sir John moved to the Bahamas. "With the advantage of hindsight now, I think there are two reasons for this success," Templeton explained.

> One is that if you're going to produce a better record than other people, you must not buy the same things as the other people. If you're going to have a superior record, you have to do something different from what the other security analysts are doing. And when you're a thousand miles away in a different nation, it's easier to buy the things that other people are selling, and sell the things that other people are buying. So that independence has proved to be a valuable help in our long-range performance.[28]

Templeton believed that a career as a securities analyst is a ministry comparable to ministers, lawyers, and doctors.

> If service for others is the motive of your life, then happiness and wealth are likely to come to you. The security analysis profession helps to provide for investors the benefits of greater security, personal freedom, mobility, and self-reliance...It is well known that the rich invest in entrepreneurship, and the poor save and conserve.[29]

Give Generously

The third mental fastener to Templeton's mental pillars was to give generously of his time, talent, and treasure. In his early years, he gave 20 percent of his earnings to charities and even more in his later years. He was most famous for his namesake Templeton Foundation program of Prizes for Progress in Religion. The cash award at its inception was larger than the Nobel Peace Prize or any other award, to reflect that progress in religion of all types is more important than progress in any other area. He believed that he would do more good with his wealth by encouraging others to use scientific methods to answer spiritual questions. As of 2013, the financial prize was £1,100,000, second only to the financial prize award by the Fundamental Physics Prize Foundation. The first recipient was Mother Teresa of Calcutta in 1973 "for her extraordinary efforts to help the homeless and neglected children of Calcutta," six years before she received the Nobel Peace Prize. Other recipients included Aleksandr Solzhenitsyn and Billy Graham.

To emphasize their sense of gratitude, John and Irene traditionally sent Thanksgiving cards on Thanksgiving Day rather than Christmas cards. Templeton credited his religious convictions with influencing his investment philosophy and success: "If people will recognize the unique prosperity and blessing of modern life and give thanks for them, it will translate into a happier life and also lead to more money…If you take seriously all the tragedies in life, you are unaware of the opportunities. Everybody finds what they are looking for."[30]

Templeton frequently reminded investors to raise their sights from everyday worries to be thankful for our economic progress: "If you do not fall down on your knees each day, with overwhelming gratitude for your blessings—your multiplying multitudes of blessings—then you just have not yet seen the big picture."[31] He observed in 1984 at a speech before the Financial Analyst Federation, that as recently as sixty-five years earlier, there was no Social Security, no unemployment insurance, no SEC, no capital gains tax, no air mail, no airlines, no antibiotics, no nylon, no frozen foods, no TV, no transistors, no lasers, no fax, no Xerox, and no nuclear energy. If he were alive today, he would also include email, the internet, Google search, biotechnology, laptops, tablet computing, and mobile phones.

As enthusiastic as Sir John was about the impact of investing, he was equally enthusiastic about religion:

What we say about investments isn't as lasting as what we say about spiritual matters. But actually, my two passions are related: economic freedom and religion go hand in hand. I've watched businesses for over fifty years. Those that succeed, help the customer. Those that cheat, fail. The way to be successful in financial affairs is to have an attitude of gratitude.[32]

The exceptions are publicized so much more rapidly and pervasively, and it is a media problem, according to Sir John.

The availability of the information (about wrongdoing) is so much more rapid and extensive than it ever was. And the fact that 999 out of 1,000 on Wall Street are straight arrows doesn't make news. The percentage of people in trouble is no higher than it was twenty years or fifty years ago. It's just that people hear about it more. Up until twenty years ago, there was no radio or television coverage of the subject of Wall Street.[33]

Sir John thought that the most important thing business schools can teach is ethics. Templeton believed in using his God given talent as long as he could and had no intention of retiring.

I have no intention of retiring, Louis. God gave every one of us some talents, not the same talents or the same quantity of talents, but some talents, and therefore, I think he expects us to use them as long as he allows. So I intend to continue to help people with investments.[34]

He added, "So I intend to work as long as God allows, trying to help people not only financially but spiritually."[35]

In summary, the ten pillars to John Templeton's mental model that supported his attitudes toward the process of investing are:

1. Be A Bargain Hunter
2. Diversify Investments
3. Invest Overseas Only in Free Enterprise Countries
4. Keep an Open Mind
5. Be Patient
6. Research Thoroughly
7. Consult Your Network
8. Think and Act Productively
9. Think Positively and Be an Optimist
10. Prepare Mentally

While these ten pillars represent Templeton's approach, it is also interesting to see how he saw his investment pillars. There is some overlap. In January 1992, Templeton penned an article for *World Monitor* where he offered his list of sixteen enduring principles for investment success. Some of these are repeated elsewhere, but together they are timeless principles that are worth revisiting more than once.

1. **Invest for maximum total real return** (after taxes, inflation, trading commissions, and fees).

2. **Invest—don't trade or speculate**. Commissions can consume your profits if you treat the market like a casino. Momentum investing— that is, simply buying recent winners and selling recent losers—ignores valuation and risk.

3. **Remain flexible and open-minded** about types of investment, i.e., Blue-chip stocks, cyclical stocks, corporate bonds, convertible stocks, U.S. treasuries, and cash.

4. **Buy low.** Simple in concept but difficult to execute. "Buy low" does not necessarily mean buy stocks that are low-priced or stocks whose price has recently declined. "Buy low" means to buy when the stock price is low relative to a company's intrinsic value as estimated by forecasting what the company's earnings and cash flow will be in five years. This is likely when sentiment has reached maximum pessimism but is not solely contrarian. Valuation is critical.

5. **Search for bargains among quality stocks**, such as a leader in sales or technology, strong management with a proven track record, low-cost producer, well-capitalized, or well-known trusted brand for a consumer product. Quality stocks, particularly those that have a predictable recurring business have staying power, and an investor has a higher conviction to forecast long-term earnings power and intrinsic value.

6. **Buy value, not market trends or the economic outlook.** Do the right thing for clients by investing only in stocks that represent good value, and don't be guided by index weights, popular holdings by competitors, peer pressure, or consensus macro worries.

7. **Diversify**—by company, by industry, by risk, and by country. Templeton said, "The only investors who shouldn't diversify are those who

are right 100 percent of the time." Diversify, but only in attractively valued stocks.

8. **Investigate before investing.** Do your due-diligence or hire experts to help. There is no substitute for hard work.

9. **Aggressively monitor your investments.** There are no stocks you can buy and forget because the pace of change is too great. Stocks may become too expensive or the company's competitive advantage may have eroded.

10. **Don't panic.** Sell when a stock is expensive or when you find a more attractive stock; otherwise don't sell, especially after a sharp market decline.

11. **Learn from your mistakes and the mistakes of others.** Determine what went wrong and how you can avoid the same mistake again.

12. **Begin with prayer so you can think more clearly**, make fewer mistakes, and make wise decisions.

13. **Recognize that outperforming the market is difficult.** The market index doesn't pay salaries to security analysts or portfolio managers and doesn't hold cash to redeem shares.

14. **Investing success is a process of continually seeking answers to new questions** as the economy, political environment, and universe of investments are always changing. Securities or industries that become popular will eventually lose their luster. Don't become complacent.

15. **Never invest purely on sentiment, analyst's recommendations, or tips.** Conviction is built upon your own work to conclude that your facts and reasoning are right.

16. **Don't be fearful or misled by media pessimism.** Sir John was eternally bullish on the drive, ingenuity, and resourcefulness of societies to advance living standards within a free market system. In his own words:

Because we have free communications here, if you're going to succeed in communications, you have to cater to the human weakness of desiring horrible things. And now communications are so much greater than it was when I became an investment counselor. At that time, there was no television. There was no program about investments on earth at that time.

Now we're just flooded with communications. As a result, we're flooded with bad news. And this bad news is making people depressed at a time when prosperity is at its greatest ever. We should be so optimistic. We have more blessings than at any time in history. And I notice it particularly in reading the newspapers. The newspapers will interpret almost anything in bearish terms. Catastrophes, murders, and so forth that happened fifty years ago in Asia were not heard of. Now they're on the front page of the newspaper. And this has a depressing effect. I believe though, that it will wear off. I believe that there's only a certain amount of bad news that we can take. As we get used to it, we will gradually learn to overlook it—just as the people in the communist nations began to overlook what was in their newspapers.[36]

CHAPTER 4

Templeton's Method
of Investment Selection

When your friends say such things as 'I'm going to buy semiconductor stocks because they have a great future,' you have to recognize that they are talking investment nonsense. It's true that semiconductors are going to have a great future, but the price of shares usually reflects that obvious expectation. So if all you know about any particular stock is that the product behind it is going to have a great future, you're nowhere near knowing whether you should buy shares.

—JOHN TEMPLETON[1]

With the table set with Templeton's mental preparation to investing, let's look more closely at how he selected his investments from the myriad of menu options.

Templeton's version of the timeless axiom, "Buy low, sell high" was "Buy at the point of maximum pessimism, and sell into maximum optimism." This advice sounds so simple in concept, but it is difficult in practice because it goes against human nature. However, Templeton pointed out that the lowest price for any security can only occur when there is rampant pessimism. If you wait until the light is at the end of the tunnel, investors will see the light also and the price will be higher accordingly. He encouraged investors to read the book written in 1841 by Charles MacKay, *Extraordinary Popular Delusions and the Madness of Crowds*.

In this chapter, we will explore how Templeton disciplined himself to apply this principle, what metrics he used to determine value, his thoughts on modern academic theory, the resources he used, his favorite list of questions for management, when he decided to sell a stock, and common mistakes to avoid.

As disciplined as Templeton was in life, he was equally disciplined in evaluating investments. Like other master investors, he sought to exploit the market's volatility driven by fear and greed. When asked how he picked stocks and whether intuition or feelings were part of his selection process, Templeton responded, "We avoid intuition. We apply arithmetic. For forty-seven years we have called ourselves quantitative security analysts. We don't buy something because it feels good, we buy something because we work out the arithmetic and it looks more promising than anything else."[2]

Templeton's Favorite Valuation Metric

Templeton used yardsticks of value to indicate bargains such as price/earnings ratios and price/cash flow ratios, but he was quick to mention that they don't all apply to each company. When asked if his valuation approach was earnings-based or asset-based, Templeton answered, "Both. You cannot neglect either. But in most cases, in assessing a company, we place more emphasis on future earnings rather than on current earnings or assets." He elaborated further:

> The yardstick of value we have used most often is price relative to probable future earnings. Others that we have used include price relative to cash flow, and price relative to true liquidating value, not book value. For different corporations, we look at different things. Most of the time we concentrate on fundamentals over technical, quantitative over qualitative. Future earnings more important than current or past, etc.[3]

Templeton also evaluated the trend of operating profit margins, liquidating value, the consistency of earnings growth, financial strength of the balance sheet, hidden assets, and he avoided hyper-rapid growth.

Templeton consistently reiterated that the most basic test he used in stock selection was to focus on the value of company derived by its long-term core earnings power relative to its current price.

> What is the lowest possible price in relation to probable long-range future earnings? There are many other (tests). We have to look at hundreds of

things, as you know. But nothing is so important as estimating what it'll earn in the long run and buying at the lowest price now.[4]

Note that Templeton's flagship fund was named the Templeton *Growth* Fund, not the Templeton Value Fund, or the Templeton Contrarian Fund. The name he chose indicated his bias that long-term, future core earnings is the key component in estimating intrinsic worth. He then maintained his discipline of buying securities priced at a discount to that value.

Many investors search for value based simplistically on low price/earnings ratios. Templeton said that "a low price/earnings multiple is *one* yardstick of a bargain. But it's too restrictive for our organization. It's only one method of dozens of approaches."[5] One of its limitations is that it is too focused on short-term results with the denominator—earnings—typically based on trailing one-year actual earnings or one-year forward estimates. Templeton was more interested in the longer-term sustainable core earnings as well as triangulating with other valuation metrics. The important point is that Templeton moved beyond Benjamin Graham's preference for historic valuation metrics. Instead, Templeton preferred valuation metrics based on future estimates with history as a guide.

Templeton used a variety of approaches and worksheets to assess value as relevant to the particular company. He was evasive about exactly how he used the worksheets.

> *I cannot be really specific about this. Besides, any method that is particularly successful only works if we keep it to ourselves…There isn't a typical one (worksheet). And they keep changing. Nothing that I want to publish. We are constantly changing the worksheets that we are using. More and more computers are being used. We partially select our security analysts on their ability to use computers in new ways.*[6]

His goal was to assess value and then determine whether the stock price was selling below its value. He was also interested in comparing his findings with other companies to get relative measures of value.

Once he discovered an anomaly where, for example, he found a company with strong growth and a low P/E ratio, he recognized that the yardstick of value was just the beginning of, not the answer to, his research.

> *I discovered years back with only a casual reading in a newspaper that the South Korean gross national product was growing three times as fast*

as America's. And then I discovered that South Korean securities could be bought in South Korea at only about four times earnings and a current yield of about 13 percent. So the combinations of a rapidly growing economy and corporations selling at very low yardsticks of value meant that I should investigate further. So I took a trip to South Korea, met with a banker who had lived there most of his life, and based on that I started studying about South Korea twelve years ago. Having a background of over one hundred yardsticks of value, any time that you find something out of line on one maybe two of these yardsticks, you go and investigate and study further. It's not intuitive, it's based on value.[7]

Favorite Questions to Ask Management

The first rule of investing, many would argue, is to understand the business that is being considered for investment. Determining a statistical bargain is one element of making an investment decision. Understanding management's strategy and competitive environment of the business are also vital steps for assessing the amount and timing of future cash flows, and for gaining the conviction necessary to make the investment. An investment, after all, is the process of allocating capital as a partner in trust to a management team that an investor expects to be an excellent steward of their capital. Templeton's process of evaluating management and its competitors included asking the following questions:

1. Do you have a long-range plan?
2. What will be your average annual growth rate?
3. If the growth rate is higher than the past, ask: Why should the future be different from the past?
4. What are your problems?
5. Who is your ablest competitor? Why?
6. If you couldn't own stock in your own company, which of your company's competitors would you want to invest in and why?[8]

Company managers have a natural tendency to be optimists about their own firm, which naturally biases their answers. Their candor, or lack thereof, is nonetheless instructive. In the early 1960s, Templeton met with the management of one of his investments in their office. The Templeton Growth Fund had made a small investment in this North Carolina company, and Templeton wanted to meet management before considering a larger position. Before he even returned home, he gave instructions to sell the stock immediately. "I've just interviewed the president and he has a great big bar in his office and a ticker tape machine and I don't trust him. Sell all of our stock."[9]

Interviewing management about their competitors' strengths and weaknesses can reveal an unvarnished and valuable perspective of the competitive landscape. Management's views can be validated from conversations with their competitors, suppliers, distributors, and customers to determine the company's true competitive position.

Influence of Benjamin Graham

At Columbia University, Templeton and Buffett were students of Benjamin Graham, who is considered the grandfather of security analysis. Graham gained notoriety beyond his students at Columbia for authoring, with David Dodd in 1934, the seminal textbook, *Security Analysis* as well as the more layman version, *The Intelligent Investor*.

Templeton valued his experience as a student under Graham, but like Buffett, was able to transition beyond his teaching. Templeton recalled:

> When I was a student under the famous Benjamin Graham, he taught me about using book values and to search for those companies selling for less than book values and to search for those companies selling for less than net-net working capital, i.e., where you subtract the liabilities from the current assets and if the result is higher than market price then you are buying cash at a discount and everything else is thrown in free. And I've used it. But it won't work today. Not in America. Because you won't find any companies selling for less than net working capital. Ben was a very wise man. He had a splendid method. But if he were alive today he would be doing something else, relying on newer and more varied concepts.[10]

When asked what tests he applied to determine value, Templeton responded, "Ordinary security analysis. Security analysis as taught by Benjamin Graham and others to arrive at evaluation of what the corporation is worth and thereby, what the share is worth, then we buy those shares that have the lowest price in relation to values."[11]

Graham's valuation approach was static based on historical balance sheet numbers that aren't subject to errors of estimation. The limitation was that the

41

net-net working capital approach ignores the earnings power of the business. The intrinsic value of any business is based on its discounted future cash flows, which incorporates its future core earnings power. Graham's approach sniffed out bargains, resulted in limited downside risk, and deserved the moniker that Buffett referred to as "cigar butt" approach to investing. Metaphorically, while there wasn't much left of the cigar, it was a bargain because the remaining puffs were essentially free. Graham's approach, however, admittedly ignored the more holistic approach of valuing the entire "cigar."

Resources

Templeton used a variety of resources to generate ideas and validate his current holdings. He used *Value Line* for its facts, not its opinions. He read *Wall Street Transcript*, which generally included lengthy interviews with portfolio managers who described their process and rationale for favorite holdings. He also read broker reports for establishing facts and paid no attention to their buy and sell recommendations. He believed that only about 1 percent of brokers thought in his terms. Brokers were typically told to send him their analyses in writing and not to call him. Templeton also studied holdings of other fund managers. When asked if he studied portfolios of other funds as a source of ideas, Templeton replied, "I do indeed…I follow about twenty of them, and every time the reports come out I go over them carefully to see what they've been able to think up."[12]

Comments on Academic Theories

Templeton was the greatest mutual fund investor of his generation. He outperformed his competitors and index benchmarks over decades with old-fashioned bargain hunting and fundamental security analysis, searching worldwide for neglected stocks that were selling for a fraction of their true worth. He was as intellectually honest as any investor and readily admitted that remaining flexible and open to new ideas were critical to future success. Templeton was aware of Modern Portfolio Theory, the Capital Asset Pricing Model, Efficient Market Theory, and Option Theory, but was skeptical about using them. Templeton's decades-long outperformance itself is a repudiation of the theory that the markets are always efficient because their prices already perfectly incorporate all known information, and that there was no advantage in attempting to beat the market.

Louis Rukeyser asked John Templeton for his views on the Efficient Market Theory, saying, "This past weekend, I was with a group of academics… and they told me that nobody can analyze stocks, that it's all just a random walk, and a very efficient market, and that the kind of advice that you people give and the kind of analyses you do is worthless. How do you reply to them?"

Templeton responded, "That's just resigning from the game. If you take the game of tennis, [there are] exactly as many losers as winners, but that's no reason to give up playing tennis."[13]

The Capital Asset Pricing Model generally describes a relationship where an investor's expected return is correlated to the risk of the company. An investor's return is expressed as the risk-free rate of return plus a premium for the risk of the security. Risk is defined as *beta*, which is defined as the historical price volatility of a stock relative to the market over a period of time. The overall market has a beta of 1.00. A stock with a beta of .80 would have been historically 20 percent less volatile in price movement than the market, and a stock with a beta of 1.30 would have been historically 30 percent more volatile in price than the market.

Templeton used beta as a measure of risk of his overall portfolio, but he had no use for beta in selecting individual stocks.

> *We find that betas are unstable and therefore not a totally reliable investment indicator. We prefer to use our fundamentally based approaches, but will, however, calculate betas on our portfolios, making revisions if necessary to reflect our objectives. In our opinion, beta is overemphasized. We do use betas later on as a check on our portfolio manager, to see what the beta of specific fund portfolios is and to make sure that no one portfolio has taken on too much risk. But we don't use it at the initial stages. Instead we look for what we call yardsticks of value which are fundamentally based measures, such as share price relative to sustainable future earnings or cash-flow per share. Everyone should read about modern portfolio theory but honestly, they are not going to make much money with it. I've never seen anybody that came up with a really superior long-term record using only modern portfolio management.[14]*

Templeton correctly pointed to a flaw in beta: they can be volatile depending on a shift in a company or industry prospects. Another flaw is that beta says nothing about whether a company is overvalued or undervalued.

Use of Technical Analysis

An advantage of finding a bargain price for a stock is that the risk of a further decline in price should be limited. The risk, from a relative performance perspective, is that it may remain a bargain for longer than desired while the rest of the market moves higher. Technical analysis is the study of historical price and volume movements of a stock to understand the historical trading pattern of a stock. Technical analysis certainly was not a driver of how Templeton selected stocks, but it did have a mild influence.

Sometimes Templeton would supplement his fundamental analysis of a company with technical analysis. Once he determined a bargain, he might wait until the stock began to outperform the market for a month before he purchased. This way he aimed to avoid sitting on "dead" money. "Now we do use technical analysis in the short range to a small extent. If we are trying to choose between twelve stocks—all of whom seem to be about equally good bargains—then we try to buy those that have the favorable technical pattern."[15]

When Templeton Sold a Stock

Templeton's rule for selling was simple: sell "the least good bargain" stock when you find a better one to replace it. In fact, he preferred to replace a stock if the new candidate had at least 50 percent greater appreciation potential from its market price to its fair value than the stock replaced. "We sell when we find a better bargain. We're constantly searching for these bargains and when you find one, if you have a lot of surplus cash, you buy it. If you don't have the surplus cash, you go through the present list of over a hundred stocks we own and sell that one which is the least good bargain."[16]

Dealing with Mistakes and Avoiding Mistakes

Mistakes in investing are inevitable. The key is to learn from our mistakes and the mistakes of others. Templeton was spot on when he said, "The only way to avoid mistakes is not to invest—which is the biggest mistake of all."

There are two types of investment mistakes: mistakes of commission and mistakes of omission. Mistakes of commission are those where an investor makes an investment and it either loses money or underperforms the market. Templeton estimated that about one-third of his investments underperform the market.

> *One-third of all the decisions we make prove to be unprofitable…no matter how hard you work…you can't expect to be right more than two-thirds of the time…in our long history there had been eight years when we lagged behind the average of other mutual funds in America. And it's going to be that way in the future. There is no way to avoid that. There are good years and bad years.*[17]

The two-thirds that outperform the market index do so "largely because we bought them at bargain prices."[18]

The mistakes of commission will inevitably try an investor's patience. The key is to determine whether the original investment rationale is still intact or whether the problem is structural. Templeton recommended Ford on public television in 1978 when it was priced at $41/share. Louis Rukeyser asked Templeton in 1980 why Ford had dropped to $33/share. Templeton responded that investors were focused too short-term and missing the bigger picture.

> *The public is still looking at the short-term trend. Ford lost around a billion dollars last year in the United States, and may lose a billion this year, and that worries people, and they say 'well, why buy Ford if it's going to lose money in the United States?' Well, the answer is that Ford is not going to lose money worldwide—they had good earnings outside of the United States. In fact, I think they're the strongest automobile company outside of the United States.*[19]

He added that he thought Ford could earn over $20/share within three or four years.

Then in 1981, Rukeyser praised Templeton for the 35 percent average return of his five recommendations in 1980. The sixth recommendation however was Ford, which had declined further to $23/share. Rukeyser nudged Templeton, "Are you sticking stubbornly with a loss or are you going to be bailed out on this one?"

A humbled but steadfast Templeton admitted:

This is a good illustration that we make hundreds of mistakes. At least a third of the things that we change from one stock to another turn out later to have been wiser to stay in the old stock. Ford is having much more trouble than we anticipated or the management anticipated, but at these low prices, it's too low to sell. I would recommend that you stay with it, because at these prices, the most you can lose is $23 a share. If things turn out well, you might make $100 to $150 a share...Ford could again earn $17 a share as it did three years ago.[20]

Ford's stock price reached $100/share four years later in 1985, $150/share in 1986 and $315/share in 1993. Earnings climbed to $45/share in 1988.

The mistake of omission is where an investor doesn't make an investment that subsequently does very well. Templeton counseled, "Nobody's going to be able to take advantage of all opportunities and nobody should fret about having missed some of them. The very nature of investing is that there will be many opportunities that you don't take part in; your job is to participate in a few good ones."[21]

Templeton cautioned investors to avoid five common investment mistakes.

1. Investing with the Crowd

"Superior investment performance is possible only if you invest differently from the crowd. If ten doctors tell you to take a certain medicine, you'd be wise to take that medicine. Or if ten civil engineers tell you to build a bridge a certain way, then you should build the bridge that way. But when selecting securities, consensus is dangerous. If ten security analysts tell you independently to buy a certain asset, stay away from it. The popularity will already be reflected in a high price."[22]

Similarly, if you buy the same securities as other investors, you will have the same results as other investors.

The main thing that people need to learn is selecting assets is totally different from almost every other activity. If you go to ten doctors and they tell you (to take) the same medicine, that's it. That's the thing to take. You go to ten engineers to build a bridge, they tell you the same thing, that's to be, but you go to ten investment advisors and they pick out the same asset, you'd better stay away from them. To say the same thing in other words, the time when an asset is selling at its best bargain price is when most people are trying to sell. There's no other reason why an asset will go down to a bargain price. And if you wait until you're through the tunnel and out into the sunshine, you'll have to pay a premium price. If you even wait until you can see the light at the end of the tunnel, you're already past the best bargain days.[23]

One could imagine Templeton's smiling approval of Apple Inc.'s memorable advertising slogan in 2007: "Think different." The ad featured footage of seventeen iconic twentieth century personalities including Thomas Edison, Albert Einstein, John Lennon, Martin Luther King, Jr., Muhammad Ali, and Alfred Hitchcock. Apple could have fittingly included John Templeton for his encouragement to "think different" from the consensus investment view.

2. Lack of Due Diligence and Too Pessimistic

> *"Most investors operate with too little knowledge and think it's too easy to make a superior performance. So they get in and out too often and without enough knowledge. Also, certainly in America it's been a custom that people are unreasonably pessimistic. Here we are at the highest point in history in terms of gross national product—the highest in stock market history. (America has) many other advantages and yet the majority of the people are unusually pessimistic now. The indexes of pessimism in America are quite high. The short interest is about the highest it's ever been. So the American people, are in my opinion, clearly too pessimistic, and that's a reassuring fact because you don't have bear markets start when most people are pessimistic."[24]*

3. Holding Too Much Cash

Cash is continually losing its purchasing power in virtually every nation due to the corrosive impact of inflation. The cost of a standard U.S. postage stamp increased from $.03 in 1954, the year Templeton started his Templeton Growth Fund, to $.49 in 2014. During this sixty-year period, the compound annual growth rate of the price of a postage stamp was 4.8 percent/year. A dollar in 1954 could have mailed thirty-three letters in 1954 but only two in 2014.

> *Money has lost purchasing power every single year for thirty-seven years. And our studies would indicate it's going to lose purchasing power every one of the next thirty-seven years.*[25]

It seems to me that one of the great mistakes that investors are making right now is their desire to own fixed income assets, cash money market funds, certificates of deposit, and bond funds. We agree that the bull market in bonds is likely to continue for a while, but all the evidence is that you will produce far better results by investing in equities—in shares—than you will be investing in cash. And yet, today the public has more cash than it has ever had in history. The average family has less than half as much in common stocks in relations to its assets than it has at other times in the past. But people are fooling themselves today to think that they play safe by holding cash assets.[26]

Inflation is a constant in the modern economic world. While it has numerous corrosive effects, investors have to prepare for it and position their investments to profit from it. Templeton said that until nations learn to balance their budgets, we're almost sure to have more and more inflation. He advocated that common stocks will continue to be the best hedge against inflation, not necessarily year by year, but long-term. Bonds, according to Templeton, are not suitable for long-term investment and were no longer for widows and orphans. At the time in 1995, he said that with 5 percent average inflation and high taxes, long bonds yielding 8 percent would produce a negative yield.

4. Selling Out at the Bottom

As we've seen, Templeton famously advised to "buy at the point of maximum pessimism and sell into maximum optimism."

If you don't have too much debt, you won't get sold out at the wrong time. But more importantly, don't get frightened out at the wrong time. For every person who's forced out, many more people are frightened out...the time to get rich is by buying when share prices are low...We welcome these fluctuations. Wide fluctuations may disturb some people. But for us, they increase the possibility that we can produce superior investment results.[27]

In November 1990, with the Dow off almost 500 points from its high and amidst gloomy investor sentiment, Templeton weighed in on his views of the futility of market timing: "We have been investment counselors for 58 years, and in all that time we have never been able to tell our clients when a bear market will start or stop."[28] He observed that stock prices have doubled about every ten years throughout the history of American markets. He added, "We are finding the best bargains in industries where there is great pessimism"[29] especially emerging growth companies that were selling at a discount to their intrinsic value such as Monsanto, Quantum, Mylan Laboratories, Millipore, and First American Financial.

5. Not Saving Enough and Investing with Borrowed Money

Never buy stocks with borrowed money or with money that you may need tomorrow. Templeton never had a home mortgage. In a bear market, borrowed money acts like weight belt to a drowning victim. Investors all too often capitulate and sell their investments when their sense of panic and financial preservation at any cost reaches a pinnacle of stress. Templeton, ever mindful of the destructive effects of debt on his father and neighbors in Winchester, Tennessee, wanted to invest without emotional "weight belts." "I want to be able to hold onto stocks I buy—forever if necessary."[30]

In Templeton's last annual meeting of shareholders of the Templeton Growth Fund before selling it to Franklin Resources, he couldn't have been more direct in his advice to be thrifty and save:

- "The thrifty will eventually own the spendthrifts."

- "This law applies equally to real estate investors, people, families, and nations."

- "Often those who buy stocks with borrowed money are later wiped out because they are forced to sell at the wrong time." (Sir John offered the same advice when asked one week after the Crash of 1987 what was the single most important lesson of the previous week, and he replied, "I would say that if you never buy investments with borrowed money you can always be comfortable. Human nature is such, we're going to have periods of enthusiasm and pessimism. Every ten years, there will be bull markets and bear markets. But if you don't have borrowed money, you don't have anything to worry about."[31])

- "Few security analysts ever become wealthy because only a few of the wise analysts are ever thrifty."

- "Studying the history of nations indicates that where the people are most thrifty, the nation becomes prosperous and powerful."[32]

On May 21, 1991, Sir John Templeton, CFA, received the first AIMR (Association for Investment Management and Research—a predecessor to the CFA Institute) Award for Professional Excellence, which recognized a member of the profession whose exemplary achievement, excellence of practice, and leadership inspire and reflect upon the profession to the highest degree. In his acceptance speech, Sir John said that the rich invest in entrepreneurship and the poor save and conserve. He urged security analysts to recognize their career as an honorable ministry by working diligently to provide superior and honest results, providing investors with the "confidence and security of the truly rich in mind and spirit…that brings dignity, personal freedom, mobility, and self-reliance."

CHAPTER 5

Portfolio Design

Diversify by company, by industry, by risk, and by country.

—JOHN TEMPLETON

Before we review Templeton's professionally managed Templeton Growth Fund, let's consider his advice for an individual's portfolio.

Portfolio for Individuals

Templeton was asked in 1988 what he would consider to be the ideal portfolio for a young family with one child and one wage earner. With the usual caveats that a professional investment counselor would need much more customized information to make a suitable recommendation, Templeton responded,

> *The optimum portfolio composition would depend on the individual's income, his expectancy to inherit, tax status, number of dependents, etc. We would have to look carefully, make recommendations, and then constantly revise. But here are some guidelines. We generally recommend cash reserves (bonds and other fixed assets) equal to about 25 percent of annual income. At present, up to two-thirds of your portfolio should be in common stocks and the remainder in real estate and life insurance. You should have no less than 10 stocks, no more than 25 percent in any one industry, and no more than 80 percent in any one nation. But this applies only to people with $1,000,000 or more in assets. Otherwise, the two-thirds component should go not into selected shares, but into well-managed equity mutual funds.[1]*

In the early years, when Templeton was focused on his investment counseling business for individuals, the proportion of stocks he held for individual clients would vary based on valuation. He would allocate up to 100 percent in stocks if stock prices were as much as 35 percent below normal valuations as measured by the current overall market price ratios for price/earnings and price/asset replacement relative to their twenty-year historical averages. Conversely, if overall stock prices were 66 percent above normal valuation levels, his stock allocation could be as low as 10 percent. He established specific stock percentage allocation ranges between these extremes with 60 percent as his baseline stock exposure when stock prices were fairly priced.

Stock Selection is Paramount

When Templeton was asked whether asset allocation or stock selection was more important in determining portfolio performance, he responded, "The latter (stock selection). We consider it far more important to find a bargain. We search throughout the world for whatever is a bargain and buy that and only later then do we say what proportion do we have in common stocks."[2]

Proportion in International Investments

Templeton suggested individuals allocate about 20 percent to 60 percent of their funds to international investments.[3] His rationalization was, "Only about one-third of all common stocks in the world are in the U.S.... So common sense suggests that's how a portfolio should be allocated...studies show that in the long run, a globally diversified portfolio yield higher returns with less volatility than a diversified, single-nation portfolio."[4]

Portfolio for Individuals Who Depend on Current Income

The dilemma facing an investor who relies on current income from their investment portfolio during a period of low interest rates, is whether to venture more heavily into stocks as a source of dividend income and capital gains, despite their higher volatility than fixed income alternatives. Several times Templeton was clear with his preference:

> *There have been numerous studies that show that investing in growth stocks in the long run produces more results, total return, than seeking high income. And so for a person who wants high income, they should invest for*

growth and then spend some of the growth, spend some of that capital gains as income.[5]

(People who need income) would come out much better if they would buy well-managed common stock fund, and then just tell the fund to send them what income they need to spend.[6]

From January of 1946 through June of 1991, the Dow Jones Industrial Average rose by 11.4 percent average annually—including reinvestment of dividends but not counting taxes—compared with an average annual inflation rate of 4.4 percent...the S&P 500 outperformed inflation, Treasury bills, and corporate bonds in every decade except the 1970s and it outperformed Treasury bonds—supposedly the safest of all investment—in all four decades.[7]

Sir John eschewed the temptation for income-oriented investors to focus almost exclusively on high yielding stocks. He explained,

This is an easy method for investing your income from investments, but it is the worst of all methods. Stocks sell at low prices in relation to current dividends usually because there are good reasons for expecting that the dividend may be reduced. Investors selecting stocks with high current yield face not only the risk of reduced dividends but also the greater risk of capital losses. A far wiser method for increasing your income is to select stocks with the highest earnings in relation to market price.[8]

In the early 1990s many investors were lured by the high dividend yields of community and money center banks. Investors who blindly placed their trust in the familiarity and perceived staying power of the banks, and who didn't look closely at their swelling loan losses and weak equity capital, were scorched by plummeting stock prices when many banks reduced or eliminated their dividends in the wake of the banking and savings & loan crisis.

Sir John advised to focus on growth stocks instead. "In the endeavor to increase your income, it is wise also to select growth stocks. Growth stocks are most likely to earn more and pay increased dividends in future years. Usually growth companies have a high rate of earnings in relation to net worth."[9] Sir John preferred growth companies with high return-on-equity (ROE).

Companies with high ROEs are more valuable because they produce more income and cash flow with relatively less invested capital. All else equal, if two companies are given capital of $100, and company A produces income of $20 in the first year, and company B only produces $10, then company A likely enjoys more favorable competitive advantages than company B. If company A's competitive advantages are sustainable, then over time, shareholders will benefit from higher compounding growth rates in income, cash flow, and intrinsic value, resulting in increased dividends and higher stock prices.

Portfolio for Templeton Growth Fund

The Templeton Growth Fund was launched in late 1954 with $6.6 million in assets under management. As we mentioned earlier, the fund was domiciled in Canada for tax reasons and was one of the first mutual funds to offer investors in the U.S. the opportunity to invest in a portfolio of non-U.S. stocks. As of April 30, 1955, the fund had over 60 percent invested in equities, 18 percent in preferred stocks, and 20 percent in fixed income securities. Canadian assets accounted for 90 percent of the fund's investments, which included twenty-seven Canadian stocks, of which one-third were in forestry and mining.

Templeton was a self-proclaimed "bottom-up" investor who prospected for bargains wherever he could find them without regard to benchmark index weights. Within this framework, he had disciplined guideposts that governed which countries he would consider suitable for his investments. He preferred countries that adopted capitalism and where government interference and inflation were minimal. He focused on nations that prized democracy, deregulation, decentralization, respect for property rights (including copyright protection) and:

- less government ownership
- wider personal share ownership
- free movement of capital across national borders
- less government regulation
- less quarrelsome labor unions
- better schools for management studies
- lower corporate and personal tax rates
- incentives for thrift and entrepreneurship.[10]

As a result, Sir John said, "out of more than 160 nations in the world, there are less than three dozen where we would feel safe enough to invest our shareholders money."[11] One of those was Japan.

Templeton's first visit to Japan was in 1935, but he didn't start to buy shares for his own account until the mid-1950s and for the Templeton Growth Fund until 1964. The Japanese were an industrious people determined to recover from World War II. He observed many of his own character traits in the Japanese, such as a strong work ethic, respect for business and education, a penchant for thrift, and a desire to save.

According to a letter to his clients in 1959, Templeton was impressed with several aspects about investing in Japan:

- Japanese exports surged into the U.S., due in part to low wages, which gave their products a low-cost producer advantage. The evidence was apparent in autos, drugs, radios, ships, dinnerware, cameras, and many other products.

- Japanese industrial production was outpacing the U.S. by over ninefold from 1951–1958.

- A tax treaty between the U.S. and Japan provided that Japan would not withhold taxes on dividends for U.S. investors. The tax treaty effectively reduced the net tax on Japanese dividend income to less than one-half of comparable U.S. dividend income.

- Japanese stocks yielded 4.4 percent compared to 3.3 percent for U.S. stocks, and high quality Japanese bonds maturing in four years yielded 8 percent compared to similar bonds in the U.S. that yielded 4.2 percent.

- Only 1.6 percent of Japanese stocks were owned by foreigners due to a Japanese rule that prevented prompt repatriation of capital.

U.S. investors were deterred by a rule that prevented capital and capital gains from being converted back into dollars for two years. Even then, only 20 percent per year could be converted back into dollars. Templeton anticipated that "if the world trade position of Japan continues to strengthen, this rule about delay in converting capital back into dollars may later be eliminated."[12] As soon as deregulation allowed repatriation of profits from Japan in 1963, Templeton began buying Japanese stocks for the mutual fund.

In 1967 the fund owned fewer than thirty investments and Templeton's global focus was becoming more evident. (As the fund grew, Templeton added more stocks. By 1983 Templeton said that "we have over a hundred stocks in our mutual fund, and we think they are all good values."[13] By 1994, the Templeton Growth Fund had 240 stocks.) His largest equity holding in 1967 at a 13 percent weight was his only Japanese holding—a cosmetic company named Shiseido. He also owned Phillips and Royal Dutch Petroleum from Holland, and one company each from Japan, Germany, Sweden, and Great Britain.

Interestingly, by 1969, fifteen years after launch, the fund had only $200,000 more in assets than it started with. Redemptions almost entirely offset investment gains that had grown five-fold since inception. In 1969, valuations were lofty enough that they caused Warren Buffett to wind down his partnership. Templeton reduced his number of holdings to twenty, with Shiseido remaining his largest position at 14.5 percent of the fund. Foreign and government bonds represented more than one-third of the value of the fund.

Concurrent with his move to the Bahamas where he "could think more clearly and creatively," and perhaps frustrated with the lack of asset growth in his namesake mutual fund despite his excellent performance, Templeton began to make his bold, career-defining, oversized investment bet on Japanese stocks where others were unwilling. The fund was small enough that it could operate without investment constraints, and the bargains in Japan were too attractive to ignore. "When we began to invest in Japan, the total market in Japan was smaller than the capitalization of IBM."[14]

Japanese stocks represented a higher proportion of Templeton's investments in 1971, when the investment restrictions were lifted in Japan, and reached its peak at 62 percent of the fund in 1974. Significant winners included Nissan Motors, Sumitomo Trust, and Bridgestone. In 1972 the Templeton Growth Fund returned 68.9 percent.

In the next two years, a combination of overvaluation of U.S. stocks, choking inflation, and the OPEC oil embargo triggered an economic slowdown and a slide in U.S. stock prices of almost 40 percent.

"At that time, when the average price-earnings ratio was 19 in the United States, we were buying stocks in Japan at only two and three times earnings, so the fact that you are looking worldwide means that you can sidestep a bear market in any one nation."[15] In the period from 1972–1974 the Templeton Growth Fund climbed 32.6 percent while the S&P 500 index fell 25.3 percent for an outperformance of almost 58 percent.

By largely sidestepping the U.S. bear market and making a prescient bet on Japanese stocks, Templeton's Growth fund soared 19.6 percent a year during the 1970s compared to 5.4 percent for the S&P 500. A $10,000 investment in the Templeton Growth fund at the beginning of 1970 would have been worth $55,900 at the end of the decade compared to $17,700 invested in the S&P 500.

Templeton later explained in 1992,

> When we did (buy shares in Japan) we picked out the best growth companies and had an average cost of only 3x earnings...when they got up to 33x earnings, we thought, well there are better bargains elsewhere. So we gradually took our profits. But we looked five years too soon. The market in Japan went on up to 75x earnings.[16]

By 1979 the prices of Japanese stocks were twice as high as U.S. stocks, and Templeton's exposure to Japan was nearly eliminated at just 5 percent. By the time Japanese stock prices reached the nosebleed height of 75x earnings in the late 1980s, he had zero exposure. A by-product of Templeton selling at expensive levels only to see Japanese prices reach incredulously expensive levels is that it caused Templeton to lag the MSCI World Equity Index (which was formed in 1974) during these years. Japan represented just 12 percent of the MSCI World Index in 1974 and reached as high as 40 percent of the index weight in 1989. During this period, the Japanese, Templeton later explained, bought stocks like they buy collectibles without regard to price or earnings. While Templeton could have made even more money by selling later, in hindsight he would have violated his investment discipline to preserve capital by investing only in bargains. He also didn't violate his principles by succumbing to the pressures of the institutional mindset to hug an index weight.

Templeton found bargains in North America and Europe in the mid- to late 1970s, and these were prominent positions until he sold the fund in 1992. In 1978 Templeton allocated about 60 percent to U.S. stocks and the other 40 percent were in Canada, Japan, England, Germany, Hong Kong and Australia. The U.S. weight of 60 percent was the highest he had in over twenty-four years. He said,

> We didn't decide to put 60 percent in the United States. We simply looked all over the world for where we could buy a stock for the lowest possible price in relation to our judgment of its value and we found them in the United States, so we gradually got up to 60 percent.[17]

He found the best bargains in oil and gas, real estate and construction, "not because we decided they are good areas but because when we are searching worldwide for the best bargains, we happen to find quite a lot of them in those industries."[18]

Templeton kept a relatively consistent exposure of 60–65 percent in U.S. stocks until he sold the fund. As bargain opportunities presented themselves, he shifted his exposure between emerging growth stocks and shares of well-known companies that would be popular with pension funds.

Templeton was particularly bullish on U.S. stocks in 1982 for the following reasons:

- Valuations were cheap. U.S. stocks were priced at just 7x earnings, which matched the lowest on record for the DJIA. The low valuation reflected pessimism surrounding high inflation and interest rates, an oil crisis, and the threat of Japanese competition from lower priced products. Templeton believed that U.S. price/earnings multiples would eventually climb to levels of other countries, such as Singapore at 16x earnings, Hong Kong at 18x earnings, and Japan at 20x earnings. Price-to-book values of less than 1x were as low as the Great Depression. Price-to-replacement values in August 1982 were lower than they had ever been before in the history of the stock market.

- There were a number of corporate takeovers that suggested prices were a bargain. Templeton rationalized that the main reason why a company was willing to pay a 50–100 percent premium to gain control of another is because they believed they were still getting a bargain.

- Corporations were buying back their own shares at a greater pace than at any previous time in history. Templeton believed that a company that repurchases its own shares "proves that those people who know the company best believe that today's share prices are a real bargain."[19]

- Templeton observed that there was more cash available for investment than he had ever seen in his life. He believed this pent up buying power would eventually drive prices higher. Sources of the cash included insurance companies, foreign investors—especially the Japanese, Germans and Arabs, and pension funds that had more than $600 billion but were expected to increase to more than $3 trillion within twelve years. He reasoned that if those funds were 50 percent invested in stocks, it would represent $1.5 trillion in common stocks, which was more than the total market value of all stocks in the U.S. in 1982 of about $1.25 trillion.

CHAPTER 6

Case Studies

People are always asking me where is the outlook good, but that's the wrong question. The right question is: Where is the outlook most miserable?

—JOHN TEMPLETON

The essence of Templeton's investment purchases is to buy at the point of maximum pessimism when the current market price is low relative to a company's fair value derived from its future normalized earnings power. The maximum pessimism condition is predicated on a prevailing concern about a company's operation. The overhanging worry is typically serious enough to trigger a wave of selling by investors who fear that at best, the stock is "dead money," and they would rather own a cleaner situation; and at worst, the company developments will only deteriorate further. The opportunity is to first discern whether the problem is real or perceived. If the problem is real, the next question to answer is whether the problem is temporary, fixable, and non-structural, or if it is a structural and permanent impairment. Ultimately these situations are potentially lucrative opportunities for investors who are willing to look beyond the current turmoil, not with blind optimism, but with facts supported by research to determine whether or not the current fundamental problem will impair the future earnings power of the company and thereby its intrinsic value.

We can appreciate Templeton's stock picking ability by looking more closely at several case studies to assess how he executed his discipline to buy at the point of maximum pessimism.

Union Carbide

Templeton recalled, "one of my best trades was Union Carbide."[1] Templeton began buying Union Carbide in 1982 because "a year ago [they] earned about $10-and-a half—only selling at $40—probably within five years will earn $20 a share—only two times today's price."[2]

On December 4, 1984, *The Wall Street Journal* reported that a poisonous gas (methyl isocyanate) was leaking from a Union Carbide pesticide plant in Bhopal, India, killing 410 people the day before and injuring more than 10,000. The seven-year old plant was 51 percent owned by Union Carbide and 49 percent owned by the Indian government. The plant contributed 2 percent of the company's revenue. The article reported that a company spokesman said that any damages would be insured. In the month of December, the stock price plummeted over 30 percent from almost $50 to $33/share. (Note that the stock subsequently split three for one. The stock prices quoted are pre-split.)

Templeton bought more stock.

Remember back in 1985 [sic 1984] when there was that horrible accident at the Union Carbide plant in Bhopal? The stock came crashing down to $32.75 from $50 on the New York Stock Exchange on fears that legal suits filed by family and relatives of the victims would put the chemical producer out of business. And we were sitting with a lot of stock. But do you know what we did? We bought some more and when the price fell further, we bought more again.[3]

On December 6, 1984, Indian officials said the death toll was at least 1,600, with unofficial estimates as high as 2,000 dead, and 50,000 suffered injuries such as chest pains, eye irritation, and vomiting. Doctors estimated that tens of thousands would suffer permanent ailments such as lung damage, blindness, and sterility. After visiting the plant, India's cabinet minister, Vasant Sathe, called the tragedy the worst disaster in the history of the chemical industry. Twenty-five years later he said one-half of Bhopal was converted into a gas chamber overnight. William Kelly, a Union Carbide spokesman, said, "We do not believe the company is likely to go under."[4] Union Carbide officials repeatedly said that the company had insurance to cover damage claims, although the company declined to disclose the amount or the insurers. Insurance company officials estimated the policies would cover the company for at least $200 million but doubted the insurance would cover potentially extensive punitive damages.

The next day, on December 7th, Union Carbide's corporate director of health, safety, and environmental affairs, Jackson Browning, said, "While the Bhopal tragedy is without precedent, it is believed that considering both the insurance and other resources available, the financial structure of Union Carbide Corporation isn't threatened in any way," and it was not seeking bankruptcy. The credit rating agencies, Standard & Poor's and Moody's, said they were reviewing Union Carbide's debt rating for possible downgrading.

The same day, *The Wall Street Journal's* "Heard on the Street" column profiled Union Carbide. It cited a money manager who sold her entire stake saying, "You don't need the aggravation. This could be another Manville (a company that was plagued for years by asbestos-related claims and eventually went bankrupt), and who needs that?" The article pointed to other analysts who thought the stock decline was an overreaction, and the potential liability for actual damages was manageable because the compensation to the victims would be lower due to the lower standard of living in India. The article quoted William Young, a chemical analyst at Dean Witter, as saying that Union Carbide had more than $200 million in insurance coverage and that claims for actual damages would amount to about $100 million, and even if $200 million in punitive damages were assessed and was not covered by insurance, Union Carbide's earnings would only fall $1.50/share (compared to overall earnings then of $4.50/share). He added, "When rational analysis is used the stock is worth more than its current price." However, he was not recommending the stock.

On December 11, 1984, *The Wall Street Journal* reported the Bass brothers of Texas acquired a 5.4 percent stake in Union Carbide at prices between $34.00–$38.52/share. The dividend yielded more than 8 percent. It was also reported that a Union Carbide technical team from the United States was allowed inside the plant for the first time.

On January 11, 1985, *The Wall Street Journal* reported that Union Carbide's CEO, Warren Anderson, said, "We can make our way through. We have all the assets and bank lines and credit we need. If we manage our company well…I think we will be all right." He also stressed that he was hoping to settle the claims within six months. The cause of the disaster would not be known publicly for another three weeks.

As of September 30, 1985, Templeton was Union Carbide's largest holder, aside from GAF Corporation, which was a chemical and building products company with about 3.4 million shares. Templeton explained,

Some people thought I had become unglued! But here was the situation. First, we figured that the insurance settlements would absorb much of the Bhopal sting. And second, Union Carbide, a company that we considered to be well run, would continue to turn out the products that the public needed. In short, we believed that the Bhopal effect would have to wear off sooner or later. Either the company would rally again to profitability or its undeniably useful business units could be sold off to a number of anxious buyers.[5]

On December 10, 1985, *The Wall Street Journal* reported that GAF Corporation, which had revenues of $731 million, or just 7.7 percent of Union Carbide's $9.5 billion in revenues, offered to acquire the 90 percent of Union Carbide it didn't already own for $68/share. Union Carbide rejected the offer and said it "will come out with both fists swinging."

Templeton recalled in 1988, "By the end of 1986 [sic 1985], GAF Corporation had offered to buy the company for almost $69.00 a share, and we just happened to have 3,000,000 of the shares! That's what I mean by buying on temporary bad news!"[6]

Templeton told colleagues at his Bahamas headquarters to hold onto the stock. "It's wise not to be in too much of a hurry to sell. The first offer mightn't be the only one." For the next three weeks, he checked the prices only once or twice a day and waited.[7]

Union Carbide countered by offering to buy back 35 percent of its stock for $20/share in cash and $65/share in debt securities for a total offer of about $72/share because the debt would trade at less than $65/share.

On December 26, 1985, *The Wall Street Journal* reported that GAF Corporation raised its offer to $74/share. In the last few days of December, Templeton lost his patience, and he unloaded his entire holding, much of it on the last day of the year.[8]

On January 3, 1986, *The Wall Street Journal* reported that GAF boosted its bid to $78/share and Union Carbide retaliated by announcing measures to reluctantly sell its prized consumer products division (Eveready batteries and Glad plastic bags), increase its debt, increase its annual dividend to $4.40 from $3.40, and alter its equity structure to fund an $85/share offer in cash and securities for 55 percent of its stock. Union Carbide's debt would double to $5.4 billion, and the debt/equity ratio would swell to 14 to 1.

Templeton lamented in early 1986, "We sold too soon."[9]

On January 9, 1986, GAF abandoned its hostile $74/share offer for Union Carbide and said it would keep its 10 percent stake.

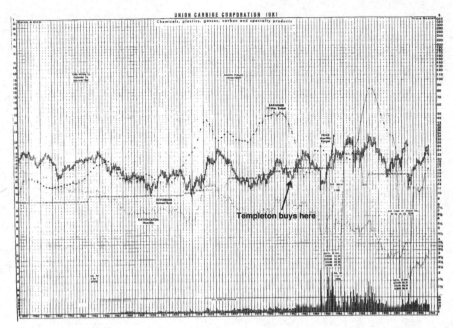

Figure 1. Union Carbide

On September 12, 1994, Union Carbide agreed to sell its 50.9 percent stake in the Indian subsidiary involved in the poisonous leak that killed at least 3,800 people and, according to a government affidavit in 2006, injured more than 500,000, to a unit of Britain's McLeod Russel Holdings PLC for $90 million. Union Carbide maintained that the cause of the leak was the work of an unidentified employee's sabotage but accepted "moral responsibility." The Bhopal factory never reopened.

Takeaways

Inevitably when holding a stock, investors are faced with a news development regarding their investment that tests their resolve. The chemical gas leak at Union Carbide's Bhopal facility has been referred to as the world's worst industrial disaster, claiming over 3,800 lives and causing over 550,000 injuries, including life-long crippling.

Templeton responded by rationally questioning what sort of liability was involved in similar instances in the past and what the potential liability would be for Union Carbide. He determined that the financial liability was reasonably covered by insurance and, to the extent insurance wasn't entirely adequate, the company could sell off unrelated, lucrative divisions to cover the rest. While it would have been easy to "sell first and ask questions later," Templeton built his conviction through rational analysis and kept buying the stock or, as he said, "kept accommodating the sellers." The result was one of his best trades. Templeton was also correct in his original assessment that Union Carbide was undervalued relative to its future earnings power. Union Carbide eventually earned nearly $15/share in 1989. Templeton first began buying the stock at less than 3x what Union Carbide earning seven years later.

Alcan Aluminum

In May 1982 Alcan Aluminum, the industry's number two producer, repealed a 6 percent price increase for sheet, the only product in high-demand use by beverage can makers. The other producers followed suit. *The Wall Street Journal* cited a buyer who said, "It's getting competitive as hell out there."[10]

On June 18, 1982, Templeton recommended Alcan Aluminum on public television.

> *"Throughout our 40 years of investment counsel, we've normally found the best bargains in the unknown companies—emerging growth stocks, but for the first time now, the big companies, such as Alcan Aluminum selling at only $16 a share, could easily earn $12 a share in the next market cycle."*

When Templeton was asked what metric he used to determine this bargain, he replied, "The standards are very widely varied, but perhaps the most important of all is how cheap is it in relation to your estimate of what it may earn in the long run."[11]

A few days later, Alcan announced plans to cut capital spending to $600 million from a previous plan of $700 million and from the previous year level of $974 million. It also froze hourly wages and postponed salary increases. Alcan's top 141 managers planned to work two weeks without pay in the second half of the year. Peter Ingersoll, an analyst at Salomon Brothers was quoted in *The Wall Street Journal* as saying, "This is by far the worst time for the aluminum industry I have lived through, even compared with 1974–1975, which was the worst downturn of the post-World War II period." Alcan was operating at 86.7 percent capacity compared to the industry rate of 76 percent because it was a lower cost producer.

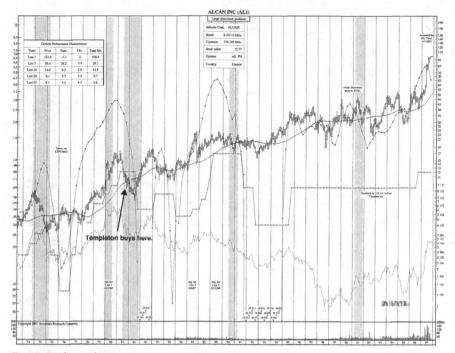

Figure 2. Alcan Aluminum

In late October Alcan reported its first quarterly operating loss ($15 million) since the early 1930s. CEO David Culver said the outlook for the near term wasn't encouraging.

In January 1983 Alcan, Alcoa, and Reynolds Metals all posted quarterly losses due to soft prices, which were generally worse than expected. But Alcoa's chairman, Krome George, said, "The price of primary aluminum appears to be firming and we are seeing a slight increase in order rates.... Assuming these trends continue, we can expect a slow, modest recovery in 1983."[12]

In June 1983 Alcan said that it expected to return to profitability in the second half of 1983 with U.S. shipments 35 percent higher than the fourth quarter of 1982 and expected a cooling off in the recent upswing in aluminum demand sometime in 1984.

By August 1983 two of the four major North American aluminum producers boosted prices for aluminum ingot for the first time in nearly three years.

In September 1983 aluminum orders were 22 percent higher than the previous year, lead times for delivery of flat-rolled aluminum products more than doubled, and aluminum ingot was trading at $0.72 per pound, up from $0.46 per pound in December 1982.

Alcan's stock doubled from where Templeton recommended it on public television just fifteen months prior. In September 1983 Alcan Aluminum announced plans to offer seven million common shares of stock.

Takeaways

Templeton was a bargain hunter. Where he found bargains varied, as did types of public company bargains. One of the ten pillars of his mental model, and a key to his long-term success, was to stay flexible and open-minded. He preferred undiscovered emerging growth stocks, but as we have seen with Union Carbide and Alcan Aluminum, he was equally comfortable with investing in cyclical industrial companies when bad news prevailed but was not life threatening.

Both Alcan and Union Carbide demonstrated his favorite bargain metric: a current market price that is low relative to the company's future potential earnings. When Templeton recommended Alcan on public television in June 1982, he thought the stock price of $16 was a bargain compared to his forecast that the company could earn $12/share in the next market cycle. He was close. Alcan earned $10/share in the next cyclical peak in 1989. Templeton bought Alcan at an extremely low price-earnings ratio of 1.6x what it earned seven years later. The stock price began discounting its earnings recovery long before it happened, as the stock doubled in a little over a year after his recommendation.

Exxon Corporation

On January 28, 1981, Ronald Reagan signed an executive order to allow petroleum product prices to be determined by free markets rather than price control. This encouraged oil production including at the Alaskan Prudhoe Bay Oil Field. The combination of declining consumption in the aftermath of the large oil prices from the energy crisis of the 1970s, energy conservation, substitution from alternative energy sources such as nuclear and natural gas, and non-OPEC overproduction caused *Time Magazine* on June 22, 1981 to declare, "the world temporarily floats in a glut of oil." These factors ultimately precipitated a five-year slide as oil prices fell from almost $40/barrel in 1981 to $11/barrel in 1986.

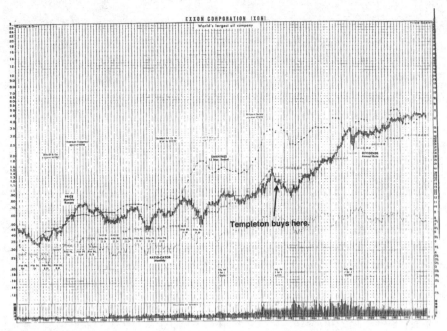

Figure 3. Exxon Corp.

In May 1981 Templeton said he was buying Exxon because it was "selling for half of its liquidating value at only five times earnings for one of the best stocks in the world."[13] Again he emphasized that the basic test he uses in picking a stock: "Nothing is so important as estimating what it'll earn in the long run and buying at the lowest price now."[14]

At the time, Exxon's dividend yield was 9 percent, earnings covered the dividend by 2x, and the P/E ratio was just 5x. Over the course of the next year, the stock slid 17 percent. In May 1982 the sponsors of the $43 billion Alaska natural gas pipeline, including Exxon, Atlantic Richfield, and Standard Oil of Ohio, announced a two-year delay due to high interest rates and slack demand for energy. Exxon also announced it was scuttling an oil shale project with Tosco because it was convinced the demand for synthetic fuels had soured.

On May 12, 1982, *The Wall Street Journal's* "Heard on the Street" column featured Exxon. It noted that the five-year total return from Exxon stock was only 0.7 percent when adjusted for inflation and was negative after taxes even though Exxon was "one of the few U.S. companies whose profits have outpaced inflation." Yet "most analysts are not recommending the stock."

The next month, Exxon offered employees incentives to resign or retire as the company stepped up efforts to cut staff costs. In June 1982, Exxon was again the subject of the "Heard on the Street" column, which noted Exxon stock had an 11 percent dividend yield—twice the corporate average and the highest among the Dow 30 stocks.

Over the next five years, Exxon stock rose 350 percent as the P/E expanded from 5x to 16x. Earnings over this period were flat. The well-covered dividend was increased 33 percent during this period, which boosted the total return.

Takeaways

Bargains can be found not only in undiscovered growth stocks, but also in familiar, high-quality companies with strong market positions, whose fundamental earning drivers may be stalled for macroeconomic reasons. The conventional view was that the stock wasn't timely because it lacked earnings momentum or a fundamental catalyst. Exxon faced a distressed situation with layoffs, stalled pipeline construction, poor demand for synthetic fuel, and slack demand for energy. But the company had staying power with a clean balance sheet and strong earnings that more than adequately covered its dividend. The 9 percent dividend yield paid Templeton while he waited for the inevitable rebound in valuation. Even though earnings didn't progress during this period, the P/E multiple tripled as investors grew confident that the natural balance of supply and demand would eventually allow oil prices to recover, and earnings would follow.

Monsanto

In October 1990 Monsanto, a diversified specialty chemical company, announced that its quarterly earnings plunged 41 percent on a slight sales increase from the prior year due to higher oil-related raw material costs. Monsanto was a large supplier of nylon for carpets and plastic for windshields that relied on oil derivatives for its raw materials. It also announced a restructuring of its agricultural products business with 300 job cuts and plans to sell its animal feed supplement division. By October 1990 oil prices had climbed 84 percent from the prior year to $35/barrel and were 177 percent higher over two years due to the impact of the Persian Gulf crisis. Monsanto reported its earnings using the LIFO accounting method which matched costs that were "last-in-first-out" against revenues. In a period of rapidly rising costs, this depressed its reported earnings.

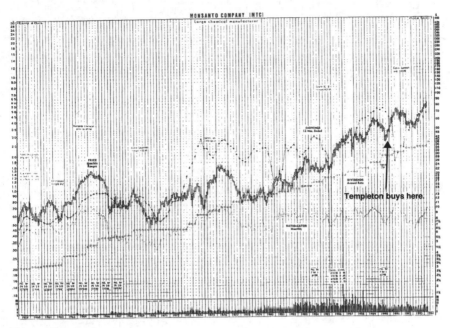

Figure 4. Monsanto

On November 5, 1990, a *Businessweek* article mentioned that with the Dow off almost 500 points from its high, Templeton was finding the best bargains in industries where there was great pessimism. "Templeton's top pick is a blue chip: Monsanto. 'It's one of the best bargains.' The company has been pulled down by selling sparked by the jump in oil prices. But long-term investors needn't worry, says Templeton. If oil prices stay high, Monsanto will eventually raise its prices. The company is trading at $42, down from a high of $62, and has a P/E of only 8.4."

Monsanto did take the lead by boosting prices to its customers to offset higher costs. Oil prices subsequently declined to a range of the mid-teens to low $20s through the end of the decade. Monsanto stock rose 78 percent to $75 in eight months.

Takeaways

Templeton found a bargain in a blue-chip specialty chemical leader whose products ranged from Saflex, an anti-shatter plastic liner used in windshields, to chemicals used in nylon as a staple for residential carpets, to Roundup herbicide. With the tailwind of an economic rebound and pricing power with differentiated products, Templeton found a company that was temporarily depressed relative to its future potential earnings. With the subsequent decline in oil prices and Monsanto's use of LIFO accounting, the lower costs quickly translated into higher earnings. Investors quickly followed Templeton's lead in anticipating the earnings recovery.

Merrill Lynch

In February 1991 Templeton said, "Our largest holdings are in out-of-favor banking, insurance, and financial services stocks. The unfavorable publicity about problems with bad bank loans had unduly depressed the stock prices of many perfectly sound and conservatively managed institutions."[15]

The economic environment in February 1991 was filled with anxiety due to a prolonged deterioration in the commercial real estate markets and soaring loan losses at banks. Junk bond giant Drexel Burnham went bankrupt, and taxpayers were presented with a $500 billion bill for the savings and loan debacle. Major banks including Citicorp, Chase Manhattan, Bank of Boston, and Chemical Bank slashed their dividend to boost capital.

Templeton said that he was bullish on Merrill Lynch, which was priced at $21/share (split adjusted price of $2.63 in the chart opposite after splitting two-for-one three times). He noted that Merrill Lynch's "conservatively stated book value is 44 percent higher than its market value. Better yet, Merrill Lynch has many assets not listed on its balance sheets. For example, it manages $100 billion in mutual funds, which should command a price of about 1.5 percent of assets under management. That's $1.5 billion, or roughly $14 a share, just for the funds."[16]

Takeaways

Templeton noticed that the entire financial services sector was tarnished with the same broad brush of fear. He seized the opportunity to align with a financial service company that was not exposed to troubled commercial loans but was being treated by the stock market as guilty by association.

Merrill Lynch's actual stated book value per share at the end of 1990 was $29.98 (pre-stock splits), which was 43 percent higher than the stock price of $21. This provided investors with a substantial cushion even if assets were written down to a lower fair value. Loans accounted for only 2 percent of total assets and 50 percent of shareholders' equity. As Templeton noted, book value

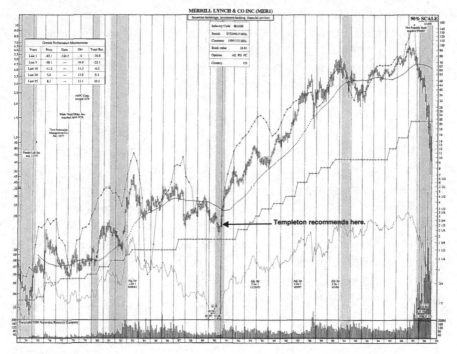

Figure 5. Merrill Lynch

was understated as the intrinsic value of Merrill Lynch Asset Management's mutual fund business was much higher than the carrying value of original cost on the balance sheet. This business alone was worth two-thirds of the stock price at the time.

Prescient Market Call

On December 8, 1983, Templeton predicted on national television that in eight years the Dow Jones Industrial Average could climb from its current level of 812 to over 3,000! He explained as follows:

> Let's say we're talking eight years ahead. In that length of time, the gross national product will almost surely double, largely because of inflation but the gross national product will double. If the gross national product doubles then the sales volume of American corporations approximately doubles. If the profit margin is the same, then the profits double. So if the profits double, how high will the stock market sell? Let's suppose, for example, that

instead of selling at seven times earnings, as it is now, it sells at fourteen times earnings, which has been the average for the last 80 years. So if their earnings double from now and then the price earnings ratio doubles also, then stock prices might be four times as high as they are now, which is over 3,000 on the Dow Jones Industrial Average.[17]

Templeton's prediction that the market could almost quadruple in as little as eight years assuredly raised eyebrows, and some may have questioned his financial sanity. The Dow Jones Industrial Average reached 3,000 on December 23, 1991, exactly eight years and fifteen days after his seemingly preposterous prediction.

Templeton's cool logic prevailed. GDP averaged 10 percent growth for the eight years preceding December 1983 and an increase of 7 percent for the next eight years. His assumption that the GDP would double in the following eight years implied a 9 percent growth rate. So, the actual rate was slightly below his prediction. The price earnings ratio rebounded as he predicted from depressed levels following the recession of 1981–1982.

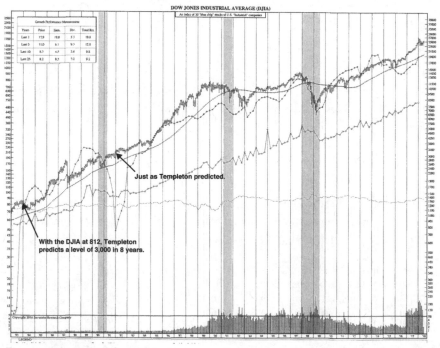

Figure 6. Dow Jones Industrial Average

In late 1985, many stock indices had reached all-time highs, and the bull market was already thirty-nine months old, which was the average length of a bull market. Before the annual meeting of the Templeton Group of Mutual Funds at that time, Templeton said that he believed the next bull market "may be a surprisingly big one."[18] He cited several bullish factors, such as the prodigious amounts of cash available that could be invested in stocks, growing investment in the U.S. by foreigners, the dwindling supply of U.S. shares due to takeovers and share repurchases, and the potential for U.S. pension funds to expand to $3–$5 trillion in ten years from $1.3 trillion. In the next ten years, $10,000 invested in the S&P 500 index rose to more than $40,000 for a compound annual return of almost 15 percent.

CHAPTER 7

Reflections

If you want to back a winner in today's rapid-paced world, study the wise and steady tortoise. He embodies the law that perseverance and self-control win the race.

—JOHN TEMPLETON[1]

The tortoise analogy is applicable to many endeavors but particularly so in investing. The law of perseverance applies to the ceaseless search for the best bargains, and the strong conviction required to stay the course with a stock in order to enjoy the power of compounding long-term results. The related law of self-control governs the principle of investing only in what you understand and resisting the powerful emotions of fear and greed in the market.

Sir John has been referred to as a hero of Wall Street, the "Old Man River" of common sense, the dean of global investing, and a trailblazing global value investor. All of these references are appropriate, but I prefer to think of Sir John Templeton as the "Capitalist Missionary" to highlight his contributions in global investing and religion. The specific symbols that come to mind for Sir John are a passport and a Bible to reflect his worldwide investment perspective and his view that financial prosperity, economic freedom, and religious passion can coexist hand in hand. Sir John believed that global investing would advance world peace. "The more international investing we have, the more we understand each other. It's a long way off, but suppose the leaders in the Kremlin had 50 percent of their money invested outside Russia. They'd have a totally different way of looking at life."[2]

Many years ago, I wrote Sir John to describe the *Empower Your Investing* project. I mentioned the research sources that I had gathered and asked him if there was anything in particular he would like emphasized. He wrote back a complimentary letter and said, "I would like to enclose a gift copy of my most recent book, *Discovering the Laws of Life*, which you may wish to incorporate in your seminar, *Empower Your Investing*."

It is noteworthy that his book, *Discovering the Laws of Life*, has nothing directly to do with investing. Instead, the book is a collection of 200 major laws of life written from Sir John's "lifetime of experience and diligent observation in the hope that it may help people in all parts of the world to make their lives not only happier but also more useful." The 200 laws include "The Golden Rule;" "You are sought after if you reflect love, joy, peace, patience, kindness, goodness, faithfulness, gentleness, and self-control;" "Pray without Ceasing;" "It is more rewarding to give than to receive;" "Enthusiasm breeds achievement;" and "Give the extra ounce." For each timeless truth in the book, Sir John elaborates why each law served him well and can serve others.

A particularly relevant law toward the end of the book is "Imitate that person in history whom you admire most, after you list the reasons why you admire that person." Sir John elaborated, "When we choose to study the lives of great men or women we can learn from them the treasured secrets of a truly worthwhile life and let their lives give life to our own. The process of selecting certain heroes or heroines to emulate will allow us to fully enjoy the treasures they bear."[3]

As a side note, I rather foolishly used Sir John's letter as a bookmark in his book. I read *Discovering the Laws of Life* on a cross-country flight and, after landing, I was crushed to discover that his letter was missing from the book. I realized the letter must have slipped out of the book while it was in the seat pocket in front of my airline seat.

Four years later in 1998, I was fortunate to meet Sir John when he was honored for his lifetime achievement award by the Independent Institute. I explained the incident about losing his letter, and he graciously signed the cover of my notes relating to his section of *Empower Your Investing*.

Still, I regretted losing his letter and wished that I could somehow see it again. When I resurrected this project, I contacted Sir John's secretary and was pleasantly surprised to find that she was still working with his foundation. She not only had access to his library, but found a copy of the letter and emailed me a scanned copy...twenty years after it was written!

This personal incident revealed more about Sir John. In the letter, he wrote, "Thank you for your good September 15 letter, which was waiting for me when I returned from Asia October 8." First, it is noteworthy that he was still traveling for research at almost 83 years of age. Second, the fact that he enclosed a gift copy of his book was a sign of his generosity. Third, even though *Empower Your Investing* was focused on investment principles, Sir John thought highly enough of sharing the *Discovering Laws of Life* that he believed his portrait wasn't complete without including the ingredients for a successful life. Investing was a means to an end for Sir John; it wasn't the end itself. Lastly, the loyalty of his secretary—remaining devoted to working for the Templeton Foundation and keeping Sir John's records intact—is a reflection of the lifelong impact Sir John had on her and countless others.

The world affectionately misses Sir John Templeton, but if we take to heart his investment principles of bargain hunting worldwide, his life lessons, laws of life, his boundless curiosity, work ethic, integrity, generosity, and graciousness, we can look forward to realizing the potential he believed in: that "the 21st century offers great hope and glorious promise, perhaps a new golden age of opportunity."[4]

PETER LYNCH

"The Tireless Prospector"

I've always believed that searching for companies is like looking for grubs under rocks: if you turn over 10 rocks you'll likely fund one grub; if you turn over 20 rocks you'll find two...I had to turn over thousands of rocks a year to find enough grubs to add to Magellan's outsized collection.

—PETER LYNCH[1]

The person that turns over the most rocks wins the game...it's about keeping an open mind and doing a lot of work.

—PETER LYNCH[2]

CHAPTER 8

Personal Background

To Carolyn, my wife and best friend for over twenty years, whose support and sacrifices have been critically important to me. To my children, Mary Annie, and Beth, whose love for each other and their parents has meant so very much. To my colleagues at Fidelity Investments, whose extra efforts have made Magellan's performance possible but who have received none of the favorable publicity. To one million shareholders in Magellan, who have entrusted their savings to me and who have sent thousands of letters and made thousands of calls over the years, comforting me during declines in the market and reminding me that the future will be fine. To Holy God for all the incredible blessings I have been given in my life.

—PETER LYNCH[3]

Similar to Sir John Templeton, Peter Lynch credits his family, friends, and faith for his achievements in life. His greatest professional achievement, many would argue, is claim to the title as the greatest mutual fund investor ever. While he managed the Fidelity Magellan fund from 1977–1990, Peter Lynch increased the per share value of the fund by twenty-fold and achieved an average annual return of 29.2 percent! In the thirteen years he managed Fidelity Magellan, he built the mutual fund from $20 million in managed assets in 1977 into the nation's largest, best known, and most successful mutual fund with managed assets of $14 billion in 1990, when he retired. Despite this rarified feat as a professional investor, Peter Lynch has been a huge advocate that the amateur can invest just as well, if not better, than the average Wall Street professional by using their power of observation to gain an edge and by doing their homework. His career and advice are invaluably instructive.

Peter Lynch was born January 19, 1944, during World War II, when Americans were encouraged to grow any vegetables they could to help ease food shortages. He was raised in a family where there was a healthy distrust of the stock market. His mother was the youngest of seven children, which meant that his aunts and uncles experienced firsthand the crash of 1929 and the impact of the Great Depression.

Peter described his father as "an industrious man and former mathematics professor who left academia to become the youngest senior auditor at John Hancock."[4] Peter's father died tragically of brain cancer when Peter was just ten years old. His mother was forced to earn a paycheck, and Peter felt compelled to help out at age eleven by working part-time as a golf caddie at the local club. The club had many corporate executives, including some from Fidelity, and some of them were buying stocks, which he noticed were going up. "So I watched it. I didn't have any money to invest, but I remember the stock market being very strong in the 1950s and so people, not everybody, but a lot of people on the golf course were talking about it."[5] The success stories he heard dispelled his long-held family fear that the market was so risky that you could lose everything.

Peter caddied through high school and into his years at Boston College. Peter avoided the usual courses to prepare for business, such as math, accounting, and science; instead, he chose liberal arts courses in logic, history, psychology, political science, religion, and Greek philosophy. Peter credits logic as the course that best prepared him for picking stocks, if only to witness the illogic of Wall Street. The illogic he referred to was the tendency by many investors to speculate about the prospects for a company without even testing a company's product, visiting its stores, or checking with or visiting the company itself. "Wall Street thinks like some of the ancient Greeks did. They'd sit around for days and debate how many teeth a horse had. The right answer is to go check a horse."[6] He also believed that investing was an art, not a science, and that relying on rigid quantitative statistics was shortsighted. Lynch observed, "All the math you need in the stock market you get in the fourth grade."[7]

Inspired by the success stories he heard caddying and armed with his savings from caddying, a scholarship, and living at home while attending Boston College, Peter had enough resources in his sophomore year to buy his first stock, Flying Tiger Line, for $7/share. The airfreight company prospered from shipping troops and cargo in the Pacific during the Vietnam War, and the stock rose more than four-fold to $32.75 in less than two years. The proceeds from gradually selling the stock all the way up to $80/share partially funded Peter's tuition for graduate school at the Wharton School of Finance at the University of Pennsylvania in Philadelphia. Lynch acknowledged that he was lucky with Flying Tiger, because his premise was simply that the company would benefit from the future of airfreight in general, and he had no idea that its subsequent involvement in Vietnam would catapult its business. "The stock went up, I think, nine or ten-fold and I had my first ten-bagger."[8] Lynch learned that stocks offered opportunities to multiply his money, and he was motivated to find more.

Peter applied for a job as a summer intern at Fidelity during his senior year at Boston College at the suggestion of its president and Peter's caddie client, D. George Sullivan, for whom he had caddied for eight years. Fidelity had an excellent reputation with its excellent marketing and the investment success of the Fidelity Trend Fund, managed by Ned Johnson, and the Fidelity Capital fund, managed by Gerry Tsai. He was hired by Fidelity as one of three out of seventy-five job applicants. It was the only job interview he ever had.

After Wharton, Peter fulfilled his ROTC Army commitment by serving two years from 1967–1969 as a lieutenant in the artillery unit in Texas and then in Korea. He returned from Korea in 1969 and rejoined Fidelity as a permanent employee and analyst. He was paid $16,000 a year to research companies and write reports following the textile, chemicals, and metals industries. In June 1974, he was promoted to director of research, and in May of 1977, at age 33, he began managing the Fidelity Magellan fund, which had $20 million in assets and forty stocks. Although Ned Johnson urged Peter to concentrate the portfolio to just twenty-five stocks, Peter increased the number of stocks within six months to 100 and soon thereafter to 150. He recalled that there were plenty of bargains everywhere. By 1990, the portfolio had ballooned to 1,400 individual stock holdings. Peter Lynch was forty-six years old when he retired, the same age as his father when he passed away, and it weighed on Peter's mind. He left behind a work ethic that consisted of a six day, 80- to 85-hour work week in order to spend more time with family and his other religious, charitable, and educational interests. When his doctor asked him then what he did for exercise before he retired, he said, "The only thing I could come up with was that I floss my teeth at night."[9]

Since 1990, Peter Lynch and his wife Carolyn, until her passing in 2015, managed their family foundation, which is focused on four areas that they believe can be effective in solving societal problems: museums, Catholic charities—especially in Boston's inner-city schools, healthcare, and education. In 1999, the Lynch's donated over $10 million to Boston College, the largest gift to the school in its history.

Peter increasingly distrusted the efficient-market theory popularly taught at academic institutions including Wharton, especially when Lynch saw his colleagues make a twenty-fold profit in Kentucky Fried Chicken and explain in advance why the stock would go up. The efficient-market theory is the belief that all known information is immediately and rationally reflected in stock prices so that an investor seeking to gain an advantage through diligent research is an exercise in futility. The theory's chief advocates are academics, most of whom have never worked in the trenches as an investor, and consequently have not experienced how the natural emotions of fear and greed move stock prices wholly separate and distinct from the value of the underlying business.

Peter Lynch had the same disdain for modern academic theory as Sir John Templeton. He was asked, "What do you think of the random walk theory?" (The random walk theory is the premise that stock moves are random and unpredictable, and that it is impossible to outperform the market without assuming additional risk.)

> Random walk is hogwash…if you believe in random walk, you have to believe my Fidelity colleagues and my success was fluke. It's hard to support a theory that says the market is rational when you know somebody who just made a twenty-fold profit in Kentucky Fried Chicken and explained in advance why it was going to rise.[10]
>
> If there were one million tennis matches this weekend, there are going to be 500,000 people who lose and 500,000 people who win. Therefore, should people not practice tennis, should they not practice their serve? Should they not practice their backhand? The question is why not be the winner than the loser? You could be a better investor if you looked at the balance sheet, if you know what the company did, if you use the information you have…What the academics are saying is that people have done a bad job investing, therefore they shouldn't invest. These people are being told they don't have a chance, it's a big casino, and they act accordingly. Then they get the bad results. It's sort of a self-fulfilling prophecy. You convince the public

that the odds are against them so they behave like they're in a casino. They go in there and buy options, which is like betting on number twenty-six. It's like poker without looking at your cards...That's like investing without doing research.[11]

CHAPTER 9

Investment Performance

My goal over a long period of time, not every year, would be to beat the market by 4 to 5 percent. I think that's a real fair objective. If I can do it, I would be very happy. I think that would be an accomplishment for my shareholders.

—PETER LYNCH

Peter Lynch's performance during his thirteen years managing the Fidelity Magellan mutual fund was Herculean, growing its assets from $22 million to over $13 billion. He navigated the fund to an average annual return of 29.2 percent in comparison to 15.4 percent for the S&P 500 index. An investment of $10,000 in Fidelity Magellan under Lynch's management would have grown to $280,000, in contrast to the S&P 500 of $64,000. The total return for thirteen years was 2780 percent, over 4x higher than the S&P 500. Magellan had a positive return every year during the thirteen-year period, and Lynch outperformed the S&P 500 in eleven of the thirteen years. The fund outperformed the average mutual fund for thirteen consecutive years, and by 1990 the fund had the best record of any mutual fund over the previous ten years. During the last five years, despite the fund being the biggest fund in the country, Magellan beat 99.5 percent of all funds, with a return of 154.4 percent in comparison to the S&P 500 of 118.0 percent. For many of the thirteen years, one out of every one hundred Americans invested in Fidelity Magellan.

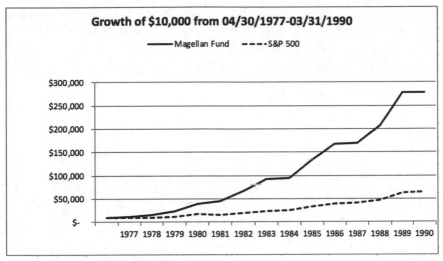

Magellan Fund Growth of $10,000

Lynch Returns					Total	Lynch
	Magellan Fund	Annual Return		S&P 500	Return	Less: S&P500
5/31/77	$ 10,000			$ 10,000		
12/31/77	$ 11,375	13.75%		$ 9,894	-1.06%	14.81%
12/31/78	$ 14,982	31.71%		$ 10,543	6.56%	25.15%
12/31/79	$ 22,732	51.73%		$ 12,487	18.44%	33.29%
12/31/80	$ 38,631	69.94%		$ 16,545	32.50%	37.44%
12/31/81	$ 44,986	16.45%		$ 15,731	-4.92%	21.37%
12/31/82	$ 66,606	48.06%		$ 19,121	21.55%	26.51%
12/31/83	$ 92,309	38.59%		$ 23,435	22.56%	16.03%
12/31/84	$ 94,183	2.03%		$ 24,905	6.27%	-4.24%
12/31/85	$ 134,786	43.11%		$ 32,807	31.73%	11.38%
12/31/86	$ 166,784	23.74%		$ 38,932	18.67%	5.07%
12/31/87	$ 168,452	1.00%		$ 40,976	5.25%	-4.25%
12/31/88	$ 206,791	22.76%		$ 47,782	16.61%	6.15%
12/31/89	$ 278,300	34.58%		$ 62,924	31.69%	2.89%
5/31/90	$ 278,160	-0.05%		$ 64,318	2.22%	-2.27%
CAGR		29.2%	2782%		15.4%	643%

Lynch Performance

One caveat deserves mention. At its inception in 1963, the Fidelity Magellan fund was an incubator fund whose investors were Fidelity insiders. The fund was not open to the general public until 1981. As an incubator fund, Lynch was able to invest unconstrained by the pressures and exposure of public mutual funds. Lynch's performance during the nine years when Magellan was available to the public was still remarkable with his annual return of 21.8 percent versus the S&P 500 return of 16.2 percent, and in the last five years before he retired, Magellan outperformed 99 percent of stock mutual funds.

CHAPTER 10

Peter Lynch's Perspective on Investing

The stock market demands conviction as surely as it victimizes the unconvinced.

—PETER LYNCH[1]

As remarkable as Peter Lynch's performance was as a professional investor, he never wavered in his fervent belief that amateur investors can have an edge over professionals. In a speech at the National Press Club in 1994, Lynch said,

> I think it is a tragedy in America that the small investor has been convinced by the media, the print media, the radio, the television media that they don't have a chance; that the big institutions, with all their computers, and all their degrees, and all their money have all the edges. That just isn't true at all. When people are convinced of this, they act accordingly. When they believe it, they buy stocks for a week, they buy options; they buy the Chilean fund this week, and next week it's the Argentina fund. And they get results proportionate to that kind of investing. That is very bothersome. I think the public can do extremely well in the stock market on their own. I think that institutions dominate the market today is a positive for small investors because institutions push stocks to unusual lows; they push them to unusual highs.[2]

While Peter Lynch urged amateur investors to not overestimate the skill and wisdom of professional investors in general, it is helpful to understand how his legendary work ethic and habits contributed to his success and why he deserves the moniker "The Tireless Prospector." Combining even a part of Peter Lynch's work ethic with the mindset of an amateur who takes advantage of his understanding of local companies is a winning combination.

The heart of Peter Lynch's work habit was his desire to gain an edge on competition, many of whom he derided for being arrogant "out-of-touch experts." Peter Lynch focused on discovering unappreciated virtues in companies he understood, and gaining the conviction necessary to have the willpower to own a stock even though it might be unpopular or unconventional.

Peter Lynch's typical day began with a commute to work with two to three doctor friends who picked him up at 6:15 a.m., which allowed Lynch to read research and chart books before arriving at the office. He arrived at 6:45 a.m. and reviewed the previous day's buys and sells of other Fidelity managers, read Fidelity analyst comments from the day before, and read *The Wall Street Journal*, all by 7:30 a.m.

> *Mr. Lynch personifies the 'keep it moving' culture at Fidelity. A former analyst, he is on the phone by 7:30 a.m., practicing the trade at Olympic speed. His attention span is short, and he constantly scribbles notes while racing to a conclusion about a company's prospects. He has been known to invest heavily in an entire industry after just a brief conversation with a corporate executive.*[3]

Lynch worked eighty to eighty-five hours each week including Saturdays after 1982 and even Sunday mornings before church. On Saturdays, he read through the "fifty inches of mail I get a day. I throw out 90 percent of it, but you have to look through 100 percent to decide on which 10 percent to read."[4] Why work so many hours? "I figure if I work about 40 percent more time, I ought to able to do 10 percent better (than competitors)."[5] He traveled on average twelve to thirteen days a month.

Throughout the day, Lynch constantly referred to stock charts. Although Lynch would describe himself as an investor focused on a company's fundamentals, he liked to refer to long-term chart books as a check to assess how the stock price trend compared to its earnings trend. "I keep a long-term chart book close to my side at the office, and another one at home, to remind me of momentous and humbling occurrences."[6]

Lynch's office was an ode to the adage, "A cluttered desk is a sign of genius." "Lynch's quarters were a monument to chaos, with stacks of annual reports and analysts' treatises partially blocking the windows…yellow legal pads with notes on hundreds of companies."[7] "The filing cabinets surrounding the room are stacked two feet high with documents and books."[8]

He admitted in 1997 that "I don't own a computer. I can't turn on a computer."[9] He did use a dumb terminal that provided stock quotes and news, which are freely available to investors today.

His personal objective was to have at least one conversation each month with a representative of each major industry group to detect early changes in business direction for better or worse. He usually ended the conversation with management by asking which of their competitors they most respected and why. He often bought the competitor's stock.

In 1982 Lynch said that in a typical year he visited over 200 companies (by 1986 it was 570 companies) and read over 700 annual reports. "Basically, it's hard work…it's 99 percent perspiration."[10] Vacation for Peter Lynch meant that he would spend the weekdays visiting companies and join his wife on weekends. Lynch had the luxury that Fidelity's headquarter office was a revolving door of companies pitching their stories. Lynch, however, relished opportunities to visit companies on their home turf where cultural signs of humility or arrogance might attract or deter further interest.

Within Fidelity, Peter Lynch revolutionized the method of accountability and sharing best ideas. In a traditional setup, fund managers chose stocks based on analyst recommendations, which allowed fund managers to blame analysts for poor performance. He required fund managers to be responsible for their own independent research and be accountable for their results. He made them roll up their sleeves and immerse themselves in primary research. There was no room for ivory tower thinkers. Analysts and fund managers met once a week to present their best picks. He presided and timed the presentations for three minutes, which got shortened to one and a half minutes. He allowed no further feedback. Listeners could follow up on leads as they pleased or feel free to ignore them. In the end, fund managers were held accountable to their results.

In a speech before individual investors with the National Association of Investors Corporation on October 15, 1998, Peter Lynch's advice covered three important points that he said would be just as important twenty days before as twenty years or more in the future. The first was to know what you own;

the second was to avoid predicting the economy, interest rates, and the stock market; and the third was to be patient with the investment process. These three and a few others that he emphasized elsewhere comprise the core of his principles for investing.

Altogether, Peter Lynch emphasized seven habits for success in investing:

1. Focus on Companies You Understand and Develop Conviction

Peter Lynch consistently emphasized that, "The single most important thing in the stock market for anyone, is to know what you own…If you can't explain to a ten-year-old why you own a stock in two minutes or less, you shouldn't own the stock…Stocks are not lottery tickets. There is a company behind every stock."[11]

Lynch was adamant that investors should only invest in what they understand: "Invest in things you know about."[12] There are plenty of attractive investment opportunities in familiar companies that have actual earnings, rather than chasing after exotic sounding opportunities that aren't profitable and are difficult to value: "Don't ignore the understandable profitable business in favor of the inexplicable venture that loses money."[13] The safer bet is to date the radiant girl or guy next door, than the shallow one full of promise, that inevitably causes regret. Lynch said,

> You hear this story, all sizzle; no steak. I have never broken-even on these long-shots. Most long-shots are no-shots.[14]
>
> This is the kind of company people like to own. They make a very simple, easy to understand product. It's a one-megabit, SRAM, CMOS, bi-polar risk, floating point data IO array processor, with an optimized compiler, 16-bit dual port memory, a double-defused metal oxide semiconductor monolithic logic chip, Unix operating system, four whetstone megaflop poly-silicone emitter, high bandwidth—that's important, you shouldn't have low bandwidth—6 gigahertz, double metallization communication protocol, asynchronous backward compatibility, peripheral bus architecture, four-way memory, token ring interchanging backplane, with 15 nanoseconds capability. Now if you own a piece of junk like that, you will never make money. Someone will come along with more megaflops or less megaflops, a bigger emitter, more nanoseconds. What do you do if you buy this at $12 and it goes to $8? Do you call the psychic hotline? What do you do if it goes down? I was lucky enough to make money in

stocks like Dunkin' Donuts, Stop 'n Shop. I could understand them. When there were recessions, I didn't have to worry about what was happening. I could go there and saw that people still go there. It's nice to know that when the market goes down as it does from time to time, that you don't have to worry about low priced foreign imports. The companies will survive. That is the single biggest principle; the most important thing (to know what you own).[15]

He reiterated,

I think you have to understand what they do. It's easy to buy a stock at $10, and when it gets to $15, you say isn't that terrific. But it doesn't always happen that way. A lot of times you buy a stock at $10, it goes to $12, and six months later, it is $6. If you don't understand what they do and you don't know why they're doing it, you don't know whether to double your bet, flip a coin, sell it; so if you don't understand a company, you shouldn't own it. You need an edge.... I probably call one company a week (in retirement) instead of five a day....[16]

When I was at Fidelity, I had this stock, Kaiser Industries. I was a new analyst. The stock had gone from $31 to $16. We bought the biggest block ever on the American Stock Exchange. We bought 7 or 8 million shares at $14.75. About two months later, I called my mother. I said, 'Mom, you ought to buy Kaiser Industries. It's gone from $31 to $10. How much lower can it go?' Thank God, she didn't listen to me. It went to $9, it went to $8, it went to $7, it went to $6, it went to $5, it went to $4. Now fortunately for me this happened rather slowly, or I would have been bagging at the Stop 'n Shop. This happened over about five months. I said I was a little early at $16, but let's go over what we own here. Kaiser Industries is at $4 now. There are 25 million shares outstanding. It's worth $100 million. They had no debt. Now this is important. It is almost impossible to go bankrupt if you don't have any debt. They owned 60 percent of Kaiser Steel, 40 percent of Kaiser Aluminum. 37 percent of Kaiser Cement, they owned all of Kaiser Sand and Gravel. They owned seven TV stations. They owned Jeep, now owned by Chrysler. They owned Kaiser Fiberglass; they own a bunch of companies. They eventually gave all the shares out to the public. They sold all the divisions. You got 55 bucks. But if you didn't know what you owned, and you said, 'how much lower can it go?' what would you have done when it went from $12 to $10, then went to $8, then it went to $6, then it went to $4. I think you would have left. So this system of asking, 'how much lower can it go?' is a big mistake.[17]

You have to know the reason why a stock should go up. Peter Lynch sincerely believed that every investor has an edge and can observe trends before they are obvious to other investors, but many people ignore them and mistakenly buy companies they don't understand. When those companies stock prices drop, the investors lock in poor results by selling in a panic because they don't know what they own. Understand what you own, and own what you understand. Anything else is just gambling.

2. Be Persistent in Prospecting for an Undervalued Gem

Similar to conducting a job search, investing is a numbers game. Peter Lynch thought that the more rocks you turn over, the more likely you will find an undiscovered nugget. When you find a reasonably priced great company, avoid the temptation to say you missed it. You are never too late with a terrific business. Peter Lynch often said that an investor has plenty of time in the stock market with great companies.

> *You could have bought Walmart ten years after it went public, you could have made 30x your money. If you bought it the year they went public, you could have made 300x your money. If you bought Microsoft four years after it went public, you could have made 50x your money. If you bought Home Depot eight years after it went public, you would have made 10x your money. With great companies, you have plenty of time. People are in too much of a hurry.*[18]

Peter Lynch would often wonder at the irony that consumers would take their time and carefully research the reliability rating and features when buying a car or a major household appliance, yet act impulsively with an investment of equal or greater cost—with predictably poor results. Since a carefully chosen investment can pay for multiple cars, the investment deserves at least as much time devoted to researching the best value.

3. Stay in Touch

"Once I buy a company, I very rarely go visit it again. I just call up and see what's cooking."[19] As previously mentioned, at least once each month, he wanted to have a conversation with a representative of each major industry group in case their business was starting to turn around or there were other developments that Wall Street had overlooked.

4. Take Copious Notes

Peter Lynch kept religious diaries of conversations and visits with companies noting dates, names and current stock prices. These notes were a handy reference for subsequent conversations to see if management followed through on their plans.

5. Focus on the Company

Lynch wasn't shy about his disdain for heady generalists who were preoccupied with matters that either weren't relevant or knowable. He wryly observed, "If all the economists in the world were laid end to end, it wouldn't be a bad thing." He added,

> Economists have predicted thirty-six of the last nine recessions. If you spend thirteen minutes a year on guessing the economy, you've wasted ten minutes of your time. I am not talking about economic facts. If I own hotels, I want to know how many hotels are under construction. I can deal with that. But if people tell you after five years of economic expansion, that next year we are going to have a recession, that's like weather forecasting.[20]

Instead of trying to understand economic predictions, focus on facts relevant to individual business. He said,

> Invest in companies, not the stock market...predicting the short-term direction of the stock market is futile...(on why others were not performing as well as he was)...Well, I think a lot of people spend so much time predicting the big picture. What the economy is going to do, what interest rates are going to do. When Alan Greenspan heads the Federal Reserve, he doesn't know what's going to happen to interest rates. So they spend too much time on that.[21]

One of the ways Peter Lynch focused on companies was to consult a chart book published by Securities Research Company,[22] which contained twelve-year and thirty-five-year charts of earnings and prices for individual companies. "It's a good idea to consult them before you buy a stock, then every six months or so thereafter."[23] Significant divergences between the trend of earnings and stock price signaled an opportunity to research further to understand the way investors perceive a company.

Just because a company's stock price strays below the earnings trend line on a chart, doesn't mean the stock is an automatic buy. "Sometimes, a stock is cheap for a good reason—the company has troubles. With every company, there is something to worry about, but the question is, which worries are valid and which are not?"[24] If your research indicates that the worries are temporary/short-term and not structural/long-term, then buying a stock that is below its earnings trend line can have a double-play effect. The stock can benefit by reverting to its higher average price/earnings ratio, and it can appreciate thereafter in line with its higher earnings.

> *I can't say enough about the fact that earnings are the key to success in investing in stocks. No matter what happens to the market, the earnings will determine the results. In thirty years, Johnson & Johnson's earnings are up seventy-fold, and the stock is up seventy-fold. Bethlehem Steel earns less today than it did thirty years ago, and, guess what? The stock sells for less than it did thirty years ago.*[25]

6. Work Hard; It's Not Magic

Lynch was once asked how he "played the market." "The word 'play' is a bad term. It's not what it is about, it is a dangerous term. People in investment clubs know that it's fun, but it's no play. Play usually means the game ends pretty soon. It's over in a couple of hours. It is usually pleasant. The stock market can be unpleasant."[26]

Peter Lynch's tireless persistence was an inspiration to his colleagues at Fidelity, his clients, and his competitors. He humbly described his sleuthing: "With every spectacular stock I've managed to ferret out, the virtues seemed so obvious that if 100 professionals had been free to add it to their portfolios, I'm convinced that 99 would have done so."[27]

> *The biggest position in my fund one time was Hanes, which owned L'eggs. It was a huge stock and was bought eventually by Consolidated Foods, and it was the best division of Consolidated Foods. It was my biggest position and they had a monopoly on L'eggs. L'eggs was a really big hit and I knew somebody would come along with a new product. Kayser-Roth introduced No Nonsense. I was worried that this thing was better, and I couldn't quite figure out what was going on. So I went to the supermarket, and I bought sixty-two pairs of No Nonsense in different colors and different shapes. They must have wondered what kind of house I had at home. I brought them into the office and passed them out to anybody that wanted these things, male or female. Just take them home and tell me how it is. They came back in about*

three weeks and said it was not as good. And that is what research is. I held on to Hanes and it was a huge stock. That is what it is all about.[28]

Hanes was bought out by Consolidated Foods, which is now part of Sara Lee. Lynch said, "It might have been a thirty bagger instead of a ten bagger, if it hadn't been bought out."[29]

7. Be Open-Minded, Flexible, and Think Like an Amateur

Peter Lynch avoided wholesale snap judgments, such as "it's too small for me to buy," "there is no track record," "there are too many union employees," and "it's not in a growth industry." He was willing to invest in obscure or underfollowed companies rather than seeking shelter in popular stocks to avoid looking bad. "Success (on Wall Street) is one thing, but it's more important not to look bad if you fail…If IBM goes bad and you bought it, the clients and the bosses will ask, 'What's wrong with that damn IBM lately?' but if La Quinta Motor Inns goes bad, they'll ask, 'What's wrong with you?'" Lynch had an open platform to invest. He wasn't constrained from a fixed menu such as an "approved list" of stocks, which is popular at banks, nor did he have to adhere to a mutual fund style-box, such as small-cap growth. "Investors who put on blinders and ignore entire categories of companies, such as stodgy utilities, or lousy airlines, or silly candy makers that only sell to a bunch of kids, are missing out on some great deals."[30]

He also recommended that you eliminate inbred biases, such as avoiding companies with union employees or companies in sleepy industries. Peter Lynch noted that "Home Depot was in a terrible industry and went up 100-fold. Sherwin Williams went up 20-fold in the last twenty years (ending 1998) in a terrible industry. There are all these prejudices and biases. Stay flexible. There are great stocks everywhere; you just have to find them." He also said, "What a terrible mistake (to avoid companies with union labor). I make a huge amount of money in Chrysler. Huge amount of money in Deere. A lot of money on Boeing. I lost money in airlines and railroads, but all told, I made a lot of money with union companies."

Optimism and Faith in Capitalism

Peter Lynch identified fifteen personality traits he believed were critical to succeed in investing: patience, self-reliance, common sense, tolerance for pain, open-mindedness, detachment, persistence, humility, flexibility, willingness to do independent research, willingness to admit mistakes, ability to ignore panic and pessimism, ability to make informed decisions, conviction, and persistent faith and optimism.

The first fourteen traits are self-explanatory. The fifteenth trait is the optimism that our country's capitalist system is conducive to product innovation, job creation, higher standards of living, and wealth creation. Peter Lynch was as optimistic as Sir John Templeton regarding the resilience and ingenuity of entrepreneurs operating in a free-market economy who can deliver innovative new products, enhance standards of living, and create wealth for shareholders. Both investors believed that the job creation and wealth opportunities created by dynamic lesser-known companies are too often overshadowed by the negative headlines of older businesses that have lost touch with their customers. Lynch said:

> In the decade of the 1980s, 500 of the largest companies eliminated three million jobs. We (America) added fifteen million jobs, despite the 500 largest companies eliminating three million jobs. In the decade of the 1990s, 500 of the largest companies eliminated, again, three million jobs. The United States added seventeen million jobs in the 1990s...It's the small companies that are growing. That is what makes America great. We have a fantastic system here. Yet people are always dumping on it...People keep telling us America is inept and they're lazy. The average American works eleven hours more per week than the average German; four more hours per week than the average Japanese. We are working twelve hours more per week than our parents. And people tell us we are lazy. And we dominate our industries. Disney is the best at what they do. We are number one in the record industry; number one in the space industry. It is staggering the country we are in. So either you believe in it or you don't. If you don't believe in it, you don't own stocks, you don't own mutual funds. Otherwise, to miss it is a great mistake.[31]
>
> Keeping the faith and stock picking are normally not discussed in the same paragraph, but success in the latter depends on the former. You can be the world's greatest expert on balance sheets or p/e ratios, but without faith, you'll tend to believe the negative headlines.... What sort of faith am I talking about? Faith that as old enterprises lose momentum and disappear, exciting new ones such as Walmart, Federal Express, and Apple Computer will emerge to take their place. Faith that America is a nation of hardworking and inventive people...and whenever I am confronted with

doubts and despair about the current Big Picture, I try to concentrate on the Even Bigger Picture...The Even Bigger Picture tells us that over the last seventy years, stocks have provided their owners with gains of 11 percent a year, on average, whereas Treasury bills, bonds and CDs have returned less than half that amount."[32]

This faith in the ability of a free market economy to rejuvenate itself is the foundation of support for seeing inevitable declines in the market as buying opportunities rather than the beginning of the apocalypse that fearful media pundits often portray.

In the eighty-seven-year period from 1928–2015, there have been ninety-three declines of at least 10 percent, the common definition of a market correction. During this time, there were thirty-four declines of 20 percent or more, which is the classic definition of a bear market. So, corrections occur on average at least once each year, and bear markets occur on average about once every three years. Lynch advised that it was futile to predict the corrections and bear markets. Instead, recognize their inevitability and take advantage of the buying opportunities with the faith that, as spring follows winter, higher earnings and cash flow will sprout, and so will corresponding stock values.

When you invest in stocks, you have to have a basic faith in human nature, in capitalism, in the country at large, and in future prosperity in general. So far, nothing's been strong enough to shake me out of it.[33]

CHAPTER 11

Selecting Stocks

Invest at least as much time and effort in choosing a new stock as you would in choosing a new refrigerator.

—PETER LYNCH[1]

Great stocks are out there. They're out there looking for you. You just have to keep your eyes open.

—PETER LYNCH[2]

Peter Lynch said the best time to buy stocks is when you have convinced yourself that you've found a solid company at a good price. His *philosophy* on investing offers a solid foundation for understanding his *method* of stock picking. From a broad perspective, Peter Lynch, like Sir John Templeton, focuses the long-term earnings power of companies to drive stock prices. "In the last 20 years, Merck and Coca-Cola have had their profits go up 15-fold and guess what, (their) stocks have gone up 15-fold...So there is a direct relationship. That's what you have to concentrate on."[3]

Peter Lynch said he thought it was a mistake to refer to Magellan as a growth fund. He refused to be pigeonholed in a style-box, but preferred to be an opportunist. He said some people say they will only buy growth stocks, but if growth stocks are overpriced it causes a problem. Peter Lynch believed there were good and bad stocks everywhere. The key is to avoid "prejudices and biases that prevent people from looking at a lot of different industries."[4]

Both Templeton and Lynch favor two types of companies: blue chip turn-arounds and smaller growth companies that can grow into larger companies. Lynch said,

I try and find basically two types of companies. One would be a major company that's had earnings problems in an industry that's been depressed, and the earnings are about to turn up, and sometime in the future, I don't know, but perhaps in the next six months or the next year, major moves in companies usually occur because there's a dramatic change in profit. The second type of company would be a small successful company that grows to a major size company over a long period of time [5]

He said the best gains come from stocks of companies that are relatively small but lead their industries, are already profitable, and have good balance sheets with little to no debt.

Lynch favored growth stocks that had the following features:

- The company already has a consistent track record
- It is a simple company that can almost run itself
- It has something inherent that can sustain its growth
- It is well-managed, low-priced, with a clean balance sheet

Retailers

Lynch has always been partial to retailers. They are not made obsolete by a competitor located across the country, they are easy to monitor, and there is great potential for expansion by cloning itself over and over.

With retailers, you can see the competitors coming, and you can see when a company has reached the saturation point with a store in every mall and on every other street corner. That's the time to think about selling the stock, but until that point is reached, a successful chain of stores can multiply its sales and its earnings at an exponential rate. It happens again and again. [6]

Lynch's checklist for retailers was:

- Increasing same-store sales
- Realistic expansion plans (fewer than one hundred stores/year)
- Strong balance sheet (low or no debt)

- Positive experience from a visit to the store
- Comparison to competition:
  —Sales per square foot
  —Prices
  —Management experience
  —Strategy
  —Business economics (Return on Equity)
  —Competitive Differences
  —Ability to call company with any concerns
  —P/E ratio less than growth rate

Seven Steps for Stock Search

The following are seven steps to Peter Lynch's search for winners with his advice on each step:

1. Generate the idea
2. Determine the impact of the product
3. Categorize the company
4. Focus on its earnings
5. Value the company
6. Develop a two-minute script
7. Check out the story

Here are each of these in more detail.

1. Generate the Idea

Lynch famously recommended investors look for leads close to home, at the shopping mall, and where you work. These are areas where an investor is likely to have an edge based on first-hand experience on Main Street, before the company is widely recognized by Wall Street.

While Lynch generated some ideas this way, he generated many ideas by persistently calling companies. "He calls hundreds of companies a year and visits the ones he believes have strong growth potential—regardless of size or industry."[7] Lynch prepared himself before calling by reading the company's annual report and quarterly reports. The key with Lynch is that he was relentless and kept calling back.

> *It doesn't happen the first time you visit. Very rarely do you see a company and they have record high order backlogs, competitors have just gone out of business, and the stock is down from $55 to $5. That rarely happens. Usually there are five negatives and five positives, and eventually if you keep calling them, some of the problems go away. So I think then at that moment in time you say to yourself this company is doing better and the stock happens to be down. So I think it is the random call, you keep working it, that makes the difference.*[8]

2. Determine the Impact of the Product or Service on the Company

Don't waste time getting excited about a company's new product or service if it's expected contribution is not material or relevant to the overall size of the company's operation. Make sure the product of interest is material to the company.

Is the particular product that you are interested in, a meaningful percentage of the company's sales and earnings?

3. Categorize the Company as One of Six Varieties

1. **Slow Grower**
   - The dividend yield is the primary component of return.
   - Focus on consistency and the dividend payout ratio, which is a measure of how much earnings cover the dividend. (The ratio is dividend per share divided by earnings per share. The lower the ratio, the better.)
   - Utilities are typically slow growing regulated monopolies that attract investors hungry for their above-average dividend yield. Lynch said that the best time to buy utilities is when the economy is entering a recession and interest rates are declining. The lower prevailing interest rates make the utilities' high dividend yields more attractive to investors. Lynch also said to consider buying utilities when they omit their dividend as yield-oriented investors capitulate and sell at depressed prices.

2. **Stalwart**
   - Mature, steady growth companies.
   - Be particularly sensitive to the purchase price.
   - Prefer a high profit-margin company for a long-term holding since it indicates a competitive strength.
   - Check the company's record during previous recessions.
   - Beware of stalwarts that diversify away from their core attractive business, which Peter Lynch refers to as "diworseifications."

3. **Fast Grower**
   - Moderately fast growers (20–25 percent) that are already profitable in non-growth industries are ideal investments.
   - Look for companies with niches.
   - Be wary of unsustainable growth such as >50 percent.
   - Look for a clean balance sheet (little to no debt).
   - If the company is a retailer, make sure the company's concept is replicable.
   - Make sure the company has room to grow and that expansion is accelerating, not slowing down.
   - The fewer institutions that own it the better.
   - Because of compounding, a 20 percent grower with a P/E of 20x is a better investment than a 10 percent grower selling at a P/E of 10x.

4. **Cyclical**
   - The strength of a cyclical company depends on the ebb and flow of the general economy. They either have large discretionary products or depend on a key commodity, such as oil, copper, or corn.
   - Timing is everything. Contrary to non-cyclical companies, buy when their price-earnings ratios are high (meaning earnings are at cyclical lows).
   - Watch inventories. Make sure they aren't increasing at a rate faster than sales, which could lead to future fire sales.

- The best time to buy is in a recession with low earnings, strong balance sheet, and positive free cash flow (cash flow from operations less capital spending and dividends).

- Anticipate a shrinking P/E multiple over time as earnings recover.

- Lynch's favorite signal that the economy is recovering is this: "I've always looked at used car prices as a great indicator... I think that's a very good indicator."[9]

5. Asset Play

- An "asset play" is a company that has valuable assets that are unrecognized by the market. The asset can be real estate, an ownership stake in another company, a tax-loss carryforward, or a multi-division company that is worth more based on the sum of its parts than in its consolidated form.

- Determine the value of the hidden assets.

- Is debt detracting from the value of the assets?

6. Turnaround

- How is it turning around?

- Do a solvency check right away. Does the company have a healthy enough balance sheet to allow it to survive long enough to work out its problems? How much cash does it have? How much debt? Time is on the company's side with more cash than debt.

- Prefer a relatively low profit-margin company for a successful turnaround.

- Has it rid itself of unprofitable divisions?

- Is business coming back?

- Are costs being cut?

- Make sure the company doesn't have an overwhelming pension obligation that it can't meet.

- "Wait until the prevailing opinion about a certain industry is that things have gone from bad to worse, and then buy the shares in the strongest companies in the group… It's senseless to invest in a downtrodden enterprise unless the quiet facts tell you that conditions will improve."[10]

4. Focus on Earnings and its Prospects to Improve Through…

- Raising prices

- Reducing costs

- Higher volume of product sold by gaining market share or benefitting from a growing market

- Revitalizing by closing or selling an underperforming operation

I think the most important thing I've learned in the last twenty years is what's happened to corporate profits. It's magic—in twenty years the Dow Jones average has tripled and the profits for Dow Jones companies have tripled. It's a direct relationship to what happens to companies' earnings, what happens to stocks; and that's the key thing, over time…in the last twenty years, Merck and Coca-Cola have had their profits go up 15-fold and guess what, (their) stocks have gone up 15-fold… So there is a direct relationship. That's what you have to concentrate on.[11]

5. Value the Company

Determine if the company is reasonably priced:

- Is the price/earnings (P/E) ratio lower than its growth rate, and is it low relative to others in the industry?

- Is the P/E excessive on an absolute level? If so, even if everything goes right with the company's operations, you may not make money.

- Compare the price line to the earnings line on SRC charts. Over the long-term they should correlate with each other. The price should not be unreasonably high relative to the earnings trend line.

- Check the net cash (cash minus interest-bearing debt) per share as a percent of the total share price.

6. Develop a "Two-Minute" Script

This is the "elevator pitch" where you should be able to explain why you like the stock so a twelve-year-old can understand. You should be able to explain what the company has to do to succeed and what risks the company may encounter.

7. Check Out the Story

Peter Lynch refers to this as doing your homework. Just as a doctor routinely checks the pulse and blood pressure to initially diagnose the health of a patient, investors should review the company's financial documents as a first step to diagnose the financial health of a company. Just as a doctor wouldn't consider a health exam complete without seeing the patient, an investor's check-up isn't complete until the investor personally kicks the tires and checks in with the company.

Read the Annual Report and More

- Is free cash flow positive? "I prefer to invest in companies that don't depend on capital spending…if cash flow is ever mentioned as a reason you're supposed to buy a stock, make sure it's free cash flow that they're talking about. Free cash flow is what's left over after the normal capital spending is taken out."[12]

- Check whether the earnings track record is consistent or erratic.

- Check the ten-year trend of shares outstanding. Is it steadily declining because the company is buying back shares, or is it increasing due to issuance of shares to finance operations and/or to issue employee stock options?

- How strong is the balance sheet, and how is its debt rated? Are cash and marketable securities higher than debt? Is the ratio of debt (net of cash) to total capital low?

- Check the pretax profit margins (pretax earnings divided by sales) within an industry. Typically, the company with the highest pretax margins is the lowest cost operator and has a better chance of surviving if business conditions deteriorate. Own a relatively high profit-margin business for the long-term and a relatively low profit-margin business for a successful turnaround.

- Evaluate the debt structure. Lots of short-term debt due on demand is negative. Non-callable long-term debt is positive.

- Check the level of inventories. Preferably they are growing at a rate less than sales growth. If inventories grow faster than sales, the company may have to discount the inventory to sell it.

- Check the dividend record. Is it consistently growing and comfortably covered with earnings? Lynch liked to keep some dividend paying stalwarts in his portfolio because their stock prices are more resilient during times of crisis.

- Check for hidden assets such as patents, brand name, investments, tax-loss carry-forwards, and land value.

- Make sure the pension liability is not overwhelming.

- *Value Line* is a good reference for a company's long-term record, especially for determining what happened to earnings and dividends during the last recession.

- Is management buying shares and is the company buying shares? Favor companies where management has a significant ownership and ideally, when several individual managers are buying at once. Look for companies that consistently buy back their shares. Peter Lynch said that investors "ought to concentrate on insider buying. Very readily available. They can see companies that are buying in their stocks, or insiders that are buying in their stocks. I find that to be a very good, reliable indicator."[13]

- Is the level of institutional ownership low?

Call the Company (better yet, visit the company)

- Get the company's reaction to your story/investment thesis.

- Ask questions that indicate that you've done your homework.

- Ask, "When was the last time an analyst visited."

- Kick the tires. Try the product or service. Before Lynch bought La Quinta, he spent three nights in their motor inns, and before he bought Pic 'N' Save, Pep Boys, and Toys "R" Us, he stopped in at one of their stores. "I owned American Motor Inns, Hospitality Inns, United Inns and I asked them, 'Who is your best competitor?' They said La Quinta

Motor Inns. I visited them (La Quinta) and made it a big position. It was a huge success. I owned it for seven to eight years."[14]

- Test competing products. "I don't mean just reading the annual reports or the quarterly reports. I'm saying if you own Chrysler, you ought to find out if somebody is coming up with a better Jeep, or somebody is coming up with a better minivan. You don't get that from reading stuff, you get that by driving the new vehicle that's coming out."[15]

Recheck the Story

- Periodically check your rationale for owning the company.

- Check quarterly and annual reports, visit stores, read interviews and quarterly conference call transcripts.

The Perfect Stock

In his book, *One Up on Wall Street*, Peter Lynch described the characteristics of the "perfect stock." In general, it was a company that had a steady, growing business with a reliable customer base and little if any competition. It would have the following attributes: dull boring name, dull boring business, disagreeable or depressing business, a spin-off, under-owned or underfollowed, suffered from unfounded rumors, was in a "no-growth" industry, had a niche product or service, its product required repeat purchases, was user of technology, insiders were buying stock, and the company was buying back shares.

Spin-offs occur when a parent company issues stock in one of its divisions and sells a small percentage in a public offering. The rest is eventually distributed to shareholders. Spin-offs tend to outperform stocks in general because the newly independent company becomes more entrepreneurial and can benefit from focus. Their cash flow can be redirected from funding parent company projects to fund innovation projects and capital improvements of its own. For example, the Justice Department required AT&T to split itself into eight parts in 1983; AT&T was to provide only long-distance service and the seven Regional Bell Operating Companies, commonly referred to as the Baby Bells, were to provide only local service. In the seven years after the break-up, the average Baby Bell stock outperformed AT&T almost two-to-one, or 349 percent compared to Ma Bell at 159 percent.

CHAPTER 12

Avoiding Mistakes and Selling Stocks

I think the single biggest mistake is they (investors) don't do research. People go to the library and they do incredible research on a microwave oven, and then they'll go out and spend $10,000 on a stock because they heard a tip on the bus.

—PETER LYNCH[1]

Selling Stocks

Peter Lynch said that if you know why you bought a stock in the first place, you will automatically have a better idea of when to sell. Recall that when Lynch bought a stock, he developed a two-minute script for: 1) why he liked the stock, 2) what had to happen for the company to succeed, and 3) what risks the company may face. If a company development occurs after you purchased a stock that violates your reason for buying the company, the decision to sell becomes easier. Re-rationalizing a deteriorating situation can become a dangerous downward spiral.

No single formula applies to selling stocks. Generally, Peter Lynch sold for one of three reasons:

1. **Price/Earnings ratio is higher than its growth rate.**
   - *"As a rule of thumb, a stock should sell at or below its growth rate."*[2]

2. **Violates Reason for Purchase**

- *"If I make a mistake, I try and sell it. If I'm looking for something to happen, some product to work, the business to get better and it's clear that I'm wrong, that is the key thing, you really have to sell it, it's difficult to do. But you don't want to just hope and pray because you can wait for years to go on."*[3]

- *"When you buy a stock, you should write down the reasons why you buy it. That's what you look at. I bought Subaru. I wish I bought it at $10, I wish I bought it at $15, it was up from $3. It was selling at 10x earnings. It had $20/share in cash. It had a great niche in the market. It was a total drive vehicle, it was fairly priced, no competition. They did not make any Subarus. It was just a distributor. Fuji Heavy Industries made the Subaru and Subaru eventually bought it out. Subaru was a public company that just distributed. It's a fantastic stock. It went from $5 to $150. I bought it at $15. But then I sold it. The reason I sold it was, guess what, one day, Ford introduced the Escort. Price discounting was on the horizon. All of a sudden there is competition that is good at a low-price level. The yen went up; Subaru (cars) went up in price. It's a car. The car wasn't a buy anymore, and guess what; the stock isn't a buy anymore. I sold the stock. That story matured. That's when I sell the stock, when the story falls apart."*[4]

3. **Better Substitute**

- *"I sell because something else is more attractive. Stock A is simply more attractive than stock B."*[5] *"But in nine times out of ten, I sell if company 280 has a better story than company 212, and especially when the latter story begins to sound unlikely."*[6]

Peter Lynch had specific reasons for selling different categories of stocks.

Selling Slow Growers

Lynch did not own many slow growers, but of those he did, he sold when there was a 30–50 percent appreciation or when the fundamentals had deteriorated even if the stock declined in price.

Selling Stalwarts

Stalwarts are typically companies with very large market capitalizations, and investors should not expect them to rise many-fold in a short period of time.

Lynch sold stalwarts when their price/earnings ratio rose too far above its historical range, and he usually replaced it with another stalwart that was more reasonably priced. Other sell signals include no officers or directors having bought stock in the last year, and if the company has managed its earnings growth by cost cutting, and future cost cutting opportunities are limited. Be especially wary of stalwarts that manage to report earnings growth within its historic trend, but the source of earnings growth comes from unusual sources like gains in "other" income, temporary lower tax rates, or a lower share count achieved by increased borrowings.

Selling Cyclicals

Stock prices discount the future, and investors in cyclical stocks usually position themselves before a turn in the cycle actually occurs. Cyclical stocks often begin to outperform before any visible sign of a turn in the cycle and begin to underperform even while fundamentals appear strong.

Peter Lynch said that "Other than at the end of the cycle, the best time to sell a cyclical is when something has actually started to go wrong."[7] He noted several warning signs:

- Costs start to increase
- Plants are operating at full capacity
- Inventories are rising
- Commodity costs are falling
- Competitors cut prices to win market share
- Union contracts are expiring and labor leaders want much more
- Demand is slowing
- Foreign producers are selling below domestic costs
- Excessive capital spending plans

Selling Fast Growers

Peter Lynch sold fast growers when their price/earnings ratios reached absurdly expensive levels, such as when Avon and Polaroid had P/Es of 50x or when the P/E is far above the company's sustainable earnings growth rate.

The main thing to watch for according to Lynch, is the end of the second phase of rapid growth. Indicators include:

- Excessively bullish Wall Street analyst recommendations
- Heavy institutional ownership
- Fawned over by national media
- Deteriorating fundamentals
- Retail stores are looking shabby and no longer relevant
- Declining same store sales
- Senior management resign to join another firm

Selling Turnarounds

The best time to sell a turnaround is after the company has turned around, all the major problems have been addressed, everyone is aware of it, and the company is its old self again. Shareholders aren't embarrassed to own it again. Other signs to indicate sell:

- Debt rises after many quarters of sequential decline
- Inventories are increasing faster than the rate of sales growth
- The p/e ratio is inflated relative to earnings prospects
- Its customer's sales are slowing

Selling Asset Plays

Often it pays to wait for an activist investor to prod management to realize the value of its assets either through an asset sale, takeover, or leveraged buyout. Asset plays can also be sold when the asset is sold for less than expected or when the company "di-worsifies" by announcing a merger financed with undervalued stock that dilutes the value of the unrecognized asset.

Stop Loss Orders

Some investors sell their stock if it drops to a predetermined percentage loss, such as 10 percent. They believe that if they limit their loss consistently, they can prevent a disastrous loss of 80–90 percent and still have the bulk of their capital to reinvest in another company. Peter Lynch said that he "detests" stop loss orders. With normal market volatility, it is almost inevitable that an investor would be forced to sell. Lynch made the point that when an investor uses a stop loss limit order, they are, in effect, admitting that they are going to sell the stock for less than it is currently worth. He also thought that selling a stock when it doubles is just as foolish. Don't let the stock price dictate your view of future prospects. As long as your original rationale for investing makes sense and the valuation is fair, then hold the stock for future gains.

Stocks Peter Lynch Avoids

Ideally a stock is purchased and held for many years with outstanding results and never has to be sold. Many times, however, a company's competitive advantage erodes, management changes for the worse, competitors become reinvigorated, and a stock that once made sense, needs to be sold. Then there are those stocks that should never be bought in the first place. Stocks that Peter Lynch says he avoids include:

- The hottest stock in the hottest industry.

  Lynch said, "If I could avoid a single stock, it would be the hottest stock in the hottest industry, the one everyone's talking about."[8] Hot industries attract hordes of smart competitors hungry for their share of the market. Sales may increase at attractive rates in what may be an intuitively obvious trend of secular demand, but profits often wither as competitor's discount prices in their struggle for market share. Hot stocks have high expectations for their continued business and stock price momentum. A company may exceed quarterly earnings estimates, but if its guidance for future revenues or sales falls short of expectations, the stock price reaction can be ugly.

- A stock touted as the "Next Something"

  A stock touted as the "next Apple" or "next Microsoft" almost never is. Copycats usually fall short. Peter Lynch says that when someone touts a stock as the next of something, it often marks the end of prosperity for not only the imitator, but also for the original to which it is being compared.

- Companies that "di-worsify"

  Profitable companies that diversify by acquiring other companies often overpay and expand beyond their core competence. The shareholder pays the price of tuition for management incompetence. Wall Street analysts typically praise the acquisition by citing opportunities for sales synergies and eliminating redundant costs. When the company eventually suffers indigestion in the form of a restructuring and unloads its former grand acquisition for a song, Wall Street analysts excuse the write-off as a "one-time" charge and praise the company for streamlining itself and becoming more focused. The company appears to win in either case, but in reality, the winners are investment bankers who broker the transactions. Instead, the profitable company is usually better off buying back its own stock at opportunistic prices.

- Whisper stocks

Whisper stocks are long shots ideas with great stories but no substance. They sound "too good to be true" and usually are. They are often communicated in hushed confidential tones and recommended for your personal account. Peter Lynch said that, "often the whisper stocks are on the brink of solving the latest national problem: the oil shortage, drug addiction, and AIDS where the solution is either very imaginative or impressively complicated."[9] These companies are high on promise but short on earnings. In fact, they normally have no earnings. Peter Lynch advises to wait until the company has established a proven record of delivering earnings. He said, "When in doubt, tune in later."[10]

The same is true of most Initial Public Offerings (IPOs) that are over-hyped new companies that are very risky because they lack a track record. The safer IPOs are companies that have been spun off from another company, and the new entity has a track record of proven performance. The new entity has a fresh focus where it can reinvest its own cash flow to reinvigorate its products as a result of being ignored as a stepchild by the former parent company.

- Companies overly dependent on a major customer

Companies that derive a material percentage of their earnings from a major customer are at a major bargaining power disadvantage. If GM tells one of its auto suppliers to jump, the supplier says "how high." The supplier is always at risk for price concessions and at a catastrophic risk of being replaced by another supplier.

- Stocks with an exciting name

Peter Lynch noted that flashy company names give investors a false sense of security. "As long as it has 'advanced,' 'leading,' 'micro,' or something with an x in it, or it's a mystifying acronym, people will fall in love with it."[11]

How Peter Lynch Deals with Losses

Peter Lynch said that stocks don't know that you own them. Yet, when a stock falls below your purchase price, it can feel like a personal affront. Reconcile yourself to the fact that mistakes are inevitable. Lynch estimated that 35–40 percent of his stocks were losers.[12] "You're going to make mistakes. You're terrific in this business if you're right six times out of ten. No method guarantees you're not going to lose your shirt. I've had stocks go from $11 to seven cents."[13]

While mistakes may be inevitable, Peter Lynch repeatedly reassured investors that one winning stock can make up for many losers:

The beauty of the stock is if you put $1,000 on a stock, all you can lose is $1,000. I mean I've proven that many times. If you're right, you can make $5,000. You can make $10,000. You don't have to be right half the time. If you're right three times out of ten, then the times you recognize the company is doing well and you understand what they do, you add to it, and you take advantage of it, you can make a lot of money.[14]

Market corrections are normal and recurring. Though they are unpredictable as to timing and can be stomach wrenching to ride through, they are as normal as the seasons of the year. The key is to focus on the long-term outperformance of stocks compared to bonds, CDs, and cash:

In this century, there have been 50 declines of 10 percent or more. So about every two years there is a 10 percent or greater correction in the market. Of those 50 declines, 15 have been 25 percent or more, (1929 and 1987 were 33 percent; and before every decline of significance, there was a high level of speculation marked by high levels of individual and foreign buying and a high level of new issues). What I am saying is that when it is below zero in Minneapolis in the winter, no one panics. But when the market goes down every couple of years, TV has it, taxi drivers are in a bad mood. To me, it is just the nature of the beast. You get declines. You usually can't find a reason for them. They just happen, and good stocks go down, and that is great. You get ready. And when the ones you liked at $18 go to $12, you say terrific… you either ride it out or, hopefully, find more money and buy some more.[15]

So on average, once every two years the market drops 10 percent, and once every six years it goes down a quarter or more.[16]

In other words, be prepared; don't panic, but be opportunistic.

For the first time in eight years in October 1987, Peter Lynch and his wife Carolyn took a vacation to Ireland, their first visit to the Emerald Isle. They left on Thursday, October 14 and the Dow Jones Industrial Average fell 58 points (2.4 percent) followed by a 108 drop (4.6 percent) on Friday. Peter said to Carolyn, "If the market goes down on Monday, we'd better go home." After spending the weekend in Ireland, the DJIA sank 508 points (22.6 percent), so they went home. There wasn't much Lynch could do, but he hurried home since he figured that it looked better if he was in his office instead of saying he was on the eighth hole shooting for par. In two business days, he lost of third of his fund from $12 billion to $8 billion.

To put the crash of '87 in perspective, Lynch noted that the market moved from 777 in 1982 to 1700 in 1986. So in four years the market rose 1,000 points. Then in nine months in 1987, the market jumped another 1,000 points to 2,700. In two months, it fell 1,000 points, 500 on the last day. So effectively the market was unchanged in twelve months, but everyone remembers the dramatic fall. He remembered,

> They (investors and the media) thought, 'Oh, my goodness, this is the crash. It's all over. It's going to go to 200 and I'm going to be selling apples and pencils,' you know. It was just a unique phenomenon because companies were doing fine. Just, you know, you'd call up a company and they would say, 'We can't figure it out. We're doing well. Our orders are good. Our balance sheet is good. We just announced we're going to buy some of our stock. We can't figure out why it's gone down so much.'[17]

Lynch wasn't scared because he concentrated on company fundamentals and had the proper market perspective.

A Baker's Dozen of the Biggest Mistakes Investors Make

Peter Lynch identified the thirteen most common and biggest mistakes investors make. Being aware of these mistakes and guarding against these "forced errors" will go a long way toward minimizing the risk of loss.

1. Not Knowing What You Own

In order to know what you own, you have to do research. There is no shortcut. Not doing homework leads to lack of conviction, which leads to lack of willpower to ride through the inevitable declines. "The worst thing an investor can do is invest in companies they know nothing about. Buying stocks on ignorance 'playing the market' is nothing more than looking for instant gratification without having to do any work. Invest in what you understand."[18]

2. Buying Potential Instead of Performance

> *I think the biggest mistake is they don't know what they own and the other is they buy on the potential of something. They hear a terrific potential story but the profits aren't there…you have to get on to some other subject because you have to tune in later on these things. I don't think you want to buy it on the potential of something. You want to buy it on the results.*[19]

In May 1999, Peter Lynch said the Internet sector was in need of a correction and described it as "La-La land." Ten months later, the bubble burst in internet stocks, many of which never survived.

3. Bottom Fishing

Wall Street pundits often say buy the dip. Buying a stock just because it drops in price without knowing whether the fundamental story has changed, is like buying a shirt from a sale rack without inspecting whether the shirt is flawed. There might be a very good reason why the stock is marked down and, even then, it might not be an attractive value.

> *Buying a stock only because it has fallen from price X to two-thirds of X (is a mistake)…A stock, Avon Products, goes from $150 to $90, on that basis alone they buy the stock and then it—you know, it can go to $18, as we know. A stock that's down combined with a good fundamental story is good. But just buying on that basis alone is very dangerous.*[20]

4. Impatience

Buying stocks is not an avenue for short-term gratification. Sound investing requires patience and a focus on the long-term. Lynch said that his big winners tend to come in the second, third, or fourth year he owned them, not the first week or first month. "I've really concentrated on the long-term. I'm surprised how much time I spent on trading. My great stocks were the third, fourth year I owned them, not the third or fourth week, and that great companies win out in the end."[21]

Let your winning stocks run. "Some stocks, go up 20–30 percent and they get rid of it and they hold onto the dogs. And it's sort of like watering the weeds and cutting out the flowers. You want to let the winners run…You have to let the big ones make up for your mistakes."[22]

5. Betting on Options

Time is not on your side with options. The clock is always ticking, and the time value of the option decays quickly as it approaches expiration. Peter Lynch said you might as well bet on the weather. He never bought a future or option in his life.

"None of the money goes to the company. It's just a bet…I don't think it serves investors or the country."[23] "It's just doing no good at all and it's a tragic thing if you're right on a company and you have a three-month option, and you put $10,000 on it and this company turns around in six months."[24]

Peter Lynch often said it was the third, fourth, fifth year he owned a stock, such as with La Quinta Motor Inns, Chrysler, Ford and Fannie Mae, that they did so well. It wasn't in the third month or sixth month period when many options expire. He said it was a tragedy if an investor bought a three-month option, and was right on why the stock would increase, but it took a year instead of three months. Instead of making multiples on the stock, they lose everything on the option.

6. Trying to Predict the Market/Dwelling on Macroeconomic Worries

Peter Lynch said, "I think market timing is a waste of time. It's futile, it's ineffective."[25] He said that investment success depends on your ability to ignore the worries of the world long enough to allow your investments to succeed:

> People always worry about something. I remember when people said oil was going to $100 and then we were going to have a depression. And the same people said oil was going to go to $5 and we were going to have a depression. We had money supply. Remember those Thursday nights when everybody worried about money figures; the M1s and the M3s? Money was going to grow so fast we were going to have a depression. Now the same people say money is growing too slow…There is always something to worry about. But it is garbage to worry about these things.[26]

Peter Lynch believed investors should not waste their time with forecasting the future, but focus on current facts. "I deal in facts, not forecasting the future. That's crystal ball stuff. That doesn't work. Futile."[27]

Related to the mistake of dwelling on macroeconomic worries is the folly of market timing. Peter Lynch observed in mid-1996 that in the past ninety-five years, the market had fifty-three "corrections" or declines of 10 percent or more. Of these, fifteen of the declines were at least 25 percent, a bear market.

So once every two years, on average, the market drops 10 percent, and once every six years on average the market sinks 25 percent or more. No one can predict when those drops will happen.

> *If you are not ready for that (market decline), you shouldn't be in the stock market. I mean the stomach is they key organ here. It's not the brain. Do you have the stomach for these kinds of declines? Is your horizon one year or ten to twenty years? What the market is going to do in one or two years, you don't know. Time is on your side in the stock market (if your horizon is long-term).*[28]

Peter Lynch compared three investors who invested in a U.S. market index from 1965–1985. The first invested at the high of the year, the second at the low of the year, and the third at the beginning of the year. After twenty years, the first investor had an 11.7 percent return, the second had a 10.6 percent return, and the third investor had an 11.0 percent return. There was almost no difference.[29] Shortly after the tragedy of September 11, 2001, Peter Lynch admitted that in the short-term, the market was likely to be choppy, but that "nobody can predict with any certainty which way the next 1,000 points will be. Which way the next 1,000 to 2,000 points in the market will go is anybody's guess, but I believe strongly that the next 10,000, 20,000 and 40,000 points will be up."[30] He pointed to innovations in healthcare, manufacturing and technology, as well as the demise of communism—the rise of free-markets for creating jobs and adding to prosperity.

7. Giving Up Too Soon

Be patient and focus on the long-term. Peter Lynch said that his best stocks rallied in the third or fourth year he owned them, not the third or fourth day or week. Lynch also recommended being patient with your winners.

> *The flip side is, if it has gone this high already, how much higher can it go? That's like cutting the flowers and watering the weeds. In fact, in 1989 I got a call from Warren Buffett about 8 o'clock at night. "This is Warren Buffett from Omaha. I love the book. I love the book. There's this quote about cutting the flowers and watering the weeds. I love it and I want to put it in the annual report. He said if you ever come to Nebraska and don't come to Omaha, your name will be mud in Nebraska; we'll put mud all over your name. So I went and saw him. He said his greatest stocks are those that*

other people sold. He bought Coca-Cola and it went up 500-fold. So, just selling stocks because they went up is a huge mistake.[31]

That one line that he (Buffett) picked in my whole book has been my greatest mistake. I visited the first four Home Depots ever built. I sold that stock after it tripled, and then it went up another fifty-fold...With great companies the passage of time is a major positive.[32]

8. Myopic Focus

Expand your investment horizon beyond the conventional growth areas. Keep a wide scope but stay with companies that you understand.

9. Investing Too Much in Fixed Income and Not Enough in Stocks

Peter Lynch was astounded that 90 percent of the nation's investment dollars were parked in fixed income instruments such as bonds, CDs, money market accounts, and cash. Lynch often compared the long-term return differences between stocks, bonds, and treasuries bills. In the 64-year period from 1926–1990, stocks returned 10.3 percent annually compared to 4.8 percent for long-term government debt. Only one decade in the last seven (the 1930s) did bonds outperform stocks. $100,000 invested in 1926 in long-term treasuries and the S&P 500 by 1990, would have been worth $1.6 million and $25.5 million respectively.

10. Thinking That You Missed a Stock

As long as the company has an open-market opportunity and has not saturated the market and the stock is reasonably priced, there is more opportunity for gains in the stock.

Peter Lynch noted that by 1980 Walmart stock had risen 20-fold since its IPO in 1970. But it still only had 276 stores in 15 percent of the country:

...and they hadn't even saturated that 15 percent. So you could say to yourself, now what kind of intelligence does this take? You could say, this company has minimal costs, they're efficient, everybody who competes with them says they're great, the products are terrific, the service is terrific, the balance sheet is fine, and they're self-funding.[33]

You could have bought Walmart in 1980 and it would have had a 30-fold gain through 1990. In 1991, Walmart rose another 60 percent, resulting in a "50-bagger" in eleven years.

11. Thinking That Watching Stock Quotes is Doing Research

Peter Lynch said he thought people, including himself, spend hours looking at what stocks are going up or down all day. He said, "that is an absolute waste of time. Great companies do well, their earnings do well, and what the stock does one week or next week doesn't matter…stocks go up when companies' earnings go up, not because of buyers and sellers. That stuff is way overrated."[34]

12. Tuning Into the Noise and Feelings Rather Than Facts

> *Don't listen to the noise. Cut out the noise. Noise is not useful. Look at facts instead. If you own an auto company, you ought to care what's happening to used-car prices, you ought to care what's happening to steel prices, you ought to care what's happening to affordability. That's what you ought to be looking at, not worrying about who's going to be the next president, and what's happening in Congress, what's happening in the Supreme Court, what's happening in the Middle East. Those are things you have no control over.*[35]

Warren Buffett had the same advice, which is why he preferred to keep his office in Omaha, Nebraska. Buffett echoed Peter Lynch's remarks by saying that investors should focus on what is relevant and knowable, not what is irrelevant and unknowable.

Recessions are inevitable, but Peter Lynch used three indicators to signal an upturn in business, rather than rely on economists or the opinions of popular media commentators. The first is the price of used cars: "I've always looked at used car prices as a great indicator."[36] Businesses are naturally reticent to rehire after a downturn due to the added benefit costs of social security, pension and healthcare. So when they do rehire, it signals a turn in business: "The average work week is a very good indicator."[37] Lastly, when the ratio of inventory to sales reached extremely low levels, it signaled a probable upturn in investment in order to rebuild inventory.

13. Don't Miss Great Opportunities Waiting for Unusual Companies to Get Dirt-Cheap.

Lynch noted that,

> *…throughout its 27-year rise from a split-adjusted $.016 to $23, Walmart never looked cheap compared with the overall market. Its price-to-earnings ratio rarely dropped below 20, but Walmart's earnings were growing at 25*

to 30 percent a year. A key point to remember is that a p/e of 20 is not too much to pay for a company that's growing at 25 percent.[38]

Technical Analysis

Technical analysis is a form of investing that believes that studying past price and volume movement of stocks, and their moving averages, can be helpful in determining future price action. Peter Lynch said that, "The problem with technical analysis is that somebody could love the stock at $12 and hate it at $6."[39] He did favor a form of technical analysis to identify when stocks had bottomed. He would use it to generate a list of companies to analyze further with fundamental research:

> It's like trying to catch a falling knife. When it's going from 50 to 8, it looks cheap at 15; it looks cheap at 12. So you want the knife to stick in the wood. When it stops vibrating, then you can pick it up. That's how I see it on a purely technical basis...From a technical standpoint, this is the only formation that would show me something.[40]

Peter Lynch emphasized that this list of companies is not a buy list but a research list for further investigation about, for instance, the strength of their balance sheet and the threat from competition.

CHAPTER 13

Portfolio Design

The current stock price tells us nothing about the future prospects of a company, and it occasionally moves in the opposite direction of the fundamentals. A better strategy, it seems to me, is to rotate in and out of stocks depending on what happened to the price as it relates to the story.

—PETER LYNCH[1]

In this chapter, we will review how Peter Lynch designed his portfolio to maximize gain and minimize risk. Lynch said that his objective was to beat the market over the long-term, not each year, by an average of 4–5 percent per year. Lynch believed that, considering the time spent researching stocks and the money spent on commissions and research publications, an active investor ought to earn 12–15 percent compounded return to make the effort worthwhile. The alternative is to invest in a low-cost index fund, which could replicate the historic long-run return for stocks of 9–10 percent per year. "I think if people aren't willing to do homework and they're not willing to do research, maybe they should buy an index fund of the Russell 2000 or the Wilshire 5000, and buy and S&P 500 index fund."[2]

Peter Lynch advised individuals to answer three questions before deciding to invest:

1. Do I own a house? If not, consider owning a house before stocks. The advantages include: the ability to buy with leverage; deferral of taxable

gains; real estate is a hedge against inflation; and you won't likely sell in a panic when the general press is negative.

2. Do I need the money? Lynch encourages individuals to only invest what you can afford to lose without that loss having any effect on your daily life in the foreseeable future.

3. Do I have the personal qualities it takes to succeed? These include patience, self-reliance, common sense, a tolerance for pain, a willingness to do independent research, an equal willingness to admit mistakes, the ability to ignore general panic, make decisions without complete information, conviction to stand by your stocks as long as the fundamental story hasn't changed, and faith and optimism about our country's capitalist system.

Number of Stocks

Peter Lynch advised only owning as many stocks as you can understand and follow, is attractively priced, and passes the research tests outlined in the previous chapter. For small portfolios, he advised owning between three and ten stocks, but he also cautioned to not rely on a fixed number of stocks, but evaluate them on a case-by-case basis.

The advantages of owning more stocks rather than fewer include: 1) increasing the odds that you own a stock that performs well beyond your expectations, and 2) increasing your flexibility to rotate funds between the stocks.

Lynch acknowledged that portfolio design should be age appropriate. Older investors with a shorter investing horizon, or who depend on income from their investments, will have a different percentage allocation than a younger investor who can afford to allocate more to higher risk, higher potential return companies. In either case, he advocates developing the conviction necessary to be willing to buy more of a stock that is down 25 percent as long as your original rationale is intact.

The ability to allocate among different categories of stocks depending on fundamental values is a key part of Peter Lynch's portfolio design to minimize risk. He typically allocated 30–40 percent to growth stocks, 10–20 percent in stalwarts, 10–20 percent in cyclicals, and the rest in turnarounds. He was constantly looking for values in all areas. For instance, when a market correction occurred, he could sell a portion of the stalwarts that held up as a safe-haven and invest the proceeds in the more volatile growth stocks that were relatively depressed in value. Conversely, when the market was euphoric, he could sell some of his overvalued growth or cyclical stocks and add to his exposure in stalwarts that had likely lagged.

> *I divide the Fidelity Magellan into two sections. One section is small growth companies and cyclical stocks that I'm hoping to hold for a long period of time—make substantial moves. The other part of the portfolio is relatively conservative stocks. When the market breaks…and the stocks I really like go from $18 to $9 and then I can sell my conservative stocks…If your whole portfolio goes from $18 to $9, you don't make much progress.[3]*

When Fidelity Magellan was opened to new investors in 1981, it had 200 stocks. Lynch increased the number of stocks as the fund grew. By 1983 it had grown to 900 stocks, reached a peak of 1,800 stocks in 1987 and fell to 1,400 in 1990 when he retired. Lynch believed that he could better monitor stocks if he owned them, even if it was just a small position. He also reasoned that if he had to sell to meet large redemptions, he could do so more easily by selling many 2,000 share positions than huge blocks of a few select stocks. Lynch said that during the first three years he ran Magellan, one-third of the shares were redeemed. "I mean there was very little interest. People didn't care. The market was doing okay and Magellan was doing well, but people were sort of recovering from their losses from the '50s and '60s, and so literally one-third of the shares were redeemed the first three years I ran it."[4]

Even though he owned as many as 1,800 stocks, he concentrated 50 percent of Magellan's weight in the top 100 stocks, and up to 75 percent of its weight in the top 200 stocks. The bottom 500 secondary stocks represented only 1 percent of the portfolio. If the story or valuation improved in one of the 500 smaller stocks, he graduated it to a primary weight.

Peter Lynch didn't try to predict the stock market or economy and was always fully invested in the Magellan fund.

Cash and Bonds

Peter Lynch was asked in February 1985 by Louis Rukeyser if he ever had any cash on hand. He replied, "Never." Rukeyser then asked, "What percent is cash right now?" and Lynch replied, "One percent."[5]

He used conservative stocks in lieu of cash.

In lieu of cash, I put 25–35 percent of the fund in conservative stocks—by which I mean that, after I make 30 percent or 35 percent in them, I want to sell and buy another that hasn't done much lately... If the market goes down and the economy worsens, I usually tend to add to the more attractive growth segments of the portfolio while cutting back on my conservative stocks.[6]

In 1982 Peter Lynch's biggest position for many months in Magellan was long-term Treasury bonds, which were yielding 13–14 percent. He said that he bought the bonds because the yields exceeded the returns that an investor would normally expect from stocks. Lynch frequently noted that, over the long haul, stocks substantially outperform bonds. He observed in 1989 that a hypothetical $1,000 investment in common stocks sixty years prior would have amounted to $272,000 and "paid off fifteen times as well as corporate bonds, and well over thirty times better than Treasury bills!" Over those sixty years, stocks returned on average 9.8 percent annually, corporate bonds returned 4.9 percent, government bonds returned 4.4 percent, and Treasury bills returned 3.3 percent. He acknowledged that stocks are risky, but so are bonds, especially during a period of rising interest rates. However, when bonds yield enough compared to the long-term expected return on stocks, it makes sense to invest in bonds. Peter Lynch offered a helpful rule of thumb to guide investors when to make the switch: "When yields on long-term government bonds exceed the dividend yield of the S&P 500 by 6 percent or more, sell your stocks and buy bonds."[7]

Technology Stocks

Peter Lynch didn't understand and preferred not to own technology stocks, which were his most consistent losers.

I've owned very few technology stocks. I tend to buy technology stocks when they're really hot. Near the top of '83 market was probably my all-time high in technology stocks...My technology group has ranged from 3 percent and 10 percent of the fund and now it's 4 percent or 5 percent, so it is not a real commitment...if you have some whiz-bang semiconductor company, how do you know if somebody else doesn't have a better semiconductor? When a stock goes down a third, I have to know if I should double my position or sell it.[8]

CHAPTER 14

Case Studies

One of the keys to Peter Lynch's investment success was his opportunism—his ability to keep an open mind, stay flexible, and invest where he saw the greatest return. The investments ranged from undiscovered smaller growth companies, turnarounds, larger stalwart consistent growth companies, and even treasury bonds. The following examples of his notable investments, and the context behind each one, may allow us to benefit from similar situations in the future.

La Quinta Motor Inns

In 1978 Lynch was referred to La Quinta Motor Inns during a phone conversation with a vice-president of United Inns, the largest franchiser of Holiday Inn, after asking the vice-president which company was Holiday Inn's toughest competitor. Lynch also owned American Motor Inns and Hospitality Inns, and they responded similarly about La Quinta as their most respected competitor. Lynch soon called La Quinta's CEO and was impressed with the company's strategy of charging 30 percent less than Holiday Inn for similar quality rooms, and it was still profitable by eliminating the wedding area, the kitchen area, conference rooms, the large reception area, and the restaurant. He liked the company's strategy of locating itself next to a Denny's or other restaurants that it didn't have to manage. He was also drawn to La Quinta's appeal to the middle-market business traveler, which was unpenetrated. La Quinta located

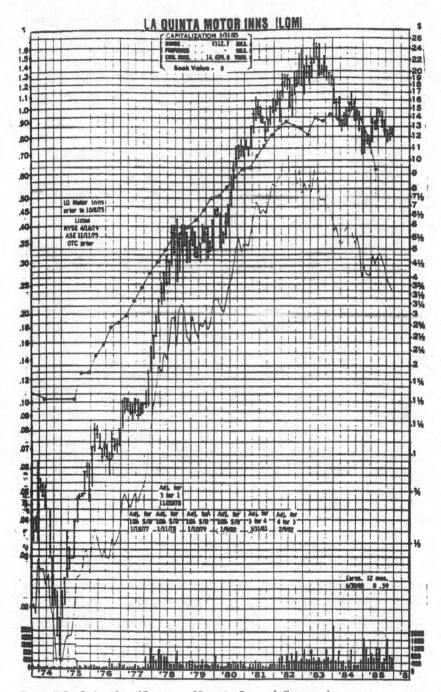

Figure 7. La Quinta Inn. (Courtesy of Security Research Company)

its units near business districts, hospitals, and industrial complexes whereas Holiday Inn targeted travelers by locating next to freeway ramps.

Lynch was also swayed by La Quinta's track record of operating for four to five years, and growing earnings 50 percent annually. The stock was priced at just 10x earnings, only three brokerage firms followed it, and institutions owned less than 20 percent of the stock. Although the motel industry was low-growth, La Quinta had found a niche and was growing its units at 20 percent per year. La Quinta began operating in Texas and had successfully duplicated its strategy in Arkansas and Louisiana. Before he bought the stock, Lynch spent three nights in their motor inns but was almost deterred from buying the stock due to recent insider selling at half the current price. Despite the stock doubling in the previous year, he bought the stock, and made eleven-fold over a ten-year period before the company suffered from its exposure to a downturn in energy producing states. "I visited them (La Quinta) and made it a big position. It was a huge success."[1]

Takeaways

One of Lynch's favorite techniques for finding promising new stocks is to ask a company who their toughest competitor is and why. This was also one of Templeton's favorite questions. Lynch discovered La Quinta Motor Inns from this method and followed up his discovery with extensive due diligence, including his own direct experience with their product. La Quinta had already demonstrated that its unit growth formula was replicable, it filled an unpenetrated niche, offered differentiated value by eliminating low margin space, was profitable and growing quickly, was underfollowed, and priced cheaply.

Chrysler

Peter Lynch said Chrysler was the most significant stock he ever owned in Magellan because no other stock represented such a large percentage of the fund while the stock rose and, with which, he made $100 million in profits for Magellan shareholders. (He also made $100 million in Ford.) The stock rose five-fold in less than two years and over fifteen-fold while Lynch owned it.

Background 1978–1982

Lee Iacocca began his career with Ford in 1946. He thrived in sales and marketing and eventually became president in 1970. He participated in the design of several successful cars including Ford Mustang, Lincoln Continental Mark II, and Ford Escort. He also advocated ideas that were rejected by the company but did achieve success when later introduced by Chrysler, such as the minivan and K-car. After a falling out with Henry Ford II, he was fired as president of Ford Motor Company in July 1978 despite bringing the company earnings to $2 billion. He was hired as Chrysler's president.

Chrysler lost $205 million largely due to recalls of its Dodge Aspen and Plymouth Volare, which Iococca later said should never have been built. Iacocca immediately began selling or closing unprofitable plants and cutting staff. Consumers were scorning Chrysler's gas guzzlers, which had generated past profits in favor of other high-mileage cars during a gas shortage and a crisis of high gas prices due to the revolution in Iran.

In 1979 Chrysler was absolutely on the precipice of bankruptcy, according to a former government official who helped draft the $1.5 billion federal loan bailout bill that Congress passed in late 1979. In return for the guarantee, Chrysler was required to reduce costs and abandon some long-term projects, and required equal sacrifice by Chrysler employees, bankers, and suppliers.

In the fall of 1980, Chrysler introduced its line of compact, fuel-efficient K-cars to capitalize on the popular high-mileage cars. By year end, Chrysler lost $1.71 billion and asked the government for $400 million more in loan guarantees. "Before granting the request, the government was required to certify that Chrysler would survive."[2] In return, Chrysler assembled $2 billion in concessions and agreed to cut future-product capital spending. Chrysler repeatedly missed legally set targets on constraining losses and maintaining cash balances. "In each case, the government tore up the rules."[3]

On an unannounced tour with government officials, blue collar workers stopped working and spontaneously applauded and cheered Iacocca. Iacocca famously appeared on TV ads as a feisty promoter of "buy American" products just as interest rates eased and gas became cheaper and more plentiful.

In December 1981 Chrysler projected that it would be profitable in 1982 for the first time since 1977, as it forecasted improved car sales in the second half and a favorable consumer response to federal tax cuts designed to spur the economy. In February 1982, most major banks lowered their prime lending rate by 0.5 percent to 16.5 percent.

Peter Lynch's Rationale for Buying in 1982

Against this backdrop, Peter Lynch concluded it was a good time to buy the autos. Importantly, he waited until Chrysler received an infusion of cash from the government bailout loan. He later said that daring investors could have bought the stock beforehand while Chrysler was on its deathbed and made 20x their investment, but they could have lost everything. Instead he bought afterward and made 10x his investment, but with less risk.

The conventional view of the economy was doom and gloom, and Lynch believed that consumers would inevitably return to the auto showrooms. Vehicle sales had declined from 15.4 million in 1977 to 10.5 million in 1982. He reasoned that the downside in car sales was limited due to two reliable indicators: used car prices and units of pent-up demand, which is the cumulative difference between actual vehicle sales and the long-term trend. He discovered this indicator from reading Chrysler's publication called *Corporate Economist*.

Peter Lynch said that he stumbled onto Chrysler after speaking with Ford, and he became convinced that Chrysler would benefit more. Lynch started buying Chrysler when it was a $6 stock (pre-split) and was impressed that its $1 billion in cash, largely from the proceeds of selling its tank division to General Dynamics, would allow it to survive for at least a couple of years. The U.S. government also guaranteed its survival, presumably to avert an endemic reaction. A Chrysler manager said at the time that a collapse "would take down banks, towns, and even some countries."

Lynch reasoned that if Chrysler was "hovering near the breakeven point when sales were slow, it had the potential to do jumbo numbers when sales picked up."[4] At the time, Chrysler's Robert Miller Jr., EVP finance, said that Chrysler should break even if it ships 1.244 million vehicles in 1982 compared to its 1981 breakeven point of 1.413 million and actual 1981 shipments of 1.283 million vehicles. Chrysler was forecasting 1.399 million units in 1982 predicated on a second half economic upturn.

In April 1982, Chrysler reported a first quarter loss from continuing operations of $89 million, which was better than analyst expectations, compared to the prior year loss of $289 million. Capital spending was only $16 million compared to $105 million in depreciation and amortization. Iacocca said, "Chrysler's operating results should improve substantially during the balance of the year with a slight moderation in interest rates and a modest improvement in industry sales."

Lynch visited Chrysler's headquarters in June 1982. He recalled, "This was probably the most important day in my 21-year investment career."[5] The scheduled interviews, planned for three hours, lasted seven hours; and a scheduled brief chat with Lee Iacocca lasted two hours. Lynch became convinced that Chrysler could survive and was impressed with its new products including the Dodge Daytona, Chrysler Laser, the G-124 Turbo Car—which was a sportier front-wheel drive New Yorker—and what Iacocca excitedly described as the "first new thing in the auto industry in twenty years, the minivan." As Lynch was buying his position in the spring of 1982 and into the summer, Wall Street sell-side analysts abandoned coverage because it was so disparaged. By June it was his largest position, and by July it was the maximum 5 percent weight at cost allowed by the SEC.

On July 19, *The Wall Street Journal* profiled Chrysler with a "Heard on the Street" article titled, "Profit Seen for Chrysler in Quarter Boosts Shares but Isn't Termed a Sign of Long-Term Prospects." The article echoed the prevailing sentiment that Chrysler's survival was questionable: "The stock closed Friday at $8.25 (pre-split), a high for the year, but a second quarter profit doesn't say much about the company's long-term chances for survival or the stock's value as anything but a speculative play."

The next day, Chrysler reported earnings of $107 million despite shipping 10 percent fewer vehicles than the previous year. Lower gas prices fueled consumer demand for mid-sized cars which increased 143 percent and even large-sized cars which rose 74 percent. Iacocca said, "I've never been so confident about this company's future," and he predicted a full year operating profit of $150 million. In contrast, the next month, Ford's EVP of North American auto operation, Harold Poling, said he "sees a basic industry in trouble and wondered about its survival."[6]

On October 29, 1982, Peter Lynch appeared for the first time on Louis Rukeyser's *Wall Street Week* weekly television show. Lynch recommended Chrysler, which later elicited reactions from friends and relatives, who said, "…'But how could you ever recommend Chrysler? Don't you know they're going bankrupt?' I remember friends of mine and relatives saying, 'That sounds crazy to me.' So it worked out fine."[7]

He articulated his rationale for owing Chrysler as follows:

Positive on the Consumer and an Auto Industry Revival

Well, I'm very optimistic on the consumer. If you look at the economy right now, I think the corporate sector is in the worst shape it's been in about 20 years, but the consumer is in excellent shape. Now he or she doesn't realize that in a lot of cases, but with inflation slowing, high level of income, a lot of money paying down debt, I think the consumer when feeling a little bit better is going to unleash some spending. I think it's going to make a big difference and I'm trying to emphasize consumer companies...the biggest example would be automobile industry...This is the first year (since) 1978 (that) auto driving peaked. People are driving cars...So, I think autos will be the largest beneficiaries of an improved economy.[8]

Improved Lineup of Vehicles

I'm buying all the auto companies, but my emphasis has been Chrysler... Chrysler is a risky situation. I'm willing to take that risk...I look at Chrysler—they have an outstanding line-up of cars with the LeBaron, the Reliant cars, the New Yorker. Next year, they have two fantastic cars. They have a car coming out, a sports car that goes zero to 60 in a half a second faster than a Porsche. And the Japanese are going to have a lot of trouble when they see that engine compared to their little lawnmower engines they have in their cars.[9]

Chrysler was no longer a car company for grandfathers.

Adequate Liquidity

I'm concerned about that (danger of bankruptcy). They have a billion dollars in cash...They have a huge tax loss carry-forward." Lynch later wrote, *"In the famous bailout arrangement, the key element was that the government guaranteed a $1.4 billion loan in return for some stock options.*[10]

Successful Cost-Cutting with Lower Breakeven

In the past two years, their auto sales are flat and they've reduced losses by $700 million. I think they've done what you can do.[11]

Reward Potential

But Chrysler's down from $52 (to $10 pre-split) and the upside is enormous... It wasn't as risky as it looked in the newspapers...At the time I bought Chrysler, if everything went right, I thought I could make 400 percent, and *if everything went wrong, I could lose 100 percent. This is something you had to recognize going in. As it turned out, I was pleasantly surprised and made 15-fold on it.* [12]

Subsequent Events

In December 1982 Chrysler stock reached $18.50/share (pre-split), and the company agreed to give its lenders common stock in exchange for eliminating $1.1 billion of preferred stock that banks and insurance companies had held since the 1981 federal bailout. Chrysler issued 29.2 million new common shares compared to its share base of 79.5 million for a dilution to existing shareholders of over one-third. The company also agreed to sell at least 8.7 million shares of the lenders stock by July 1983 for at least $12/share. A January 17, 1983, *The Wall Street Journal* "Heard on the Street" article noted that Peter Lynch owned both the common and the preferred stock.

A February 18, 1983, *The Wall Street Journal* "Heard on the Street" article titled "Auto Makers Ride High on Fast Track, But Two Analysts Believe Mileage Nears Peak" quoted PaineWebber analyst Maryann Keller as saying, "History has demonstrated the wisdom of abandoning auto stocks early." The article also mentioned that she and David Healy, an analyst at Drexel Burnham, as "…especially noncommittal toward Chrysler, primarily because its recently announced financial restructuring will cause substantial dilution…they predict 1983 earnings (for) Chrysler of $2 a share."

The stock would proceed to jump ten-fold in less than five years. Chrysler reported EPS of $5.79 even after writing down a $222 million write-down on its 15 percent stake in Peugeot. The company had reduced its debt from $2.1 billion at the beginning of the year to less than $1 billion, it had $1 billion cash, and it couldn't meet demand for some of its vehicles, including the minivan.

Chrysler reported 1985 EPS of $18.88/share. Its first quarter profit alone of $706 million exceeded any previous full year profit due to brisk sales of heavily equipped, high-margin minivan and sports cars in addition to cost cutting, higher prices, and Japanese import quota protection.

In 1986 Lee Iacocca told the Federal Election Commission that he was not running for president and formally disavowed the work of two committees who tried to draft him. Chrysler had almost $3 billion in cash, and the company had a goal of repurchasing 37.5 million shares, or 25 percent, of its base of 147 million shares outstanding. Chrysler was shrinking its share base as the business was improving.

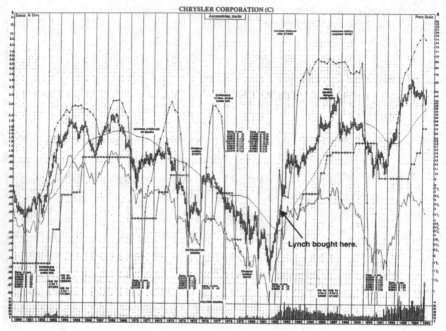

Figure 8. Chrysler (Courtesy of Security Research Company)

In 1987 Chrysler bought Renault's stake in American Motors, which gave Chrysler the highly profitable Jeep line, a modern $675 million production plant and access to a 1,300 dealer Jeep/Renault distribution network. The new plants relieved Chrysler's capacity problem since its facilities were running at nearly 100 percent of capacity. In April 1987 it was reported that Iacocca earned $20.6 million in salary, bonuses, stock grants, and stock options in 1986 compared to Ford's Donald Petersen's $4.4 million. Iacocca's response when asked to explain his compensation when the firm was cutting costs in part by limiting compensation for white-collar employees, he said, "That's the American way. If little kids don't aspire to make money…what the hell good is this country? You gotta give them a role model, right?"

Lynch reduced his Chrysler, Ford, and other auto stocks in 1988, "because I sensed that the great car buying spree that began in the early 1980s was about to end…the debt was paid and the rot was cleaned out, and Chrysler was back to being a solid, cyclical auto company."[13] The pent-up demand from the early 1980s was satisfied as 74 million new vehicles were bought in five years. Chrysler was no longer a turnaround. Lynch adhered to his adage that the best time to sell a turnaround is after it's turned around, all the troubles are over, and everybody knows it.

Takeaways

Peter Lynch's seminal investment in Chrysler demonstrated that his conviction—based on facts and reasoning, and personal experiences with the company's management and products—overwhelmed conventional fears that the company was destined for bankruptcy. Lynch wasn't deterred from buying Chrysler despite the fact that the stock had doubled in the past year. He said he treated each potential investment as though it had no history and focused on Chrysler priced at $6 with the prospect of earning $5–$7 per share. Perhaps more than any other stock, Peter Lynch's experience with Chrysler echoed John Templeton's advice to buy at the point of maximum pessimism and Warren Buffett's advice to be fearful when others are greedy, and be greedy when others are fearful. Lynch's conviction allowed him to not only initiate the position against conventional wisdom but convinced him to stay with the position despite the naysayers' warnings all the way up until the stock peaked.

Fannie Mae

In 1987 Peter Lynch began to lighten his weight in autos as he believed the economic recovery was long in the tooth, and analysts had expectations for the auto companies that he thought were excessive. He boosted his weight in financial companies, particularly Fannie Mae and the savings and loans. Fannie Mae was the largest weight in Fidelity Magellan during Peter Lynch's last three years at the helm. Fidelity shareholders made more than $1 billion in Fannie Mae stock and warrants during the 1980s, and Lynch touted the company in a *Barron's* interview in 1986 as "the best business, literally, in America."[14] In his annual roundtable interview with *Barron's*, Peter Lynch recommended Fannie Mae for ten consecutive years.

Fannie Mae, formally known as Federal National Mortgage Association, was founded in 1938 and is a government-sponsored enterprise that first sold stock to the public in 1968. Its charter is to expand the secondary mortgage market by buying mortgages and securitizing them into mortgage-backed securities. Lenders can benefit by selling their loans to Fannie Mae, reinvest their assets into more lending, and allow investors that bought tranches of mortgage-backed securities the benefit of geographic diversification. Its function was to provide liquidity in the mortgage market by buying mortgages from banks and savings and loans.

Lynch first invested in Fannie Mae in 1977 when it was borrowing with short-term debt and investing in higher fixed-rate mortgages. He sold it a few months later when he saw interest rates rising, which he viewed as a threat to their interest margin and growth. Sure enough, in 1978, while Fannie Mae was earning 7–11 percent on long-term mortgages issued in the mid-1970s, Fannie Mae's funding cost ballooned to 12–16 percent when short-term rates skyrocketed. The stock fell to $2 and was rumored to go bankrupt.

Peter Lynch bought the stock as a minor position in Magellan for the second time in late 1982 as interest rates were falling. The prime rate had dropped to 15 percent from over 20 percent in 1981. Earlier in the year, David Maxwell, an attorney and former insurance commissioner, was hired as Chairman and CEO. He was determined to make the company's earnings more stable and reliable by eliminating the company's practice of borrowing short and lending long, and by packaging loans, which was already being done by Freddie Mac (Federal Home Loan Mortgage Corporation).

In 1983 Fannie Mae still owned $60 billion of mortgages yielding 9.2 percent while its average cost of debt was 11.9 percent. The stock was just 0.1 percent of Magellan. In 1984 Fannie Mae began to match funds by offering three-, five-, and ten-year bonds at higher interest rates, which penalized earnings in the short-term but removed the risk of rising interest rates. By year-end, Fannie Mae was 0.37 percent of Magellan.

After visiting with David Maxwell in Washington in May 1985, Lynch increased Fannie Mae's weight to 2 percent of Magellan, becoming one of his top ten holdings by mid-year. Lynch figured that the company could earn $7/share by making a 1 percent spread on its $100 billion portfolio and pay for its overhead with the proceeds on fees from servicing mortgage-backed securities, which would give the stock a price/earnings ratio of only 1x. Fannie Mae reported 1985 EPS of 0.52 compared to a loss $0.87 in 1984.

In 1986 Fannie Mae significantly tightened its lending standards on new mortgages after losing money in Texas in the oil-patch boom the year before and reported EPS of $1.44. In his interview in January with *Barron's*, Peter Lynch said, "If you want the real whoopee though, though it's Federal National Mortgage, which is my third-largest position...if you believe in flat rates, this is the best business, literally in America."[15] He articulated his rational as follows:

- It had low overhead with just 1,200 employees, which had an expense ratio of just 20 basis points or 20 hundredths of a percentage point. He later wrote in *Beating the Street* that it had one-quarter the employees as Fidelity had, with ten times the profits.
- It was the lowest-cost borrower in the U.S. at one-tenth of a percentage point over the government rate.
- He believed that within two years, Fannie Mae could make 1 percent return on assets which would be $1 billion or $16/share before tax. He noted that the mortgages they had booked in the last four years were already earning 1 percent on assets.
- He estimated that Fannie Mae's business arm, which serviced mortgages that Fannie Mae had sold off, should earn $1.00–$1.25 in 1985, $1.50 in 1986, and $1.75 in 1987. He figured that business alone could be worth $20/share.

A few months later, Chairman David Maxwell predicted in *The Wall Street Journal* interview that Fannie Mae's results in 1986 would show a "very healthy increase (from 1985) due to lower interest rates, a better maturity match between the company's debt and assets, and its increased reliance on certain fee income."[16]

In 1987 Fannie Mae represented Lynch's second largest position at 2–2.5 percent of Magellan throughout the year. His target price was $80, and the stock was $13. In October, David Maxwell told Lynch that if interest rates were to rise three percentage points, the company's earnings would only fall $0.50. Fannie Mae's match funding was working, and its transformation would be evident in its more consistent, better quality earnings. Moreover, its ninety-day delinquency rate was falling, which was a leading indicator that its foreclosures had peaked. After the 1987 stock market crash, Fannie Mae announced it was buying back up to 5 million shares.

In 1988 Fannie Mae was 3 percent of Magellan for most of the year, one of his largest positions along with Ford. Lynch explained why he liked Fannie Mae again in his February 8 roundtable interview with *Barron's*:

- **Low cost producer.** Fannie Mae "borrows at 15–20 (basis) points over governments, and they have only 12 or 15 basis points of cost."

- **Better earnings quality.** The quality of earnings improved "dramatically" according to Lynch because the accounting for Fannie Mae's commitment fees, which had ranged from $30–$100 million per quarter and led to volatile earnings, was being changed to a rolling fifteen-year average to smooth quarterly earnings.

- **Market potential.** "The mortgage industry is enormous. I think it is bigger than the stock market. Ten years ago, banks would take in mortgages and hold them forever. Now they sell them off. They're constantly selling them back and forth."

- **Valuation.** Lynch noted that the stock was about the same price as five years earlier even thought it was a much better company in 1988 because they figured out five years earlier that borrowing short and lending long was not a good business. Lynch estimated EPS of over $5 share in 1988 and over $7 a share in 1989. He thought the stock deserved "a 10 multiple because it now should be a steady grower of earnings."

In 1989 Lynch boosted Fannie Mae to reach the maximum cost weight of 5 percent of Magellan. He noted that Warren Buffett owned 2.2 million shares. The stock rose 260 percent from $16/share to $42/share in 1989 as investors finally understood Fannie Mae's transformation and grasped its market potential. From Lynch's pivotal interview with David Maxwell in May 1985 until his retirement in 1990, Fannie Mae rose more than sixfold. Peter Lynch continued to recommend Fannie Mae in his annual roundtable interview with *Barron's* until 1995, during which the stock more than doubled, largely because earnings grew to over $7/share, as Peter Lynch predicted it could in 1988.

Takeaways

Peter Lynch liked to maintain many small positions in Magellan to keep on his radar screen. He continued to monitor their progress as prospects to be drafted from the minor league to the majors with a greater weight in the fund. Fannie Mae began as a 0.1 percent weight, and as Lynch's conviction in Fannie Mae strengthened after visiting with the company, he matched it by eventually making it his largest position. The prevailing opinion of Fannie Mae was that it was still a volatile and vulnerable company. Its strategy was to borrow money with short-term debt and buy fixed-rate mortgages at higher rates. When

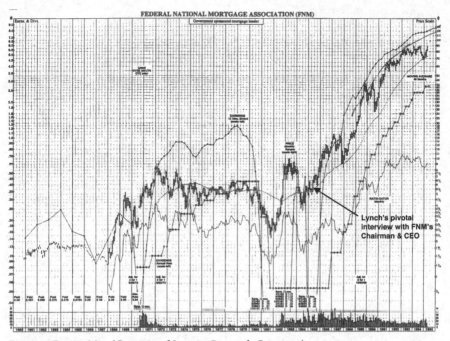

Figure 9. Fannie Mae (Courtesy of Security Research Company)

short-term rates skyrocketed, it exposed Fannie Mae's structural weakness. As the company transformed itself to match the maturity of their mortgage investments with debt of similar maturities, investors remained skeptical because the matching process was constrained by the maturity schedule of its mortgage investments acquired at unfavorable rates in the 1970s. The transformation was an evolution, and the company's scars from its near bankruptcy left many doubters. By borrowing at higher long-term rates, Fannie Mae was penalizing earnings in the short-term. Investors didn't have the required patience to see the long-term benefit. Peter Lynch was rewarded with his differentiated view. As he wrote in *Beating the Street*,

> *You have to know the story better than they do, and have faith in what you know. For a stock to do better than expected, the company has to be widely underestimated…When the prevailing opinion is more negative than yours, you have to constantly check and recheck the facts, to reassure yourself that you're not being foolishly optimistic.*[17]

General Public Utilities

The Three Mile Island accident was a partial nuclear meltdown that occurred on March 28, 1979, at a reactor owned by General Public Utilities. In February 1980, General Public Utilities omitted its dividend. Lynch bought it after the situation stabilized, earnings had recovered, and he realized that the tragedy was perceived to be worse than it was. According to the American Nuclear Society, the average radiation exposure to people living within ten miles of the plant was about equal to the radiation from a chest X-ray. A variety of epidemiology studies concluded that the accident had no observable long-term health effects. Lynch bought the stock in 1985 after General Public Utilities announced that it was planning to start up the sister reactor and that other utilities were going to share in the cost of cleaning up from the meltdown. Lynch figured the utility was going to survive its difficulties, was not going out of business, and still had a lot of room to recover. Magellan made $69 million on this stock.

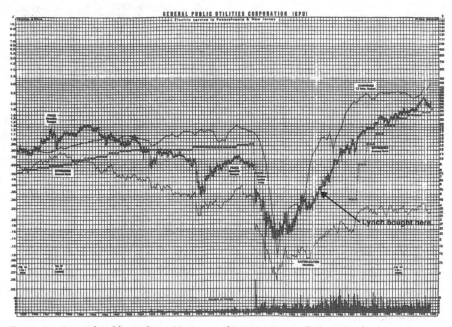

Figure 10. General Public Utilities (Courtesy of Security Research Company)

Takeaways

Lynch was open to turnarounds as a way to find opportunities in distress. He kept monitoring the Three Mile Island development dispassionately for several years after the initial meltdown. Lynch bought General Public Utilities years after it omitted its dividend but after its earnings had recovered, which was two years before dividend payments resumed. Lynch liked to showcase this as an example of how investors don't have to be early to do well and how lucrative it can be to buy utilities after their dividend is eliminated.

Merck

Merck is an example of a quality, steady Eddie, blue-chip growth stock that Peter Lynch favored as a core stalwart section of Magellan. He added to it when investors lost interest and trimmed it as valuation warranted. In July 1985 he said,

> I've been buying a lot of the drugs in the last six months — they're now almost 7 percent of the fund. They've rallied in the last year, but on a 10-year basis, they were quite depressed. I don't know if you ever looked at Merck. Merck

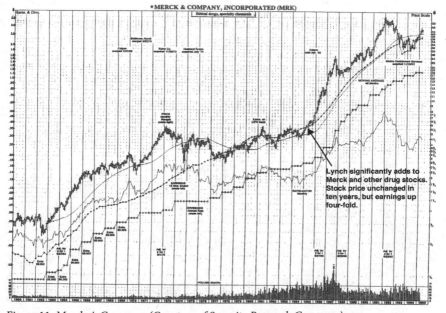

Figure 11. Merck & Company (Courtesy of Security Research Company)

was at $100 ($5.55 split adjusted on this chart) ten years ago, and it was $100 four months ago. But earnings have gone up fourfold. And again, I'm hoping the dollar might weaken, and so that would be a plus for drugs.[18]

Coca-Cola

Peter Lynch often cited Coca-Cola as another quality, mature, stalwart that provided ballast to a portfolio during stormy markets. In 1992, however, Lynch commented that a great company is not necessarily always attractively priced.

Big companies to me need a rest. In the last ten years, Coca-Cola went up 15-fold in price. Fifteen-fold! Earnings went up 5-fold. It's a great company. I'd like to own it in the next ten years. It's a twenty-five times next year's earnings. It needs a rest. Earnings have to catch up with the stocks.[19]

Coca-Cola stock went sideways for the next year and a half and then proceeded to climb four-fold over the next four years while earnings rose 70 percent. The price climbed to such dizzying heights in 1998 that it wasn't until sixteen years later, in 2014, that the stock reclaimed its old high.

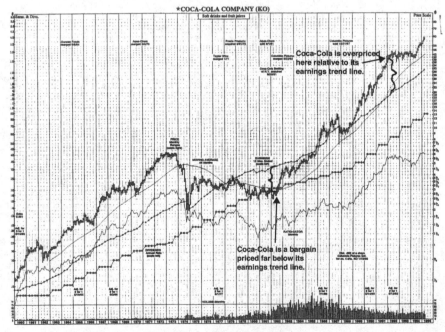

Figure 12. Coca-Cola (Courtesy of Security Research Company)

Takeaways

The takeaway is that price matters, even with great brand name companies. Another takeaway is that Peter Lynch loved to refer to these charts as tools to guide him as to whether a stock is under- or over-priced relative to its history of earnings.

Johnson & Johnson

In 1993 President Bill Clinton set the cornerstone of his first-term agenda: a task force on national healthcare reform. He asked his wife, Hillary, to head the task force to emphasize his commitment. The Clinton health care plan, nick-named "Hillary-care," required healthcare coverage by all Americans; would contain the growth of health care costs, which were growing at twice the rate of inflation; and would promote responsible health insurance practices, such as not denying enrollees for pre-existing conditions. Hillary Clinton defended the bill before Congress in September 1993. Despite a Democratic-controlled Congress, the bill was defeated for being overly bureaucratic, complex, coercive, restrictive of patient choice, and rife with restrictive regulations and guidelines. A compromise bill introduced by Senate Majority leader George Mitchell in August 1994 also failed to generate support.

Against this backdrop, Peter Lynch recommended Johnson & Johnson and Pfizer in the annual roundtable *Barron's* interview in January 1995. He reasoned,

> Both stocks are relatively depressed on a five-year basis. Johnson and Johnson was $58 in 1991; it is now $54. In 1992, J&J earned $2.46; this year will be at least 50 percent higher. Next year, net will probably be over $4 a share. So earnings are up dramatically and the stock has gone sideways to down for the last three to four years. It's a fantastic company. They have only one product that over 1 percent of earnings–Tylenol is 6 percent. That's not growing here, but it's growing nicely overseas. They spend something like $1.3 billion a year on R&D. There's not a lot of R&D needed in baby shampoo and Band-Aids. So they spend a lot on their drugs, have a great drug product line and are cutting costs…Neither of these companies has anything substantial coming off-patent. Pfizer has net cash and so does Johnson & Johnson. They have gorgeous balance sheets. They are going to do well.[20]

The stock jumped over 6-fold over the next seven years.

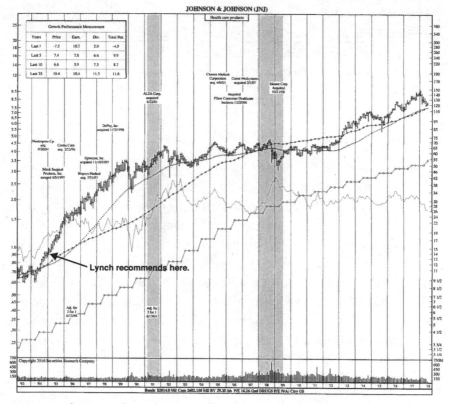

Figure 13. Johnson & Johnson (Courtesy of Security Research Company)

Schlumberger

After Peter Lynch retired from managing Fidelity Magellan, he wrote a series of articles in *Worth* magazine expressing his thoughts on the market and offering specific stock recommendations. In February 1995, he wrote a column titled "The Next Oil Boom," where he made the case that the oil industry was much closer to a shortage than the prevailing view of a glut.

He noted that it had been more than a decade since the previous oil boom. By the end of 1994, oil prices had declined four consecutive years by a cumulative one-third to $15.66/barrel, and by almost 60 percent from the price in 1980. The prevailing wisdom was that "OPEC can't stick to its quotas, and once Iraq starts pumping, it will flood the market with 3 million extra barrels a day."[21]

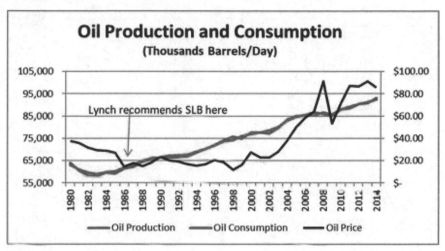

Oil Production and Consumption

However, Peter Lynch correctly noted that world consumption was increasing by 1.5 percent annually, which meant that supply would have to increase by one million barrels per day to meet demand. Even if Iraq flooded the market, its supply would be completely absorbed in three years. North American oil rigs had declined from over 4,000 in 1981 to approximately 1,100 by 1994, a decline of 75 percent. The severe decline in rigs augured well for the owners of rigs, who could name their price when demand rebounded. Since the equipment was already paid for, the higher prices would fall straight through to earnings. Lynch said that the best-positioned companies to benefit from a rebound in oil prices were oil service companies that had the best high-tech capability such as 3-D seismic mapping and smarter drills that go horizontal and around contours of submerged rock. The crown jewel in this field was Schlumberger, which was profitable, buying back stock, and had acquired GeoQuest, a leader in seismic services. The stock was in the bottom-end of its trading range of $50–$70 where it had been for several years.

Schlumberger stock tripled in the next two and a half years from $14 to $46. As Peter Lynch later remarked, "It turned out that the survivors shook off the rust and ironed out the balance sheets—which was a pleasant surprise to investors in Schlumberger..."[22]

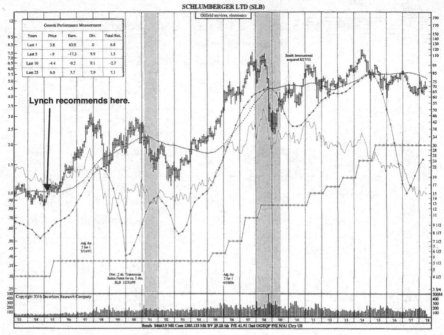

Figure 14. Schlumberger Ltd. (Courtesy of Security Research Company)

Takeaways

When your facts are right in an industry poised for a turnaround, it pays to invest in the highest quality company with a clean balance sheet and that has staying power. Schlumberger was already profitable and buying back its own stock before it tripled. A colleague once said that it is hard to go bankrupt if you have no debt. This is especially true for turnarounds. The fact that Schlumberger was buying back its own stock was a sign of financial health and an indication that they believed the stock was undervalued.

CHAPTER 15

Reflections

As we've seen, Peter Lynch was as passionate about his own work ethic for investing as a "tireless prospector" as he was for empowering amateur investors with tools and knowledge. He felt that they could get as good or better investment results than many professionals by applying common sense to investing. His salient principles are: use your natural observational skills to your own advantage; know what you own and why you own it; and do the necessary research to build conviction that the company has an enduring competitive advantage.

One of Peter Lynch's protégés, Will Danoff, who manages the Fidelity Contrafund, spoke glowingly of Peter Lynch's work ethic and open-minded approach to investing: "Peter is an exceptional human being. He's a really hard worker, smart, a great individual. He's a walking encyclopedia of corporate knowledge and business history."

When Danoff was an analyst and pitched a stock, some portfolio managers were focused on other things and weren't interested. But Danoff recalled,

> But Peter would say 'That sounds interesting. Let's call them.' Or 'Let me know the next time you're calling them so I can hear it. Can I come with you for a visit?' Peter was all about: When in doubt, call the company. Find out the facts. When you have facts, you can make better decisions. He says, 'Keep flexible. Keep looking forward. Call companies.'[1]

Peter Lynch's fact-finding process focused primarily on determining whether the company was financially sound. Does the company have more cash than debt? Does it have earnings and free cash flow or only hope? What is the trend?

He invested only when the stock was underappreciated and attractively priced. He looked for a reward/risk ratio of at least three to one. He checked whether insiders were also buying. He thought it was better to invest in the third inning after the company had proven itself, than to buy too early with unnecessary risk and invite disappointment.

He had faith in the market and the U.S. capitalist economy. He urged investors to be an optimist, think long-term, and don't predict the market or the economy. Peter Lynch said, "the stock market is an index of faith in this country. People think if the market goes down for three months, the world is ending, but it's the market's long-term trend that's the bellwether of faith in the economy."[2]

In 1997 he added,

> We've had nine recessions since World War II, we've had two presidents shot, one died and one made it, President Reagan. We've had changes in the Supreme Court, we've had changes in Congress, we've had wars. You've had all sorts of things happening since World War II. And the stock market has gone up, you know, over that period of time. So, trying to predict all these events is just not worth it.[3]

Former Fidelity portfolio manager and colleague of Peter Lynch, George Vanderheiden, said of Lynch, "He always had a positive attitude. He would come to work feeling that the market was going to be up that day…that there were stocks that would double in the next year."[4]

Peter Lynch's most rewarding stocks made their greatest gains in the third or fourth year he owned them. He was always quick to remind investors that if you invest $1,000, all you can lose is $1,000; but if you are right, you can make many multiples of $1,000. There is a strong correlation between corporate profits and stock prices in the long run. In 2001 Peter Lynch noted this correlation as follows: "Since World War II, despite 9 recessions and many other economic setbacks, corporate earnings are up 63-fold and the stock market is up 71-fold."[5]

You may not have six plus days a week to devote to investing research like Peter Lynch did at Fidelity, but then you are probably not managing 1,500 stocks. You may not be so obsessed with the stock market that you would spend your first date with your spouse-to-be talking only about exciting companies, as did Peter Lynch. He suggested, however, that an individual investor only needed to follow about ten companies and know them well, which is manageable even while working another full-time job. As he says, all you need is a few good stocks in your lifetime.

While Peter Lynch's accomplishments as a mutual fund manager are unparalleled, he is just as remarkable for his genuine honesty, modesty, and humility. Peter Tanous mentioned in his book, *Investment Gurus*, that during his noon interview with Peter Lynch in the Fidelity office, he was offered a sandwich while Peter Lynch ate his, which he brought from home in a little brown bag.

I attended Peter Lynch's presentation before the National Association of Investors Corporation in 1998 and met him as he graciously signed several of his books. He was bright, witty, positive, insightful, and genuinely passionate about sharing his investment wisdom to empower the average American investor.

Peter Lynch said he wanted to be remembered for trying to teach people to be careful with their money. He said, "When you own a stock, you own a piece of a company. It's not a lottery ticket. The company does well, the stock does well."[6] He urged investors to do it right, or don't do it at all.

As an acknowledged hero investor, Peter Lynch was once asked who his heroes were. His response was insightful and instructive. He said his heroes were those who start businesses. They are unsung heroes, some of whom take the risk and fail, but many of who begin as small businesses and grow to become medium-size and even large-sized businesses. Large-sized businesses are often criticized for being complacent, lazy, and out of touch with reality. When they adjust and downsize to become more productive, they are criticized for being soulless and greedy, and it makes front-page news. The media, however, ignores the underlying growth of dynamic companies that create jobs and make America strong. He was fond of repeating that eighteen million jobs were created in the decade of the 1980s, and seventeen million jobs were created in the 1990s despite the 500 largest companies eliminating up to three million jobs in each decade. The leaders of the companies that provide those job opportunities are the unsung heroes that make America great. Lynch said when he joined Fidelity, it had sixty employees and by 1995, it had 9,000. He said the American capitalist system works, but the public has been convinced that it doesn't.

Peter Lynch said he was humbled and motivated knowing that he made a difference in the financial lives of commonplace Americans. "There were people that I'd meet in airports and they had made a total of $7,000 and they were ecstatic about it, it made a difference in their lives. It was fulfilling to meet these folks. That's why I worked so hard."[7]

Thank you, Peter Lynch for making a positive difference in the lives of Magellan shareholders and for the beneficiaries of your charitable giving. Thank you for your time and energy as an advocate for the amateur investor who you inspire and empower through your generous teaching in books, articles, interviews, and lectures. Investors are wiser and wealthier by your example.

WARREN BUFFETT

"The Incomparable"

I've been extremely fortunate in life to have a tremendous group of heroes, and none of them have ever let me down. You're lucky in life if you have the right kind of heroes.

—WARREN BUFFETT[1]

CHAPTER 16

Personal Background

Someone is sitting in the shade today because someone planted a tree a long time ago.

—WARREN BUFFETT

Warren Buffett is arguably the greatest investor of all time and appropriately deserves the moniker, "The Incomparable." Buffett's original $100 investment in his Buffett Partnership in 1956 grew to a value of over $25 million in 1969 when he closed the partnership. This astounding increase came from Buffett reinvesting earnings from his 25 percent share of annual profits above a 6 percent required return for his limited partner investors. The Buffett Partnership's average annual return from 1957–1969 was 29.5 percent compared with the Dow Jones Index average annual return of 7.4 percent. In 1964, he took control of a nearly bankrupt textile mill, Berkshire Hathaway, and grew its market value to become one of the five most highly valued companies in the U.S. In the fifty-four years ending 2018, the market value of Berkshire Hathaway increased an average of 20.5 percent per year, more than double the Standard & Poor's 500 index average of 9.7 percent. A $1,000 investment in Berkshire Hathaway in 1965 would have been worth $24 million by 2018.

As astonishing as his investment record is, Warren Buffett is also renowned for his business integrity, generous philanthropy, his role as a teacher of business and investment wisdom, his ability to inspire loyalty among his managers, and the clear and clever analogies he uses to communicate his investment philosophy.

Warren Edward Buffett was born to Leila and Howard Buffett on August 30, 1930, as a seventh-generation Buffett in Omaha, Nebraska. His father, Howard, was a four-term congressman and was frugal with his money. Howard once returned his salary increase from $10,000 to $12,500 back to the government because he thought the government was more in need of the money. After Howard's fourth term, he returned to the brokerage firm, Harris Upham, a predecessor to Smith Barney. He was also an editor of the *Daily Nebraskan* newspaper.

Warren's mother, Leila Stahl, set type in the family print shop, and her father was an owner/editor of a weekly newspaper in West Point, Nebraska. The newspaper influence from Warren's parents impacted his subsequent appreciation of the power of a local newspaper as a virtual monopoly.

Warren was the second of three children and had two sisters. Warren's illustrious business mind was formed early. His business career began at the tender age of six when he began selling Juicy Fruit gum packs at a profit of $0.02 per pack of five pieces. He also bought a six-pack of Coca-Cola for $0.25 from his grandfather's grocery store and sold each bottle for $0.05, and made $0.05 per pack. Buffett said he first started reading about investment when he was six.[2] When he was seven, at Christmas he asked Santa Claus for a book called *Bond Salesmanship*.[3]

By age eleven, he was marking prices on the slate in the boardroom of his father's office and had read every book in the Omaha public library on investing or on the stock market. He bought his first stock in April 1942 in the midst of World War II: three shares of Cities Services Preferred at $38 per share. He also convinced his sister to buy three shares. It promptly fell to $27 per share, and she badgered him daily about it. Finally, the stock rose to $40, where he and his sister sold. Within two years, the preferred stock was called for $212. "It went on to be called at $212 a share or something like that not long thereafter. So, I decided from there on not to talk to anybody about what I did and just think by myself."[4] He learned three lessons: first, don't be influenced by what others say; two, if you accept clients, don't tell them what you are buying or selling; and three, investing requires patience.

When he was thirteen years old, Warren filed his first tax return and deducted his bike as a work expense for $35. He worked odd jobs, such as retrieving lost golf balls and selling them; delivered almost 500 newspapers/

day for the *Washington Post* and *Washington Times Herald*; and published a handicapping sheet on horses called *Stable Boy Selections*.

By age fifteen, he made $175/month selling *Washington Post* newspapers and saved $1,200 to buy a 40-acre farm in Omaha, Nebraska. When he was seventeen, he joined his friend Donald Danley to start a company named Wilson Coin-Operated Machine Company. They bought a pinball machine for $25 and installed it in a barber shop. They were soon netting $50 per week with several machines. Buffett later remarked, "I hadn't dreamed life could be so good." The total earnings from all his jobs and the farm totaled over $9,000, which he used to pay for his college tuition.

Warren attended University of Pennsylvania's Wharton School for his first two years in 1947–1949, then transferred to University of Nebraska where he was the circulation manager for the *Lincoln Journal*. He graduated in 1950. During this time, he studied and tried many investment methods including point and figure technical analysis. "I went the whole gamut. I collected charts, and I read all the technical stuff. I listened to tips. And then at nineteen years old (in 1950 while he was a senior) I picked up (Benjamin) Graham's *The Intelligent Investor*. That was like seeing the light."[5] He also said, "I don't want to sound like a religious fanatic or anything, but it really did get me."[6]

Warren applied for graduate business school at Harvard and, after a ten-minute interview, was rejected. He later realized that Harvard would not have been a good fit, but he was crushed for fear of disappointing his father. His father responded with "only his unconditional love…an unconditional belief in me."[7]

The following year, he studied under Benjamin Graham and David Dodd at Columbia University. Warren believes this was the best decision in his life. There, he received his MBA in 1951 and was Graham's only A+ student. Graham and Dodd are the co-authors of the bible of value investing, *Securities Analysis*. After David Dodd's passing at 93, Buffett paid tribute to him saying, "The proof of his talent is the record of his students: No other teacher of investments has sent forth so many who have achieved unusual success. When students left Dave's classroom, they were equipped to invest intelligently for a lifetime because the principles he taught were simple, useful, and enduring."[8]

After graduating from Columbia, Warren sought career advice from the two people he most admired: his father and Benjamin Graham. Both thought the Dow, then at 200, was too high and encouraged Buffett to wait awhile. Many years later, Warren reflected that had he listened to their advice, he would probably still have the same $10,000 he had when he sought their advice. Warren offered to work for Ben Graham's New York-based company, Graham-Newman Corp, for free, but Graham rejected the idea. Warren returned to work with his father's brokerage firm in Omaha, Buffett-Falk, as an investment salesperson while still corresponding with Graham about his investment ideas.

Warren's persistence paid off in 1954 when Graham offered him a job as an analyst for $12,000 a year in New York; the firm had $6 million of client assets under management at that time. Two years later, Graham retired and closed his partnership. Buffett's savings had grown from $9,800 to $140,000.

Warren returned to Omaha with his wife Susan and bought a house for $32,500, where he still lives today. Working from Omaha offered several advantages: 1) Warren could focus on what was important rather than what was urgent or fashionable; 2) he could be in New York or Los Angeles in three hours; and 3) "This is a good place to live. You can think here. You can think better about the market and you don't hear so many stories, and you can just sit and look at the stock on the desk in front of you. You can think about a lot of things."[9] He also added, "You don't have the static and all the noise that you get in a place like Wall Street. I worked in Wall Street for a couple of years, and people came up whispering to me every ten seconds, and I got overstimulated. You really only need one good idea a year, and Omaha's a good place to get it."[10]

On May 5, 1956, at the age of twenty-five, he formed a $105,000 investment partnership called Buffett Associates, Ltd. He was the general partner, and the limited partners initially were four family members and three close friends. Buffett took no salary but earned 25 percent of profits exceeding 6 percent per year. For six years, he worked alone out of a spare bedroom in his house. He had no calculator and wouldn't reveal his holdings because he didn't want to waste his time with clients' suggestions or concerns. He later said that it would have been like a surgeon carrying on a running conversation with a patient during an operation. "All I want to do is hand in a scorecard when I come off the golf course. I don't want you following me around and watching me shank a three-iron on this hole and leave a putt short on the next one."[11]

When Warren was twenty-nine, a mutual friend, Edwin Davis, introduced him to Charlie Munger, who would later be his famed business partner and vice-chairman of Berkshire Hathaway.

In 1961, at the age of thirty-one, he was managing a total of seven partnerships all from his home: Buffett Associates, Buffett Fund, Dacee, Emdee,

Glenoff, Mo-Buff, and Underwood. The partnerships were worth several million dollars. Buffett bought Dempster Mill, which was a windmill manufacturing company, for his first million-dollar investment. Buffett earned a board seat with Sanborn, a map company he invested in 1958 when the stock price was $45 and the value of its investments alone were $65 per share.

In 1962 he merged the partnerships into one and renamed it as Buffett Partnerships, Ltd. At that time, Charlie Munger introduced Buffett to Harry Bottle, CEO of Dempster. Bottle turned around Dempster by cutting costs and reducing the workforce. Buffett began buying Berkshire Hathaway, a Massachusetts textile company, as a turnaround for $8 per share when it had working capital of $19 per share. He was able to buy the value of the fixed assets for free. The Buffett Partnership became Berkshire's largest shareholder.

In 1963 Buffett sold Dempster for a $2.3 million gain, a three-fold gain of his original investment. In 1964 and 1965, Buffett invested in a 5 percent ownership stake each in American Express and Walt Disney. American Express and Walt Disney will be discussed in detail in the chapter on case studies.

In 1965 Buffett took complete control of Berkshire Hathaway, and the following year he closed the Buffett Partnership to new money. His personal investment in the partnership was worth $6.8 million. Two years later, the Buffett Partnership was worth $65 million and Buffett's personal stake was worth $10 million, due in part to making $20 million on a $13 million investment in American Express.

In 1969, after lamenting for two years that he was unable to find good investments in a raging bull market, he closed his $104 million partnership, of which his share was $25 million. He explained to his limited partners,

> I am out of step with present conditions. When the game is no longer played your way, it is only human to say the new approach is all wrong, bound to lead to trouble, and so on…On one point, however, I am clear…I will not abandon an approach whose logic I understand (although I find it difficult to apply) even though it may mean forgoing large, and apparently easy, profits to embrace an approach which I don't fully understand, have not practiced successfully, and which possibly could lead to substantial permanent loss of capital.[12]

Buffett dissolved the Buffett Partnership for four main reasons. First, the market was overpriced. Second, he refused to sell certain businesses he was fond of. "I was developing relationships with the operating people in our owned businesses and I simply didn't want to have their duration determined by whether I got an exceptionally good bid that morning."[13] Third, accepting more than one hundred limited partners would require him to register as an investment advisor, which would have limited his style by revealing his transactions publicly. Lastly, he was relieved of the administrative end of managing his limited partners.

Three years later, the market suffered its severest drop in decades. During the 1973–1974 bear market, Buffett grabbed several bargains saying, "I'm like a sex-starved guy in a harem."[14]

Warren and Susie Buffett had two sons, Peter and Howard (named after Warren's father), and a daughter Susan (named after his wife). Howard is a businessman, farmer, and conservationist. He has been a director of Coca-Cola since 2010, and a director of Berkshire Hathaway since 1992. Upon Warren's death, Howard will become non-executive chairman. Peter is a musician, composer, author, and philanthropist. He is an Emmy Award winner and *The New York Times* bestselling author. Susie Buffett is the oldest of the three and is a philanthropist focused on grants in public education and social justice. Interestingly, none of the three graduated from college.

Susan and Warren Buffett separated in the 1970s, although they remained married until her death in 2004. Susie occasionally performed as a cabaret singer and was an active philanthropist focused on civil rights, abortion, and population control. Neil Sedaka encouraged her to pursue a singing career, and in 1977 she left Warren and moved to San Francisco. Warren was heartbroken with her move, but they vacationed together and attended public functions as husband and wife. In 1978, Susan introduced Warren to Astrid Menks, who moved in with Warren in their Omaha home; Astrid married Warren two years after Susan's death in 2004. Prior to Susan's death, they signed Christmas cards, "Warren, Susie, and Astrid." Susie was a director of Berkshire Hathaway and was president of the Buffett Foundation.

Warren is famous for his diet of junk food, hamburgers, and his daily intake of five cherry Coca-Cola's per day. In 1985, after forty-eight years of drinking Pepsi, he switched to the new Cherry Coke, naming it the official drink of Berkshire. This was four years before his hugely successful investment in Coca-Cola.

No one is more respected for his investing intellect; his Berkshire annual reports are considered classics. Many people, myself included, consider a reading of his reports to be worth at least as much as any two-year MBA program.

Depending on the price of Berkshire stock, Warren Buffett has at times been the wealthiest person in the world. He has consistently said that he intended to give his wealth back to society, but Bill and Melinda Gates convinced him to not wait until the end. For many years he believed he could do the most good for society if he accumulated as much wealth as possible during his lifetime and then give it away at the end.

> *I hear children of the rich or the rich themselves talk about the debilitating effect of food stamps on welfare mothers and they say, it's terrible, you know, you hand them all these food stamps and it causes the cycle to perpetuate itself. But, of course, when a very rich child or one who's going to inherit a lot of money if born, when they leave the womb, they're handed this lifetime supply of food stamps, only they—and they have a welfare officer, he's called a trust department officer and the food stamps are little stocks and bonds. And nobody seems to notice the debilitating effects of that particular form of lifetime supply of food stamps. I think that by and large that if I'm going to be a sprinter, I will become a better sprinter in life if I sprint against everybody else leaving the starting blocks at the same time than if they say because I'm Jesse Owens's child or something I get to start on the 50-yard line.*[15]

In 1990 he said, "I think I should give it back to society. I see no reason why I should create some dynasty of wealth that can sit around fanning themselves for 50 years."[16]

In 1996 Buffett, then the world's wealthiest person, pledged to give all of his Berkshire Hathaway stock to philanthropic foundations. He pledged to give away 99 percent of his wealth, with the largest amount to the Bill and Melinda Gates Foundation where he is a board member. The Gates Foundation is committed to enhancing healthcare, reducing poverty, expanding educational opportunities, and expanding access to information technology. Buffett pledged 10 million shares of Berkshire Hathaway Class B stock to the Gates Foundation over a period of time through annual contributions. The gift has three conditions: 1) Bill or Melinda Gates must be alive and active in the administration; 2) it must continue to qualify as a charity; and 3) each year, the foundation must give away a minimum amount equal to the value of the entire previous year's gift from Buffett plus 5 percent of the foundation's assets. The Gates Foundation typically receives 5 percent of the remaining earmarked shares each July. Buffett also pledged $2 billion of Berkshire Hathaway stock to each of his children's foundations. Buffett's personal charitable aims include population control and limitations on nuclear weapons.

Warren Buffett is almost entirely focused on business except when he spends ten hours a week playing bridge online. The "Oracle of Omaha" has a humble, awe-shucks affable manner with a gregarious laugh that belies his sharp focus, analytical mind, and photographic memory. He has an uncanny ability to quickly discern the three criteria he values most in a business partner: integrity, intelligence, and energy. Among his eighty-plus operating companies within Berkshire, the division heads are typically founding managers who delight in working for Warren even though they are already wealthy and don't need to work. They do it because they are passionate about building their business, Warren trusts them to run their company without his interference, and Berkshire has no mandatory retirement. In return, his managers are fiercely loyal. He charges a cost of capital to motivate his managers to return their excess cash flow to Warren so he can allocate capital toward new investments. Buffett says he tap dances to work, and his investors have surely danced a jig of their own.

Approaching 90 years of age, Buffett still does what he loves: reading massive volumes each day to satisfy his boundless curiosity and thirst for business wisdom in leading a model of business and ethical excellence with his legacy company Berkshire Hathaway.

CHAPTER 17

Investment Performance

Over the years, I will be quite satisfied with a performance that is 10 percent per year better than the averages.

—WARREN BUFFETT[1]

W arren Buffett is famously known for his astounding record as a master CEO and capital allocator at Berkshire Hathaway. Prior to Berkshire, he gained renown for his phenomenal record of performance as the general partner of his Buffett Partnership.

After Benjamin Graham closed his partnership at Graham-Newman in 1956, Warren Buffett returned to Omaha and formed the first of several Buffett Partnerships to invest for family and friends. Buffett was the general partner and his investors were limited partners. The limited partners received 6 percent interest on their investment each year plus 75 percent of the profits above the 6 percent threshold; whereas Warren Buffett kept 25 percent of the gains. If there was a loss, Buffett absorbed 25 percent of the loss and was obligated to pay back cumulative losses before he could earn 25 percent of the gains above 6 percent.

The gross returns for the Buffet Partnership (before fees to the limited partners) averaged 29.5 percent per year compared with 7.4 percent for the Dow Jones index. The net-of-fee average annual return to the limited partners was still an amazing 23.8 percent. In thirteen years of managing the partnership, Buffett posted positive returns every year, despite five years of negative returns for the Dow Jones. A limited partner who invested $10,000 with Warren Buffett at the beginning of 1957 would have over $160,000 by 1969, when the partnership was dissolved. On May 5, 1956, seven limited partners (four family members and three close friends) contributed $105,000 to the predecessor partnership, and Warren Buffett contributed a mere $100. By 1969, the partnership had grown to $100 million of assets through the miracle of compounding returns and from additional partner investments. Warren Buffett's personal stake was worth $20 million by the time he "retired" in 1969.

	Buffett Partnership Results	Limited Partner Results	Dow Jones
1957	10.4%	9.3%	−8.4%
1958	40.9%	32.2%	38.5%
1959	25.9%	20.9%	20.0%
1960	22.8%	18.6%	−6.2%
1961	45.9%	35.9%	22.4%
1962	13.9%	11.9%	−7.6%
1963	38.7%	30.5%	20.6%
1964	27.8%	22.3%	18.7%
1965	47.2%	36.9%	14.2%
1966	20.4%	16.8%	−15.6%
1967	35.9%	28.4%	19.0%
1968	58.8%	45.6%	7.7%
1969	6.8%	6.6%	−11.6%
CAGR	29.5%	23.8%	7.4%

Buffett offered several reasons for retiring:

Fewer Bargains

Opportunities to invest using Benjamin Graham's quantitative methods to identify statistically cheap balance-sheet bargains had "virtually disappeared after steadily drying up over the past twenty years." Buffett said, "…the exploding ranks of security analysts brought forth an intensified scrutiny of issues far beyond what existed some years ago."[2]

Size

Buffett's assets under management had grown to $100 million, and he believed that the size further prohibited investing in "a large portion of this seemingly barren investment world." Buffett found many gems among obscure, under-followed companies that were priced below their liquidation value. These "cigar-butts" worked well with small sums. Buffett later admitted in his 2014 Berkshire Hathaway letter,

> My cigar-butt strategy worked very well while I was managing small sums. Indeed, the many dozens of free puffs I obtained in the 1950's made the decade by far the best of my life for both relative and absolute performance... But a major weakness in this approach gradually became apparent: Cigar-butt investing was scalable only to a point. With large sums, it would never work well.

He explained that commitments of less than $3 million would not have a real impact on performance, and his size ruled out companies with a market value of less than $100 million.

Speculative Frenzy

Buffett faced an increasingly short-term oriented and speculative market that was a looming trap for the unwary. Buffett described the financial scene in his July 1968 letter to partners, "We live in an investment world, populated not by those who must be logically persuaded to believe, but by the hopeful, credulous and greedy, grasping for an excuse to believe." In his January 1969 letter, Buffett quoted an investment manager who oversaw $1 billion as, "Securities must be studied in a minute-by-minute program." Buffett was both fascinated and appalled, and said tongue-in-cheek, "This sort of stuff makes me feel guilty when I go out for a Pepsi." He presciently said, "I am not attuned to this market environment and I don't want to spoil a decent record by trying to play a game I don't understand just so I can go out a hero."

A few years later from January 1973 to December 1974, the Dow Jones crashed over 40 percent, the worst slide since the Great Depression. The so-called "Nifty Fifty" blue-chip steady growers including McDonald's, Coca-Cola, and Avon were stratospherically priced at 83x, 63x, and 47x trailing earnings. In less than two years by October 1974 when the market bottomed,

McDonalds, Coca-Cola, and Avon stock prices sank 72 percent, 69 percent and 85 percent respectively.

Personal Considerations

In his October 9, 1967 partnership letter, Buffett said his personal considerations were the most important factor in changing his investment objective. He softened his investment goal from ten percentage points above the Dow to the lesser of 9 percent per year or a five-percentage point advantage over the Dow. He said, "My own personal interests dictate a less compulsive approach to superior investment results than when I was younger and leaner." Buffett was enjoying the business stimulation and satisfying relationships with the managers of his 100 percent-owned businesses and was reluctant to trade that experience for, as he said, "the possible irritation, aggravation or worse for potentially higher returns."[3] Ironically, he said in his May 1969 partnership letter that "I know I don't want to be totally occupied with out-pacing an investment rabbit all my life...I do know that when I am 60, I should be attempting to achieve different personal goals than those which had priority at age 20."

Terms of Liquidating the Partnership

Buffett offered three options to his limited partners when he liquidated the partnership and transferred their assets to his partners. First, he wanted all partners to have the option to receive cash and the possibility of readily marketable securities where he still liked the price and prospects, but where his partners could convert to cash if they wished.

Second, he recommended two alternative money managers that he admired as investors and as people: Bill Ruane and David "Sandy" Gottesman. Gottesman was an early investor in Berkshire, and Ruane was a former classmate of Buffett at Columbia University and student of Ben Graham. Buffett admired them for their integrity, ability, temperament, and intellect. Buffett also considered Charlie Munger, whom he met in 1959, but he wasn't interested in expanding his investment business. Ruane established the Sequoia mutual fund in July 1970 to accommodate investors of all sizes. Interestingly, although the Sequoia fund trailed the S&P 500 for each of its first few years, its long-term record under Bill Ruane, who passed away in October 2005, was exemplary with a compound annual gain of 16 percent compared to the S&P 500 of 11.7 percent.

Third, he wanted his partners to have the option of maintaining their proportionate interest in the Buffett Partnership's two controlled companies; Diversified Retailing Company (DRC) and Berkshire Hathaway (B-H). The securities in these companies were not freely marketable, but Buffett offered his partners the option of taking a cash equivalent. However, he was reluctant to sell controlled businesses where he liked and respected management, found the business stimulating, and where the business earned worthwhile returns on capital: "I strongly like all of the people running our controlled businesses" and "I certainly have no desire to sell a good controlled business run by people I like and admire, merely to obtain a fancy price."[4]

Buffett Takes Control of Berkshire Hathaway

Buffett began buying Berkshire Hathaway at $7.60/share in 1962 and acquired control in the spring of 1965 after heavy purchases earlier in the year, which lifted his average cost to $14.86/share. Buffett viewed this as a prototype Benjamin Graham balance sheet value, since the company had net working capital value (excluding the value of plant and equipment) of $19/share. Theoretically, he was buying the liquidating value of the cash, accounts receivable, and inventory less debt at $0.78 on the dollar and getting the plant and equipment for free.

By 1969 Buffett redeployed capital from Berkshire Hathaway as a pure textile operation into a smaller textile operation, an insurance division conducted by National Indemnity and National Fire & Marine, and a bank operated by Illinois National Bank and Trust. Buffett acknowledged that the textile business was not satisfactory because its return on capital was below its cost of capital, but he was loyal to management since they had worked hard to improve the business under difficult conditions; he expected to continue the textile business as long as it produced at then current levels. Buffett said that the combined insurance and banking business produced a return on tangible capital of 13 percent "with good prospects for growth."

In the understatement of the century, Buffett advised his limited partners,

My personal opinion is that the intrinsic value of DRC and B-H will grow substantially over the years. While no one knows the future, I would be

disappointed if such growth wasn't at a rate of approximately 10 percent per annum...I think both securities should be very decent long-term holdings and I am happy to have a substantial portion of my net worth invested in them. I think that there is a very high probability that I will maintain my investment in DRC and B-H for a very long period...[5]

Investors who heeded Buffett's advice and held Berkshire have enjoyed compound annual returns averaging more than 20 percent for more than fifty years.

We will explore in the next chapter how Buffett's investment process during his Buffett Partnership period evolved and formed the foundation for his astounding capital deployment success during his Berkshire years.

Berkshire's Performance vs. the S&P 500		
Annual Percentage Change		
In Per-Share Book Value of Berkshire	In Per-ShareMarket Value of Berkshire	In S&P 500 with Dividends Included
1965	23.8	49.5	10.0
1966	20.3	(3.4)	(11.7)
1967	11.0	13.3	30.9
1968	19.0	77.8	11.0
1969	16.2	19.4	(8.4)
1970	12.0	(4.6)	3.9
1971	16.4	80.5	14.6
1972	21.7	8.1	18.9
1973	4.7	(2.5)	(14.8)
1974	5.5	(48.7)	(26.4)
1975	21.9	2.5	37.2
1976	59.3	129.3	23.6
1977	31.9	46.8	(7.4)
1978	24.0	14.5	6.4
1979	35.7	102.5	18.2
1980	19.3	32.8	32.3
1981	31.4	31.8	(5.0)
1982	40.0	38.4	21.4
1983	32.3	69.0	22.4
1984	13.6	(2.7)	6.1
1985	48.2	93.7	31.6

Investment Performance

1986	26.1	14.2	18.6
1987	19.5	4.6	5.1
1988	20.1	59.3	16.6
1989	44.4	84.6	31.7
1990	7.4	(23.1)	(3.1)
1991	39.6	35.6	30.5
1992	20.3	29.8	7.6
1993	14.3	38.9	10.1
1994	13.9	25.0	1.3
1995	43.1	57.4	37.6
1996	31.8	6.2	23.0
1997	34.1	34.9	33.4
1998	48.3	52.2	28.6
1999	0.5	(19.9)	21.0
2000	6.5	26.6	(9.1)
2001	(6.2)	6.5	(11.9)
2002	10.0	(3.8)	(22.1)
2003	21.0	15.8	28.7
2004	10.5	4.3	10.9
2005	6.4	0.8	4.9
2006	18.4	24.1	15.8
2007	11.0	28.7	5.5
2008	(9.6)	(31.8)	(37.0)
2009	19.8	2.7	26.5
2010	13.0	21.4	15.1
2011	4.6	(4.7)	2.1
2012	14.4	16.8	16.0
2013	18.2	32.7	32.4
2014	8.3	27.0	13.7
2015	6.4	(12.5)	1.4
2016	10.7	23.4	12.0
2017	23.0	21.9	21.8
2018	0.4	2.8	(4.4)
Compound Annual Gain 1965–2018	18.7%	20.5%	9.7%

Buffett Explains Why Popular Funds Underperform

Buffett frequently peppered his partnership letters with comparisons of his performance with four of the largest diversified mutual funds whose performance not only paled to Buffett's, but failed to achieve performance superior to the Dow Jones index despite charging hundreds of millions in fees and being run by bright, energetic people. In his January 1965 partnership letter, Buffett attributed their lack of performance success, and inversely, attributed his own success, to five factors:

1. *Group think.* Buffett believed "that it is close to impossible for outstanding investment management to come from a group of any size with all parties really participating in decisions."

2. *Conformity.* Many trust departments and other large investment companies adhere to approved lists of stocks that are widely regarded as "safe" due to their staying power and popularity.

3. *Closet indexing deemed safe.* Many institutions regard index-like performance as safe and discourage straying too far from the index. In fact, many institutions quantitatively monitor the level of active risk and penalize investors for straying beyond acceptable bounds. To outperform an index, an investor has to invest independent of the index. However, the penalty for underperformance in many cases is much greater than the reward for outperformance.

4. *Irrational diversification.* Many institutions adhere to diversification policies that Buffett says are "irrational." For instance, some mandate that they invest with the same sector weights as an unmanaged index but hope to outperform through stock selection. Buffett said, "Diversification is a hedge against ignorance, but if you don't feel ignorant, the need for it goes down drastically."[6]

5. *Inertia.* Some investment firms believe they serve their clients well by adhering to rigid allocations to various countries or styles without understanding the underlying securities.

Conventional vs. Conservative Investing

Buffett eased possible concern from his clients over his concentrated investments by explaining that, while it may not be conventional investing, conservative investing does not depend on whether many people agree with you or whether important people agree with you. Buffett believes that conservative investing should be measured by whether the investor's reasoning and facts proved correct, especially in down markets. He contends that conservative investing has little to do with portfolio concentration. Conservative investing means subjecting the investor to much less temporary or permanent loss in value.

In November 1965, Buffett informed his limited partners that he might invest up to 40 percent in a single security if he believed that his facts and reasoning had a high probability of being correct, coupled with a low probability of a risk of permanent loss of value. The catalyst for this level of concentration was Buffett's confidence in American Express. Buffett's target was to limit declines in his portfolio to less than one-half of the decline in the Dow.

> It is unquestionably true that the investment companies have their money more conventionally invested than we do. To many people conventionality is indistinguishable from conservatism. In my view, this represents erroneous thinking. Neither a conventional nor an unconventional approach, per se, is conservative. Truly conservative actions arise from intelligent hypotheses, correct facts, and sound reasoning. These qualities may lead to conventional acts, but there have been many times when they have led to unorthodoxy... We derive no comfort because important people, vocal people, or great numbers of people agree with us. Nor do we derive comfort if they don't. A public opinion poll is no substitute for thought.[7]

Qualities of Investment Managers

Years later Buffett articulated the qualities that he looked for in hiring his investment management lieutenants at Berkshire Hathaway, Todd Combs and Ted Weschler. By describing these qualities, Buffett is also describing the criteria for selecting an investment manager in general, the qualities for success for any investor, and, indirectly, himself. He looks for an excellent track record, investors that view stocks as businesses, and can evaluate risk.

> I looked at what they'd done. It isn't just an investment record that impressed me, it's how the investment record was achieved...But Todd and Ted look at investments very much like I do. They look at stocks not as stocks. They look at them as pieces of businesses, and they evaluate businesses. They're

really business analysts, when you get right down to it. Then they translate that into investment decisions...[Todd and Ted] both have a fundamental soundness to them—it's a combination of soundness and brilliance. And you want both. And they think about things that haven't happened yet in terms of problems. They're not in terms of dreaming about great projects that are pie in the sky, but they're always thinking about the downside.[8]

CHAPTER 18

Influences and Perspectives on Investing

Someone is sitting in the shade today because someone planted a tree a long time ago.

—WARREN BUFFETT

Warren Buffett said that he won the ovarian lottery by being born in United States in 1930 where democracy prevailed, capitalism was rewarded, he didn't have to overcome the barriers of race or gender, and where the U.S. economy progressed to $50,000 GDP per person, six times higher than when he was born. While Buffett acknowledges his luck, millions of others were equally lucky, and yet his accomplishments are unique and extraordinary. Buffett may have been blessed by winning the ovarian lottery, but he distinguished himself with his voracious desire and ability to learn from five heroes in his life, all of whom shaped his investment success. They are Howard Buffett, Benjamin Graham, Phil Carret, Phil Fisher, and Charlie Munger.

Howard Buffett

Before Warren was born, his father, Howard, was a securities salesman for Union Street Bank, which strained the Buffett household. Those burned by the crash feared repeating their experience with stocks. Two weeks before Warren was born, the Great Depression claimed Union Street Bank as a victim. Shortly afterward, Howard and his partner, George Sklenicka, formed Buffett, Sklenicka & Co. to sell stocks and bonds, with offices in the same Union State Bank building.

Howard's father, Ernest, a tight-fisted grocer, belittled investing in stocks as a fool's game. As president of the Rotary Club, Ernest advised his fellow Rotarians not to give Howard business, claiming his son didn't know much about stocks. Howard's commissions from selling securities were few and far between during Warren's young years. Howard worried that his family would starve. Ernest comforted his son, who inherited his father's aversion to debt. "Don't worry about food, Howard. I'll just let your bill run." Warren's mother, Leila, stopped going to her church circle and skipped meals to help provide for her family.

Howard resolved that he would raise his son with a far better experience than being shamed by his own curmudgeon father. Howard had principled ethics that Warren admired. Howard didn't smoke or drink, taught Sunday school religion, and served on the local school board and in the U.S. Congress. Howard even refunded favored clients if their investments lost money by repurchasing the securities for his own account. Warren was nicknamed affectionately "Fireball" by Howard, who allowed ten-year-old Warren to visit his now-thriving brokerage firm, which had moved to the Omaha National Bank building. Warren also visited the Harris Upton brokerage, two floors below in the same building, where they allowed Warren to chalk the prices of stocks on the blackboard when the market traded for two hours on Saturday mornings. Warren devoured "The Trader" column in *Barron's* as well as investment books on his father's bookshelf.

Howard gave each of his three children an opportunity to travel with him to New York when they turned ten years old. Warren was seared with two positive impressions of the possible wealth of Wall Street. Howard introduced Warren to Sidney Weinberg, a senior partner of Goldman Sachs. Saying good-bye after a half-hour conversation, Warren never forgot his awestruck feeling when Sidney cared enough to ask him, "What stock do *you* like, Warren?"

Then Warren and Howard visited the New York Stock Exchange, where they had lunch with a member of the Exchange. After lunch, Warren was impressed with the evident wealth that justified hiring a server to offer various tobacco leaves to make custom cigars.

Warren appreciated his father and forever revered him for his integrity and for keeping what Warren referred to as an inner scorecard, which was his own measure of character rather than what others thought of him. Armed with a model of character who introduced him to the possibilities of wealth and independence, Warren had an epiphany. "It could make me independent. Then I could do what I wanted to do with my life. And the biggest thing I wanted to do was work for myself. I didn't want other people directing me. The idea of doing what I wanted to do every day was important to me."[1] The next year at age eleven, he began his journey toward self-reliance by buying his first stock, Cities Services Preferred.

Benjamin Graham

Warren Buffett said, "To me, Ben Graham was far more than an author or teacher. More than any other man except my father, he influenced my life."[2]

Benjamin Graham was born in 1894. His father died when Ben was nine, and his mother's savings were wiped out in a market panic of 1907. Experiencing poverty, Ben was driven to contribute to the household by working odd jobs and studying hard. In 1914, at the age of twenty, he graduated as salutatorian of his class at Columbia. He turned down offers to instruct in three of the college's departments: English, Mathematics, and Philosophy. Instead, he heeded the advice of a dean and began his career on Wall Street.

Graham's introduction to Wall Street was similar to Buffett's—chalking prices on a blackboard. In those days, there were no securities analysts, only statisticians. Graham nevertheless pursued a quantitative approach to systematically determine whether a stock was cheap compared to its net assets. Thinking the worst was over after the Crash of 1929, when the Dow dropped 35 percent from September until year-end, Graham borrowed on margin and invested heavily in stocks only to see the Dow fall another 34 percent in 1930 and plummet another 53 percent in 1931. From the peak of 381 in September 1929 until the bottom in July 1932, the Dow crashed 89 percent. By 1932 Graham's portfolio declined 70 percent, and he would have quit if not for the generosity of a relative of his partner, Jerome Newman, who contributed $75,000 of capital to enable their firm to survive.

In an investing environment in the early 1930s where cheapness and value appeared elusive and where momentum investing and anticipating market psychology were rampant, Graham and his colleague David Dodd co-authored the seminal textbook, *Security Analysis,* a guide to rationally valuing a stock as a business. The streamlined layman version, *The Intelligent Investor,* was published in 1949, and Warren Buffett read it in early 1950 as a college senior. Buffett devoured every book on investing in the library, but *The Intelligent Investor* changed his life forever and earned Buffett's highest praise: "It is by far the best book on investing ever written." The books represented a fresh structural approach to a market that was overrun by a gambling mindset.

In the rubble of the crash, many stocks were priced at less than the underlying business's liquidation value, including some that were quoted at less than their cash value alone. Graham and Dodd's books offered investors a logical systematic guide for navigating the murky waters of investing. Buffett later said the book "brought structure and logic to a disorderly and confused activity."[3] For the first time, investors had a framework for investing based on sound quantitative analysis that differentiated underlying business value from fickle market prices.

Graham and Dodd advocated a "margin of safety" where investors had a prescription for downside protection. What mattered most was not the allure of making a killing on an investment, but preserving capital and not losing it. They explained that a business had an intrinsic value based on its physical assets that was separate and distinct from its quoted market price.

Buffett said the most valuable and enduring lessons he learned about investing were from Ben Graham.[4] Buffett said *The Intelligent Investor* had three cornerstone ideas that shaped everything he has done:

1. View Stocks as a Stake in a Business

The first is to regard stocks as part of a business rather than ticker symbols that go up or down. Stocks represent a partial ownership stake in a business and should represent the fractional ownership of what an investor would be willing to pay for the entire business. Graham astutely wrote, "Investment is most intelligent when it is most businesslike…every corporate security may best be viewed as an ownership in, or a claim against, a specific business enterprise."[5]

2. Margin of Safety

The second lesson is what Buffett refers to as the three most important words in investing, *margin of safety*. An investor should insist on a wide margin of safety; that is buying a $1.00 bill for $0.50. Buffett says if you are going to be driving 10,000-pound trucks across a bridge, build it to handle 15,000 pounds, not 10,001 pounds. This safety net offers downside risk protection while still allowing significant upside to fair value. Graham advocated buying when the stock price was quoted for two-thirds or less than the company's working capital less long-term debt per share. He figured in a worse case, if the stock price was below the value of liquidating a company's current assets and paying off its debt, in theory, an investor would receive the plant and equipment and other long-term assets for free. The deeper the discount between the stock price and the company's net-working capital, the larger the margin of safety.

3. The Market is Your Servant

The third timeless principle is the notion that the market is there to serve the investor with volatile market quotes, and the investor shouldn't fear the volatility, but capitalize on it. Graham personified the market as "Mr. Market" whose emotions vacillated between moody and depressed, and excitable and euphoric. Graham advised,

> *The investor with a portfolio of sound stocks should expect their prices to fluctuate and should neither be concerned by sizable declines nor become excited by sizable advances. He should always remember that market quotations are there for his convenience, either to be taken advantage of or to be ignored. He should never buy a stock because it has gone up or sell one because it has gone down.*[6]

Buffett summarized this principle with his famous mottos, "Mr. Market is your servant, not your master," and "Be greedy when others are fearful; and fearful when others are greedy." Capitalize on the folly of the market rather than participating in it and becoming a victim.

After graduating from the University of Nebraska-Lincoln, Buffett leafed through graduate school catalogs and to his delightful surprise, found that Benjamin Graham and David Dodd were instructors at Columbia. Buffett enrolled and had the advantage of practically memorizing *Security Analysis* before class even started.

> *The truth was that I knew the book even better than Dodd. I could quote from any part of it. At that time, literally, almost in those whole seven or eight hundred pages, I knew every example. I had just sopped it up. And you can imagine the effect that would have on the guy, that somebody was that keen on the book.*[7]

175

Buffett was the star student. Buffett wanted to learn as much as he could about his hero. He looked Graham up in *Who's Who* and found that Graham was the chairman of Government Employees Insurance Company, or GEICO. Curious to find out more, Buffett took a train to Washington D.C. on a Saturday morning without an appointment and banged on the locked door until a janitor answered. He explained that he was a student of Benjamin Graham and wanted to see if anyone could explain GEICO's business to him. The janitor took Buffett to the sixth floor to meet GEICO's financial vice president, Lorimer Davidson. Davidson thought, as a favor to Graham, he would spend five minutes with Buffett. Five minutes turned into four hours after Davidson admired Buffett's mature and insightful questions. Later Davidson recalled,

> *After about ten to twelve minutes of his questions, I realized that I was talking to a highly unusual young man. The questions he was asking me were the questions that would have been asked by an experienced insurance-stock analyst. His follow-up questions were professional. He was young, and he looked young. He described himself as a student, but he was talking like a man who had been around a long time, and he know a great deal. When my opinion of Warren changed, I began asking him questions. And I found out that he had been a successful businessman at age sixteen. That he had filed his own income tax at age fourteen and every year since then. That he had had a number of small businesses.*[8]

Buffett was enamored with Graham and offered to work for him for free after graduation. Graham turned him down—since other Wall Street firms in the 1950s wouldn't hire anyone who was Jewish, Graham reserved his few hires for them. Warren returned to Omaha to become a commissioned stockbroker with his father's firm, Buffett-Falk & Co., over the preference of his father and Graham, who both advised him to wait until the market was more attractively valued.

Warren was less interested in the macro issues and more interested in the bounty of cheap stocks that he could buy and convince others to buy. As a stockbroker, Warren struggled to convince others to buy his favorite stocks, as they dismissed his youth and inexperience. Warren didn't enjoy making small talk and, even more, didn't like the conflict of interest that rewarded stockbrokers for commissions on quantity of trades rather than on the quality of their advice to hold stocks for long-term gains. He was performance driven, not commission driven, and wanted to be aligned with his customers instead of at odds with them. He was more comfortable combing through the *Moody's Manuals* looking for bargains. "I went through the *Moody's Manuals* page by page. Ten thousand pages in *Moody's Industrial, Transportation, Banks* and *Finance Manuals*—twice. I actually looked at every business—although I didn't have to look very hard at some."[9] Years later at a Berkshire Hathaway annual meeting, a shareholder asked him how he might amass such a database of knowledge. Warren encouraged him to use the same approach: "Well, start with the As."

As Warren found bargains, he would forward his stock ideas in his correspondence with Ben Graham. His persistence paid off when he was hired to start in September 1954. He was so excited to work with his idol he showed up a month before his official start date.

As much as Warren believed in Ben's gospel of value investing, Warren had differences. Warren didn't subscribe to Ben's practice of over-diversification with as many as one hundred different securities that Ben used to protect himself from possible value traps. Warren preferred to concentrate his bets in companies where he had high conviction, as he did with GEICO. Ben was only interested in the quantitative calculation of value and discouraged meeting with management, believing they weren't to be trusted. Warren wanted to know as much as he could about the company's competitive advantage and the character of its management.

In the spring of 1956, Graham notified his partners of his retirement plan to move to California, teach at UCLA, write, ski, and study the classics. His investment record for the previous eleven years matched the S&P 500. Ironically, if the GEICO shares that were distributed to Graham-Newman shareholders were included, their return doubled that of the S&P 500. Although Graham offered Buffett an opportunity to become a general partner of the firm, Warren didn't like New York, and he liked even less the idea of working as a junior partner to Jerry Newman's son Mickey.

Now armed with the experience of observing Graham-Newman's method of identifying bargains with limited downside risk in stocks, arbitrage situations, liquidations, and hedges (buying a convertible bond and simultaneously shorting the common stock), overlaid with Buffett's bias for concentrating with conviction, Buffet was ready to apply his craft on his own terms back home in Omaha.

Philip Carret

In 1991 Warren Buffett said that "Phil (Carret) has the best long-term investment record of anyone in America." Two years later, he wrote to Carret, "You are the Lou Gehrig of investing and, like him, your record will never be forgotten." Buffett later said that Carret would be included in a Hall of Fame of investment managers if one were to exist.

Carret and the Dow Jones Industrial Average were both born the same year, 1896. He passed away in May 1998 at the age of 101. His investment career spanned eight decades, during which he witnessed more than thirty bull markets, twenty bear markets, twenty recessions, the Depression, and two stock market crashes. He remembered when there were no electric lights, no Securities and Exchange Commission, and no Federal Reserve.

He graduated from Harvard in 1917 with a chemistry degree and enlisted in the Army Signal Corps (a predecessor to the Air Force), but World War I ended before he saw combat. After the war, he was a financial reporter for the *Boston News Bureau* and for *Barron's*. In 1928 he pooled $25,000 from friends and family to start an investment pool that evolved into the Pioneer Fund, the third oldest U.S. mutual fund. During the fifty-five years Carret managed the Pioneer Fund, a $10,000 investment would have grown to $8 million compared to the Dow Jones Industrial Average of $3.8 million.

Starting his investment management in 1928 and surviving through the trying years of the crash and depression shaped his moral principle of avoiding debt. "I never borrow money. If you don't borrow money, you can't go broke."[10] He added that borrowed money is the most common way smart people go broke.[11] He also preferred his companies to have little to no debt.

In the mid-1940s he traveled to Omaha to visit Howard Buffett, who recommended investing in a barrel maker, Greif Brothers Corporation. He bought the stock at a split adjusted price of $0.68/share, and Carret & Co. still held 4 percent of the company stock before he died at a price of about $36/share.

Carret thought Warren Buffett was one of the two greatest investors he'd seen and believed he was the smartest man in the U.S. Carret was a long-time shareholder of Berkshire Hathaway and frequently attended Berkshire's annual meetings. I was present at one of them when Buffett identified him as "one of my heroes."

Carret was a value investor, a prolific writer, and continued to commute from his home in Scarsdale, New York into Manhattan five days a week until he passed away. He wrote several investment books, including *Buying a Bond*, *The Art of Speculation*, and *A Money Mind at Ninety*. His general investment guidelines were to buy steady growers with steady management at a reasonable price and patiently hold them for many years. He abhorred arrogant management and was a voracious reader of annual reports. He didn't watch TV. "I'd rather read books."[12]

He bought enduring quality companies with steadily growing earnings, strong balance sheets, honest and devoted managers, and held them for the long term. He said, "Trading in and out of the market is the pinnacle of stupidity."[13] Louis Rukeyser on *Wall Street Week* in April 1995 asked Carret, then ninety-nine, to mention the one thing he had learned over the past 75 years on Wall Street. Carret replied, "Patience. I buy things for myself and my clients to hold for five years, ten years…" Even at ninety-nine years of age.

Similar to Buffett and Lynch, he looked at each stock as a share of a business and encouraged investors to prospect with products or services an investor likes and understands. Carret said one of the most profitable investments he ever made started in the bathroom at the Bostonian Hotel where he liked the small cake of Neutrogena soap. After discovering that Neutrogena Corporation was a public company whose niche high-end products didn't compete directly with the large consumer product companies, he visited the company and bought the stock. The stock rose from a split-adjusted $1 in 1979 to $35.75 when Johnson & Johnson acquired it in 1994.

In *A Money Mind at Ninety*, Carret identified six key questions to assess in determining the quality of an investment candidate:

1. Does the company have a long record of earnings, with an unbroken, or almost unbroken, record of rising earnings for at the least the past ten years?

2. Has the company's growth been financed by borrowing money, by issuance of additional shares of stock, or has it been financed entirely by plowing earnings back into the business?

3. Does the company, thanks to having prudently husbanded rather than distributed its earnings, have a debt-free or almost debt-free balance sheet?

4. Is the company a leader, preferably *the* leader, in its field?

5. How long has that the company's management been in power? How secure is their tenure?

6. Finally, is there a reasonably broad market for the company's shares?[14]

At the 1996 Berkshire Hathaway annual meeting, Warren Buffett said, "The main thing is to find a wonderful business, like Phil Carret, who's here today, always did. He's one of my heroes, and that's an approach he used."

Phil Fisher

In an interview in 1969 with Forbes, Warren Buffett described himself: "I'm 15 percent Phil Fisher, and 85 percent Benjamin Graham."[15] Buffett credits Phil Fisher for finding great businesses held for the long-term. "Phil Fisher opened my eyes a little more toward trying to find a wonderful business. Charlie (Munger) did more of that than Phil did, but Phil was espousing that entirely, and I read his books in the early 60s."[16]

In the 2004 Berkshire Annual Meeting, a shareholder asked Buffett about Fisher's influence; Fisher had recently passed away. "Phil was a great man...As with Graham, you could really get it all through their books." Fisher's classic books, *Common Stocks and Uncommon Profits* (which initially impressed Buffett) and *Conservative Investors Sleep Well*, were published in 1958 and 1975. Buffett had only met Fisher once, in 1962, but "the writing was so clear, you didn't need to meet him." Buffet said that both he and Charlie Munger were "preaching a similar doctrine."

Fisher's doctrine was that since it was hard to find really good investments; concentrate on a few and hold them for a long time. "The greatest investment reward comes to those who by good luck or good sense find the occasional company that over the years can grow in sales and profits far more than industry as a whole...when we believe we have found such a company we had better stick with it for a long period of time."[17]

In Common Stocks and Uncommon Profits, Fisher outlined fifteen valuable points to look for in a stock, five things to avoid, and some insights into his research process.

Fifteen Points to Look for in a Common Stock

1. Does the company have products or services with sufficient market potential to make possible a sizable increase in sales for at least several years?

2. Does the management have a determination to continue to develop products or processes that will still further increase total sales potentials when the growth potentials of currently attractive product lines have largely been ignored?

3. How effective are the company's research and development efforts in relation to its size?

4. Does the company have an above-average sales organization?

5. Does the company have a worthwhile profit margin? (Fisher said that the greatest long-range investment profits are never obtained by investing in marginal companies, but with companies having among the best profit margins in the industry.)

6. What is the company doing to maintain or improve profit margins?

7. Does the company have outstanding labor and personnel relations?

8. Do company executives have outstanding relations with lower echelon personnel?

9. Does the company have depth to its management?

10. How good are the company's cost analysis and accounting controls?

11. Are there other aspects of the business, peculiar to the industry, which will give the investor clues as to how outstanding the company may be relative to its competition?

12. Does the company have a short-range or long-range outlook in regard to profits?

13. In the foreseeable future will the growth of the company require sufficient equity financing so that the larger number of shares then outstanding will largely cancel the existing stockholders' benefit from this anticipated growth?

14. Does the management talk freely to investors about its affairs when things are going well but "clam up" when troubles and disappointments occur?

15. Does the company have a management of unquestionable integrity?

Five Things for Investors to Avoid

1. Don't buy into promotional/early stage companies. Fisher says that while it may be tempting "to get in on the ground floor," there is much

greater probability of error in assessing potential strengths and problems. Stay with established companies.

2. Don't ignore a good stock just because it is traded over-the-counter.

3. Don't buy a stock just because you like the "tone" of its annual report. A slick public relations department may create an impression in print and in pictures that may reflect a close-knit, harmonious, and enthusiastic management team when the truth is something altogether different.

4. Don't assume that the high price at which a stock may be selling in relation to earnings is necessarily an indication that further growth in those earnings has largely been already discounted in the price. New sources of earnings power may warrant maintaining the price/earnings premium.

5. Don't quibble over eighths and quarters. Buy "at the market" if the company is the right one and the price is reasonably attractive. Being penny-wise may be pound-foolish by missing huge profits in a stock you correctly identified that had great potential.

Fisher's Research Process

Fisher realized that 80 percent of his best stocks were sourced from other outstanding investment advisors, not from industry sources. In conversations or reading material, he could readily determine whether the identified company met his basic fifteen criteria mentioned above. His two principle concerns at this early stage of discovery were to determine whether the company had an opportunity for unusual growth in sales and whether the company was insulated from competition. Fisher then reviewed the SEC Form 10-K and proxy statement to understand management's background and the company's product lines and competition.

Next, he would use his famed "scuttlebutt" approach and try to have a phone conversation with every key customer, supplier, competitor, ex-employee, commercial banker, or professional in a related field that he knew or could approach through mutual friends. Only after the scuttlebutt approach helped answer at least 50 percent of his fifteen points did Fisher feel he was ready to call on management to determine their competency. When he visited management, he made sure that he met decision-makers, not just the investor relations officer.

Fisher believed his research standards were so rigorous that he bought one company for every two companies he visited. I recall sitting in a small group meeting with management of Motorola, and Phil Fisher was seated right next to management. He was an intent listener and asked very few but pointed questions.

At eighty-nine years of age in 1996, Phil Fisher granted an interview with *Forbes* where he said he had under a dozen clients, some of them fifth-generation clients, and he operated without a computer, quote machine, or analysts. He just had a phone and a part-time secretary. His portfolio consisted of just six stocks, with one each purchased in 1957 (Motorola), 1969, 1977, 1986, and two in 1988. He emphasized the importance of management in a company with a differentiated product. "I have stressed management, but even so, I haven't stressed it enough. It is the most important ingredient...It's not what industry you're in, it's what you're doing right that your rivals haven't figured out yet...and are just starting to have potential."

Buffett said when he started his career, "and for a long time, I used to do a lot of what Phil Fisher calls the "scuttlebutt" method. And I don't think you can do too much of it."[18]

Differences between Graham and Fisher

There are many similarities between Phil Fisher's investment strategy and Charlie Munger's as we will see, but at this point it is instructive to see the differences between Ben Graham and Phil Fisher. Ben Graham's paramount concern was whether the stock was statistically cheap, whereas Fisher was willing to pay a reasonable price. Graham diversified his investments among dozens of "cigar-butts" whereas Fisher concentrated on less than a dozen. Graham discouraged meeting with management, whereas Fisher insisted on sizing up management firsthand to determine their candor, integrity, and competence. Graham was less concerned with the quality of the business as long as it was cheap, whereas Fisher prized first-class leaders. Graham's method tolerated high turnover, whereas Fisher was willing to hold outstanding companies for decades to enjoy their compounding returns.

Charlie Munger

Warren Buffett met Charlie Munger in 1959 through an introduction by one of Warren's clients. Warren was 29 and Charlie was 35. Munger was a Harvard

Law School graduate working as an attorney in Pasadena, California, and happened to be in Omaha to settle his father's estate; his father had also been an attorney.

Munger was raised in Omaha and had ironically worked for Warren Buffett's grandfather at the Buffett grocery store but hadn't known Buffett. Munger realized that he wouldn't become rich by practicing law. He augmented his earnings by working on real estate deals on the side early in the morning before his law practice. He said, "Like Warren, I had a considerable passion to get rich. Not because I wanted Ferraris—I wanted the independence. I desperately wanted it."

Buffett recalled, "When I first met Charlie, he had a number of clients, his father had a number of clients, and he had thought about the businesses of each one of those clients, probably in a more perceptive way than most of them thought about it themselves."[19]

Like Buffett, Munger was an avid reader and studied mental models of accomplished leaders, especially his role model, Ben Franklin. Unlike Buffett, Munger expressed his self-assurance in a blunt, semi-arrogant, aloof, unvarnished, judgmental way that some interpreted as offensive until they understood that he was uncannily dead right.

Like Warren, he has an impeccable sense of humor and is the perfect complement to Warren. From the moment they first met, they had an immediate kinship of like-minded intellect. Munger believed the bond came from a similar Omaha background, intellectual curiosity, the enjoyment of competing in games, and the love of ideas. Buffett was enamored of Munger when they first met; he encouraged Munger to pursue a career in investment management if he wanted to make real money. By 1962 Charlie had his own investment partnership, which he ran until 1975. According to Buffett's essay, *Superinvestors of Graham-and-Doddsville*, Munger generated a compound annual return of 19.8 percent for the fourteen-year period compared to 5.0 percent for the Dow.[20]

During the Buffett Partnership and early Berkshire years, Buffett and Munger consulted with each other over the phone on almost a daily basis. In later years, they spoke less frequently.

Despite their kinship, Munger respected Ben Graham but was not a disciple. He believed that Graham's flaw was that he pessimistically valued businesses as dead rather than alive. Graham's focus was on statistically cheap businesses based on their liquidation value. Munger preferred to look through the windshield at opportunity rather than in the rear-view mirror at cheap but

Charles Munger			
	Average Annual Total Return		
Period Ending 12/31	Overall Partnership	Limited Partners	Dow Jones
1962	30.1%	20.1%	-7.6%
1963	71.7%	47.8%	20.6%
1964	49.7%	33.1%	18.7%
1965	8.4%	6.0%	14.2%
1966	12.4%	8.3%	-15.7%
1967	56.2%	37.5%	19.0%
1968	40.4%	27.0%	7.7%
1969	28.3%	21.3%	-11.6%
1970	-0.1%	-0.1%	8.7%
1971	25.4%	20.6%	9.8%
1972	8.3%	7.3%	18.2%
1973	-31.9%	-31.9%	-13.1%
1974	-31.5%	-31.5%	-23.1%
1975	73.2%	73.2%	44.4%
Compound Annual Gain	19.8%	13.7%	5.0%

dying businesses. Munger was interested in determining whether a company could sustain good sales growth, assessing the quality of management, evaluating whether the company had a durable competitive advantage, gauging barriers-to-entry, and measuring how much free cash flow a company generated relative to its capital. These criteria echoed those of Phil Fisher. Munger had four simple, common-sense filters for his investments: 1) a business he understands, 2) a business with characteristics that gave it a durable competitive advantage, 3) management with integrity and talent, and 4) a sensible price that incorporated a margin-of-safety.

When asked where his view of buying great businesses came from, Munger responded in his own colorful manner, "I have a habit in life, which is [that] I observe what works and what doesn't, and I'd seen so many idiots get rich at easy businesses. Naturally I wanted to be in easier businesses."[21] Munger explained why he was averse to buying a business in order to turn it around by replacing poor managers: "If you want to ruin your life, spend it trying to change your spouse. It's really stupid." Buffett added, "Marrying someone to change them is crazy, and I would say hiring someone to change them is crazy, and becoming partners with them to change them is as crazy."[22]

Buffett credited Munger for influencing his purchase of American Express stock in his partnership and their purchase of the entire company of See's Candy as part of Berkshire Hathaway. The See's Candy purchase was a seminal event for Berkshire that paved the way for buying other wonderful businesses. We will cover these more in detail later.

Charlie Munger highlighted an important advantage regarding owning wonderful companies: time is on your side as an investor in a wonderful company but not so in a mediocre company.

> Over the long-term, it's hard for a stock to earn a much better return than the business which underlies it earns. If the business earns 6 percent on capital over 40 years and you hold it for 40 years, you're not going to make much different than a 6 percent return—even if you originally buy it at a huge discount. Conversely, if a business earns 18 percent on capital over 20 or 30 years, even if you pay an expensive looking price, you'll end up with a fine result.[23]

Munger will readily admit that prices can sometimes dramatically overshoot even a wonderful company, as they did in the "Nifty Fifty" 1974 period. Therefore, paying a fair price for a wonderful company will generally prove more lucrative over the long-term than holding out for a bargain price in a mediocre company.

Munger once asked Buffett how he wanted to be remembered and Buffett said, "As a teacher." Munger remarked, "Who else in America who is a CEO wants to be remembered as a teacher? I like it." He was then asked how he wanted to be remembered and he said, "I wouldn't mind being remembered as a teacher, but I won't be. I may be remembered as a wise-ass."[24]

Munger has been Buffett's closest business partner for over fifty years. He has been Berkshire's long-time vice-chairman and is the reason why Buffett evolved from a Graham-style bargain hunter to a value buyer of wonderful businesses. Buffett said "I'm willing to pay more for a good business and for good management than I would twenty years ago. Ben tended to look at the statistics alone. I've looked at the intangibles."[25] He famously elaborated, "It's far better to pay a fair price for a wonderful business than a wonderful price for a fair company."

Buffett later admitted that buying Berkshire Hathaway was a mistake because the company was a lousy textile business—perhaps his biggest mistake. It was cheap quantitatively but it was a mistake to hold it for twenty years because it was still a lousy business, and the original business did not compound. Buffett said that "time is the friend of the wonderful business" because they keep doing more business, and they keep making more money. He added the corollary, "time is the enemy of the lousy business," and staying with Berkshire was a mistake. He said that he would have been better off investing in other businesses with a new entity he could have set up rather than using Berkshire as the platform. Buffett credits Munger for his conversion.

When pressed for his top three major influences, in order Buffett credits his father, Ben Graham, and then Charlie Munger. Howard Buffett "taught me to do nothing that could be put on the front page of a newspaper. I have never known a better human being than my Dad." Ben Graham gave Buffett "an intellectual framework for investing and a temperamental model, the ability to stand back and not be influenced by a crowd, not be fearful if stocks go down." Last but certainly not least,

> Charlie made me focus on the merits of a great business with tremendously growing earnings power, but only when you can be sure of it.[26] Charlie shoved me in the direction of not just buying bargains, as Ben Graham had taught me. This was the real impact he had on me. It took a powerful force to move me on from Graham's limited views. It was the power of Charlie's mind. He expanded my horizons.[27]

Circle of Competence

An important key to Buffett's success is that he only invested in businesses that he understood. Buffett has often said that you don't get paid for the degree of difficulty in investing. He added, "I would say the most important thing in business and investments, which I regard as the same thing, from our standpoint, is being able to accurately define your circle of competence."[28] Buffett said as early as 1967 that "We will not go into businesses where technology, which is way over my head, is crucial to the investment decision. I know about as much as semi-conductors or integrated circuits as I do of the mating habits of the chrzaszcz."[29]

When Buffett liquidated his partnership, he emphasized the importance of investing only in what he understood—his circle of competence—and ignoring outside pressures to do otherwise,

If I can't understand something, I tend to forget it. Passing an opportunity which I don't understand—even if someone else is perceptive enough to analyze it and get paid well for doing it—doesn't bother me. All I want to be sure of is that I get paid well for the things I do feel capable of handling— and that I am right when I make affirmative decisions.[30]

It isn't important how wide the circle of competence is, but rather knowing where your lines are that define the circle and having the discipline to stay within those lines. Charlie Munger reinforced Buffett's bias for staying within his lines when he reminisced about Berkshire's first fifty years, "Berkshire…(is) averse only to activities about which it could not make useful predictions."[31]

Market Timing

In November 1965 Buffett delineated his ground rules for investing in the Buffett Partnership. Rule No. 6 said, "I am not in the business of predicting general stock market or business fluctuations. If you think I can do this, or think it is essential to an investment program, you should not be in the part-nership." Buffett said he didn't buy or sell stocks based upon what *other people* think the *stock market* was going to do, but upon what *he* thought the *company* was going to do. He added that he would be in trouble if he began letting his guesses or emotions dictate whether he would or wouldn't buy stock in a company where he had a long-run edge.

The barriers to owning a stock are low. It only takes a few seconds to execute a trade online. But the barriers are much higher to understanding what you own. The effort to understand a company's competitive advantages and risks builds the conviction necessary to resist the inevitable temptations to sell due to false rumors, misperceptions, and capricious shakeouts to stay the course for the long-term reward. I wonder how many investors sold in a panic during four occasions when Berkshire Hathaway stock suffered vicious sell-offs ranging from 37 percent to 59 percent and never reaped the reward of Berkshire's long-term growth in value.

It may be tempting to anticipate short-term market direction and override business valuation for the promise of quick gains. But that is like forecasting tomorrow's weather by simply extrapolating today's weather. Buffett says "you can't get rich with a weathervane."[32] Forecasting short-term market movement isn't investing—it is speculating. Some people have a strong instinct for overnight riches, but Buffett says he doesn't know how to do it. He advocates getting rich slowly. Buffett says the real test of whether an investor is speculating—that is, just focused on the price action of a stock—or investing is whether they care if the stock market is open.

Buffett says he doesn't care if the market is closed for a couple of years when he buys a stock because he is looking to the *business* to produce returns for him in the future. He says buying a stock should be no different in your mind than buying income-producing farm land or rental property. All of these investments ultimately derive their value from their ability to generate income, not from how a speculator thinks the weathervane will shift tomorrow. Borrowing and lending for speculation is a delusional toxin that can lead to a financial grave. "Once you start lending money, big time, to people where your hope of getting your money back is that the asset goes up rather than the asset produces enough to service the loan, I mean that's very dangerous, whether it's farmland, whether it was oil in Texas. It creates lots of problems."[33]

Buffett had a few armchair quarterback investors who, after a market decline, suggested that they thought stocks were going a lot lower. Buffett said these comments always raised two questions: 1) why didn't they inform him earlier of the impending decline; and 2) if they didn't accurately predict the current decline, how do they know now that it will decline further? The future, as Buffett points out, is never clear.

The great fortunes were built on single wonderful businesses by those who believed in their company. You don't see market timers among the Forbes 400 wealthiest people. Buffett said,

> *I've never made any money by predicting the stock market. I don't spend any time thinking about it. I really look at individual businesses...I try to figure out what the business is worth. The real fortunes in this country have been made by people who have been right about the business they invested in, and not right about the timing of the stock market.*[34]

CHAPTER 19

Evolution of Buffett's Stock Selection Method

We're adapting reasonably to a business that's gotten very much more difficult.

—CHARLIE MUNGER[1]

The last chapter discussed the influences on Warren Buffett's stock picking philosophy. This chapter explores the evolution of Buffett's investing style. His investments followed three distinct phases:

1. **Early Buffett**: Mediocre smaller companies bought at bargain "cigar-butt" prices in the classic style of Benjamin Graham, which emphasized buying companies priced at a discount to tangible assets on the balance sheet. Graham had his limitations. In 1988 Buffett told *Fortune* magazine columnist Carol Loomis, "Boy, if I had listened only to Ben, would I ever be a lot poorer." Buffett conceded at the 1996 Berkshire Hathaway annual meeting that one of his biggest mistakes was not paying up for quality businesses.

2. **Later Buffett**: Quality businesses, in the style of Charlie Munger, Phil Fisher, and Phil Carret, which were not selling at prices related to tangible assets, but were attractively priced relative to their future

earnings power based on a qualitative assessment of the durability of a company's competitive advantages. In Buffett's terminology, he assessed whether the company's "castle" was surrounded by a wide protective moat and whether the company's product had pricing power. These companies typically generated high returns on capital (ROIC) and required little incremental capital to grow.

> *The principles of buying value and margin of safety and the detachment from the market I learned from Ben. You might say that I learned the proper temperamental set from Ben. The stocks I buy are entirely different from what Ben would buy if he were alive today.*[2]

Buffett also believed that Ben Graham's method wouldn't scale with large sums of money at Berkshire.

During this period, Buffett evolved toward Charlie Munger's influence of buying excellence; especially companies with strong brand loyalty and pricing power. Often these brands were much more valuable than their tangible assets, but the value of their intangible brand didn't appear on their balance sheet. Graham relied on quantitative bargains based on tangible assets, and Buffett transitioned to quantitative bargains based on future cash flows. Graham had no interest in predicting earnings because he didn't have confidence about those predictions. Unlike Buffett, Graham followed Yogi Berra's advice that it is tough to make predictions, especially about the future. Fortunately, Buffett was a fan of another baseball hall of famer, Ted Williams, who advised to wait for the right pitch. Buffett said "we mostly buy stocks for future earnings"[3] and those stocks have to be a fat pitch. Otherwise, he will stand with the bat on his shoulder.

3. **Modern Buffett**: Large, capital-intensive companies with stable, recession-resistant returns in the mature Berkshire phase. Warren Buffett admitted that:

> *You can't expect to get returns in the utility business (that you get in other businesses). It's not a great business; it's a good business. And the more money we can put in good businesses, the better I like it. Our utility business 10 or 20 years from now will be a whole lot bigger than it is now.*[4]

Buffett believes a consistent 10 percent-plus return in a capital intensive but mature business, such as a utility or a railroad, may not knock the cover off the ball, but at Berkshire's size he is content to hit singles and doubles consistently. The huge capital requirement of these businesses essentially puts Berkshire on autopilot for a large portion of its future capital allocation.

> *In earlier days, Charlie and I shunned capital intensive businesses, such as public utilities. Indeed, the best businesses by far for owners continue to be those that have high returns on capital and that require little incremental investment to grow. We are fortunate to own a number of such businesses, and we would love to buy more. Anticipating, however, that Berkshire will generate ever-increasing amounts of cash, we are today quite willing to enter businesses that regularly require large capital expenditures. We expect only that these businesses have reasonable expectations of earning decent returns on the incremental sums they invest. If our expectations are met—and we believe that they will be— Berkshire's ever-growing collection of good to great businesses should produce above-average, though certainly not spectacular, returns in the decades ahead.[5]*

Unconstrained investors don't have to be satisfied with *decent* results by investing in *good* businesses, but may want *excellent* results by investing in *great* business, which generally have high returns on capital, strong growth, little to no debt, and generate cash led by owner-oriented management.

Early Buffett: Investing During the Buffett Partnership Years

Buffett returned to Omaha in 1956 after working in New York for his mentor Ben Graham. Buffett wasted no time establishing his own partnership in May and began painting his own investment masterpiece. Buffett's stated goal was to outperform the "averages" by at least 10 percent per year with minimal exposure to long-term loss of capital. He preferred to be judged by how he performed in a bear market while saying he would be content to match the index in a bull market. The average Buffett referred to was the Dow Jones Industrial Average, which was popular, had a long history, and generally reflected the average experience of investors. He preferred his results to be measured over a five-year period, but felt that three years were a bare minimum test.

Evolution of Buffett's Stock Selection Method

His first limited partners consisted of his father-in-law; Buffett's college roommate and his roommate's mother; Buffett's aunt Alice; and his sister Doris and her husband, Truman. An original investment of $10,000 in the first partnership, assuming the limited partner elected to transfer their investment in Berkshire stock when the partnership was liquidated in 1969, today would be worth over $500 million.

The colors Buffett chose initially for his painting came from the same paint set as Ben Graham. In 1957, 85 percent of Buffett's investments were in undervalued situations and 15 percent were in workouts. Workouts were investments that depended on a specific corporate action for its profit, such as a sale, merger, liquidation, or tender offer. Buffett was already diverging from Graham's practice of portfolio diversification.

In 1957 Buffett's largest position was 10–20 percent of his various partnerships with a goal of reaching 20 percent in due course. In 1958 he revealed that the investment was a "very well-managed" bank, Commonwealth Trust Co. of Union City, New Jersey, which, at $50/share, was priced at just 5x earnings of $10/share. Buffett estimated the company's intrinsic value at $125/share. Over time, Buffett acquired 12 percent of the shares outstanding to become the second largest shareholder. The problem was lack of liquidity as the stock averaged only two trades per month. Buffett eyed a control opportunity where he could become the largest shareholder, and he found a buyer who was willing to pay $80/share for Buffett's influential block of shares even though the market price was about $67.

Next, in 1958, Buffett redirected 25 percent of his assets into Sanborn Map Co., where he was the largest shareholder. The company was an investment trust that owned thirty to forty high-quality securities and was priced at a substantial discount to the market value of its investment portfolio and the value of its operating map business. This stake had the obvious advantage of allowing Buffett to more directly influence the realization of the investment value than having to wait for the market to recognize the value, which could take years. By 1959, Sanborn represented 35 percent of Buffett's assets.

Sanborn's core business was publishing detailed U.S. city maps that were primarily sold to insurance companies. Sanborn operated as a quasi-monopoly for seventy-five years, but over the prior decade, a competitive method eroded Sanborn's annual profits by 80 percent to $100,000. Fortunately, the company had accumulated an investment portfolio of 50 percent bonds and 50 percent stocks that was valued at $65/share compared to the stock price of $45/share.

The stock price was just 70 percent of the investment portfolio alone, and the operating business was essentially thrown in for free. Buffett joined with two other large shareholders as a team of activists and triggered value creation by distributing the equity securities in the investment portfolio to shareholders. This transaction contributed to Buffett's largest annual outperformance in 1960 with a gain of 22.8 percent vs. the Dow Jones *loss* of 6.3 percent.

Three Categories

In January 1962 Buffett elaborated on his investment strategy. He divided his investments into three categories. He referred to the first category as "generals," which were "generally undervalued securities." These were passive investments in securities where he usually allocated 5-10 percent in each of five or six stocks and smaller positions in another ten to fifteen. This was Buffett's largest category. In 1964 Buffett further explained that while qualitative factors, such as good management and a decent industry were important, before he invested he "demanded" that the stock price was a quantitative bargain compared to what a private owner would be willing to pay. In this category, the timetable for stock prices to reach parity with their underlying values was subject to the whims of the market.

In 1965 Buffett further subdivided the "general" category into "Generals-Private Owner Basis," which is similar to the original "general" definition, and "Generals-Relatively Undervalued," which were securities that were cheap relative to comparable securities of similar quality. Both categories sought to limit price risk. In both categories, Buffett sought businesses that were "understandable and where he could verify competitive strengths and weaknesses thoroughly with competitors, distributors, customers, suppliers, ex-employees, etc."[6] Buffett admitted having success with this subcategory where he felt that insisting on a private owner value to estimate intrinsic value to be too restricting. He pointed out in his January 1966 letter that "results in this category were greatly affected for the better by only two investments," later revealed to be American Express and Walt Disney.

The second largest category was "workouts," which as we previously explained, depended on a corporate action, such as a publicly announced merger, liquidation, reorganization, or spin-off, and had a specific timetable for determining outcome. Buffett usually invested in ten to fifteen workouts and enhanced his returns with borrowed funds limited to 25 percent of the partnership net worth. The predictability of outcome and the short holding period to expected outcome resulted in attractive annualized rates of return. In the earlier years of Buffett's partnership, he invested 30–40 percent of assets in this category, but the increased size of the partnership assets precluded earning consistently high returns.

The last category of investments was "control" situations where Buffett either controlled a company with a majority ownership or he had significant influence with a large position. These situations occurred when the stock price of a "general" was relatively flat for an extended period of time, allowing Buffett to accumulate a sizable ownership position. The second and third categories produced returns and typically behaved independent from the performance of the Dow Jones Average.

Altogether, Buffett usually owned about fifteen to twenty issues. The division among categories was mostly accidental based on opportunities, but all of the categories offered good investment opportunities. In 1966, Buffett's portfolio weights were: Generals-Relatively Undervalued 44 percent; Controls 35 percent; Workouts 15 percent; Generals-Private Owner 3 percent; and U.S. Treasury Bills 3 percent. Buffett's flexibility to shift among categories to the most promising opportunity was a key to his success.

Performance in the Categories

The Generals-Relatively Undervalued category ballooned to 44 percent due to American Express. Buffett never mentioned the security in his partnership letters but revealed it years later in interviews. (We will discuss American Express as a case study in a later chapter.) In 1966 Buffett celebrated his tenth anniversary of the partnership with the largest outperformance margin of 36 percent, when his partnership rose 20.4 percent compared to the Dow index loss of 15.6 percent. The outperformance was largely due to American Express.

> *Our relative performance in this category was the best we have ever had—due to one holding, which was our largest investment at year-end 1965 and also year-end 1966. This investment has substantially outperformed the general market for us during each year (1964, 1965, 1966) that we have held it. While any single year's performance can be quite erratic, we think the probabilities are highly favorable for superior future performance over a three- or four-year period... We spend considerable effort continuously evaluating every facet of the company and constantly testing our hypothesis that this security is superior to alternative investment choices.[7]*

The gift of American Express kept on giving in 1967 as the "General-Relatively Undervalued" category leaped 72 percent due in large part to this single security. After four years of astounding gains, Buffett finally trimmed most of his 40 percent weight, "Our holdings of this security have been very substantially reduced and we have nothing in this group remotely approaching the size or potential which formerly existed in this investment."[8]

Buffett's first control situation was Dempster Mill Manufacturing Company, which manufactured farm equipment and waters systems. Buffett first began buying the stock in 1956 at $18/share when the net working capital (current assets less all liabilities) per share was $50/share. Buffett bought the stock in small segments for five years at prices in the $16–$25 range. Buffett was a director of the company during most of those five years. By mid-1961 Buffett owned 30 percent of the company. The combination of large purchases and a tender offer resulted in Buffett owning 70 percent of the stock by January 1962. He acquired his total position at an average price of $28 compared to the company's net working capital of $53/share, and the investment represented 21 percent of his partnership assets.

After an attempt to work with existing management to improve operations proved futile, Buffett called Charlie Munger for advice, and he referred Buffett to Harry Bottle who was hired as president in April 1962. Buffett praised Bottle in his January 1963 partnership letter as "unquestionably the man of the year" for converting Dempster's assets into cash at a faster and more productive rate than Buffett anticipated. Buffett redeployed the cash into a stock portfolio worth $35/share, which alone was worth more than Buffett's original investment of $28/share. In addition, the remaining operating net assets of Dempster was worth $16/share for a value of $44/share.

By July 1963 Bottle had reduced inventory, valued at $4.2 million in November 1961, to just under $900,000. The proceeds were used to retire $1.2 million in debt and redeployed into investments in marketable securities. Bottle also eliminated redundant overhead expenses, closed five branches that were hemorrhaging, and negotiated better contracts with suppliers and distributors. Just prior to the end of 1963, Buffett sold Dempster for $80/share, almost triple his average cost of $28.

Buffett used this case study to explain that his investments required patience and secrecy. He could not have acquired his controlling stake at dormant prices if he were telegraphing what he was buying.

Buffett's most famous "control" situation, Berkshire Hathaway, was first publicly disclosed in his November 1, 1965, partnership letter. Buffett began buying Berkshire as a "general" investment in 1962. From a peak operation in 1948 of eleven textile mills, 11,000 employees, and earnings of $29.5 million, by 1965 Berkshire was losing money, had 2,300 employees and was operating only two mills. Buffett was comforted however with his bargain price and "excellent management" led by Ken Chace, despite presciently acknowledging that "there is no question that the state of the textile industry is the dominant factor in determining the earning power of the business."[9]

Qualitative School or Quantitative School of Investing?

The quantitative school of investing believes that if a stock is purchased at a low enough price, the downside risk is limited, and the stock, even in a poor business, will take care of itself. The qualitative school of investing believes that if you buy the right company with excellent management, prospects, competitive advantages, and industry conditions, the stock will also take care of itself. The year 1967 was a watershed year for Warren Buffett. He wrote to his investors that although he still identified himself in the quantitative school of investing since "the more sure money tends to be made on the obvious quantitative decisions," he acknowledged "the really big money tends to be made by investors who are right on qualitative decisions." Buffett learned this from his success with American Express: "the really sensational ideas I have had over the years have been weighted toward the qualitative side where I have had a 'high-probability insight'... Much of our good performance during the past three years has been due to a single idea of this sort."[10]

Buffett's assets under management had grown to $69 million by October 1967 from his humble beginning eleven years earlier of $105,100. The growth was due to compounding returns and additional contributions by investors. He said the combination of his much larger capital base and the virtual disappearance of statistical bargains, which had been over-prospected by a growing legion of security analysts, caused him to reset his longer-term investment goal to the lesser of 9 percent per year or a five-percentage point advantage over the Dow. His longstanding goal was at least a ten-percentage-point advantage over the Dow, which he handily achieved by mid-July with a cumulative annual compound rate of return of 29.6 percent versus 9.1 percent for the Dow.

Later Buffett

The shift in investment emphasis from quantitative investing, or "early Buffett," to qualitative investing, or "later Buffett," coincided with a transition in Buffett's bias to invest in controlled companies that, according to Buffett, may not offer the highest returns but were "reasonably easy, safe, profitable, and pleasant." Buffett enjoyed the stimulation and fulfillment of working with managers who were intelligent, passionate, energetic, and had high integrity. This shift in investment emphasis presaged Buffett's structure at Berkshire Hathaway where he favored marrying an acquired business for life, rather than dating businesses in a revolving door of short-term trades. By marrying acquired businesses for life, Buffett attracted sellers who wanted assurance that they could still operate their businesses independently and that their carefully crafted cultures would stay intact under the Berkshire umbrella.

Buffett articulated his preference for a healthy exposure to controlled operating businesses:

> When I am dealing with people I like, in business I find stimulating, and achieving worthwhile overall returns on capital employed (say 10–12 percent), it seems foolish to rush from situation to situation to earn a few more percentage points. It also does not seem sensible to me to trade known pleasant personal relationships with high grade people, at a decent rate of return, for possible irritation, aggravation, or worse at potentially higher returns.[11]

See's Candy Shops, Incorporated

Buffett credits his purchase of See's Candy in 1972 as the watershed event that led to his bias for acquiring and investing in quality businesses—defined as possessing pricing power, requiring little capital reinvestment, and generating free cash flow. Charlie Munger echoed the impact of this transformative deal. "Not only did the purchase work out well in its own right, but our favorable experience helped us 'pay for quality' more and more as the years unfolded."[12] Buffett has repeatedly emphasized that the most important factor in assessing the strength of a business is its pricing power:

> The single-most important decision in evaluating a business is pricing power. If you've got the power to raise prices without losing business to a competitor, you've got a very good business. And if you have to have a prayer session before raising the price by a tenth of a cent, then you've got a

terrible business. I've been in both, and I know the difference.[13] *The ability to raise prices—the ability to differentiate yourself in a real way, and a real way means you can charge a different price—that makes a great business.*[14]

See's Background

Warren Buffett and Charlie Munger controlled Blue Chip Stamps, which acquired See's Candy Shops on January 3, 1972. Blue Chip Stamps was subsequently merged into Berkshire Hathaway in 1983. Blue Chip Stamps sold trading stamps to retailers, and the retailers in turn would hand the stamps to their customers with their purchase. When customers had enough stamps posted into their booklets, they could redeem the booklets for gifts such as a toaster oven or blender. Buffett and Munger admired Blue Chip for its "float." Blue Chip enjoyed the advantage of receiving funds from the retailers long before having to pay for token gifts. Furthermore, Blue Chip Stamps was a monopoly in California, which was formed by retailers who didn't want to

be aligned with the national leader, Sperry & Hutchinson, more commonly known then as S&H Green Stamps. Blue Chip Stamps became a dying business as housewives found their time was more valuable than licking and posting trading stamps. The company needed a transformative acquisition.

For over ninety-five years, See's made candy using only the highest quality and freshest ingredients, and some candies are still made using the original recipes from the iconic Mary See. Mary See's son, Charles A. See, emigrated with his family from Canada in 1920 to Los Angeles, where he founded the first See's Candy Shop. At 135 N. Western Avenue, he made candy by hand using his mother's home recipes and emphasized friendly customer service in the distinctive black and white stores.

The mark of See's motto, "Quality Without Compromise," is branded on the indulgent palette of its loyal customers and is reinforced every Valentine's Day, Halloween, Easter, and Christmas. Mary See's warm photo on every box of See's candy evokes old-world charm, quality, and service.

Acquisition Price

See's Candy was acquired for $35 million when it had $18 million in shareholder's equity and $10 million of excess cash. Had the See's family insisted on their asking price of $40 million, Buffett would have walked away. Fortunately, one of Charlie Munger's friends, Ira Marshall, offered sage advice that changed Buffett and Munger's mind: "You guys are crazy. There are some things you should pay up for—human quality, business quality, and so forth. You're underestimating quality." This advice in hindsight was a watershed event that transformed the focus of Berkshire to wonderful companies at fair prices rather than fair companies at wonderful prices. Buffett said, "One of the questions we asked ourselves—and we thought the answer was obvious—was, 'If we raised the price $0.10 a pound, would sales fall off a cliff?' And of course, the answer, in our view at least, was no. There was untapped pricing power in the product."[15]

Buffett and Munger immediately paid the $10 million of excess cash to Blue Chip, so the effective price was $25 million for $8 million of assets. Berkshire paid an effective price-earnings multiple of 11x; $25 million net of cash divided by fiscal-year ended August 31, 1971 net income of $2.2 million. This represented a 9 percent earnings yield with the promise of much higher yields once See's unleashed its pricing power.

Buffett and Munger agreed to install Charles "Chuck" Huggins as CEO of See's. Chuck Huggins began his fifty-five-year career at See's twenty years earlier, which started, in his words, a "love affair with a business that was to become a most important part of my life and of my immediate family."[16] Huggins was mentored by Edward G. Peck, who was hired by Charles See initially as sales manager in 1931 and who "made a monumental contribution to the growth and quality image of See's Candies"[17] in his forty-one-year tenure. Huggins respectfully and fondly always referred to his mentor as Mr. Peck, who impressed Huggins as someone who "practiced and preached honesty and integrity, and [demonstrated] why a handshake could be as binding as a legal contract."[18] When Huggins said that he treasured "the value of relationships built upon honesty and integrity which involve associates in all departments of the company (which) have meant so much to me over the years,"[19] one can sympathize with Buffett when he said that it took him about fifteen seconds to realize Chuck Huggins was the person for the CEO position. In later years, Buffett wondered why it took him so long.

Buffett paid tribute to Huggins in Berkshire's 2005 annual report when Chuck Huggins passed the CEO reigns to Brad Kinstler.

> Our retailing category includes See's Candies, a company we bought early in 1972 (a date making it our oldest non-insurance business). At that time, Charlie and I immediately decided to put Chuck Huggins, then 46, in charge. Though we were new at the game of selecting managers, Charlie and I hit a home run with this appointment. Chuck's love for the customer and the brand permeated the organization, which in his thirty-four-year tenure produced a more-than-tenfold increase in profits. This gain was achieved in an industry growing at best slowly and perhaps not at all.

I had an engaging and delightful conversation with See's V.P. Marketing, Richard "Dick" Van Doren, in October 1995. Dick, who would devote fifty-two years to See's, spoke highly of Warren Buffett's uncanny ability to size up people very quickly where integrity was all-important. He recalled that Buffett prized the combination of moral values and success, and that he was concerned with family. In my thank you note for the interview, I wrote: "It is rare in business to find the values of honesty, integrity, and devotion to quality practiced so consistently at all levels. Those values were reinforced in our conversation and it is obvious that they are perhaps the most important ingredients in the recipes that make See's candy so cherished."[20]

Although Buffett and Munger were impressed with See's brand reputation and customer loyalty born of See's "passion to please," they were salivating over See's pricing power. Buffett said,

> We thought it had untapped pricing power. See's was selling candy for about the price of Russell Stover at the time, and the big question in my mind was, if you got another fifteen cents a pound, that was two and a half million dollars on top of four million dollars of earnings. So you really were buying something that perhaps could earn six and a half million dollars at the time, if just priced a little more aggressively.[21]

When See's was acquired, the company had revenues of $28 million and sold sixteen million pounds of candy for an average price per pound of $1.75. Ten years later in 1982, See's sold 24.2 million pounds for $123.7 million in revenues for an average price per pound of $5.11. Revenues grew on average 16 percent per year driven by growth in pounds of 4 percent and an 11 percent increase in price charged per pound. Buffett wasted no time in raising the price, which he did every year the day after Christmas. Pretax income sweetened from $4.6 million to $22.8 million for a 17 percent average growth rate. As of June, 2018, the price per pound of a box of standard assorted chocolates was $20.50. This represents an average annual increase of 4 percent in the thirty-five years since 1982, well above inflation. Clearly customers have been willing to pay up for See's quality candy, and its customers are as sticky as See's peanut brittle.

Blue Chip Stamps vs. See's

In the next twenty years after 1972, trading stamp sales by Blue Chip fell from $102 million to $1.2 million in 1991 while See's candy sales increased an average of 10 percent annually from $29 million to $196 million. See's income grew even faster at an average annual rate of 12.3 percent from $4.2 million in 1972 to $42.4 million.

Buffett reflected on the valuable lesson he learned from See's in the Berkshire 1991 annual report:

Charlie and I have many reasons to be thankful for our association with Chuck (Huggins, manager) and See's. The obvious ones are that we've earned exceptional returns and had a good time in the process. Equally important, ownership of See's has taught us much about the evaluation of franchises. We've made significant money in certain common stocks because of the lessons we learned at See's.[22]

Berkshire made significant money in See's also. Buffett recalled, "Even at what I then considered a fancy price, we paid only 5½ times pre-tax earnings for See's. Better yet, earnings steadily increased after our purchase; over our 43 years of ownership, pre-tax earnings have totaled about $1.9 billion. So long cigar butts, hello quality."[23] Buffett's emphasis on quality control extends to his regular sampling of See's candy, with a box delivered to his office every month. The quality purchase of See's led to subsequent purchase of quality businesses with powerful brands, including Coca-Cola, Gillette, GEICO, and many others.

Charlie Munger acknowledged that while Benjamin Graham's investing method—buying companies for less than two–thirds of their working capital—incorporated a huge margin of safety, was rational and appropriate for his time, it was no longer relevant:

He was, by and large, operating when the world was in shell-shock from the 1930s—which was the worst contraction in the English-speaking world in about 600 years...Ben Graham could run his Geiger counter over this detritus from the collapse of the 1930s and find things selling below their working capital per share and so on...If we'd stayed with the classic Graham the way Ben Graham did it, we would never have had the record we have... The bulk of the billions in Berkshire Hathaway have come from the better businesses. Much of the first $200 or $300 million came from scrambling around with our Geiger counter. But the great bulk of money has come from the great businesses. And even some of the early money was made by being temporarily present in great businesses. Buffett Partnership, for example, owned American Express and Disney when they got pounded down.[24]

Return on Tangible Assets

If pricing power is the single most important element in assessing the strength of a business, the single most important financial metric is return on tangible assets.

What a business can be expected to earn on unleveraged net tangible assets, excluding any charges against earnings for amortization of goodwill, is the best guide to the economic attractiveness of the operation. It is also the best guide to the current value of the operation's economic goodwill.[25]

Buffett consistently referred to this metric in assessing how productive a business is relative to its contributed capital. In 1991, See's earned a return on tangible assets of 168 percent ($42.4 million/$25 million). Buffett explained,

For an increase in profits to be evaluated properly, it must be compared with the incremental capital investment required to produce it. On this score, See's has been astounding: The company now operates comfortably with only $25 million of net worth, which means that our beginning base of $7 million has had to be supplemented by only $18 million of reinvested earnings. Meanwhile, See's remaining pre-tax profits of $410 million were distributed to Blue Chip/Berkshire during the 20 years for these companies to deploy (after payment of taxes) in whatever way made most sense.[26]

Buffett even uses return on investment capital for executive compensation at Berkshire. "It's really astounding what's done in compensation (by other companies). The only logical way to do it is to tie it to returns on capital."[27] Basically Buffett ties executive compensation to the manager's ability to generate returns above their cost of capital.

Modern Buffett

Berkshire's size compelled Buffett to seek investment "elephants" rather than "gazelles." Buffett concedes that the ideal business is an unregulated one that generates a high return on invested capital and requires little incremental investment to grow. But Berkshire's size and ability to generate free cash flow of over $2 billion per month forced Buffett to invest in or acquire businesses that weren't necessarily spectacular, but were still good businesses with staying power that moved the needle at Berkshire.

At the 1988 Berkshire Hathaway annual meeting Buffett said, "We're pretty negative on capital intensive businesses. We like businesses that dispense cash rather than consume it. It's amazing how many businesses actually consume it."[28] But by the 2016 annual meeting, Buffett explained the drawbacks of Berkshire's size. "Increasing capital acts as an anchor on returns in many ways. One is it drives us into businesses that are much more capital intensive." Buffett rationalizes allocating capital to capital intensive businesses as long as he believes he can earn more than a dollar in present value for each dollar invested.

There may be two other motives for investing in capital intensive businesses by Buffett, who is always mindful of the long-term. The first comes from a sense of responsibility for the many investors whose primary asset is Berkshire, to ensure that Berkshire's operating businesses are dominated by relatively predictable and impregnable businesses that enjoy near monopoly status and whose competitive positioning is likely to remain as indispensable in the distant future as they did when they were acquired. The other reason may be to make the internal capital allocation decision simpler, more turnkey, and less discretionary for future Berkshire CEOs.

Berkshire directed a huge amount of capital to two major operations that are both regulated and capital-intensive: Berkshire Hathaway Energy (BHE) and Burlington Northern Santa Fe (BNSF). By 2016 these two businesses accounted for one-third of Berkshire's after-tax operating earnings and they represented nearly 70 percent of Berkshire's total capital spending of $13 billion.

Berkshire Hathaway Energy (BHE)
(Originally Named MidAmerican Energy Holdings Company)

In March 2000 Berkshire purchased a 76 percent economic interest and a 9.7 percent voting control of the utility company MidAmerican Energy, where Buffett's good friend Walter Scott, Jr., a director of Berkshire, was also a director.

The Public Utility Holding Company Act limited Berkshire to a 9.9 percent voting control. Buffett warned in his 1999 annual Berkshire letter that Berkshire might make large additional investments in the utility. At the time of the investment, MidAmerican provided electric service to 1.8 million customers and natural gas service to 1.1 million customers in the U.S. and in the U.K., and owned major generating facilities in California and the Philippines as well as the second-largest real estate brokerage business in the United States. MidAmerican was the major provider of electricity in Iowa and the U.K.'s third largest distributor of electricity. The real estate brokerage business was called HomeServices of America but is now called Berkshire Hathaway HomeServices.

Buffet's interest in the utility was driven by MidAmerican's diversified stream of stable, recession-resistant regulated earnings, its essential monopoly status, and the opportunity to deploy capital at reasonable, albeit not exceptional, rates of return. For the first time, in Berkshire's 2009 annual report and coinciding with the purchase of Burlington Northern Santa Fe railroad, Buffett acknowledged that Berkshire's growing size compelled it to redirect capital to "good but not great businesses."

> *Anything that Berkshire Hathaway Energy (MidAmerican) does, anything that BNSF does takes lots of money. We get decent returns on capital, but we don't get the extraordinary returns on capital that we've been able to get in the businesses that are not capital intensive. We have a few businesses that earn actually 100 percent a year on true invested capital. Clearly that's a different sort of operation. Berkshire Hathaway Energy may earn 11 percent or 12 percent on capital, and that's a very decent return, but it's a different animal than the businesses that are very low capital intensity.*[29]
>
> *In earlier days, Charlie and I shunned capital-intensive businesses such as public utilities. Indeed, the best businesses by far for owners continue to be those that have high returns on capital and that require little incremental investment to grow. We are fortunate to own a number of such businesses, and we would love to buy more. Anticipating, however, that Berkshire will generate ever-increasing amounts of cash, we are today quite willing to enter businesses that regularly require large capital expenditures. We expect only that these businesses have reasonable expectations of earning decent returns on the incremental sums they invest. If our expectations are met—and we believe that they will be—Berkshire's ever-growing collection of good to great businesses should produce above-average, though certainly not spectacular, returns in the decades ahead.*[30]

Buffett presciently predicted in the Berkshire 1999 Annual Report that "Though there are many regulatory restraints in the utility industry, it's possible that we will make additional commitments in the field. If we do, the amounts involved could be large."

After a subsequent purchase in February 2002 for a cumulative investment of $2 billion, Berkshire owned a fully-diluted 80.5 percent economic interest of MidAmerican Energy Holdings, and Buffett referred to the company as a "key part of Berkshire." Following the purchase of two gas pipelines, Kern River and Northern Natural Gas, which allowed the company to transport 8 percent of all gas in the U.S., and three acquisitions during 2002, including Prudential California Realty, Buffett said that Berkshire "stands ready to inject massive amounts of money" into MidAmerican Energy Holdings. Again in the Berkshire 2006 annual letter, Buffett predicted "A decade from now, HomeServices will almost certainly be much larger (by purchasing additional brokerages)."

In March 2006 MidAmerican Energy acquired PacifiCorp, a utility serving six Western states, primarily Oregon and Utah, for $5.1 billion cash. As part of this transaction, Berkshire increased its stake in MidAmerican to 86.6 percent. Buffett rationalized the purchase in his 2005 Berkshire annual letter by admitting that "you can't expect to earn outsized profits in regulated utilities, but the industry offers owners the opportunity to deploy large sums at fair returns— and therefore it makes good sense for Berkshire." He warned that he was looking for more "very large purchases in the utility field." These investments were in part due to the fact that MidAmerican, unlike most utilities, does not pay a dividend, but its cash income has been reinvested to earn what Buffett says is a "fair return on huge sums we have invested."[31] By 2013, MidAmerican retained more earnings than any other American electric utility, which was a huge competitive advantage.

In August 2005, the Public Utility Holding Company Act was repealed as part of the Energy Policy Act of 2005, which allowed Berkshire to consolidate the financial statements of the utility into Berkshire beginning February 2006.

In 2007 MidAmerican's per-share earnings, excluding a non-recurring tax benefit, was $15.01 compared to $2.59/share in 1999—the year that Buffett agreed to buy the company—for a compound annual growth rate of 24.6 percent!

Additional acquisitions from MidAmerica included NV Energy, parent company for Nevada Power and Sierra Pacific Power, which supplies electricity for about 88 percent of Nevada's population, in December 2013 for $5.6

billion cash. In December 2014, MidAmerican, now referred to as Berkshire Hathaway Energy Company (BHE), acquired AltLink, a regulated electric transmission-only business in Calgary, Alberta, for $2.7 billion cash.

By 2015 BHE had invested $16 billion in renewable wind and solar generation. It ranked number one of all states in percentage of capacity that comes from wind at 7 percent and had six times more megawatts of wind generation than any other regulated electric utility in the country. It also generated 6 percent of the U.S. solar generation.

By 2016 Berkshire held a 90 percent ownership interest in BHE, and its wind generation produced 55 percent of all megawatt-hours sold to its Iowa retail customers. Berkshire expects that figure will increase to 89 percent by 2020. From 2006–2016 Berkshire's capital spending at BHE amounted to $43.7 billion, which was almost double BHE's cumulative pretax earnings of $22.9 billion.

The fruits of Berkshire's massive capital spending and efficiency initiatives bore fruit as evidenced by the utility holding its kilowatt-hour (KwH) rate even for over sixteen years while the industry raised rates by 44 percent. BHE's retail KwH was 7.1 cents in 2015 compared to 9.9 cents for its competitor in-state and 9–10 cents in neighboring states.[32] Also, the rate of injuries at BHE dropped from 7 percent at acquisition to 0.8 percent in 2015. While pretax margins have increased from 13.9 percent in 2006[33] to 16.6 percent in 2016, its productivity is evidently constrained by its spending, as its pretax return on tangible assets has dropped by 5.8 percent in 2006 to 4.4 percent in 2016 and is far below the high ROIC businesses influenced by Berkshire's watershed purchase of See's Candy. The Berkshire division Service and Retailing Operations, which includes See's Candy, had a pretax return on tangible assets of 36 percent in 2016 compared to the good, but less wonderful, capital intensive operations of BHE at 4.4 percent and Burlington Northern Santa Fe of 10.5 percent.

Burlington Northern Santa Fe (BNSF)

Warren Buffett's investment transition toward capital intensive businesses was reinforced in November 2009 when Berkshire agreed to acquire Burlington Northern Santa Fe (BNSF) for $26.5 billion, which was Berkshire's largest investment to date. Buffett began accumulating BNSF stock in 2006 and by 2009 had owned 22.5 percent of the nation's largest railroad. According to Berkshire's 2007 annual report, Berkshire's initial purchases averaged $77.77/

share for a stake of 17.5 percent which, as the following chart indicates, was after the stock had already doubled in the prior two years. Berkshire indicated in the 2010 annual report that, prior to the acquisition, it owned 76.8 million shares of BNSF with a carrying value of $6.6 billion, which implies an average cost of $85.95/share. Berkshire paid $100/share on February 2010 for the 77.5 percent of BNSF that it didn't already own in a combination of 60 percent cash and 40 percent Berkshire stock. The price represented a 31 percent premium to the previous closing price, but was only a 10 percent premium to the previous closing high price reached the year before. The stock portion of the deal was 30 percent of the overall cost after considering the initial 22.5 percent ownership that was purchased in the market for cash.

Buffett agreed to buy BNSF a year after the financial crisis had triggered the worst U.S. recession in over seventy years. He said, "It's an all-in wager on the economic future of the United States. I love these bets." Rails are a vital artery to the nation's health as Buffett explained, "Our country's future prosperity depends on it having an efficient and well-maintained rail system." Railroads have many advantages including: a massive barrier-to-entry with pricing power, releasing fewer pollutants than trucks, and diminishing highway congestion. Two train employees can drive a 9,000-foot, 300-car train compared to a trucking company that needs to hire 300 truck drivers to move the same freight. Since BNSF was concentrated in the mid and western U.S., it was well positioned for trade with Asia. Buffett was confident that BNSF would carry more carloads in ten years and that there would be no substitute. Buffett said that he should have figured out that railroads, in particular BNSF, had improved dramatically over the previous fifteen to twenty years, and he believed that the company's infrastructure could not be replaced for three to six times what he paid for the company.

Railroads had become much more efficient. Railroads moved 90 percent more ton-miles than twenty-five years prior on 40 percent less track with less inflation adjusted cost. Buffett noted in the 2012 annual meeting that the railroad industry after World War II had 1.7 million employees, and in 2012 there were less than 200,000. BNSF moved one ton of goods 500 miles on one gallon of diesel compared to trucks, which use four times as much fuel. This would prove to be a valuable competitive advantage as surging demand in a recovering economy drove oil prices higher.

BNSF is not a utility, but it has a utility aspect to it. Similar to MidAmerican, it depends on regulators for a reasonable rate of return on the massive capital spending it takes to merely stay in the same competitive place. Buffett was characteristically optimistic on the U.S. economy and the railroad.

> *It (BNSF) has to do well if the country does well, and the country is going to do well. So, you know, I don't know about next week or next month or even next year, but if you look at the next 50 years, this country is going to grow, it's going to have more people, it's going to have more goods moving, and rail is the logical way for many of those goods to travel, and probably a greater percentage all the time, just in terms of, of cost efficiency, in terms of fuel efficiency, in terms of environmentally friendly. So there's no way rail is going to lose share, and I think the pie is going to grow, and I think the rail share of the pie is going to grow.*[34]

The aggregate price paid for BNSF was $42.7 billion, comprised of $6.6 billion of initial investments for 22.5 percent interest, $26.5 billion for the remaining shares to obtain control, and the assumption of BNSF's net debt as of December 31, 2009, of $9.6 billion. When Buffett agreed to buy 100 percent of BNSF in November 2009, he would have analyzed the 2008 annual financial statements, which reflected EPS of $6.06. At $100/share Buffett was paying about 17x trailing earnings with the tailwind of a recovering economy.

What has happened since the acquisition? Although BNSF benefited from the tailwind of a steadily improving economy, its revenues were impacted by lower traffic of crude oil and related petroleum products; pipelines displacing rail traffic of crude oil; and lower coal volumes due to displacement by low prices for natural gas. As you can see in the table that follows, operating margin increased nearly ten percentage points due to the lower cost of fuel. Return on tangible equity was steady in the low double-digits. If BNSF was capital intensive before the acquisition, it became a highly capital-intensive railroad post-acquisition, as Berkshire doubled capital spending in the seven years (ending 2016) since owning it compared to the prior seven years. Buffett acknowledged that capital spending would be a lot more than depreciation to stay in the same (competitive) place for a long time, and that is a negative.[35]

Nonetheless, BNSF generated $17 billion in free cash flow for the first seven years of Berkshire's ownership from 2010–2016. When compared with Berkshire's total acquisition cost of $42.7 billion, the free cash flow has returned on average almost 6 percent per year and reached 9 percent in 2016.

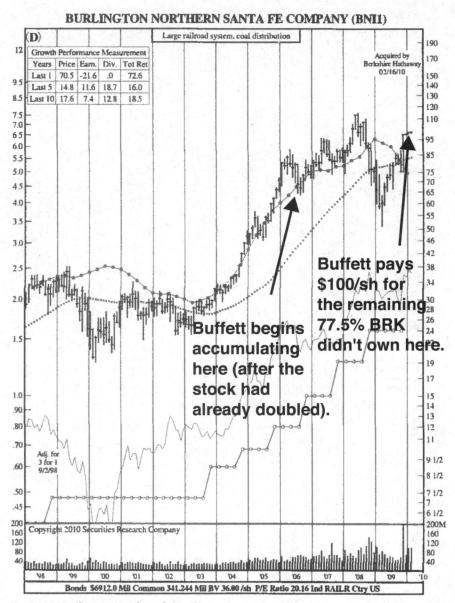

BURLINGTON NORTHERN SANTA FE COMPANY (BNI1)

Large railroad system, coal distribution

Acquired by
Berkshire Hathaway
02/16/10

Growth Performance Measurement

Years	Price	Earn.	Div.	Tot Ret
Last 1	70.5	-21.6	.0	72.6
Last 5	14.8	11.6	18.7	16.0
Last 10	17.6	7.4	12.8	18.5

Adj. for
3 for 1
9/2/98

Buffett begins accumulating here (after the stock had already doubled).

Buffett pays $100/sh for the remaining 77.5% BRK didn't own here.

Copyright 2010 Securities Research Company

Bonds $6912.0 Mil Common 341.244 Mil BV 36.00 /sh P/E Ratio 20.16 Ind RAILR Ctry US

Figure 15. Burlington Northern Santa Fe

Evolution of Buffett's Stock Selection Method

BNSF

Income Statement (per BNSF 10-K)

($ millions)	2016	2015	2014	2013	2012	2011	2/13/10- 12/31/10
Revenues	$ 19,278	$ 21,401	$ 22,714	$ 21,552	$ 20,478	$ 19,229	$ 14,835
Operating Expenses							
Compensation and benefits	4,717	4,994	4,983	4,615	4,472	4,288	3,544
Fuel	1,934	2,656	4,478	4,503	4,459	4,267	2,687
Purchased services	2,037	2,056	2,167	2,064	2,122	2,009	1,787
Depreciation & amortization	2,115	1,993	2,117	1,968	1,888	1,807	1,531
Equipment rents	766	801	867	822	810	779	670
Materials and other	1,072	1,134	1,108	912	764	808	652
Total Operating expenses	12,641	13,634	15,720	14,884	14,515	13,958	10,871
Operating Income	6,637	7,767	6,994	6,668	5,963	5,271	3,964
Interest expense	50	35	44	57	55	73	72
Other expense, net	(192)	(111)	(31)	(72)	(46)	(22)	(7)
Income before taxes	6,779	7,843	7,041	6,683	5,954	5,220	3,899
Income tax expense	2,519	2,928	2,644	2,412	2,234	1,947	1,517
Net Income	$ 4,260	$ 4,915	$ 4,397	$ 4,271	$ 3,720	$ 3,273	$ 2,382
Operating Margin	34.4%	36.3%	30.8%	30.9%	29.1%	27.4%	26.7%
Return on Tangible Equity	10.9%	13.2%	12.6%	13.3%	12.4%	11.4%	

BNSF 10-K

Cash Flow (per BNSF 10-K) ($ millions)	2016	2015	2014	2013	2012	2011	2/3/10 - 12/31/10	Cumulative Total
Net Income	$ 4,260	$ 4,915	$ 4,397	$ 4,271	$ 3,720	$ 3,273	$ 2,382	
Net Cash provided by op. activities	$ 7,638	$ 7,984	$ 7,005	$ 6,205	$ 5,900	$ 6,177	$ 4,585	
Capex excluding equipment	3,225	4,398	3,734	2,975	2,596	2,726	1,953	
Acquisition of equipment	614	1,226	1,509	943	952	763	445	
Total Capex	$ 3,839	$ 5,624	$ 5,243	$ 3,918	$ 3,548	$ 3,489	$ 2,398	$ 28,059
Free Cash Flow	$ 3,799	$ 2,360	$ 1,762	$ 2,287	$ 2,352	$ 2,688	$ 2,187	$ 17,435
Return on total $42.7B purchase price	8.9%	5.5%	4.1%	5.4%	5.5%	6.3%	5.1%	5.8%

BNSF 10-K Cash Flow

Takeaways

There are several takeaways from Buffett's evolution of investment style.

1. Buffett's track record on a percentage basis was most impressive when he handled smaller sums and followed Ben Graham's model of buying cheap companies based on balance sheet values.

2. Buffett added the most dollar value to Berkshire while applying his "Later Buffett" style of valuing companies based on the power of their brand and related earnings power.

3. Buffett always insisted on buying value but evolved in his definition of value. Checklists are important in a repetitive situation where safety is paramount such as flying a plane or piloting a ship. An investment checklist is useful for consistently applying an investment discipline, but common sense must prevail in assessing investments. Buffett has a mental model in assessing investments, but does not slavishly follow a checklist. Reflecting on the bond ratings company, Moody's, Buffett explained,

   > ...I would not want the cop-out, really, of 'I was relying on a rating agency.' And the rating agencies, they have models, and we all have models in our mind, you know, when we're investing. But they've got them all worked out, with a lot of—a lot of checklists and all of that sort of thing. I don't believe in those, myself. All I can say is, I've got a model in my mind. Everybody has a model in their mind when they're making investments. But reliance on models, you know, work 98 percent of the time, but it's—they never work 100 percent of the time. And everybody ought to realize that, that's using them.[36]

4. Buffett adapted over time but he was consistent in evaluating his investment ideas by assessing three questions:

   - Do I understand the business and does the business have a sustainable competitive advantage?

   - What is the quality and capability of management?

   - Is the price sensible after considering what is an appropriate margin of safety?

213

5. Buffett was always looking ahead with fresh eyes. Even though BNSF had recently doubled in price prior to his initial purchases, he recognized that the stock was still attractively valued given how the industry had consolidated and become more efficient, and how the company was poised for a boost from the economy.

CHAPTER 20

Case Studies

Two roads diverged in a wood, and I—I took the one less traveled by, and that has made all the difference.

—ROBERT FROST, *The Road Not Taken*

John Templeton, Peter Lynch, and Warren Buffett all shared Robert Frost's intrepid hiker's tenacity, willingness to explore new horizons, and independent thinking. They pursued roads less travelled, which made all the difference to them, and it can for you too.

Will Danoff has managed the Fidelity Contrafund for more than twenty-seven years, and his average annual return of 12.9 percent has outperformed 95 percent of U.S. diversified stock funds, according to Morningstar, Inc.[1] He trained under Peter Lynch and sought investment advice from Warren Buffett. Danoff recalled Peter Lynch's tenacity, "Peter believed in turning over more rocks than anybody else. The more companies you see, the more opportunities you will find."[2] As the Contrafund grew to more than $100 billion in asset size, he sought advice from Warren Buffett on how to manage the large sum, and Buffett advised him to "bet big on his best ideas."[3]

Berkshire benefitted from betting big on Buffett's best ideas, including putting 40 percent of his net worth into American Express in the mid-1960s. Many of Buffett's bold bets were in companies with a product characterized by repeat purchases, or a "tollgate," with strong consumer loyalty, whose future earnings power was undervalued. A careful study of Buffett's notable investments and the context behind each one is an instructive way to recognize and capitalize on similar opportunities in the future.

As we've already seen, there are common threads to his key investments:

Predictable businesses he understands: Buffett looks for businesses where he understands the product, the nature of competition, and what can go wrong over time, to allow him to reasonably predict what the business will look like in ten years. This leads him to predictable businesses with consistent earning power with little or no debt.

> *Charlie and I in managing Berkshire try to put money in things that we understand. And when I say "understand," I mean where we think we know in a reasonable way what the economics will look like in five or ten or twenty years... We'll stick to within what we consider to be our circle of competence.*[4]

Buffett recommends that investors understand the business and stay with businesses where surprises are few:

> *"Charlie and I avoid businesses whose futures we can't evaluate, no matter how exciting their products may be... We stick with businesses whose profit picture for decades to come seems reasonably predictable."*[5]

In situations where the investment may be popular, but not transparent, such as collateralized debt obligations (CDOs), even though they may be rated highly by Wall Street analysts or credit rating agencies, if you don't understand it, leave it alone. CDOs poisoned the financial crisis. "Anybody that is investing in something they consider opaque should just walk away, I mean, whether it's a common stock or a new invention or whatever it may be."[6]

Buffett uses *Value Line* as a snapshot of facts for reviewing the historical profile of a company.

> *I don't know what we pay for Value Line. Charlie and I both get it in our respective offices. We get incredible value out of it because it gives us the quickest way to review a huge number of key factors that tell us whether we're basically interested in a company.*

Buffett identifies the key variables in a particular business and evaluates how predictable they are. Assuming they were predictable, he would then evaluate the company's future earnings stream to determine whether its earnings power over the medium- to long-term would be worse, as good, or better than the past. If Buffett didn't know what would likely happen to the company in the future, he passes.

Views stock as part of a business: Even when buying a part of a company, Buffett thinks in terms of buying the entire company because it enables him to think as a businessman instead of a stock speculator. A stock is nothing more than a piece of a business. He evaluates the stock the same way he would any business including competition, what can go wrong, and its long-term earnings power.

Share of Mind: Buffett views share of mind just as important—if not more—than share of market, especially for consumer product companies. American Express is an interesting case study.

> *We always think in terms of share of mind versus share of market—because if the share of mind is there, the share of market will follow. American Express had a very special position in people's minds about financial integrity over the years—and ubiquity of acceptance.*[7]
>
> *Get in the mind of the consumer, Coca-Cola means something to most people in the world. RC Cola doesn't mean anything. Coke is where you are likely to have a smile on your face. Disney is the same way. It is about trust. It is about a favorable meaning. Does your face light up? Are memories and associations good? Will it be true 5–10 years from now?*[8]

Economic Moat: Buffett's most important assessment of a business is evaluating its competitive advantage and determining whether that advantage is strong and durable. He refers to the competitive advantage—what differentiates the product or service—as a moat around the business.

> *We think of every business as an economic castle. And castles are subject to marauders. And in capitalism, with any castle—razor blades, soft drinks, or what have you—you have to expect and even want the capitalistic system to work in a way that millions of people out there with capital are thinking about ways to take your castle away from you and appropriate it for their own use. Then the question is, 'What kind of moat do you have around that castle that protects it?' See's Candy has a wonderful moat around its castle…We tell our managers we want the moat widened every year.*[9]

A company has a wide moat if a competitor were handed $1 billion and they still couldn't impair the fortunes of the company. Competitive advantages, or moats, can include being a low cost producer, such as GEICO; high switching costs where it is too troublesome to switch to another company's product, such as Microsoft's Office; scale advantage, such as Coca-Cola; intangible assets that prevent other companies from duplicating its products, such as patents; network effect that increases as more people use the product, such as Facebook; and a reputational advantage for product quality and value, such as Costco, Amazon, and in 1964, American Express.

Buffett noted that several industries that transformed society such as television, autos, radios, and airlines failed to deliver rewards to investors. He emphasized that,

> *The key to investing is not assessing how much an industry is going to affect society or how much it will grow, but rather determining the competitive advantage of any given company and, above all, the durability of that advantage. The products or services that have wide, sustainable moats around them are the ones that deliver rewards to investors.*[10]

The true test of a business with an insulated competitive moat is whether the company has pricing power. Buffett said, "We like buying businesses where we feel that there's some untapped pricing power."[11] Additionally, as we saw in the case of See's Candy, the best businesses are those that generate the most cash with the fewest assets.

In sum, the businesses most attractive to Buffett had pricing flexibility, high returns on capital, were predictable, generate cash, and preferably were buying back shares.

Management: Buffett looks for the same qualities in managers of partially owned businesses as he does in Berkshire's managers: people that have intelligence, passion, and integrity, whom he likes, trusts, and admires. He wants management to view shareholders as partners in the business, and this is reflected in how they are compensated and how candid they are in communicating with shareholders. "To carry the castle analogy further, we not only look for a great economic castle, but we look for a great knight in charge of that castle…And of course the question is, 'How much of the castle does the knight get for doing that?'"[12] Just as Buffett stays within his circle of competence, he wants the management of Berkshire's wholly owned companies to stay within theirs too. Buffett's key filter is to determine whether the manager loves the business or the money. He isn't interested in buying from a seller who just wants to get rich; he wants to solve a problem for the seller. He can promise the seller that the business will never be resold and that they will continue to run their business their own way as though they still owned the entire business.

Buffett wants management that have a strong work ethic, have fun, and enjoy what they do. He looks for good communicators who do more than they are asked. The same filter can apply to partially owned companies. Does management have the passion, integrity, intelligence, experience, and dedication to excel; or does management's love of money and arrogance distract them from key business fundamentals? "If the seller cares more about the money when selling their business, it probably won't work out. Go for people who are nuts about what they do."[13] "We look for brains, energy, and integrity in our people."[14]

Price: Lastly Buffett decides on an appropriate price to pay for the stock relative to his estimate of intrinsic value of the company. Intrinsic value is the present value of all future cash flows of the company. Buffett uses the risk-free, long-term government bond rate as a constant yardstick to discount his estimate of future cash flows. He doesn't split hairs over the discount rate but focuses instead on understanding and being right about the business, which means having conviction about where the business will be in ten years. To assess profitability and productivity, Buffett compares owner earnings to tangible assets. Owner-earnings is equal to normalized (excluding unusual items) earnings plus amortization of intangibles. Tangible assets exclude intangibles, primarily goodwill. Return on tangible equity is the same as return on tangible assets for companies without debt. Ultimately, he is buying future earnings power at a reasonable to bargain price. Buffett explained, "We're basically looking—we don't find them very often—for things that just scream at us. We're looking for things where if our calculations are off, it's still obvious the investment is wise."[15]

When Buffett believed he was staring at a fat pitch where the market price was much lower than his estimate of the company's intrinsic value, he swung hard and bought in quantity. Charlie Munger elaborated,

> *It's not given to human beings to have such talent that they can know everything about everything all the time. But it is given to human beings who work hard at it—who look and sift the world for a mispriced bet—that they can occasionally find one. And the wise ones bet heavily when the world offers them that opportunity. They bet big when they have the odds. And the rest of the time, they don't. It's just that simple. That is a very simple concept. And yet, in investment management, practically nobody operates that way. We operate that way—I'm talking about Buffett and Munger.*[16]

Buffett added, "A great investment opportunity occurs when a marvelous business encounters a one-time huge, but solvable, problem as was the case many years back at both American Express and GEICO. Overall, however, we've done better by avoiding dragons than by slaying them."[17]

American Express

In American Express's 1964 annual report, President Howard Clark candidly acknowledged that "we will remember 1964 as much for the very gratifying improvement in sales and the record net earnings as for the warehousing problem which occupied much of our attention." As indicated in the following table, the average annual growth for the previous decade for revenues and EPS was 12 percent and 10 percent respectively. In 1964, revenues accelerated to 17.7 percent growth while EPS grew 11.5 percent, driven by growing awareness abroad of the value of the American Express Travelers Cheque, which was universally accepted as a trusted and accepted form of safe money. International appeal for the Travelers Cheque was clearly evident as, for the first time in its seventy-three-year history, international sales of its Travelers Cheques almost equaled sales from its domestic offices.

Sales were also booming for the American Express credit card. Credit card billings leaped 42 percent to $344 million in 1964 and had more than doubled in three years. Total cards in force grew 20 percent to 1.225 million as 1964 marked the first time consumers could use the company's credit card to charge airline tickets. American Express started its credit card business in 1958 against the incumbent pioneer Diners Club. The strength of American Express's brand and its pricing power were already evident in 1961, when the company raised the price on its charge cards 33 percent to $8 from $6 a year, and on its supplemental cards to $4 from $3. These were priced at a premium to Diners Club rates, which charged $5 a year for the primary card and $2.50 a year for supplemental cards. In 1962, American Express's credit card division was profitable for the first time.

Against this backdrop of vibrant growth in its respected mainline business, American Express was a victim of fraud on a grand scale in its small-field warehousing division. The fraud is commonly referred to as the "salad oil scandal." American Express established its field warehousing division as a way for the company to make loans to businesses who stored their inventory of commodities. Tino De Angelis, through his company Allied Crude Vegetable

American Express						
($ 000)	1964	1963	1962	1961	1960	10 year CAGR
Revenues	$ 118,144	$ 100,418	$ 86,771	$ 77,378	$ 74,709	12.1%
Net Income	$ 12,541	$ 11,264	$ 10,131	$ 9,204	$ 9,007	9.7%
EPS	$ 2.81	$ 2.52	$ 2.27	$ 2.06	$ 2.02	9.7%
Dividends/share	$ 1.40	$ 1.40	$ 1.25	$ 1.20	$ 1.20	9.1%
Shareholders Equity	$ 83,613	$ 78,696	$ 68,356	$ 63,805	$ 60,102	
ROAE	15.5%	15.3%	15.3%	14.9%	15.5%	
% change EPS	11.5%	11.0%	10.2%	2.0%	6.9%	

Oil Refining Corporation, was a customer, and American Express gave him warehouse receipts for his millions of pounds of stored vegetable oil. The receipts could then be taken to a bank and exchanged for cash, and the lender, such as Bank of America or Procter & Gamble, would own the oil as collateral, or so they thought. American Express's seal of approval as custodian vouched for the inventory. The American Express subsidiary, American Express Warehousing Ltd., had a storage facility on the same property as Allied Crude and was reportedly storing about $80 million of soybean oil in four separate tanks. The fraud occurred when De Angelis substituted water for most of the oil, and he deceived inspectors by strategically placing just enough oil at the inspection location of the tank to pass the audit. He also shuttled the same oil through a maze of pipes to several tanks to convince inspectors there was more oil in storage than was really present.

De Angelis tried to corner the soybean oil market by using cash from exchanging its warehouse receipts issued by American Express, and loans from Wall Street banks, to buy massive futures in oil. At the time, Allied Crude was the nation's largest exporter of vegetable oil. Eventually inspectors were informed about attempted bribery and failed deliveries. Upon more thorough inspection, they found 90 percent water, which exposed the scandal and resulted in a crash in the futures market. Allied Crude filed for bankruptcy in November 1963 for failure to meet a margin call of $19 million, and the swindle eventually defrauded fifty-one lenders out of $150 million.

In January 1964 American Express Warehousing, a limited liability corporation, filed for Chapter 11 bankruptcy as "a step toward obtaining an over-all forum for the orderly determination of the validity and amount of claims against the subsidiary company."[18] The company added that, although it wasn't legally liable to the holders of the warehouse receipts, it felt "morally bound to do everything it can, consistent with its overall responsibilities to see that excess liabilities are satisfied should the subsidiary be held legally liable for amounts in excess of its insurance coverage and other assets."[19] American Express was defending its public confidence and the goodwill of its franchise.

Buffett urged American Express not to ignore the claims against its subsidiary even though it had legal justification to do so:

> I would be willing to testify, at my own expense, to the fact that we would not have purchased our 70,000 shares of stock if we had thought the parent company was going to ignore the claims against the subsidiary, because our feeling would be that the long-term value of the enterprise would be substantially reduced. In other words, it is our judgment that American Express, by making a fair and perhaps even generous offer, is an enterprise that is worth very substantially more than American Express disclaiming responsibility for its subsidiaries' acts.[20]

Buffett astutely saw the long-term reputational benefit to American Express to stand behind its "promise to pay" far outweighed the short-term cost of the salad-oil claim.

Although American Express Warehousing's LLC structure meant that the parent company wouldn't be legally liable for its debt, the parent company, American Express, was an unincorporated joint stock enterprise, which technically meant that its shareholders could be assessed as partners for any debt not covered by its assets. Although no such assessment had been levied in nearly a century of operation, and was generally understood to be an academic matter, it didn't prevent four mutual funds, including Putnam Growth Fund and Fidelity Capital Fund, from disgorging a collective 2.5 percent of American Express's 4.46 million shares outstanding in the last quarter of 1963. With shareholder's equity in 1963 of $78.7 million as backstop, the stock sank to $35 from a pre-scandal high of $62.375 in 1963. While other institutional shareholders fled in fear, Buffett bought. It was particularly honorable that Buffett encouraged American Express to pay the claims, even though it was possible that, as a shareholder under American Express's unique corporate form, he could have been assessed personally to cover the company's shortfalls if the company went broke.

On April 9, 1964, American Express offered to pay $58 million to settle claims totaling $126 million. Terms included a payment of up to $45 million by American Express on the condition that the payment was tax deductible and the remainder was in insurance proceeds. Twelve insurance companies that carried $30 million in policies refused to acknowledge that the policies covered losses due to fraud. President Howard Clark said the amount of the offer was determined by a "careful examination by the directors in relation to the amount the parent could afford to pay."[21] After eighteen months of negotiations, American Express settled for most of the $144 million claims for $90 million, including: a payment of $58 million by American Express over a six-year period with an initial payment of $30 million; a promise to give creditors the first $20 million of any insurance recovery; $5.9 million raised from selling oil recovered in the scandal. Tino De Angelis was sentenced to twenty years in federal prison for conspiracy and interstate transport of forged receipts.

Warren Buffett bought 5 percent of American Express during 1964 for $13 million, which was 40 percent of his capital. even though his previous policy was to commit no more than 25 percent of the partnership's capital to any one investment. Buffett said, "American Express—the name only is a great franchise...American Express had over 80 percent of the traveler's check market nationally, and nothing could shake it."[22] Buffett convinced himself that American Express's fundamental business advantage and the tremendous float of the traveler's check business was still intact by sitting behind the cashier in Ross's Steak House restaurant in Omaha to see how many American Express receipts were used to pay for dinner. He also toured many Omaha banks to verify whether the scandal dented the use of American Express traveler's checks.

This purchase was made after extensive investigation among Travelers Cheque users, bank tellers, bank officers, credit card establishments, card holders, and competitors in these various lines of endeavor. All confirmed that American Express's competitive vigor and preeminent trade position had not been damaged by the salad oil problem.[23]

President Howard Clark personally acquired 2,500 shares in December 1965, which increased his holdings by 22 percent to 13,740, and this may have been another signal of confidence to Buffett.

Buffett later recalled in the Berkshire Hathaway 1980 annual report that American Express was a one-of-a-kind company, temporarily reeling from the effects of a fiscal blow that did not destroy their exceptional underlying economics. The American Express brand and its traveler's checks, which stood for financial integrity as a money substitute, were not harmed. He said that the company was not a turnaround, but an extraordinary business franchise with a "localized excisable cancer (needing to be sure, a skilled surgeon)." Buffett sold the stock in 1967 for a $20 million profit or a 154 percent gain. The stock quintupled from a low of $35/share to $189/share in five years.[24] Also during those five years, the cost of the charge card grew to $20 in five years with no loss of acceptance.

Takeaways

Buffett's purchase of American Express in 1964 was a classic case of taking advantage of a stock sell-off driven by a non-structural, temporary, and solvable problem. The issue involved a minor division of the company that wasn't a core business, and the division's liability exposure was capped due to its limited liability structure. American Express was not legally bound to compensate the victims of the fraud, but it correctly believed it was ethically bound to fund the liability to preserve its hallowed trust and reputation that underscored the currency value of its travelers check. As far as Buffett was concerned, "that $60 million was a dividend they'd mailed to the stockholders, and it got lost in the mail."[25]

The confidence to view $60 million as a lost check in the mail and not disruptive to American Express's consumer allegiance came from Buffett's first-hand research.

> I had learned that from a fellow name Phil Fisher who wrote this great book called Common Stocks and Uncommon Profits. And he calls it the scuttlebutt method. And Phil was a remarkable guy. I first used it back in 1963 when American Express had this great Salad Oil Scandal that people worried about bankrupting the company. So I went out to restaurants and saw what people were doing with their American Express card, and I went to banks to see what they were doing with travelers' checks and everything. And clearly American Express had lost some money from this scandal, but it hadn't affected their consumer franchise.[26]
>
> American Express still had two-thirds of the worldwide market after 60–70 years despite charging more than these other well-entrenched, well-known competitors. Any time you can charge more for a product and maintain or increase market share against well-entrenched, well-known competitors, you know that you have something very special in people's minds...You could see this dominance prevail. It told you what was in

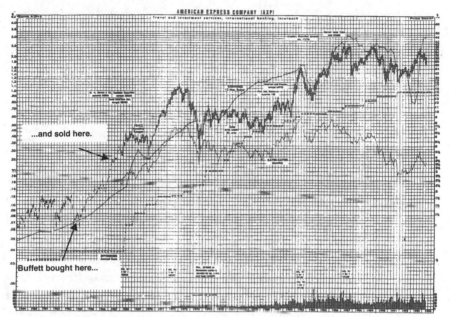

Figure 16. American Express

people's minds—which is why I bought into the stock in 1964. We bought 5 percent of the company—which was a huge investment for us at the time. I was only managing $20 million at the time. But you could see that this share of mind—this consumer franchise—had not been lost.[27]

Assuming Buffett didn't buy American Express at its all-time low of $35/ share but close to it, say $40/share, he would have paid 14x 1964 EPS of $2.81. This is equal to an earnings yield of 7 percent that was growing at a double-digit rate, and the company was earning a respectable mid-teens ROAE (return on average equity).

Buffett's purchase of American Express broke the mold of following Ben Graham's model of buying tangible assets statistically cheap in a diversified portfolio. The value of American Express was not in any tangible asset, but in customers' goodwill because of its inherent promise to make good on the cash value of its traveler's check and the acceptance of its credit card. Failure to make good on its non-core warehouse receipts may have caused doubt about its foundational promise to make good on its core traveler's check. Buffett was convinced that consumers were unfazed by the salad oil scandal and were still loyal to the travelers check and to its credit card.

Buffett bet big on his best idea where he had conviction. It wasn't diluted among many other cigar butts. Recall that in November 1965 Buffett informed his limited partners that he might invest up to 40 percent in a single security if he believed that his facts and reasoning had a high probability of being correct and coupled with a low probability of a risk of permanent loss of value. One could argue that he should have held it longer, but he did revisit American Express years later with success.

American Express (The Sequel)

The Salad Oil Scandal in 1964 threatened American Express's hallowed reputation for its "promise to pay," and twenty-seven years later in 1991, the company faced a crisis that threatened its reputation of honoring its commitments. President Howard Clark's goal was to minimize American Express's economic vulnerability by diversifying into other areas related to travel and financial services. In 1966 American Express acquired an investment bank specializing in underwriting government bonds, W.H. Morton & Co.; and in 1968 it acquired the large property and casualty insurer, Fireman's Fund Insurance Company. James D. Robinson III became Chairman & CEO in 1977 during an embarrassing period when four of American Express's acquisition attempts failed. In 1981 American Express acquired one of the nation's leading brokerages, Shearson Loeb Rhoades Inc. Shearson, which operated as an independent division, then acquired Atlanta-based brokerage Robinson-Humphrey among others. Sanford (Sandy) I. Weill became president of Shearson in early 1983, and he immediately expanded the financial services supermarket by acquiring Ayco, a financial counseling firm. In 1984 American Express acquired the financial planning company Investors Diversified Services, more commonly known as IDS, and also added Lehman Brothers Kuhn, Loeb & Co. Sandy Weill left in August 1985 when he realized he was not going to be CEO.

The empire became unwieldy as price wars in the property and casualty insurance arena led to declining earnings and the need to spend $430 million to boost Fireman's reserves. American Express spun off the insurance company in a series of public stock offerings from 1985–1988. The funds were allocated for Shearson to acquire E.F. Hutton in 1988. The aftermath of the 1987 Crash impacted Shearson's credit write-offs, and American Express had to boost Shearson's loan-loss reserves by $900 million. By 1990, Shearson's balance sheet was leveraged 100:1 with tangible equity of $627 million and assets of $66.5 billion.

Meanwhile, American Express's core traveler's check and charge card business was under siege. The traveler's check faced competition from no-fee bank cards and debit cards. The charge card faced intense competition and pressure from Visa and MasterCard, who charged lower fees and were gaining market share. Merchants complained the supposed higher-value American Express customer wasn't worth the higher fee. A group of restaurants in Boston staged a revolt referred to as the Boston Fee Party to protest high rates. Pressured to cut costs in the midst of the 1990 recession, many merchants stopped accepting the American Express card.

Standard & Poor's downgraded Amex senior debt to AA- from AA in July 1991, despite asset sales at Shearson and plans to securitize and sell as much as $1 billion of charge card receivables.

With this backdrop, Warren Buffett's close friend and head of Fund American Cos. (formerly known as Fireman's Fund Insurance), John J. "Jack" Byrne, also a board member of American Express, suggested to James Robinson III that Buffett might be interested in an investment. Robinson called Buffett and within a week, on August 1, 1991, they struck a deal for Buffett to invest $300 million for a private issue of convertible preferred stock (called a Preferred Equity Redemption Stock—or Perc). The preferred stock carried a fixed dividend of 8.85 percent, but since 70 percent of dividend income was exempt from corporate taxes, the taxable equivalent yield was more than 11 percent. The preferred was to be converted into common stock three or four years after issuance, representing a 2.5 percent stake in the company, at the option of American Express with no floor and with a maximum capped upside of 38 percent. The deal benefitted American Express with Buffett's halo effect of an equity infusion without immediately diluting its shareholders.

Buffett originally offered to invest $500 million but American Express wanted to minimize its potential share dilution, and they agreed to $300 million. Buffett admired the American Express franchise; he was familiar with and understood the business, and he respected CEO James D. Robinson III. "We're buying to be in with Jim."[28]

In 1993 Harvey Golub became CEO, and he orchestrated an aggressive restructuring with the sale of Shearson's retail brokerage and asset management business to Primerica, headed by Sandy Weill. In May 1994 American

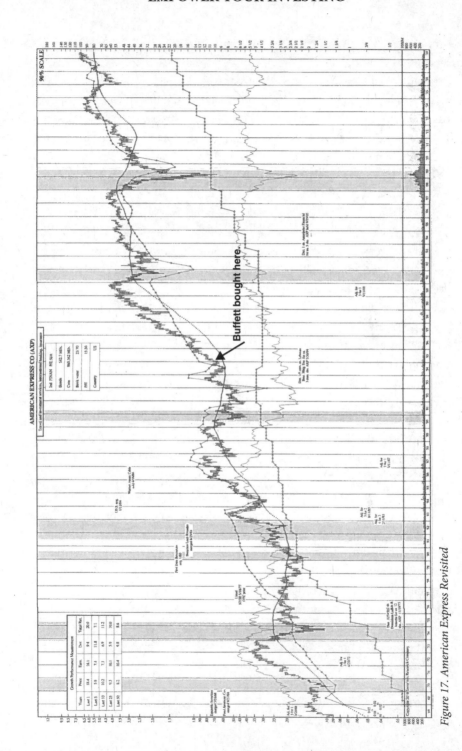

Figure 17. American Express Revisited

Express spun off the remaining investment banking business of Shearson as Lehman Brothers Holdings (which later became the posterchild of the financial crisis in 2008 when it filed for bankruptcy). Golub also instituted massive cost cutting and refocused its credit card business. Buffett remained impressed with the company's strong global brand name: "American Express is synonymous with financial integrity and money substitutes around the world."[29]

Buffett explained why he not only retained the converted shares but quadrupled his position.

> *Our Percs were due to convert into common stock in August 1994, and in the month before I was mulling whether to sell upon conversion. One reason to hold was Amex's outstanding CEO, Harvey Golub, who seemed likely to maximize whatever potential the company had (a supposition that has since proved true—in spades). But the size of that potential was in question: Amex faced relentless competition from a multitude of card-issuers, led by Visa. Weighing the arguments, I leaned toward sale.*
>
> *Here's where I got lucky During that month of decision, I played golf at Prouts Neck, Maine, with Frank Olson, CEO of Hertz. Frank is a brilliant manager, with intimate knowledge of the card business. So from the first tee on, I was quizzing him about the industry. By the time we reached the second green, Frank had convinced me that Amex's corporate card was a terrific franchise, and I had decided not to sell. On the back nine I turned buyer, and in a few months Berkshire owned 10 percent of the company.[30]*

Frank Olson told Buffett that his company was still paying 8 percent for Amex fees, and they felt compelled to continue paying.

Buffett was also impressed with Amex's announcement in September 1994 that it authorized the repurchase of up to 20 million shares—about 4 percent—and in the last quarter of 1994, had repurchased $555 million. Berkshire Hathaway converted its preferred for a 2.5 percent stake in American Express in August 1994. By the end of the year, Berkshire owned 5.5 percent of the company through open market purchases. Buffett continued buying aggressively and, by February 1995, Berkshire owned 9.8 percent of the company; and by September 1995, Berkshire owned 10.1 percent of American Express.

Takeaways

Buffett was familiar with American Express, had tracked it for a long time, and understood its products well:

My American Express history includes a couple of episodes: In the mid-1960s, just after the stock was battered by the company's infamous salad-oil scandal, we put about 40 percent of Buffett Partnership Ltd.'s capital into the stock—the largest investment the partnership had ever made. I should add that this commitment gave us over 5 percent ownership in Amex at a cost of $13 million. As I write this, we own just under 10 percent, which has cost us $1.36 billion. (Amex earned about $12.5 million in 1964 and $1.4 billion in 1994.)

My history with Amex's IDS unit, which today contributes about a third of earnings of the company, goes back even further. I first purchased stock in IDS in 1953 when it was growing rapidly and selling at a price-earnings ratio of only 3. (There was a lot of low-hanging fruit in those days.) I even produced a long report—do I ever write a short one?—on the company that I sold for $1 through an ad in The Wall Street Journal.

Obviously American Express and IDS, (recently renamed American Express Financial Advisors) are far different operations today from what they were then. Nevertheless, I find that a long-term familiarity with a company and its products is often helpful in evaluating it."[31]

In early 1995 Buffett was not deterred from paying a price close to Amex's previous all-time high, which had been reached about seven years earlier before the 1987 Crash. In 1995 Amex reported core EPS from continuing operations of $3.11. At a split adjusted price of $33 in early 1995, Buffett paid an attractive price about 11x core earnings for a company that was more focused on its core travel and charge card business after divesting a volatile and troubled brokerage, was generating robust cash flow, and was embarking on an aggressive share repurchase program. Buffett's conviction was reinforced from his scuttlebutt research conversation over golf with Hertz's CEO Frank Olsen.

Walt Disney

Buffett bought Disney in 1966 using a sum-of-the-parts valuation, but the parts were not based on physical equipment or inventory, but intangibles. Buffett invested $4 million in Disney when the entire company had a market value of $80 million. Buffett observed that the cost of several of Disney's animated movies, such as *Snow White, Bambi* and all those other cartoons had been written off the books. They alone were worth that much ($80 million). You had Disneyland to boot, and Walt Disney as a partner for nothing."[32] He estimated that Disney was then worth $300–$400 million.

Buffett was attracted to Disney because it had a valuable movie vault, which represented a perpetual royalty that could be recycled every seven years, was written down to $0 by the company, and wasn't valued by Wall Street. Moreover, the movie vault was even more valuable due to a hugely popular new release of *Mary Poppins*.

> We bought 5 percent of the Walt Disney Company in 1966. It cost us $4 million. $80 million bucks was the valuation of the whole thing. It had 300 and some acres in Anaheim. The Pirate's Ride had just been put in. It cost seventeen million bucks. The whole company was selling for $80 million. Mary Poppins had just come out. Mary Poppins made about $30 million that year, and seven years later you're going to show it to kids the same age. It's like having an oil well where all the oil seeps back in...in 1966 they had 220 pictures of one sort or another. They wrote them all down to zero—there was no residual values placed on the value of any Disney picture through the '60s. So you got all of this for eighty million bucks, and you got Walt Disney to work for you.
>
> It was incredible...in 1966 people said, 'Well, Mary Poppins is terrific this year, but they're not going to have another Mary Poppins next year, so the earnings will be down.' I don't care if the earnings are down like that. You know you've got Mary Poppins to throw out in seven more years, assuming kids squawk a little. I mean there's no better system than to have something where, essentially, you get a new crop every seven years and you get to charge more each time...I went out to see Walt Disney. He'd never heard of me. I was 35 years old. We sat down and he told me the whole plan for the company—he couldn't have been a nicer guy...Essentially, they (Wall Street) ignored it because it was so familiar. But that happens periodically on Wall Street.[33]

Takeaways

Buffett invested in Disney when the entire company's market value was priced less than what a Disney blockbuster movie grosses in an opening weekend today. Buffett recognized that despite an accounting standard that forced Disney to write down its older movies to zero value, the film vault was extremely valuable since the movies could be resurrected and monetized every seven years with a new generation of kids. Even though Buffett could easily see how the company was worth so much more than its market value, he still traveled to meet the engaging founder, who passed away several months after

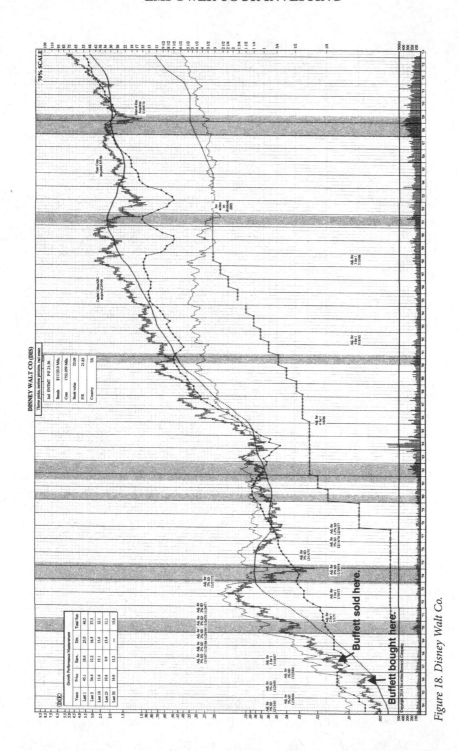

Figure 18. Disney Walt Co.

Buffett made his investment. Sometimes opportunities to find hidden value lie waiting to be discovered even in the most familiar companies. Buffett sold Disney one year later for a 50 percent gain.

Coca-Cola

Warren had a long-time favorable appreciation of the commercial appeal of Coca-Cola. He recalled having his first Coca-Cola in either 1935 or 1936. The enterprising Buffett collected over 8,000 used silver bottle caps from gas station coolers and found that Coca-Cola was the overwhelming favorite of consumers. Over 50 years later, he swallowed over a 6 percent stake in the company, which was his largest investment ever.

Buffett reported his first investment in Coca-Cola in Berkshire's 1988 annual report at 14,172,500 shares for a cost of $592,540,000. He paid an average price per share of $41.81 for a 3.9 percent ownership stake. In March 1989, *The Wall Street Journal* reported that Buffett acquired a 6.3 percent stake. Buffett explained,

> *Coke is exactly the kind of company I like... I like the products I can understand. I don't know what a transistor is, for example... More and more in recent years, their superb decision-making and the focus of their strategies have emerged more clearly to me... (and the purchase) is the ultimate case of putting your money where your mouth is.*[34]

Let's review a few of the developments that occurred prior to Buffett's purchase to better understand what attracted him to the beloved American brand, Coca-Cola. Coca-Cola was invented in 1886 by Dr. John Pemberton, a pharmacist in Atlanta, Georgia. He was a Civil War veteran with a morphine addiction looking to cure his ailment. His unique recipe for syrup and carbonated water, originally marketed as "Delicious and Refreshing," has remained a closely guarded secret ever since. In 1923 Robert Woodruff became president of Coca-Cola, where he remained an active leader for more than sixty years. He is legendary within the company for his order at the beginning of World War II "that every man in uniform get a bottle of Coca-Cola for 5 cents, wherever he is and whatever it costs the company." Military men and women around the world consumed more than 5 billion bottles of Coca-Cola during the war. After the war, Coca-Cola became a symbol of friendship and refreshment, which sparked worldwide growth.

J. Paul Austin, chairman of the board and chief executive officer, was a Harvard educated attorney who began his career in 1949 in Coca-Cola's legal department. He transferred to South Africa in 1954 to run Coke's operations and eventually became president of Coca-Cola in 1962, CEO in 1966, and chairman in 1970. To his credit, Austin led a nearly tenfold increase in Coca-Cola's net income in his eighteen years of control. However, in 1980 Pepsi's market share surged ahead of Coke in the prized category of supermarket sales driven by the "Pepsi Challenge" blind taste test, which indicated that consumers preferred Pepsi's sweeter taste. Coke had also become a far-flung conglomerate with operations in water purification, shrimp farming, wine, coffee, plastic cutlery, and plastic bags. Austin twice tried to acquire American Express, but the Coke board was skeptical over valuation and operational compatibility. The lure supposedly was to attract James R. Robinson III, Amex's Chairman and fellow Coke board member, to succeed Austin. In the ten years before Roberto Goizueta became CEO, Coke's total return to investors averaged less than 1 percent a year.

In June 1980 Roberto Goizueta was named president of Coca-Cola, and on March 1, 1981, he succeeded J. Paul Austin as chairman of the board and chief executive officer. Roberto Goizueta was born in Cuba in 1931, graduated at the top of his secondary school class in Havana, and earned a chemical engineering degree from Yale. Goizueta walked away from lucrative opportunities to work with either his father managing his mother's family sugar mill and refinery or with his wife's family wholesale food business, which catapulted his in-laws to one of the wealthiest families in Cuba. He wanted no part of nepotism but wanted to compete and be evaluated on his own merit. Instead, he responded to an anonymous ad from a food enterprise that wanted to hire a chemical engineer. Compensation, however, was one-half what he could make with his father, and there would be lots of travel. The food enterprise was Coca-Cola. Goizueta's father advised Roberto to buy one hundred shares of Coca-Cola with his $8,000 loan saying, "You shouldn't work for someone else. You should work for yourself."[35] The one hundred shares were custodied in New York where they remained until he died. Those 100 shares through stock splits grew to 29,000 shares worth more than $1 million. It was the only asset that he was able to keep when his family fled Cuba in 1960 following Castro's takeover.

Austin had tapped Goizueta to upgrade, modernize, and standardize Coke's engineering division at headquarters so that they could be standardized and adopted as best practices globally. Goizueta's assignment for Austin revealed Goizueta's focus on accountability, planning, pay for performance, and collaborative decision making. He instituted what are now commonly referred to as roving corporate black-belts. These headquarters-trained engineers ensured best practices by traveling to a division to solve manufacturing problems using analytical thinking and then training locals to execute in a standardized manner. Success with the corporate re-engineering project led Goizueta to become Coca-Cola's youngest vice president ever at age thirty-five.

Goizueta's fast-tracked career at Coca-Cola included spearheading the ultra-secret lab work developing Diet Coke. Austin had killed the project due to fears over cannibalizing Coke's diet drink, Tab.

Goizueta's first move as Chairman & CEO was to name Don Keough as president. Keough was president of Coke's North America operations and had a reputation as a charismatic salesman and savvy marketer. In 1958 Keough bought the house across the street from Warren Buffett as a young family man. Two years later Buffett invited Keough to join Buffett's newly formed investment company named Berkshire Hathaway with a $10,000 investment, but Keough regrettably declined. The two remained friends for life. The combination of Goizueta's focus on financial discipline and Keough's marketing finesse proved to be a symbiotic winning team.

In his first annual letter to shareholders in the 1980 annual report, Goizueta publicly stated that Coca-Cola's goal during the 1980s was to exceed Coca-Cola's record during the decade of the 1970s of growing its sales and earnings at 12–13 percent and to achieve higher return on assets.

> [He conducted an] intensive global review of operating expense budgets during 1980 to reinsure that our operations are being run as efficiently as possible. We also are reexamining the way we manage our working capital requirements to provide added funds for reinvestment…(and) we will be looking closer than ever before at the management of productivities—of assets and of people.[36]

What Goizueta and Keough discovered during the global review was shocking. Coke was adrift without a strategic plan. Goizueta said, "The company had no sense of direction whatsoever. None."[37] Previously, division heads waited for their goals to be set by corporate headquarters and followed marching orders. Goizueta expected each division head to defend a three-year plan, with specific goals for which they were held accountable, including justification for capital spending and their expected returns.

Goizueta and Keough discovered that only the soft drink business earned more than the company's cost of capital. The wineries, water purification business, plastics, and food business all earned less than 10 percent of capital employed. Furthermore, he discovered there was no coordinated strategic planning or coordination. Decisions were reactionary without a framework for consistent financial accountability. Goizueta developed an analytical matrix that evaluated each of Coke's businesses based on key performance metrics,

"It's simple," says Goizueta. "You make a chart. Across the top you put your businesses: concentrate bottling, wine, foods, whatever. Then you put the financial characteristics on the other axis: margins, returns, cash flow reliability, capital requirements. Some, like the concentrate business, will emerge as superior businesses. Others, like wine look lousy."[38]

Goizueta was far ahead of his time in assessing each business for what is now called Economic Value Added (EVA). EVA is simply evaluating the excess return a division generates above their cost of capital. Goizueta judged all of the company's operations based on their after-tax operating profit in excess of a charge for capital. Goizueta explained,

> When you get right down to it, what I really do is allocate resources—capital, manpower. And I learned that when you start charging people for their capital, all sorts of things happen. All of a sudden, inventories get under control. You don't have three months' concentrate sitting around for an emergency... We're not just financial people, but until 1981, none of our operating executives could even read a balance sheet. What we've insisted on is weaving a strong financial thread into the marketing fabric of this company.[39]

In 1981 Coke sold its water purification business Aqua-Chem. In 1982 Coke sold its wine division and its private label instant coffee and tea business, and opened its first bottling plant in China since World War II. The company embarked on an aggressive plan of investments and joint ventures to restructure and consolidate its bottler system, to upgrade their machinery, and prepare them for more aggressive growth. In July 1982 the company introduced Diet Coke and quickly captured 17 percent of the U.S. diet soft drink market. By the end of 1983, it became the fourth largest-selling soft drink and the leading low-calorie drink in North America. Eventually, in 2010, its market share would outrank Pepsi and only trailed Classic Coke.

Goizueta hired a consulting firm to recommend how Coke could diversify from soft drinks, and establish domestic income parity with its dominant international operations, through a friendly acquisition with earnings that were predictable and non-dilutive. Coke bought Columbia Pictures in 1982 for $692 million with the idea of injecting its marketing know-how to film distribution. Despite movie successes such as *Tootsie, Gandhi, Karate Kid,* and *Ghostbusters*, Goizueta concluded the film business was difficult to manage and wasn't reliable and predictable. In 1987 Coke spun off 51 percent of Columbia as a taxable dividend to shareholders. In November 1989 Coke sold its 49 percent interest to Sony for $1.55 billion, a net gain of $509 million.

Coca-Cola introduced Cherry Coke in 1985 and Buffett praised the soda in Berkshire's 1985 annual report:

"After 48 years of allegiance to another soft drink (Pepsi), your chairman, in an unprecedented display of behavioral flexibility, has converted to your new Cherry Coke. Henceforth, it will be the Official Drink of the Berkshire Hathaway Annual Meeting."[40]

This was before Berkshire owned a share of the company. Buffett drinks five to six servings of Coke each day—Classic Coke at the office and Cherry Coke at home.

Several other notable events preceded Buffett's purchase of Coca-Cola:

- **Trimming fat:** Coca-Cola announced that it would lay off 8 percent of its 2,500 domestic soft drink division staff due to the consolidation of its independent bottlers, which had shrunk to 185 from 365 over the prior ten years. (Jan. 1988)

- **Accelerated share repurchases:** Coca-Cola announced 1981 earnings increased 15 percent and said it intended to use excess cash flow for share repurchases and that the share buyback pace might accelerate. (Feb. 1988)

- **Robust EPS and buybacks:** Coca-Cola reported 1Q 1988 EPS rose 16 percent and said that it expected the full-year EPS growth to mirror its excellent first quarter. The company repurchased 3.2 million shares in the quarter for a cumulative 9.7 million purchased under authorization to buy as many as 40 million shares by 1990. (April 1988)

- **WSJ touts cheap stocks:** *The Wall Street Journal's* "Heard on the Street" article, "Major Consumer-Staple Stock Issues Offer Buying Opportunities, Some Analysts Believe" touted Coca-Cola, McDonald's, Pepsi, and Anheuser-Busch as buying opportunities since many were selling at just a point or two above the market P/E of 12.5x estimated 1988 earnings compared to historical premiums to the S&P 500 of 25–35 percent. (September 8, 1988)

- **Deserved promotion:** Coke promoted Ira Hebert to president of the USA division to resurrect a slumbering giant that had become complacent to Pepsi. Hebert was credited with architecting Coke's memorable advertising campaigns, "It's the real thing," and "I'd like to buy the world a Coke." He said, "We need to add more excitement to the advertising."41 (October 1988)

- **Re-entering India:** Coca-Cola announced plans to re-enter India after an eleven-year absence when a new government began to open up to foreign investment. Coca-Cola had operated in India for twenty-seven years until 1977 when the Indian government that deposed Indira Gandhi ruled that foreign companies couldn't own more than 40 percent of their Indian subsidiaries and would have required Coke to hand over its secret concentrate formula. Coke walked and Pepsi also left. Now Coke was excited about re-entering the world's second most populated nation with 800 million people and where Coke enjoyed a 3:1 lead over Pepsi in international competition. (November 1988)

- **Coca-Cola Classic:** Tired of losing U.S. market share to Pepsi's sweeter cola driven by the "Pepsi Challenge," in 1985 Coke introduced "New Coke" which radically reformulated the original Coca-Cola with a much sweeter flavor. A large contingent of loyal original Coke consumers clamored for the return of their favorite American iconic drink. The uproar surprised Coke, and to their credit, the company remedied their marketing misstep, bringing back the original soda called "Coca-Cola Classic." It soon outsold New Coke and Pepsi. Buffett surely would have noticed the fiercely loyal consumers who opposed tampering with their slice of Americana in the distinctly shaped contoured bottle, which reinforced the power of its brand.

- **Cola dominance:** Cola's share of the soft drink market surged to 70 percent in 1988 from 64 percent in 1980, according to Wheat, First Securities, due in part to flavor fatigue from orange and root beer flavors and due to the addictive nature of caffeine in cola. Coke's worldwide market share of carbonated soda reached an all-time high of 45 percent in 1988, and Coke's unit volume rose a healthy 7 percent.

International operations contributed almost 80 percent of soft-drink operating profit, and unit volume was growing 8–10 percent internationally and 4.5–5.5 percent in the U.S.

The day after it was reported that Buffett acquired a 6.3 percent stake in Coca-Cola for more than $1 billion, his largest investment ever, *The Wall Street Journal's* "Heard on the Street" column noted that Coke's P/E multiple of 15.6x estimated 1989 earnings represented a 40 percent premium to the S&P 500's P/E of 11.1x and was far higher than Coke's previous five-year P/E premium of 16 percent. The article quoted Roy Burry, a beverage analyst at Kidder Peabody, who had a "hold" rating on Coke and said that "Warren Buffett was holding what is now 'very expensive stock.'"[42]

Buffett famously explained his purchase at that time, "It's like when you marry a girl," he said. "Is it her eyes? Her personality? It's a whole bunch of things you can't separate."[43] Buffett bought another 9.2 million shares in 1989 which brought his ownership to 23.35 million shares for a 6.75 percent ownership for a cost of $1,023,920.

He elaborated on what attracted him about Coca-Cola, his largest investment, in the 1989 annual report: "Only in the summer of 1988 did my brain finally establish contact with my eyes," Buffett humbly acknowledged after observing Coke blanket the world for fifty-two years with a product that had "extraordinary consumer attractiveness and commercial possibilities."

> *What I then perceived was both clear and fascinating. After drifting somewhat in the 1970s, Coca-Cola had in 1981 become a new company with the move of Roberto Goizueta to CEO* (new management). *Roberto, along with Don Keough, once my across-the-street neighbor in Omaha* (including an admired long-time friend), *first rethought and focused the company's policies* (instituted financial accountability) *and then energetically carried them out. What was already the world's most ubiquitous product* (valuable brand franchise) *gained new momentum, with sales overseas virtually exploding.*
>
> *Through a truly rare blend of marketing and financial skills, Roberto has maximized both the growth of his product and the rewards that this growth brings to shareholders. Normally, the CEO of a consumer products company, drawing on his natural inclinations or experience, will cause either marketing or finance to dominate the business at the expense of the other discipline. With Roberto, the mesh of marketing and finance is perfect and the result is a shareholder's dream.*

Of course, we should have started buying Coke much earlier, soon after Roberto and Don began running things. In fact, if I had been thinking straight I would have persuaded my grandfather to sell the grocery store back in 1936 and put all of the proceeds into Coca-Cola stock. I've learned my lesson: My response time to the next glaringly attractive idea will be slashed to well under 50 years.[44]

A common theme among Buffett's purchases is that he loves his companies to buy back stock opportunistically below intrinsic value. It adds economic value to the company, and it increases Buffett's share of future earnings. Berkshire's ownership in Coke grew to 6.98 percent in 1990 from 6.5 percent the year before without Buffett buying another share. "When Coca-Cola uses retained earnings to repurchase its shares, the company increases our percentage ownership in what I regard to be the most valuable franchise in the world."[45]

Buffett elaborated further in Berkshire's 1993 annual report what he admired about Coca-Cola, in which Berkshire's ownership grew to 7.2 percent due to further stock repurchases by Coke:

It's never too late with great companies

In 1938, more than 50 years after the introduction of Coke, and long after the drink was firmly established as an American icon, Fortune did an excellent story on the company. In the second paragraph the writer reported: 'Several times every year a weighty and serious investor looks long and with profound respect at Coca-Cola's record, but comes regretfully to the conclusion that he is looking too late. The specters of saturation and competition rise before him.'

Yes, competition there was in 1938 and in 1993 as well. But it's worth noting that in 1938, the Coca-Cola Co. sold 207 million cases of soft drinks (if its gallonage then is converted into the 192-ounce cases used for measurement today) and in 1993 it sold about 10.7 billion cases, a 50-fold increase in physical volume from a company that in 1938 was already dominant in its very major industry. Nor was the party over in 1938 for an investor: Though the $40 invested in 1919 in one share had (with dividends reinvested) turned into $3,277 by the end of 1938, a fresh $40 then invested in Coca-Cola stock would have grown to $25,000 by yearend 1993.[46]

As an update, Coke's unit case volume almost tripled to 29.6 billion cases in the twenty-five years to 2018 from 10.7 billion in 1993 for an average annual growth rate of 4.0 percent.

Prefers long-held dominant market shares

Is it really so difficult to conclude that Coca-Cola and Gillette possess far less business risk over the long term than, say, any computer company or retailer? Worldwide, Coke sells about 44 percent of all soft drinks, and Gillette has more than a 60 percent share (in value) of the blade market. Leaving aside chewing gum, in which Wrigley is dominant, I know of no other significant businesses in which the leading company has long enjoyed such global power.

Market shares that are growing with a competitive advantage

Moreover, both Coke and Gillette have actually increased their worldwide shares of market in recent years. The might of their brand names, the attributes of their products, and the strength of their distribution systems give them an enormous competitive advantage, setting up a protective moat around their economic castles.

Confidence in management's competence and character

The impressions I formed in those days (as a neighbor) about Don (Keough) were a factor in my decision to have Berkshire make a record $1 billion investment in Coca-Cola in 1988–89. Roberto Goizueta had become CEO of Coke in 1981, with Don alongside as his partner. The two of them took hold of a company that had stagnated during the previous decade and moved it from $4.4 billion of market value to $58 billion in less than 13 years. What a difference a pair of managers like this makes, even when their product has been around for 100 years.[47]

Roberto Goizueta and Don Keough stated their primary objective was to increase shareholder value over time. Goizueta admitted to checking the market price of Coke four or more times a day. They celebrated their first decade managing Coca-Cola in 1990, a year when the market value of the company grew by $5 billion, which was greater than the *entire* market value of the company in 1981 when they assumed responsibility.

A $1,000 investment in Coca-Cola at the end of 1980 would have been worth $12,110 including dividends by 1990, which outpaced the S&P 500 more than by 3:1. This represented a sizzling average annual return of 28 percent. Shareholders rewarded Coke's average annual growth in sales of 8 percent, operating income of 11 percent, and net income of 13 percent. Common shares outstanding were reduced 10 percent from 1980 funded from cash flow, increased borrowings to lower the company's cost of capital, and from lowering the dividend payout ratio to 39 percent from 63 percent. Shareholders appreciated the company's sharpened focus on its core soft drink business that sold 226 billion eight-ounce servings in 1990 and was just getting started. Even Warren Buffett hadn't finished buying shares yet.

On April 2, 1993, more commonly known as Marlboro Friday, Philip Morris announced a 20 percent price reduction to their Marlboro cigarettes in reaction to losing market share to cheaper generics. The company said it expected its operating income from U.S. tobacco sales would fall as much as 40 percent. Philip Morris stock sank in one day 23 percent following the news, and suddenly investors questioned the durability of all prominent consumer brands, including Coca-Cola. Nervous investors panicked and dumped Coke stock which dropped 10 percent over the following two weeks.

Coca-Cola stock traded between $40–$45/share throughout 1992 and leading up to Marlboro Friday. Buffett reacted by selling puts on five million shares of Coke exercisable at $35/share over the following eight months. Berkshire collected a $1.50 premium for selling the puts for a total of $7.5 million, but would have been obligated to purchase $175 million ($35 x 5 million shares) of stock if the price fell below $35. Coke's stock price troughed at $37.50 in 1993, so Berkshire kept the $7.5 million premium.

What gave Buffett the conviction to opportunistically embrace the stock while others feared that Coke could also fall victim to generics? Buffett determined that after years of price increases, Philip Morris smokers paid an extra $500 a year to smoke Philip Morris brand cigarettes vs. generics. The price umbrella was huge, which naturally attracted competition:

> Philip Morris cigarettes got to where they were selling for $2.00 a pack. The average consumer uses something close to ten packs a week. Meanwhile, the generic was at $1 or thereabouts. So you really have a $500 a year differential in cost per year to a ten pack a week smoker. And that is a big annual cost differential.[48]

Buffett noted that Coca-Cola sold about 250 billion eight-ounce soft drink servings worldwide in 1993. The same year Coke made $2.2 billion pretax, which equals about one penny per serving and does not leave a huge price umbrella especially when generic manufacturers would incur at least the same cost for aluminum cans, sugar, distribution and inventory costs.

He also noted that the price of soft drinks had changed very little over almost one hundred years:

Interestingly, a 6½-ounce Coca-Cola was $.05 way back in 1990 or so. Now the standard unit is generally 12 ounces in a can and it's not difficult at all to buy those in the supermarket on Saturday for $0.25 for 12 ounces. It's true you can't buy a 12-ounce can in a vending machine for a quarter. But if you buy the bigger bottles—2 liters and so forth—you get the cost down to $.02 an ounce pretty easily which would have been $0.13 for the old 6½-ounce bottle that was selling for a nickel in 1900. So you've essentially gone from 8/10 of a cent per ounce (in 1900) to $.02 per ounce during a time in which the price index has advanced at a much higher rate. It's been one of the lowest items there is in terms of inflation in price... I can't think of too many food items where prices have increased as little as they have for soft drinks and Coke.[109]

Charlie Munger added,

Warren would say that what you're buying when you buy a soft drink is the taste, the availability and the image...The image is important because there's a certain festivity to it and a certain ritual and so on. And if Coca-Cola is only making a penny a serving, that does not leave a huge margin for other people to come in and deliver the same availability, image and what have you. A lousy penny a serving is all that Coke is taking out of it.[109]

Fast forward to 2016, Coke sold 703 billion eight-ounce servings, or almost two billion per day, which is almost triple the number of servings in 1993. Yet Coke is still making just less than $0.01 per eight-ounce serving (2016 net income of $6.5 billion/703 billion servings).

The stock price of Coca-Cola by May 1994 had drifted sideways for two years. *Barron's* cover story on May 9 asked, "Has Coca-Cola Lost Its Fizz?" The article cited several challenges including: the competitive threat of private label in the aftermath of Marlboro Friday and the popularity of noncarbonated drinks such as Snapple, ready-to-drink teas, sports drinks, and flavored waters.

The article also challenged the sustainability of two growth drivers that contributed to Coke's 18 percent EPS growth rate. Coke fueled about two percentage points of its growth rate by lowering its tax rate from 44 percent in 1980 to 31 percent in 1993 from locating much of its production of concentrate in Puerto Rico and Ireland. The article supposed that this tailwind was largely exhausted.

The article was also suspect of Coke's ability to continue passing on price increases to its bottlers, who were losing money and reeling in debt. When Goizueta assumed control of Coke, he was frustrated that Coca-Cola was at the mercy of its different bottlers, who had low-margins and were capital intensive, but had become complacent with their perpetual contracts. Goizueta and Keough architected a strategy to invest up to 49 percent in a number of bottlers to gain more influence by consolidating them into larger, more efficient, and accountable companies. This strategy gave Coke leverage to dictate pricing. From the perspective of the bottlers, Coke benefitted in two ways: Coke crammed down hefty price increases benefitting its reported revenues; and since Coke limited its ownership to 49 percent, accounting rules allowed Coke to report its minority ownership in the bottlers as a one-line equity investment. Coke's balance sheet remained pristine without having to consolidate the burdensome debt of its bottlers. In short, Coke enjoyed pricing power, but had its influence run its course?

Goizueta was interviewed for the article, and he countered with the enormous opportunity for consumption from three billion thirsty people in developing countries including China and India. Only two eight-ounce servings of Coke products were consumed on average by every person in China compared to more than 300 in the U.S. and Mexico.

Buffett was a board member of Coke and enjoyed insider knowledge. Though the stock had lulled for two years, it wasn't cheap at 26x 1994 EPS. Nevertheless, Buffett focused on the long-term opportunity of the universal appeal of Coke's simple moment of pleasure, driving increasing worldwide case sales. Higher case sales combined with continuing share buybacks would effectively increase Berkshire's economic share of Coke's future worldwide servings.

Buffett invested an additional $275 million in 1994 for an additional 6.6 million shares, bringing Berkshire's total share count to a neat 100 million. This was Berkshire's last purchase of Coke stock. In the next four years Coke stock quadrupled. Touché *Barron's*.

Berkshire currently owns 400 million shares due to subsequent stock splits and its ownership has increased from 7.8 percent in 1994 to 9.4 percent in 2018, entirely due to Coke reducing its share count from buybacks. This more than tripled Berkshire's effective ownership of daily servings of Coke drinks over twenty-three years to more than 180 million servings per day, without Berkshire buying another single share.

Coca-Cola hosted an investor day in 1996 in conjunction with its sponsorship of the summer Olympics, which were held in Coke's backyard in Atlanta, Georgia. During one of the breaks, I introduced myself to Roberto Goizueta, who was clearly proud of his accomplishments and of sponsoring the Olympics. The effects of being a chain smoker for most his life was evident in his purple-tinged hands. I mentioned that it must be wonderful to have the sponsorship and board contribution of Buffett and he responded, "Well, Warren isn't perfect, remember the airline." Goizueta was referring to Berkshire's $358 million investment in U.S. Air preferred stock where the high cost airline, facing low-cost competitors such as Southwest, suspended its dividend that year and Berkshire wrote down its investment by 75 percent.

Unfortunately, Roberto Goizueta's heavy smoking afflicted him with lung cancer, and he passed away at sixty-five the next year. Under his reign, Coca-Cola's market capitalization exploded from $4 billion to $84 billion, and he prided in never selling a share. Warren Buffett paid tribute to Goizueta in Berkshire's 1997 annual report:

> In last year's annual report, I discussed Coca-Cola, our largest holding. Coke continues to increase its market dominance throughout the world, but, tragically, it has lost the leader responsible for its outstanding performance. Roberto Goizueta, Coke's CEO since 1981, died in October. After his death, I read every one of the more than 100 letters and notes he had written me during the past nine years. Those messages could well serve as a guidebook for success in both business and life.
>
> In these communications, Roberto displayed a brilliant and clear strategic vision that was always aimed at advancing the well-being of Coke shareholders. Roberto knew where he was leading the company, how he was going to get there, and why this path made the most sense for his owners— and, equally important, he had a burning sense of urgency about reaching his goals. An excerpt from one handwritten note he sent to me illustrates his mind-set: 'By the way, I have told Olguita (his wife) that what she refers to as an obsession, you call focus. I like your term much better.' Like all who knew Roberto, I will miss him enormously.[49]

Berkshire's 400 million shares cost $1.3 billion and, as of the end of 2018, were worth $18.9 billion. Coke stock peaked in 1998 at $44.47/share, a level it wouldn't surpass for another sixteen years. In retrospect, perhaps Buffett should have sold the stock priced at over 60x earnings. Meanwhile, Berkshire

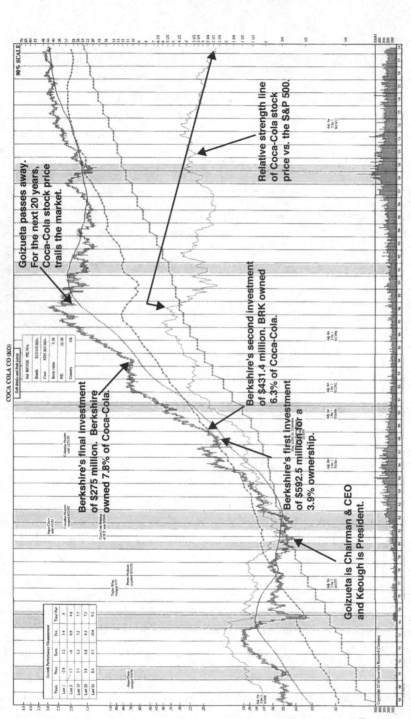

Figure 19. Coca-Cola

collected $640 million in dividends from Coke in 2018 which, in just the one year, was almost one half of Berkshire's original cost…and counting.

Takeaways

Warren Buffett admitted a big mistake with Coca-Cola. He witnessed first-hand as a seven-year-old entrepreneur how a cold bottle of Coke created a simple moment of happiness and refreshment for his neighbors on a sweltering Omaha summer day when there was no air conditioning. But he didn't put the money he made selling Coke into buying Coca-Cola stock. "His brain finally connected with his eyes" years later, in part because of his early and frequent experiences enjoying Coke's satisfying appeal, and to many, a happy addiction. Coke is a wonderful brand with a product that he understood and appreciated. Buffett focused on evaluating three important metrics with Coca-Cola: 1) unit case sales advancing at a healthy clip, 2) earnings per case, and 3) declining shares outstanding from company repurchases.

Buffett's other regret with Coca-Cola was that he didn't invest sooner when he learned that Roberto Goizueta and his long-time friend Don Keough took control. They were a formidable duo, with one focused zealously on financial discipline, economic value-add, ROIC, and shareholder value, while the other was a marketing all-star and a well-loved emissary for the company. Buffett described Keough as

> …one of the most extraordinary human beings I've ever known—a man of enormous business talent, but, even more important, a man who brings out the absolute best in everyone lucky enough to associate with him. Coca-Cola wants its product to be present at the happy times of a person's life. Don Keough, as an individual, invariably increases the happiness of those around him. It's impossible to think about Don without feeling good. The impressions I formed in those days about Don were a factor in my decision to have Berkshire make a record $1 billion investment in Coca-Cola in 1988–89.[50]

The result: a forty-fold increase in stock price during their seventeen-year reign. Buffett liked, trusted, and admired Goizueta and Keough.

Coca-Cola was a wonderful business at a fair price. Coca-Cola was wonderful because it didn't require much capital to run the business (the independent bottlers absorbed this), and it earned an attractive after-tax return-on-invested capital. Buffett liked how Coca-Cola was using its cash flow to buy back its own shares and that it was rationally evaluating its managers based on their return on capital. Buffett bought Coke in three steps. The first, and largest at $592.5 million in 1988 was when Coke's ROIC was 19 percent, its P/E was 15x and its free cash flow yield was 5 percent. The second tranche was the next year when Coke's ROIC climbed to 22 percent, its P/E was 22x, and its free cash flow yield was 3 percent. The last tranche in 1994 was when Coke's ROIC climbed to 33 percent, its P/E was 26x, and its free cash flow yield was 3.5 percent.

Buffett also salivated over Coke's attractive long-term prospects. International earnings contributed 80 percent of the entire company and yet, developing countries with populations multiples of the U.S. had per-capita consumption rates that were a fraction of the U.S. and Mexico. Buffett told Coke's then CEO Muhtar Kent at Coke's annual meeting in 2015, "I'm the kind of guy who likes to bet on sure things. No business has ever failed with happy customers…and you're selling happiness."[51]

The essence of the investment case for Coke was fairly simple for Buffett. Coke's case sales grow every year due to population growth and a growing penetration of the world's desire to satisfy their need for eight servings of liquid each day. As Coke's daily servings grow, Berkshire's share of those servings increase as Coke reduces its shares with its abundant free cash flow, thereby increasing Berkshire's share of Coke's daily servings.

Buffett was so enamored with the prospects and competitive advantage of Coke's brand and distribution system, he anointed it as one of "The Inevitables" and said, "If you gave me $100 billion and said take away the soft drink leadership of Coca-Cola in the world, I'd give it back to you and say it can't be done."[52]

Coke has continued to dominate the mindshare of the soft-drink market, but a dominant company does not necessarily make a great investment if its stock price far exceeds its intrinsic value. Buffett hinted at this when he warned,

> You can, of course, pay too much for even the best of businesses. The overpayment risk surfaces periodically and, in our opinion, may now be quite high for the purchasers of virtually all stocks, The Inevitables included. Investors making purchases in an overheated market need to recognize that it may often take an extended period for the value of even an outstanding company to catch up with the price they paid. [53]

Buffett's warning in 1996 was prescient because Coke's stock price has lagged the market ever since.

At the time, Coke stock was priced at $54 with reported earnings of $1.40 for a P/E of 39x. Two years later Coke's stock price reached $89 with earnings of $1.42 for a P/E of 63x! Loyalty and a steep capital gains tax penalty prevented Buffett from selling. He was willing to wait an extended period time for its intrinsic value to catch-up to the stock price, because his horizon is very long-term, and he had confidence in Coke's future prospects.

Another inevitable is that investors will be tested with their conviction. Buffett was tested with the question of the durability of consumer brands on Marlboro Friday. He responded by logically assessing whether the challenge facing Philip Morris was applicable to Coca-Cola, and whether the sympathetic sell-off in Coca-Cola was justified. Buffett concluded that Philip Morris's price gap compared to generic competitors was significant, whereas Coca-Cola's price gap was minimal as it only made a penny of profit per serving. Buffett responded by "being greedy when others were fearful" and bought more stock, which quadrupled in the next four years.

The old adage for making money by investing is to "buy low and sell high." With extraordinary businesses, Buffett would say, "buy low and don't sell." Robert Woodruff, whom Buffett described as the "business genius who built Coca-Cola over many decades and who owned a huge position in the company" and was a mentor for Roberto Goizueta, never sold Coke stock. Roberto Goizueta never sold a share of Coca-Cola stock. Neither has Buffett.

GEICO

Eager to absorb everything about his hero, Benjamin Graham, who would shortly be his instructor at Columbia, Warren Buffett looked up Graham in *Who's Who in America* and discovered that he was chairman of the board of Government Employees Insurance Company; later renamed GEICO. The school librarian then referred Buffett to Best's Fire and Casualty insurance manual, where he learned that GEICO was based in Washington D.C. Today GEICO is one of the nation's largest private-passenger auto insurance underwriters that sells insurance directly to consumers and avoids paying commissions to agents.

Buffett recalled his transformative meeting with Lorimer "Davy" Davidson who was the senior investment officer of GEICO and would later become CEO.

Davy had no reason to talk with me, but I told him I was a student of Graham's and he then spent four or so hours answering unending questions about the insurance industry in general and GEICO specifically. Davy couldn't have been more helpful to me that day and for decades thereafter. It really changed my life.[54]

Buffett remembered,

I just kept asking questions about insurance and GEICO. He didn't go to lunch that day—he just sat there and talked to me for four hours like I was the most important person in the world. When he opened that door to me, he opened the door to the insurance world.[55]

Davidson explained that GEICO's competitive advantage was its direct selling model through mailers which gave it a huge cost advantage over competitors that customarily sold through agents. GEICO's expenses for underwriting and claims were typically just 25 percent of premium revenues compared to 35–40 percent expense ratio for insurance companies that sold through commission paid agents. GEICO sought to limit its underwriting risk by only marketing to government employees, who were thought to be more responsible drivers. Buffett was fascinated by GEICO's unique business model of bypassing the traditional insurance agent by marketing through the mail directly to government employees who were lower risk policies. By avoiding commissions to agents and by insuring a lower risk group of drivers, GEICO sold insurance at a 30–40 percent discount to conventional rates. Over the ten-year period ending 1950, GEICO's policyholders grew, on average, 19 percent per year, and it was only licensed in fifteen states. GEICO targeted a high-quality customer pool with a product that had a "tollgate/repeat purchase" feature, because auto insurance was a required annual purchase. Moreover, GEICO generated high returns on capital since it had a capital-light business model; it didn't need to make large investments in inventory, receivables, or plant and equipment.

When Buffett returned to New York, he found that GEICO's lower cost distribution advantage resulted in profit margins that were four times the average insurer. GEICO's number of policy holders had grown at a 19 percent average rate for ten years ending 1950 and had less than 1 percent market share.

Buffett was also intrigued with how insurance companies were able to invest their customers' premiums before their claims came due, and his passion for insurance float was born. GEICO's market cap was only $7 million with a market share of less than 1 percent, but in 1950 it had an underwriting profit of 18 percent compared to 3 percent for its competitors. The stock price of $42/share was 8x depressed earnings, which was less than its much larger competitors, and given GEICO's growth prospects, Buffett thought the stock could double in five years. He said, "It appears that no price is being paid for the tremendous growth potential of the company."[56]

The next business day after meeting Davidson, Buffett sold three-quarters of his portfolio and bought GEICO stock; the first of four times in 1951 for a cumulative total of 350 shares at a cost of $10,282. By year-end Buffett's GEICO stock was worth $13,125 and it represented 65 percent of his net worth. Buffett was already demonstrating both a fascination with Graham and a departure from him, since Graham advocated a broadly diversified portfolio. Graham also disdained projections, which Buffett used to support his investment case.

Buffett said that he was more excited about GEICO than he had ever been about a stock.[57]

> *It was a company selling insurance at prices well below all the standard companies, and making 15 percent profit margins. It had an underwriting cost then of 13 percent or so, whereas the standard companies had probably 30 percent to 35 percent cost. It was a company with a huge competitive advantage, managed by the guy that was my God.*[58]

Buffett was so enthused he wrote a one-page report in 1951 about GEICO for *The Commercial & Financial Chronicle* column called, "The Security I Like Best."

Buffett sold GEICO the next year for $15,259 and almost a 50 percent gain to swap into the insurer Western Insurance Securities that was selling for 1x its current earnings. Buffett didn't own GEICO for another 25 years. Buffett recalled that "in the next twenty years, the GEICO stock I sold grew in value to about $1.3 million, which taught me a lesson about the inadvisability of selling a stake in an identifiably-wonderful company."[59]

GEICO was founded in 1936 by Leo Goodwin in San Antonio, Texas. Goodwin was an insurance company accountant who concluded after analyzing accident statistics that government and military employees were safer drivers than the general public. He also realized that by eliminating costly agent commissions, he could sell policies cheaper directly to consumers. He capitalized the company with $25,000 of his money and $75,000 from Fort Worth

Reprinted from

The COMMERCIAL and FINANCIAL CHRONICLE

Thursday, December 6, 1951

The Security I Like Best

WARREN E. BUFFETT
Buffett-Falk & Co., Omaha, Nebr.

Government Employees Insurance Co.

Warren E. Buffett

Full employment, boomtime profits and record dividend payments do not set the stage for depressed security prices. Most industries have been riding this wave of prosperity during the past five years with few ripples to disturb the tide.

The auto insurance business has not shared in the boom. After the staggering losses of the immediate postwar period, the situation began to right itself in 1949. In 1950, stock casualty companies again took it on the chin with underwriting experience the second worst in 15 years. The recent earnings reports of casualty companies, particularly those with the bulk of writings in auto lines, have diverted bull market enthusiasm from their stocks. On the basis of normal earning power and asset factors, many of these stocks appear undervalued.

The nature of the industry is such as to ease cyclical bumps. Auto insurance is regarded as a necessity by the majority of purchasers. Contracts must be renewed yearly at rates based upon experience. The lag of rates behind costs, although detrimental in a period of rising prices as has characterized the 1945-1951 period, should prove beneficial if deflationary forces should be set in action.

Other industry advantages include lack of inventory, collection, labor and raw material problems. The hazard of product obsolescence and related equipment obsolescence is also absent.

Government Employees Insurance Corporation was organized in the mid-30's to provide complete auto insurance on a nationwide basis to an eligible class including: (1) Federal, State and municipal government employees; (2) active and reserve commissioned officers and the first three pay grades of non-commissioned officers of the Armed Forces; (3) veterans who were eligible when on active duty; (4) former policyholders; (5) faculty members of universities, colleges and schools; (6) government contractor employees engaged in defense work exclusively, and (7) stockholders.

The company has no agents or branch offices. As a result, policyholders receive standard auto insurance policies at premium discounts running as high as 30% off manual rates. Claims are handled promptly through approximately 500 representatives throughout the country.

The term "growth company" has been applied with abandon during the past few years to companies whose sales increases represented little more than inflation of prices and general easing of business competition. GEICO qualifies as a legitimate growth company based upon the following record:

Year—	Premiums Written	Policyholders
1936___	$103,696.31	3,754
1940___	768,057.86	25,514
1945___	1,638,562.09	51,697
1950___	8,016,975.79	143,944

Of course the investor of today does not profit from yesterday's growth. In GEICO's case, there is reason to believe the major portion of growth lies ahead. Prior to 1950, the company was only licensed in 15 of 50 jurisdictions including D. C. and Hawaii. At the beginning of the year there were less than 3,000 policyholders in New York State. Yet 25% saved on an insurance bill of $125 in New York should look bigger to the prospect than the 25% saved on the $50 rate in more sparsely settled regions.

As cost competition increases in importance during times of recession, GEICO's rate attraction should become even more effective in diverting business from the brother-in-law. With insurance rates moving higher due to inflation, the 25% spread in rates becomes wider in terms of dollars and cents.

There is no pressure from agents to accept questionable applicants or renew poor risks. In States where the rate structure is inadequate, new promotion may be halted.

Probably the biggest attraction of GEICO is the profit margin advantage it enjoys. The ratio of underwriting profit to premiums earned in 1949 was 27.5% for GEICO as compared to 6.7% for the 135 stock casualty and surety companies summarized by Best's. As experience turned for the worse in 1950, Best's aggregate's profit margin dropped to

3.0% and GEICO's dropped to 18.0%. GEICO does not write all casualty lines; however, bodily injury and property damage, both important lines for GEICO, were among the least profitable lines. GEICO also does a large amount of collision writing, which was a profitable line in 1950.

During the first half of 1951, practically all insurers operated in the red on casualty lines with bodily injury and property damage among the most unprofitable. Whereas GEICO's profit margin was cut to slightly above 9%, Massachusett's Bonding & Insurance showed a 16% loss, New Amsterdam Casualty an 8% loss, Standard Accident Insurance a 9% loss, etc.

Because of the rapid growth of GEICO, cash dividends have had to remain low. Stock dividends and a 25-for-1 split increased the outstanding shares from 3,000 on June 1, 1948, to 250,000 on Nov. 10, 1951. Valuable rights to subscribe to stock of affiliated companies have also been issued.

Benjamin Graham has been Chairman of the Board since his investment trust acquired and distributed a large block of the stock in 1948. Leo Goodwin, who has guided GEICO's growth since inception, is the able President. At the end of 1950, the 10 members of the Board of Directors owned approximately one - third of the outstanding stock.

Earnings in 1950 amounted to $3.92 as contrasted to $4.71 on the smaller amount of business in 1949. These figures include no allowance for the increase in the unearned premium reserve which was substantial in both years. Earnings in 1951 will be lower than 1950, but the wave of rate increases during the past summer should evidence themselves in 1952 earnings. Investment income quadrupled between 1947 and 1950, reflecting the growth of the company's assets.

At the present price of about eight times the earnings of 1950, a poor year for the industry, it appears that no price is being paid for the tremendous growth potential of the company.

This is part of a continuous forum appearing in the "Chronicle," in which each week, a different group of experts in the investment and advisory field from all sections of the country participate and give their reasons for favoring a particular security.

Buffett: The Security I Like Best

banker, Cleaves Rhea and his family, in a partnership created by none other than investment banker Lorimer Davidson. In 1948 the Rhea family sold its 75 percent ownership to Graham-Newman and a small group of private investors.

Graham-Newman purchased its 50 percent share of GEICO for $712,000. In 1949 Graham-Newman was forced to distribute the stock to its shareholders under a consent order by the SEC. Graham-Newman inadvertently violated a rule that prohibited open-ended investment companies from acquiring more than 10 percent of an insurance company. GEICO thus became a publicly-traded company at about $27/share.

GEICO flourished under Leo Goodwin's leadership; he retired in 1958, becoming the founder chairman. Premiums grew from $104,000 in 1936 to $36.2 million in 1957, and the value of GEICO stock grew almost fifty-fold in the ten years ending 1958. Goodwin chose Lorimer Davidson to succeed him as CEO. Davidson was similarly successful at growing GEICO profitably. GEICO's premiums grew from $40 million to over $250 million—a compound growth of 16 percent during his tenure as CEO. He retired in 1970 and was succeeded by president and COO Ralph Peck.

By 1972 Graham-Newman's original purchase of $712,000 in 1948 was worth $400 million! With a 20 percent weight in a single illiquid stock, Graham was already violating his own advice to adequately diversify by limiting an investment to a 5 percent weight.

> *It did so well that the price of its shares advanced to two hundred times or more the price paid for the half-interest. The advance far outstripped the actual growth in profits, and almost from the start the quotation appeared much too high in terms of the partners' own investment standards. But since they regarded the company as a sort of 'family business,' they continued to maintain a substantial ownership of the shares despite the spectacular price rise. A large number of participants in their funds did the same, and they became multimillionaires through their holding in this one enterprise, plus later-organized affiliates. Ironically enough, the aggregate of profits accruing from this single investment-decision far exceeded the sum of all the others realized through 20 years of wide-ranging operations in the partners' specialized fields, involving much investigation, endless pondering, and countless individual decisions.*[60]

It is amazing that the gain from one stock, GEICO, was larger than all of Graham-Newman's other gains combined.

Leo Goodwin's death in 1971 presaged massive problems for GEICO. Inflation in the U.S. exploded from 3.2 percent in 1972 to 11.0 percent in 1974. For insurance companies and GEICO in particular, this was a perfect storm. Insurance policies underwritten when inflation was low single-digits was now unprofitable as accidents proved more costly because of inflation. The cost of paying auto insurance claims also jumped due to more lenient juries awarding generous claims, and from new no-fault laws, which provided that an insurer pay medical bills and lost earnings if a policyholder is in a car accident, regardless of who was at fault for the accident.

Also, the market value of GEICO's bond portfolio was hammered by rising inflation and interest rates and its equity portfolio was decimated by the vicious bear market of 1973–1974. Accounting rules allowed GEICO to avoid writing down the value of its bond portfolio as long as the bonds were not sold. This handcuffed GEICO from paying for claims with bonds. Finally, many states mandated that they approve rate increases to prevent insurers from overcharging. This restricted GEICO from adequate pricing. Peck sought to pay claims by marketing to higher-risk drivers at old prices in order to attract fresh cash. This ultimately proved disastrous, especially when management severely under-reserved for future claims. At its worst, GEICO was in denial and failed to disclose its deteriorating finances even to the SEC.

In early 1976, GEICO reported its first operating loss in thirty-two years of $126.5 million for the year 1975, compared to 1974 earnings of $26 million. Capital declined to $36.9 million from $144 million in 1974 and the company stopped paying dividends. Trading was suspended from February 24 to April 19, 1976. The shocking plight of GEICO reached a crescendo at its three-hour annual meeting in April, attended by over 400 angry shareholders. The stock price had fallen from the previous year price of $42 to $5, and bankruptcy fears loomed. A month later Peck was gone, and John ("Jack") J. Byrne, Jr., a respected insurance veteran at Travelers Insurance, was named chairman, president, and CEO. Norman Gidden, chairman, took early retirement at the end of March 1977.

Byrne was a high-energy bulldog, decisive, and focused. He appealed to the District of Columbia's Insurance Superintendent Max Wallach, who insisted that GEICO raise the necessary capital to meet regulatory and rating agency standards by June. Wallach also insisted that GEICO reinsure its policies with other insurance companies to limit the company's exposure to losses. In effect, Byrne had to humbly ask its competitors for a lifeline. The motive for GEICO's competitors was that it was better to proactively share the underwriting risk than to incur the wrath of regulators, ultimately forcing the competitors to pay for the potentially larger sins of GEICO. State Farm and Travelers bailed out, betting that a dead GEICO was better for them in the long-run.

Although Buffett didn't own a share of GEICO, he followed the situation closely and was distressed to see the company on a path toward bankruptcy. Buffett felt a sense of responsibility to rescue the company for the retired Lorimer Davidson and for his hero Ben Graham, both of whom still held their shares. Claim frequency was mounting with higher-risk drivers and claim severity spiraled higher with rising inflation. "I looked again at GEICO and was startled by what I saw after a few rule-of-thumb calculations about loss reserves. It was clear in a sixty-second examination that the company was far under-reserved and the situation was getting worse."[61] The stock, which had fallen to $2/share, was a bargain *if* it could avoid bankruptcy, but that was a big *if*.

Before making a commitment that depended so heavily on the success of a turnaround manager, Buffett first had to meet Byrne to evaluate his ability to understand and fix the problem, and his ability to convince investors to add capital and other insurers to reinsure. The conversation lasted until three in the morning, and by then Buffett was a believer in Byrne and in the core cost advantage of GEICO. A few hours later, Buffett bought 500,000 shares at $2.125 each. Soon thereafter he bought more shares for a total investment of $4.1 million for 1.294 million shares at an average price of $3.18/share.

Buffett spun into action and personally appealed to Max Wallach to extend the June deadline. Buffett was counting on his reputation as an investor to help make his case. Byrne convinced other insurance companies to reinsure, but their condition was that GEICO raise new capital. The large Wall Street equity powerhouses all turned GEICO down. Salomon Brothers was a bond specialist interested in dipping its toe in a lucrative equity underwriting. John Gutfreund at Salomon grilled Byrne and finally agreed to underwrite a $76 million convertible stock offering. The stock offering was thought to be so risky that no other Wall Street sell-side firms joined the syndicate.

Buffett was willing to buy the entire deal, and he instructed Salomon to buy any available shares in the aftermarket. Buffett's backing helped sell the deal to other investors and Buffett ended up owning 25 percent of the offering, or $19.4 million, for a total investment in GEICO of $23.5 million. Once the capital was raised, twenty-seven other insurers agreed to reinsure GEICO. With confidence restored, the stock quadruped to more than $8/share in six months. Buffett was grateful to Gutfreund for stepping up when no one else would.

Buffett later explained his rational for investing in GEICO:

> It wasn't essentially bankrupt but it was heading there. It was 1976. It had a lot of great business franchises that had not been destroyed by a lot of errors that had been made in terms of exploiting that franchise. And it had a manager who I met the night before I bought the first five hundred and some thousand shares who I felt had the ability to get through an extraordinarily tough period and to re-establish the value of that franchise. They still were the low-cost operator. They made all kinds of mistakes. They still didn't know their costs because they didn't know what their loss reserves should be and they got captivated by growth; they did all kinds of things wrong but they still had the franchise.
>
> It was similar to American Express in 1963 when the salad oil scandal hit. It did not hurt the franchise of the travelers check or the credit card... And GEICO with no net worth was worth a tremendous amount of money too, except it might get closed up the next day because it had no net worth. But I was satisfied that the net worth would be there...[62]

Byrne demanded rate increases and cleaned the cobwebs of sloppy underwriting. In New York, he was approved for a 35 percent rate increase. In New Jersey, Byrne personally pleaded for a rate hike and, after getting rejected by the state insurance commissioner, Byrne threw GEICO's license on the commissioner's desk and stormed out saying, "We are no longer a citizen of the state of New Jersey."[63] He then fired 700 employees in the state and cancelled 300,000 policyholders. Altogether he closed one hundred offices, reduced the workforce nearly in half, cancelled 40 percent of its customers, sold half of its profitable life-insurance affiliate, and retrenched to just seven states and the District of Columbia. By the end of 1976, GEICO's capital surplus was a record $250 million, and they returned to profitability in 1977. Unfortunately, just as GEICO was being rescued from near-death, Ben Graham passed away on September 21, 1976.

Buffett's appraisal of Bryne's character proved spot-on. Buffett later recalled his focus, energy, and skills:

> It was like he had trained all his life for that position. It was like he'd been genetically designed for that particular period of time. If you'd searched the country you could not have found a better battlefield commander. He had to

assemble a team of people, he had to chop thousands of heads, and he had to change the thinking of those heads that stayed around. It was a Herculean job. Nobody could have done it better than Jack. He was a tough, disciplined thinker about pricing and reserves and he demanded rational business principles and actions. Everybody knew exactly what GEICO was about, and he worked extraordinary hours focused on a single objective. He was always interested in what made sense rather than what had been done in the past.[64]

Jack Bryne was equally complimentary of Buffett:

I'd ask him all kinds of things. He showed me sensible ways to finance. He was generous with his time. But he never—ever—made suggestions. Warren figured out a long time ago that he could make a lot more money for Berkshire by being a benevolent shareholder. This guy made a lot of money by backing up the truck.[65]

By the time Byrne left GEICO in 1985 to resurrect Fireman's Fund Insurance Company, GEICO stock had soared to over $70/share.

Turnarounds seldom turn, Buffett concluded after his decades of experience observing attempted turnarounds, "With few exceptions, when a management with a reputation for brilliance tackles a business with a reputation for poor fundamental economics, it is the reputation of the business that remains intact."[66]

However, GEICO was an exception. Jack Byrne was a brilliant manager that resuscitated a gasping company, but GEICO was far from having "a reputation for poor fundamental economics." Its core economic advantage was intact. As Buffett described, GEICO had a "very hard to duplicate business advantage (low cost producer) with an extraordinary management whose skills in operations are matched by skills in capital allocation."[67] GEICO in the previous two years repurchased 37 percent of its stock. Buffett made subsequent purchases in 1980, and by year-end his cumulative investment of $47.1 million of 7.2 million shares was worth $105.3 million and represented a one-third ownership of the company. Additionally, Buffett estimated that Berkshire's share of GEICO's core annual earnings power was $20 million, which represented an astounding 43 percent (and growing) *annual* return on his investment.

When a former blue-chip company stumbles, the question is whether the problem is temporary and fixable or whether it is a long-term sustainable situation that permanently erodes the company's earnings power. In GEICO's case, it was the former.

(GEICO's) "fundamental business advantage—an advantage that previously had produced staggering success—was still intact within the company, although submerged in a sea of financial and operating troubles... The GEICO and American Express situations, extraordinary business franchises with a localized excisable cancer (needing, to be sure, a skilled surgeon), should be distinguished from the true "turnaround" situation in which the managers expect—and need—to pull off a corporate Pygmalion.[68]

Buffett added, "It was clear to me that GEICO would succeed because it *deserved* to succeed."[69] Buffett said he was attracted by GEICO's low-cost method of distribution, a low-risk book, and a high renewal rate. He added, "I love to buy businesses that I can't compete with."[70]

For the next fifteen years, Buffett did not buy any additional shares of GEICO but Berkshire's ownership increased from 33 percent to 51 percent solely because GEICO repurchased its own stock. By 1995, Buffett's original investment of $45.7 million had a market value of $674.7 million. At the Berkshire annual meeting in 2006, Buffett said that the purchase of the first half of GEICO for $40 million (he was rounding) was his single best investment. Years later, Berkshire bought the remaining half of GEICO for $2 billion.

Dual CEOs began leading GEICO in 1993: Tony Nicely and Louis Simpson. Nicely focused on the underwriting operations of GEICO, and the investment activities were handled by Lou Simpson. Nicely joined GEICO in 1961 while attending college and rose through the ranks, becoming president in 1989. Nicely tutored under Jack Byrne, and he recalled his experience working with Byrne:

Jack was unmerciful on me. He liked picking on young, aggressive people. But he taught me a lot and I will always be indebted to him. He taught me to think of the business as a whole, not separate functions like underwriting or investing. I learned the importance of a disciplined balance sheet.[71]

Nicely began to expand the customer base with national advertising. He outlined his five operating principles for investors in GEICO's 1986 Annual Report as:

- Be fanatics for good service
- Achieve an underwriting profit
- Be the low-cost provider
- Maintain a disciplined balance sheet
- Invest for total return

Simpson was previously president and CEO of Western Asset Management and an economics professor at Princeton. Unlike Buffett, Simpson avoided the limelight, but his investment method was Buffett-like in his conservative and concentrated stock selection. Simpson articulated his investment criteria in the GEICO's 1986 annual report, which remained unchanged thereafter:

- Think independently
- Invest in high-return businesses run for the shareholders
- Pay only a reasonable price even for excellent businesses
- Invest for the long-term
- Do not diversify excessively.

He later elaborated on his investing approach in an interview with the *Chicago Confidential*:

> "My approach is eclectic. I try to read all company documents carefully. We try to talk to competitors. We try to find people more knowledgeable about the business than we are. We do not rely on Wall Street-generated research. We do our own research. We try to meet with top management."

He once went undercover at the Manpower temporary agency to learn its training methods. Similar to Buffett, Simpson leaned toward companies that have a high free cash flow yield relative to interest rates. Also like Buffett, Simpson concentrated his investments. Just before Berkshire acquired GEICO, Lou Simpson invested GEICO's $1.1 billion insurance portfolio in just ten companies, and he typically kept 50–60 percent of assets in his best four ideas.[72]

Buffett devoted a full section in Berkshire's 2004 annual report to highlight Simpson's unsung investment record as "a cinch to be inducted into the investment Hall of Fame." From 1980–2004 Simpson achieved a compound annual gain of 20.3 percent compared to 13.5 percent for the S&P 500, with only three down years out of twenty-five. Simpson retired from GEICO at the end of 2010 at seventy-four years of age. Buffett left Simpson to operate autonomously and never asked him to pre-approve his transactions. Buffett said that he learned of Simpson's transactions about ten days after the end of the month when they are reported internally. Buffett added that "sometimes he silently disagrees with his decisions. But he's usually right."

In August 1995 Berkshire agreed to acquire the remaining 49 percent ownership in GEICO it didn't own for $2.3 billion cash, or $70/share, which

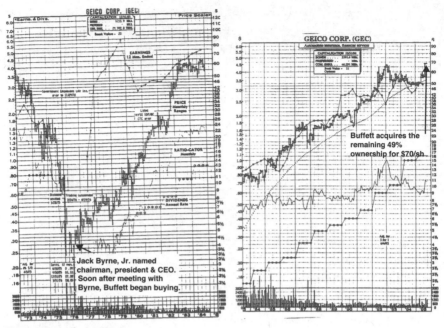

Figure 20. Buffett GEICO

was a 25 percent premium over the previous closing price of $55.75, but equal to the price in 1992—three years earlier.

The $70/share price was 19x the 1995 EPS of $3.66 which Buffett admitted was a "steep price."[73] The merger was consummated on January 2, 1996. Buffett explained at the time, "What they do extremely well is deliver low-cost auto insurance."[74] In a press release at the time, Buffett said he invested more than half his net worth in GEICO in 1951, when he was twenty. "I felt very comfortable with that commitment and I feel equally comfortable with the major commitment that Berkshire Hathaway has made today." In Berkshire's 1996 annual report, Buffett elaborated,

> GEICO's sustainable cost advantage is what attracted me to the company way back in 1951, when the entire business was valued at $7 million. It is also why I felt Berkshire should pay $2.3 billion last year for the 49 percent of the company that we didn't own.

GEICO's stock rose from the panic low of $2.25/share in 1995 to a split-adjusted price of over $300/share. Before Buffett agreed to acquire GEICO, he would have read the 1994 annual report and observed the following:

- Premium growth averaged 8.8 percent for the previous five years.

- GEICO's underwriting history was excellent. The underwriting ratio, which measures expenses and underwriting losses as a percentage of premiums, was 96.4 percent in 1994 and 99.1 percent in 1993 even though catastrophe losses (Northridge, California earthquake, and Hurricane Andrew) inflated expenses by 1.3 percent each year. This meant that GEICO was profitable on a standalone basis with its insurance underwriting operation before investment gains and losses. This also meant that its $3 billion of "float" was, in essence, free capital to invest that had no cost.

- GEICO's 1994 consumer satisfaction score was 94 percent for its auto policy service and 90 percent for its auto claim service.

- GEICO's core (excluding investment gains) EPS was $2.83 in 1994. Buffett's $70/share offer implied a rich 24.7x price/earnings multiple, but earnings were depressed due to the catastrophe losses, which made the acquisition opportunistic. This is also evident in GEICO's three-year rolling return on equity, which fell to 16.4 percent in 1994 from 27.8 percent in 1990. Without unusual catastrophe losses, Buffett had to believe that GEICO's EPS and return on equity would normalize higher.

- GEICO's book value/share of $21.17 had grown 12 percent annually for the previous five years. The $70/share purchase price was a relatively high price of 3.3x book value but fair given its growth prospects, depressed earnings, and normalized return on equity. GEICO's share count shrank 10 percent through share repurchases from 75.9 million in 1989 to 68.3 million in 1994.

- GEICO's cash flow from operating activities of $460.6 million less capital spending of $28.2 million generated free cash flow of $432.4 million or $6.33 per share. Even at a "steep" $70/share purchase price, this meant that the free cash flow yield was a hefty 9 percent, with the promise of higher cash flow growth thereafter.

Buffett was hungry to acquire the entire company for several reasons: GEICO's $3 billion of "float" would almost double Berkshire's total; Buffett liked Nicely's "brains, energy, integrity and focus;"[75] he admired Simpson and said that his presence assured him that Simpson could run all of Berkshire's investments if something were to happen to Buffett and Munger. Buffett wanted to accelerate GEICO's focus on its core direct selling of auto insurance and divest noncore home and aviation insurance operations. He also recognized its unlimited potential to capture share of the auto-insurance market where every auto-owner wanted to save money on this required major expenditure.

The timing of Berkshire's purchase of the remaining 49 percent of GEICO was probably influenced by the coincident timing of Walt Disney Company's $19 billion bid to acquire Capital Cities/ABC Inc., in which Berkshire owned 13 percent or twenty million shares. Berkshire's twenty million shares of Cap Cities/ABC, which cost $345 million, was then worth $2.5 billion. Disney paid $65/share cash plus one share of Disney stock for each Cap Cities/ABC share. Flush with these resources, Buffett was more emboldened to consider paying the $2.3 billion to fully control his sentimental favorite auto insurer.

When Berkshire acquired 100 percent of GEICO, it was the seventh largest auto insurer in the U.S., with 3.7 million cars insured. Buffett immediately adopted a new incentive compensation plan that was simple, measurable, easily understood, focused on key value drivers, and directly controllable by the individuals responsible for their area of responsibility. The plan for the top executives in the underwriting operation was based on just two variables: (1) growth in voluntary auto policies, and (2) underwriting profitability on auto business in place for more than one year. On the investment side, Lou Simpson received 10 percent of the excess over the S&P 500 performance measured over a staggered three-year period. The key point is that Buffett tied incentive compensation directly to accountable behavior and responsibility.

In 1994, the full year prior to Buffett's agreed-upon buyout, GEICO spent $31 million on marketing. Buffett fanned the flame of GEICO's advertising, which spawned the iconic beloved gecko and the irrepressible GEICO caveman to drive awareness and trumpet its comparatively low prices. GEICO's tag line, "15 minutes could save you 15 percent or more on car insurance" is familiar to nearly everyone. GEICO now spends over $1 billion a year on advertising, and its brand has become a household name. GEICO can afford to outspend multiples of other car insurers since it doesn't have the expense of paying commissions to agents. The results are telling. GEICO's brand earned the number one ranking in YouGov BrandIndex's 2016 Ad Awareness Ranking, beating out Verizon, McDonalds, and AT&T.

As you can see in the table below, GEICO has gained market share and is now second only to State Farm's 18 percent share in a still fragmented market. GEICO's growth in autos insured, premiums earned, and float has compounded for over twenty years at or near double-digit rates. GEICO has become even more efficient as the premiums per employee more than doubled since Berkshire acquired the company. The most comparable public company is Progressive (PGR), which had premiums earned in 2016 of $23.4 billion compared to GEICO's $25.5 billion. Progressive had a market capitalization of $25 billion in 2017. GEICO's implied valuation of at least $25 billion represents over a ten-fold increase in total value compared to Buffett's all-in cost for GEICO of $2.4 billion. GEICO still has a long runway of growth ahead, even with the distant prospect of self-driving cars.

GEICO	1995	2016	CAGR
Market Ranking	7th	2nd	—
Share of industry volume	2.5%	12.0%	—
# cars insured (M)	3.7	24.0	9.3%
Premiums earned ($B)	$ 2.79	$ 25.5	11.1%
# of employees	8,575	36,085	7.1%
Premiums/employee	$ 325,015	$ 706,665	—
Float ($B)	$ 3.0	$ 17.1	8.7%

Takeaways

The significance of Buffett's experience with GEICO cannot be underestimated. Buffett was asked by Becky Quick, a CNBC commentator, on March 13, 2013, which company he would keep if he could only keep one company that Berkshire owned partially or entirely. Buffett's response was,

> *I would keep GEICO… Sixty-two years ago it changed my life. It's also a wonderful company… if I hadn't gone to GEICO when I was twenty years old and had a fellow there explain the insurance business to me, my life would be vastly different. So… I'd have to choose GEICO.*

Buffett's experience with GEICO demonstrated his:

Insatiable Curiosity to Learn

Reading *Security Analysis* by Benjamin Graham several times whetted Buffett's appetite to learn more about his mentor. As a student at Columbia, Buffett discovered that Graham was chairman of GEICO. A company that merited

Graham's position as chairman deserved further study. Buffett wasn't satisfied with a passive read of GEICO in the library, so he personally visited the company.

In 1976 Buffett sought out Jack Byrne to evaluate his ability as CEO to make the tough decisions that were required to rescue GEICO. Backed by a deep conviction based on a first-hand conversation, he wasted no time in making a large investment.

Willingness to Bet Big on His Conviction

At the age of twenty, Buffett was so convinced about the underappreciated growth prospects for GEICO after his conversation with Davidson that he promptly invested more than half his net worth in GEICO.

One might question the prudence of investing such a large weight in one company. Buffett later advised, "Risk comes from not knowing what you're doing," and "Diversification is a protection against ignorance. It makes very little sense for those who know what they're doing." Buffett would argue that investing in conventional or popular stocks does not mean investing is conservative. Whereas investing in GEICO with unbridled growth opportunity, especially led by a passionate, competent, and honest founder, at 8x earnings is conservative though it may not be conventional.

The first time Buffett bought GEICO in 1951, his broker colleagues rejected his recommendation even though he touted it as *The Security I Like Best*. Buffett was just as resolute with his conviction in 1976 when he was willing to buy the entire $76 million convertible stock offering, even though the traditional large equity-oriented Wall Street investment banks turned down the offering as too risky.

Focus on an Enduring Competitive Advantage

Buffett looks for companies that enjoy an enduring competitive advantage. He refers to this competitive advantage as a "moat" that surrounds and protects the company's castle from marauding competitors. GEICO's underlying low-cost competitive advantage was sustainable. At times, it was buried under a misguided attempt to diversify into other types of insurance and in substandard underwriting. But its underlying low-cost moat was durable because the tradition-bound competitors would not relinquish their commission-based agent model. GEICO's competitive advantage is as alive today as it was at its founding.

Sense of Responsibility and Loyalty

In 1975 GEICO was unraveling as its stock was falling precipitously. Buffett said, "I looked again at GEICO and was startled by what I saw after a few rule-of-thumb calculations about loss reserves."[76] Buffett didn't own any shares, but he dropped in to see Norm Gidden, the chairman at the time. Buffett recalled, "He was friendly, but he had no interest in listening to my comments. They were in deep denial. He really sort of hustled me out of the office and would not respond on the subject."[77]

That he was unceremoniously ushered out of GEICO's offices likely emboldened Buffett's resolve to become more involved. He felt compelled to save the company because, as he said, it *deserved to be saved*. Its underlying unique competitive advantage was still intact, and he wanted to preserve the legacy of two of his favorite mentors, Ben Graham and Lorimer Davidson, who never sold their shares.

After Buffett made his $4 million investment with Jack Bryne at the helm, Buffett tried to help Byrne's cause by personally visiting with Max Wallach, the District of Columbia regulator, to extend the June deadline for securing reinsurance.

Faith in 'Float'

Lorimer Davidson's generous time with Buffett on a cold wintry Saturday morning was rewarding for not just exposing Buffett to the valuable low-cost moat of GEICO but also for introducing Buffett to the concept of float.

Today Buffett says Berkshire's most important sector is insurance because insurers receive premiums upfront and pay claims later. The collect-now, pay-later model is referred to as "float." Float allows insurers to invest the premiums. If Berkshire's insurance companies can earn an underwriting profit after its claims losses, as they usually do, then Berkshire actually gets paid to keep the float. The investment income derived from investing the float is purely additive to earnings. By contrast, many insurers subsidize underwriting losses with their investment income from float. In this case, float is not free.

This free float capital is hugely valuable in the hands of an astute investor like Buffett. Float doesn't bear interest costs like bank debt nor does it dilute existing shareholders by issuing additional shares in a secondary stock offering. As Yogi Berra once said, "They give you cash, which is just as good as money." It is no wonder why Buffett was never more excited about a stock after he heard Lorimer Davidson's pitch.

The benefit to Berkshire has been enormous. Berkshire's float has exploded from $39 million in 1970 to more than $120 billion in 2018. It's enough to make a gecko drool.

Ability to Identify and Surround Himself with Management All-Stars

Benjamin Graham led to Lorimer Davidson, which led to Jack Byrne, which led to Tony Nicely and Lou Simpson. They are part of Buffett's equivalent line-up of the 1927 Yankees. Individually they are very different, but they all shared a passion for excellence in their chosen field. When Buffett bought the remaining 49 percent of GEICO, it was well-run, profitable, generated excess cash, and already came with best-in-class and high-integrity management. Buffett would replicate this model with success in Berkshire's other 100 percent-owned companies.

Wells Fargo

The inscription on the gravestones of the Savings & Loan Crisis and Drexel Burnham Lambert were barely dusted-off when fresh graves were being dug for many large financial institutions in the late 1980s and early 1990s. In the four-year period from 1988–1991, U.S. bank and S&L failures totaled $250 billion. They ranged from Bank of New England in Massachusetts to American Savings in California. In California alone, S&Ls with $75 billion of assets went bankrupt, including former stalwarts Gibraltar Savings, Imperial Savings, Columbia Savings, and Lincoln Savings. In the ten years ending 1995, one-third of the more than 3,200 S&Ls failed, which cost $160 billion; $132 billion of that was borne by taxpayers.

Many S&Ls issued long-term mortgage loans at fixed rates and funded the loans from variable short-term deposits. In response to rising inflation, the Federal Reserve raised the discount rate from 5.25 percent in the summer of 1977 to 14 percent in 1981. As inflation and interest rates spiked, the cost of deposits eventually exceeded rates earned on loans. The investment bank, Drexel Burnham Lambert, was only too eager to provide a solution to offset losses from core lending. Drexel popularized investments in high-yield bonds used to finance below investment-grade companies. While high-debt leverage may have been a creative way to finance steady cash flow generators, such as the telecom company MCI Communications and the tobacco and snack-food company RJR Nabisco, when it was used to finance cyclical and unproven companies, defaults mounted, and investment losses added to credit losses. The seductive appeal of higher yields proved fatal to investors when they underestimated the flip-side of higher yields—higher risk. Also contributing to the demise of financial institutions charmed by excess leverage were questionable ethics, bad loans to developing countries, competition for deposits from mutual funds and for loans from Wall Street investment banks, a looming recession, and short-cut analysis.

Warren Buffett denounced one such short-cut financial metric. He warned that the popular metric known as EBITDA (earnings before interest expense, taxes, depreciation and amortization) was flawed. "Trumpeting EBITDA is a particularly pernicious practice."[78] EBITDA was and still is used as a short-cut metric for cash flow. Debt/EBITDA was, and also still is, a popular but crude metric used to convince investors that debt coverage was more manageable than deserved. EBITDA is flawed because it ignores the very real cost of depreciation. The better measure of a company's ability to service its interest and principal payments on debt is EBIT (earnings before interest expense and taxes) less maintenance capital spending. However, in the era of the 1980s and early 1990s, greed overwhelmed prudent analysis, and EBITDA was used to justify high debt.

The strain of lax lending and short-sighted investment analysis resulted in bankruptcies for the worst offenders, and layoffs and dividend eliminations for many others. But green shoots were evident by early 1989. Bank of America, for instance, resumed paying dividends. For three years, it had eliminated dividends because of significant losses, laying off 9,000 employees, selling its prized headquarters property at 555 California Street, and its Charles Schwab discount brokerage subsidiary.

Wells Fargo was unique—it maintained its dividend throughout the challenging decade of the 1980s. Wells Fargo delivered for its shareholders, who were accustomed to the company's famed reliability ever since 1852, when Henry Wells and William Fargo founded the bank to safeguard the gold miner's treasures and to ferry mail to the gold fields on its iconic stagecoach.

In 1989 Wells Fargo's then fifty-eight-year-old Chairman and CEO Carl Reichardt echoed this reliability and his frustration with the valuation of the company.

We've been in business for 137 years and to the best of my knowledge this company's never lost money. It bugs the hell out of me that the industrials are on average selling at twelve times earnings, and here's a company that has a great deal of predictability, selling at seven or eight times earnings.[79]

Reichardt joined Wells Fargo in 1970 from Union Bank after cutting his teeth making loans to real estate developers and commercial builders. He became chairman and CEO of Wells Fargo in 1983 and was known for his direct, tough-minded, no-nonsense management style with a maniacal focus on productivity. "We do have almost a fetish about this expense control thing."[80] He even eliminated the bank's tradition of putting up a large Christmas tree on the executive's twelfth floor since few if any customers visited that floor. Reichardt was proud that Wells Fargo's average compensation per employee was the highest among California banks, but Wells had the best efficiency ratio, a measure of operating expenses as a percent of revenue.

Reichardt brought with him a close colleague from Union Bank, Paul Hazen, who became Reichardt's right-hand man as Wells's president and chief operating officer. Hazen's soft-spoken nature complemented Reichardt's direct, outspoken, salty manner. As different as they were in personality, they shared a similar competitive passion for running a profitable and efficient bank. Reichardt's strategy was to focus Wells Fargo's lending primarily in California, the world's sixth largest economy, concentrate on a few core businesses, and relentlessly cut costs. He wrote off billions in foreign loans originated by his predecessor, closed all of its overseas offices, purchased several California banks, including cross-town rival Crocker National and Barclays Bank of California, sold off marginally profitable businesses, and laid off thousands of employees. After acquiring Crocker National in 1986, Wells would double its profits from Crocker in four years.

Reichardt shifted Wells Fargo's loan portfolio toward what he knew best: commercial, construction, and real estate development. Despite a loss record on its construction and real estate portfolio that was better than Wells's overall loss record, investors were nervous about the bank's relatively large exposure at more than 18 percent of total loans. As of late 1989, Wells's profitability was measurably higher than other banks, as its return on assets was 1.26 percent compared to the national average of .88 percent and California's average of 0.94 percent. Its return on equity of 25 percent in 1989 and 1990 would be the envy of any company.

In 1990 California's market for office buildings, shopping centers, hotels, and industrial buildings was softening due to overbuilding, especially in

Southern California. The national average office vacancy rate was 20 percent while California was 15–22 percent. Some Wall Street analysts predicted that California's slumping housing prices could have an impact on banks in the same way that oil-related loans decimated Texas banks. In July 1990 Moody's countered by predicting that a softening market would hurt real estate lenders, but it didn't foresee a New England-style real estate recession. Moody's noted that Wells Fargo still ranked among the nation's top-rated banks.[81]

In Washington, the FDIC and other regulators were advocating repealing laws that limited interstate banking. The longer-term promise in banking was that loan losses would accelerate mergers among the nation's 10,000 banks, which would favor the most cost efficient acquiring banks. Moreover, the Federal Reserve would likely lower interest rates to stimulate the economy and boost the bank's net interest margins.

Investors were polarized on Wells Fargo stock. The skeptics pointed out that in 1990, Wells had the highest percentage of commercial real estate loans of any major bank in the country, at almost 5x common equity. Four other major California banks were much lower, ranging from 1.6–2.9x. Wells also had a large portfolio of leveraged buyout loans, although Reichardt said that the bank only invested in senior debt and that the debt was secured by tangible assets, such as a company's factories and equipment.

The bears were charging with bared teeth in late 1990 at the prospects of defaults from California real estate prices, which had slid 15–20 percent.[82]

The Feshbach brothers of Palo Alto were short Wells Fargo stock. Tom Barton, a Dallas money manager for Feshbach Brothers, said, "I don't think it's right to call them a bankruptcy candidate, but I think it's a teenager," meaning that the share price could drop into the teens from 43 7/8. He added, "It has one of the highest exposures to real estate of any bank."[144]

A Prudential-Bache Securities bank analyst, George Salem said, "California could become another Texas… (Wells Fargo) has more to lose. They are smarter than other banks, but they are more leveraged to California real estate."[144]

Merrill Lynch bank analyst Livia Asher downgraded the stock to neutral from buy. She "wasn't forecasting a serious 'deterioration in the company's fundamentals;' rather, she thinks the stock price may suffer because of 'a real glut of negative press reports' on California real estate."[144]

Against this backdrop, Berkshire disclosed in October 1990 that it purchased 9.8 percent of Wells Fargo common stock. Berkshire was limited to less than 10 percent ownership without approval from the Federal Reserve

Board. In Berkshire's 1990 annual report, Buffett reported that it paid $289.4 million for five million shares. Berkshire acquired about one-sixth of its five million shares in 1989 and the rest in 1990. The highlights of Buffett's reasoning behind his purchase as he explained in the 1990 report are as follows:

Management Team

- **Likes, trusts, and admires:** The Wells Fargo senior management team was then highly regarded as Buffett described: "superbly-managed" and "we think we have obtained the best managers in the business." (Note that Carl Reichardt retired as chairman and CEO from Wells Fargo in December 1994 and from the Wells Fargo board in April 1998. During his twelve-year tenure as chairman and CEO from 1983–1994, the total return for Wells Fargo common stock was 1,668 percent compared to 396 percent for the S&P 500.[83])

- **Terrific fit together:** Carl Reichardt and Paul Hazen: "each partner understands, trusts, and admires (each) other" and the "pair is stronger than the sum of the parts."

- **Pays well for top performers and has minimal waste:** They "abhor having a bigger head count than is needed."

- **Ongoing cost vigilance:** "Both attack costs as vigorously when profits are at record levels as when they are under pressure."

- **Stay within their circle of competence:** "Both stick with what they understand and let their abilities, not their egos, determine what they attempt."

- **Revered culture:** For many years, Wells Fargo executives were more avidly recruited than any others in the banking business.

Business

- **Well-managed:** When banks commonly "have assets that are 20x equity, mistakes that involve a small portion of assets can destroy a major portion of equity" which is why "the banking business is no favorite of ours. Because leverage of 20:1 magnifies the effects of managerial strengths and weaknesses, we have no interest in purchasing shares of a poorly-managed bank at a "cheap" price. Instead, our only interest is in buying into well-managed banks at fair prices."

- **High-return:** Wells Fargo "has been earning more than 20 percent on equity and 1.25 percent on assets."

- **Risk Assessment:**

  - *Earthquake:* "California banks face the specific risk of a major earthquake." While the risk is real, the likelihood of widespread damage is low.

  - *Systemic (low risk):* A financial panic that impacts every bank. A real but also low risk.

  - *Vulnerability of Wells to a fallout in California real estate:* "The market's major fear of the moment is that West Coast real estate values will tumble because of overbuilding and deliver huge losses to banks that have financed the expansion."

  - *Quantified minimal risk:* "Wells Fargo currently earns well over $1 billion pre-tax annually after expensing more than $300 million for loan losses. If 10 percent of all $48 billion of the bank's loans—not just its real estate loans—were hit by problems in 1991, and these produced losses (including foregone interest) averaging 30 percent of principal, the company would roughly break even. A year like that—which we consider only a low-level possibility, not a likelihood—would not distress us. In fact, at Berkshire we would love to acquire businesses or invest in capital projects that produced no return for a year, but that could then be expected to earn 20 percent on growing equity."

Wells Fargo & Co. (in millions)	1990	1989	1988
Net Interest Income	$ 2,313.9	$ 2,158.6	$ 1,972.1
Provision for loan losses	(310.0)	(362.0)	(300.0)
NonInterest Income	908.6	778.7	682.2
NonInterest Expense	(1,717.3)	(1,574.5)	(1,519.1)
Pretax Income	$ 1,195.2	$ 1,000.8	$ 835.2
Buffett's worse case scenario:			
Total Loans:	$ 48,000.0		
Problem Loans: 10%	$ 4,800.0		
Average loss rate: 30%	$ 1,440.0		

Price

- **Purchased at less than 5x earnings** and less than 3x pre-tax earnings due to industry-wide fears of losses from inadequate loan loss reserves.

  Our purchases of Wells Fargo in 1990 were helped by a chaotic market in bank stocks. The disarray was appropriate: Month by month the foolish loan decisions of once well-regarded banks were put on public display. As one huge loss after another was unveiled—often on the heels of managerial assurances that all was well—investors understandably concluded that no bank's numbers were to be trusted.[84]

- **Conviction is tested after a 50 percent drop in price:** Buffett mentioned that after buying Wells Fargo stock in 1989, the price fell almost 50 percent within a few months during 1990, which didn't deter him from buying more. "We welcomed the decline because it allowed us to pick up many more shares at the new, panic prices."

- **Don't buy a stock simply because it is unloved; know why you own it:**

  The most common cause of low prices is pessimism—sometimes pervasive, sometimes specific to a company or industry. We want to do business in such an environment, not because we like pessimism but because we like the prices it produces. It's optimism that is the enemy of the rational buyer. None of this means, however, that a business or stock is an intelligent purchase simply because it is unpopular; a contrarian approach is just as foolish as a follow-the-crowd strategy. What's required is thinking rather than polling. [85]

Richard "Dick" Fredericks, a bank analyst at Montgomery Securities who had been bullish on Wells Fargo since 1974 said, "Buffett loves franchises. There is a tremendous franchise in the (big) California banks…The four top banks (in the state) have 60 percent to 70 percent of the deposits." In addition, Mr. Fredericks said, "Mr. Buffett is a friend of Wells Fargo's chief executive officer, Carl E. Reichardt… who …would be a powerhouse manager in any business."[144] But even Dick Fredericks admitted "to being edgy."

Shortly after the Berkshire's disclosure of its purchase of Wells Fargo stock, *The Wall Street Journal* staff reporter John Dorfman summarized the bullish case. He praised the management, who had anticipated credit problems and beefed-up loan loss reserves. He quoted a Wells Fargo spokeswoman who said, "We have a proven track record in managing real estate in California and elsewhere." Dorfman pointed out that the "fifteen-year track record included two of the worst real estate downturns the country has seen, the recession of 1973–1975 and the real estate disaster brought on by excruciatingly high interest rates in 1981–1982." Furthermore, the stock price already discounted bad news as it had fallen 50 percent to just 81 percent of book value and was only 3.6x trailing twelve-month earnings.

When Buffett bought over 80 percent of his first five million shares in 1990 for an average price of $57.89/share, he would have closely analyzed Wells Fargo's 1989 annual report. In it, Carl Reichardt and Paul Hazen reported that Wells Fargo's EPS grew 20 percent to $11.02/share, and that its return on assets of 1.26 percent and its return on a common equity of 24.5 percent were all-time highs. The annual dividend increased 20 percent in 1989 to $3.60/share, which generated a yield of over 6 percent for Berkshire. Furthermore, the dividend had grown at a 25 percent rate over the previous five years.

Reichardt and Hazen referred to 1989 as a turbulent year for the industry, but a year where they increased concentration on its core banking franchise. They sold or charged off the last of its developing country loans, sold its general equipment leasing business, and agreed to close its offices in Hong Kong, Seoul, and Singapore. Altogether, Wells eliminated $1.7 billion of developing country loans over the prior two years to reduce its risk and shifted its loan mix to in-market home mortgages. It also acquired three in-market banks, which added nearly 10 percent to its retail branch base in prime growth markets of Southern and Central Valley, California. They defended their exposure to highly leveraged transaction loans by being selective on a case-by-case basis, diversifying among many small- to medium-sized transactions, and protecting itself with senior or secured loans.

They also demonstrated a desire to delight its customers by being more accessible. Wells was the first major California bank to offer twenty-four-hour, person-to-person phone banking. It began offering home computer online banking and introduced 9:00 a.m. to 6:00 p.m. banking hours as well as Saturday hours from 10:00 a.m. to 4:00 p.m. Wells also offered a "Five Minute Max" service guarantee for customers. If they had to wait longer in line, they received a $5 credit to their checking account.

Core customer deposits, including non-interest-bearing deposits, interest-bearing checking accounts, savings accounts, and savings certificates funded 69 percent of deposits, which lessened the bank's reliance on deposits from less reliable, higher cost commercial paper funding, and senior and subordinated debt capital was strong enough for Wells to repurchase two million shares of common stock, which represented almost 4 percent of shares outstanding.

Commercial real estate loans of $11.8 billion represented 30 percent of total loans. Of these, roughly two-thirds were in California. Highly leveraged transaction loans (HLTs) were $4.2 billion, or 10.7 percent of total loans.

Berkshire effectively paid 1.2x Wells Fargo's book value of $48.08/share in its first reported purchase in 1989–1990. Since Wells reported an ROE of 24.5 percent in 1989, it effectively meant that Berkshire's implied return was over 20 percent (24.5 percent/1.2x).

The next two years tested the resolve of Wells Fargo. California was in a recession, and many traditional high-growth industries experienced lower production and laid-off employees, which pressured credit quality. Consequently, bank regulators recommended significant increases in loan loss reserves from $310 million in 1990 to $1.3 billion in 1991 and $1.2 billion in 1992. Buffett's worse-case scenario of break-even pretax earnings became reality in 1991, when Wells earned a mere $54 million compared to $1.2 billion the year before.

However, pretax, pre-provision income—a popular metric used by investors to measure the core earnings power of a bank that eliminates cyclical swings in the somewhat arbitrary loan loss provision—reflected a healthier underlying company. While reported pretax income dropped in half from 1990 to 1992, pretax, pre-provision income actually increased from $1.5 billion to $1.7 billion.

Wells Fargo & Co. (in millions)	1992	1991	1990
Net Interest Income	$ 2,691	$ 2,520	$ 2,314
Provision for loan losses	(1,215)	(1,335)	(310)
NonInterest Income	1,059	889	909
NonInterest Expense	(2,035)	(2,020)	(1,717)
Pretax Income	$ 500	$ 54	$ 1,196
Add back Provision	1,215	1,335	310
Pretax Preprovision income	$ 1,715	$ 1,389	$ 1,506

Net interest income increased steadily due to a wider spread between interest rates earned on loans and the rates it paid on deposits and borrowings used to fund its loans. Non-interest income, which includes more predictably recurring service charges and fee-based services, increased over the two-year period.

Reflecting later on this trying period Buffett conceded, "I underestimated the severity of both the California recession and the real estate troubles of the company."[86] Reichardt was convinced the loans would be sound and that reserves were more than adequate:

> Call them nonperforming loans, call them substandard loans, call them whatever you want, but the cash is still going to flow. Our reserves are now 6.2 percent (in October 1993) of our total loan portfolio, which is the second-highest of the major banks in the industry. If you take our single family loans, which historically have had no losses, then we have a reserve of 8 percent. Our losses have never been that high.[146]

In addition to conservative reserves for loan losses, most of the company's nonaccrual loans were fully secured by real estate collateral. Also, Wells Fargo's $42 billion of loyal, low-cost deposits and its 626 retail branch network were valuable assets.

Bruce Berkowitz was an investor and senior vice president at Lehman Brothers. His concentrated bets later earned him fame when he was named mutual fund manager of the decade by Morningstar in 2010. In 1992, he had nearly one-third of his liquid net worth in Wells Fargo and he articulated the bull case:

> The argument's simple. Wells has had fantastic earning power in the past. And I just don't see any reason why it won't continue. In fact, it's growing. Its earnings power has been disguised by the intense provisioning for loan losses. But when the provisioning gets back to a normal level, you'll start to see that incredible earning power come down to the bottom line. And it's as simple as that… And they're the low-cost operator. We're also talking about a business that'll be earning well over 20 percent on equity when the recession finally ends… Wells is earning $33 pretax and pre-provision per year right now. Just thinking about it gives me the shakes.[87]

The bull case for Wells Fargo recognized that California accounted for 13 percent of U.S. GDP with a diverse economy that wasn't dependent on a single commodity, unlike Texas and its oil. Although 25 percent of the aerospace and defense jobs in Southern California were eliminated in 1991–1992 and resulted in 25 percent office vacancies in San Diego, California's exposure to electronics, entertainment, biotechnology, finance, agriculture, and food processing would make California resilient to a recession.

Resilient it was. After nine consecutive quarters of increasing problem loans, peaking at $3 billion in September 1992, they fell to $1.5 billion by year end 1993 and further to $871 million in 1994. California's economy began stabilizing in 1993, and a general recovery was underway in 1994. Wells never posted an annual loss during this challenging period. By 1994 Wells Fargo earned $14.78/share, its ROE of 22.4 percent approached its 1989–1990 level of 25 percent, and its ROA of 1.62 percent exceeded its 1989 level of 1.26 percent. Much of the earnings improvement resulted from a lower loan loss provision as loans classified as nonaccrual returned to accrual status. In other words, Wells Fargo's underwriting standards were proving bank examiners wrong, and their borrowers were weathering the economic storm. The loan loss provision dropped from $1.2 billion in 1992 to just $200 million in 1994.

Wells Fargo & Co. (in millions)	1994	1993	1992
Net Interest Income	$ 2,610	$ 2,657	$ 2,691
Provision for loan losses	(200)	(550)	(1,215)
NonInterest Income	1,200	1,093	1,059
NonInterest Expense	(2,156)	(2,162)	(2,035)
Pretax Income	$ 1,454	$ 1,038	$ 500
Add back Provision	200	550	1,215
Pretax Preprovision income	$ 1,654	$ 1,588	$ 1,715

Berkshire's bet on Wells Fargo's management paid-off. Buffett later explained,

> I knew something about Carl Reichardt and, to a lesser extent at that time, Paul Hazen, from having met them and also from having read a lot of things they'd said. They were certainly different than the typical banker. Then the question was how much that difference would impact how they would run the place. And they ran into some very heavy seas subsequently. And I think those human differences that were perceived earlier were probably what let them come through as well as they did.[88]

Charlie Munger added to Buffett's recollection of Wells' handling of the recession:

I might add to that slightly—because that Wells Fargo bank is a very interesting example. They had a huge concentration of real estate lending—a field in which there was the biggest collapse in over fifty years. If they had been destined to suffer the same sort of average loss from real estate loans as an ordinary bank would have suffered, the place would have been broke.

We were basically betting that their real estate lending was way better than average. And indeed, it was. And they also handled it on the way down way better than average. Everybody else was looking at this horrible concentration of real estate loans in this sea of troubles in the real estate field and in bankers to that field. And they just assumed Wells Fargo was going to go broke. We figured that since their loans and collection methods were way higher quality than others that it would be all right. And so it worked out.[89]

Buffett had the final word on the importance of assessing management, "If we hadn't gone a little further, though, than just looking at numbers, we would not have been able to make that decision."[90]

After Berkshire's initial investment in Wells Fargo of $289.4 million in 1989–1990, Berkshire invested an additional $12.4 billion in Wells Fargo, which by the end of 2016 was worth $27.6 billion. Berkshire is Wells Fargo's largest shareholder with a 10 percent ownership stake. Berkshire's 10 percent ownership stake in Wells Fargo remained relatively unchanged from its initial purchase in 1989–1990, despite buying $12.4 billion more stock due to three events that diluted Berkshire's stake. The first was Wells Fargo's merger with Norwest in 1998, where former Wells Fargo shareholders owned about 52.5 percent of the combined company. The second was Wells Fargo's $15.1 billion all-stock merger with Wachovia in 2008 when Wells issued 422.7 million additional shares to finance the deal, which was the largest non-initial public offering single issue of common stock in U.S. history. The third was in reaction to the financial credit crisis of 2008–2009 when Wells Fargo issued additional stock in a series of secondary stock offerings to boost capital.

Takeaways

Wells Fargo surpassed Coca-Cola in 2012 as Berkshire's largest holding, and its market value in 2016 more than doubled Berkshire's cumulative purchase price. Five years after Berkshire's first purchase, when influential skeptics either shorted or downgraded their stock rating over Wells Fargo's exposure to commercial real estate, Wells Fargo stock more than tripled.

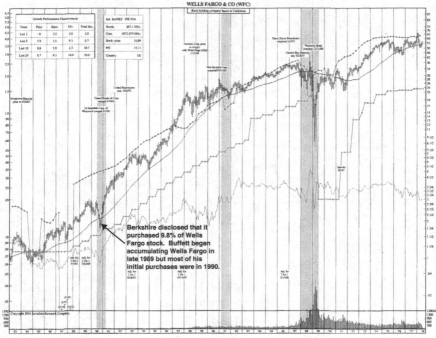

Figure 21. Wells Fargo

Bet on Management

Warren Buffett said, "If you don't know jewelry, you better know the jeweler." The same applies to banking. Some investors refuse to invest in banks because they can't assess the quality of loans. While it is true that an investor cannot know for certain the ability of every borrower to repay, investors can assess: the bank management's experience and track record; the character and consistency of the bank's lending culture; how proactive the bank is with customer service; the cost and composition of deposits; the bank's cost discipline; and whether management's actions are shareholder-minded or ego-centric empire builders.

Carl Reichardt demonstrated success in real estate development and commercial loans at Union Bank for over ten years before joining Wells Fargo. By focusing on California real estate loans, he was staying within his circle of competence. Loans to developing countries were not in Reichardt or Hazen's wheelhouse. Many other banks hemorrhaged billions in losses from defaulted loans to highly indebted countries.

Buffett personally met with Reichardt, which boosted his conviction that Reichardt was no aloof stuffed shirt. Reichardt was a no-nonsense, practical, cost-conscious businessman who was passionate about staying close to his customers, rewarding top performing colleagues, and rewarding shareholders with prudent growth and opportunistic share buybacks. These characteristics compelled Buffett to say they were the best managers in banking. Though the average investor may not have personal access to CEOs, investors can assess their candor and performance in interviews, as well as attend annual meetings to observe their conduct and even ask questions.

Margin of Safety

Buffett astutely quantified the downside risk in Wells Fargo *before* he bought the stock, which established his margin-of safety. He estimated that, in a worse-case scenario, Wells Fargo would still break even even if 10 percent of all its loans were problematic/nonaccrual and if 30 percent of those loans produced losses. Buffett's worse case did happen, and Wells Fargo essentially broke even in 1991. It is important to remember that those break-even results were primarily due to an oversized loan loss reserve, which proved ultra-conservative when those reserved-for losses were subsequently reversed. Those real estate and highly-leveraged transaction borrowers proved to be sound credits, a testimony to Wells Fargo's strong underwriting standards and credit culture.

Conviction is Tested

Wells Fargo stock fell 50 percent after Berkshire's first purchase in 1989. Undaunted, Buffett and Munger bought five times as much in 1990. After Berkshire disclosed its first investment in October 1990, George Salem, a bank analyst at Prudential-Bache Securities said, Mr. Buffet "is a famous bargain hunter and long-term investor. He picked the management that underwrites real estate the best. But the one thing he didn't realize is that even (the former Olympic swimming star) Mark Spitz can't swim in a hurricane in the middle of the ocean."[91]

While no one would mistake Carl Reichardt for seven-time Olympic gold medalist Mark Spitz, the mustached swimmer never had to navigate the under-tow of the 1973–1975 recession, the energy crisis, S&L crisis, and double-digit unemployment and inflation. Reichardt and Hazen gold-medaled in these choppy waters even before arriving at Wells Fargo. They were proven hall-of-famers when they encountered the tsunami impact of the stock market crash of

Black Monday in October 1987, which precipitated the turbulent recession in the early 1990s. Buffett and Munger had the courage to bet that Reichardt and Hazen's experience and track record would prevail against the doubters who sent the stock down 50 percent in the short-term. Their courage was based on conviction in management and in quantifying downside risk. Reichardt and Hazen did gold-medal once again, and their names are etched—not in gravestones like so many S&Ls—but in the lore of Wells Fargo's storied history.

CHAPTER 21

Ethics and Mindset

It takes 20 years to build a reputation and five minutes to ruin it. If you think about that, you'll do things differently.

—WARREN BUFFETT

Ethics

Berkshire Hathaway

One of the moral principles that Warren Buffett cherishes is "Your word is your bond." Breaking that bond in business dealings with him has severe consequences. That maxim was glaringly evident in May 1964 when Seabury Stanton, then CEO of the textile manufacturer Berkshire Hathaway, asked Buffett what price he would sell his partnership's shares. Buffett's Partnership, which then managed $7 million, had accumulated about 110,000 shares for a 7 percent ownership in Berkshire at $7.50/share. Buffett was attracted by the wide price discount to Berkshire's working capital per-share of $10.25 and book value per-share of $20.20. Buffett was enticed by Berkshire's habit of buying back shares with the proceeds of liquidating one of their textile mills. The U.S. textile business had already been in a secular decline, but Buffett figured that he could make a small profit by tendering the stock after they closed another mill. Berkshire had recently closed two mills and was positioned to repurchase more shares. When Stanton asked Buffett what price he would sell his holdings, Buffett answered $11.50/share. According to Buffett, Stanton replied, "Fine, we have a deal."[1] On May 6, 1964, Buffett received the offer letter from Berkshire to buy 225,000 shares for $11.375/share—an eighth of a point less than verbally agreed.

Though the offer price was 50 percent higher than Buffett's cost, Buffett was enraged by Stanton's ethical lapse at chiseling the offer by $0.125/share. Though the lower offer meant that Buffett would receive about $14,000 less than their verbal agreement, it was tougher to swallow the reputational loss as a patsy to someone who broke his handshake deal. Incensed, Buffett fought back by acquiring about 283,000 more shares for a total ownership of 39 percent by April 1965, which was enough to control the company by the May 1965 board meeting. Buffett fired Stanton and found himself "in a terrible business about which I knew very little."[2] He added, "the truth is I had now committed a major amount of money to a terrible business."[3]

In the Berkshire Hathaway 2014 annual report, Buffett referred to this as a "monumentally stupid decision." Upon taking control, Berkshire had no excess cash and owed its bank $2.5 million. The textile business was a financial and managerial albatross that diverted time and resources for the next two decades before Buffett finally surrendered to inevitable competitive dynamics. In an interview in 2010, Buffett thought that Berkshire then would be worth double, or $200 billion more than its current value, had he put the money directly in the insurance business.[4]

With this experience Buffett concluded that, "When a manager with a reputation for brilliance meets up with a business with a reputation for bad economics, it's the reputation of the business that remains intact." He added that, "if you get in a lousy business, get out of it."[5] A major appeal of a Buffett-controlled Berkshire is its appeal to businesses that are considering being acquired by Berkshire. Buffett promises that their culture will remain intact and that their business will find a permanent home in Berkshire. Buffett won't play gin rummy with 100 percent-owned businesses by selling them after he tires of them or when they don't fit his current business model. He won't leverage them with massive debt, cut personnel to the bone, and then repackage it to sell. The only exception where Buffett would consider selling or closing a 100 percent owned business was if it expected to lose Berkshire money permanently, or if the business had major labor difficulties. When asked at the 1998 Berkshire Hathaway annual meeting what criteria he used to sell a stock, Buffett responded, "Just hang on to great businesses for dear life."

Was Buffett prideful and stubborn at refusing a little more than a dime less per share than Stanton's agreed upon terms? Was he foolish to honor an ethical principle—that your word is your bond—by owning a terrible business that even a brilliant manager couldn't save? Was he even more stubborn by holding onto this dying business for two decades, or was he instead loyal to an honest, hardworking workforce?

Buffett's actions with Berkshire's textile business are a testament to his integrity, trust, honesty, and loyalty. He has said that he wants to do business with those that he likes, trusts, and admires. Buffett couldn't trust Stanton after he tried to chisel his shareholders by one-eighth of a point. For Buffett, the right course was to spare Berkshire shareholders further abuses by removing Stanton. He removed the deceitful captain without carefully considering if the vessel itself was seaworthy. Buffett brilliantly bolstered and expanded the ship for a memorable journey but not before experiencing at least two other episodes of evident and apparent deceit.

Salomon, Inc.

Warren Buffett believes so strongly about the importance of placing a client's interests above the firm, and of adhering to the ethical rules of conduct and the spirit of those rules, that before every Berkshire Hathaway annual meeting, he replays a video of his opening statement presented to a Congressional Subcommittee on May 1, 2010, regarding the activities of Salomon, Inc.:

> *I have asked every Salomon employee to be his or her own compliance officer. After they first obey all rules, I then want employees to ask themselves whether they are willing to have any contemplated act appear the next day on the front page of their local paper, to be read by their spouses, children, and friends, with the reporting done by an informed and critical reporter. If they follow this test, they need not fear my other message to them: Lose money for the firm, and I will be understanding; lose a shred of reputation for the firm, and I will be ruthless.*

His experience with Salomon is a timeless reminder to do what is right for the customer, be timely and transparent in communicating any transgressions, and avoid self-serving temptations. Buffett treasures trust and integrity. He has little to no patience when those bonds are broken.

Several key Salomon senior officers demonstrated self-destructive behavior in illegal trading and withholding this information, which almost cost the jobs of thousands of other ethical employees if not for the heroic actions and reputation of Warren Buffett in his role as interim chairman.

Background

During its merger with Salomon, Minerals & Resources (Minorco), a Bermuda-based investment holding company controlled by South African mining giant Anglo American Corp., received 21.2 million shares of Salomon stock in 1981 as consideration for its interest in an energy and commodities company, Phibro Corp. With its 21.2 million shares—a 14 percent stake—Minorco was Salomon's largest shareholder and had two of its own directors on Salomon's board.

Minorco was frustrated with its significant passive stake in Salomon as the securities firm stock price fell from the high $50s in 1985 to the low $30s by April 1987. Salomon suffered from large bond-trading losses, and it didn't have sufficient investment banking fees to offset the bond trading losses. Compounding the problem, Salomon had boosted its securities division staff by 40 percent just when revenue growth softened. In response to the decline, Salomon was nearly finished with a strategic review that was likely to lead to sweeping changes.

In April 1989, Minorco informed Salomon's Chairman and CEO John H. Gutfreund that it wanted to sell its block of stock. Gutfreund didn't want the stock to end up in unfriendly hands, and he didn't want Minorco's stock to be sold in periodic open-market sales, since that would further depress its stock price. Gutfreuend was also hamstrung because Salomon couldn't afford to erode its already highly leveraged capital base by reacquiring its own stock. With no evident progress, Minorco pressed the issue of selling its stake by filing its intention with the SEC in September 1989.

Ronald O. Perelman, chairman of Revlon, Inc. and a known corporate raider, approached Minorco and was close to an agreed-upon price. Gutfreund met with Perelman, and Perelman said he thought Salomon was undervalued, and he expected two seats on the board in return for a standstill agreement that would limit his interest to no more than 20–25 percent. Gutfreund and Salomon's directors rebuffed Perelman. Gutfreund explained,

> I don't really know these folks at Revlon, but I do know they ran a bootstrap operation that was financed by Drexel (Burnham Lambert—renowned aggressive junk-bond financier) to make some heady acquisitions. I feel that our clients would be totally uncomfortable with them.[6]

When they met again in Gutfreund's Manhattan apartment on Saturday, September 26th, Gutfreund was firm. "I told him I would not work for him and that I thought our people wouldn't work for him."[7] In a people-intensive business like a brokerage firm, a hostile deal is fraught with risk, since the acquired assets, namely people, can walk right out the door and never come back.

After Perelman left, Gutfreund agreed with Minorco that Salomon would match Revlon's tentative bid of $38/share or $809 million, which represented a premium to the previous day's close of $32/share.

Warren Buffett had a fond relationship with John Gutfreund since the 1970s when Gutfreund had agreed to underwrite a stock offering for GEICO. Sensing an urgent situation and a desperate seller, Buffett called Gutfreund to express his interest in buying a stake in Salomon and they agreed. On October 1, 1987, Berkshire invested $700 million in a cumulative convertible preferred security that paid a 9 percent annual dividend and was convertible at $38 a share. This was Berkshire's largest investment to date. Warren Buffett and Charlie Munger replaced the two Minorco directors on Salomon's board. A preferred security ranks above equity shareholders in the event of a liquidation or bankruptcy but ranks below bond holders. The cumulative feature obligated Salomon to make up any dividends that might be skipped. The preferred shares allowed Berkshire to have a 12 percent voting interest in Salomon, and Berkshire had the right after three years to convert its preferred shares into common stock at $38 a share compared to Salomon's stock price of $30. Salomon also agreed to repay Berkshire 20 percent of the preferred issue each year after eight years. Berkshire in return agreed to limit itself to no more than 20 percent control of Salomon's voting control for seven years and would vote its shares in accordance with the Salomon's board recommendations as long as Gutfreund or someone "satisfactory to Berkshire Hathaway" was CEO of Salomon.

Berkshire's investment was attractive based on the fixed income feature alone. The conversion option was icing on the cake. The real attraction was Buffett's confidence in Gutfreund, which he described in Berkshire's 1987 annual report:

> We, of course, have no special insights regarding the direction or future profitability of investment banking. By their nature, the economics of this industry are far less predictable than those of most other industries in which we have major commitments. This unpredictability is one of the reasons why our participation is in the form of a convertible preferred.
>
> What we do have a strong feeling about is the ability and integrity of John Gutfreund, CEO of Salomon Inc. Charlie and I like, admire, and trust John. We first got to know him in 1976 when he played a key role in

GEICO's escape from near-bankruptcy. Several times since, we have seen John steer clients away from transactions that would have been unwise, but that the client clearly wanted to make, even though his advice provided no fee to Salomon and acquiescence would have delivered a large fee. Such service-above-self behavior is far from automatic in Wall Street.

Although Salomon's equity shrank by more than $100 million ($700 million Berkshire proceeds less the $809 million payoff to Minorco), the company gained a huge reputational stamp of approval from Buffett and put a significant share stake into friendly hands. Salomon shareholders applauded and pushed the stock price higher by nearly $5 within two days to $36.875.

The preferred dividend arrangement was designed to allow Berkshire to collect a handsome $63 million a year largely tax-free, since corporations are exempt from 70 percent of their dividend income from preferred stocks. Therefore, Buffett negotiated a much more favorable arrangement from Salomon for Berkshire than if he negotiated with Minorco to buy its stake directly. Little did Buffett know that a mere eighteen days later, the stock market would plummet 23 percent on Black Monday, and Salomon's stock would eventually be cut in half. To make matters worse, Salomon's board voted to lower the exercise price of its employees' stock options as a retention policy over Buffett and Munger's objection. If shareholders suffered a price drop, why shouldn't employees share in the pain and have a stronger incentive to work even harder to drive the stock above the former exercise price?

Buffett would also buy similar preferred stocks in Gillette, U.S. Airways, and Champion International to help these companies thwart corporate raiders. In the case of Salomon, the preferred investment allowed Berkshire to patiently wait for Salomon to resurrect itself, or so Buffett thought.

Misdeeds: Bid-Rigging and Cover-Up

When business school students asked Buffett where they should go to get wealthy after college, he holds his nose and points to Wall Street. Not one to mince words, Charlie Munger elaborated,

Wall Street attracts and rewards what I call a locker room culture filled with people who just have to win at football or soccer or something like that. They are just so competitive that whatever A is doing they have to be as good, or better than A. Of course, Warren and I don't have those compulsions. I would rather live my way than theirs. They do enormous damage to the rest

*of us with their damn locker room culture that has to win, and is [sic] not
very squeamish about what they have to do to win.*[8]

It isn't the competitive nature alone that is so offensive to Munger, but
the unsavory manner in how they compete. Investment bankers at Salomon,
not unlike many others, were motivated by lucrative investment banking fees
earned by underwriting deals and then pumped the securities to clients. Get
the deal done, and caveat emptor—let the buyer beware—was the maxim
many lived by. Buffett disdained Wall Street's enabling junk bond-aholics:

> *As usual, the Street's enthusiasm for an idea was proportional not to its
> merit, but rather to the revenue it would produce. Mountains of junk bonds
> were sold by those who didn't care to those who didn't think—and there was
> no shortage of either.*[9]

Salomon traders were infamous for their aggressive fratboy behavior on
the smoky trading floor where they barked orders into their phone and swore
in frustration at their computer screens. The pressure to make split-second
profitable trading decisions on thin bid-ask bond spreads was in stark contrast
with Buffett's office in Omaha, where he didn't have a computer, read at least
five hours a day, and patiently waited for the right pitch each year.

Michael Lewis penned the best seller *Liar's Poker* in 1989, in which he
colorfully described his experience working for four years at Salomon Brothers, with first-hand experience in the company's testosterone-stoked culture,
encouraged by none other than CEO John Gutfreund. If Buffett knew the
extent of this subculture, he would likely have reconsidered his investment.
Lewis described an iconic scene where Gutfreund proposed playing a hand
of liar's poker against John Meriwether for $1 million. Liar's poker is a game
where two square off and bet their hand using the serial number on a dollar
bill. The game celebrates handicapping, bluffing, probability forecasting, and a
steely temperament—skills that were prized on the bond trading desk where
eighths of a point on billions of dollars traded could mean millions in trading
profits for the firm and lucrative bonuses for the traders. John Meriwether was
a brilliant mathematician and senior executive valued for his bond trading.
Meriwether sensed this proposal was a no-win scenario, since even if he won
the game, he would lose the war by losing against his boss. Meriwether countered by saying he would only play for $10 million and Gutfreund backed off.
Though this game was off, the macho freewheeling casino culture was on.

Traders were hired guns, willing to work for the highest Wall Street bidder. Between trades, the traders played practical jokes and one-upped each other with vulgar jokes and ordered up strippers. The culture of arrogance and bravado was as pungent as the billowing smoke from Gutfreunds's ever-present cigar.

The U.S. Treasury smelled smoke when they instituted a rule in 1990 that prevented any single Wall Street firm from bidding for more than 35 percent of treasury securities being auctioned. The U.S. Treasury wanted to prevent any one firm from unfairly exercising its bond trading negotiating power by cornering the market in any obligation of the U.S. Treasury. Smoke indeed led to fire when Salomon's managing director Paul Mozer broke this rule that he loathed—in December 1990 and again in February 1991. He bid up to Salomon's limit of 35 percent and added to this by submitting bids for Salomon clients, unbeknownst to them, for the excess. He then transferred the funds to Salomon's own account in an attempt to avoid detection. Sensing his scheme was about to be discovered in late April 1991, Mozer owned up to his infraction to his boss, John Meriwether, by showing him a letter from a federal regulator to a Salomon client whose name Salomon used to bid without permission. To Meriwether's credit, he immediately informed Salomon's president, Tom Strauss, of the news and, a few days later, discussed it with Strauss, Gutfreund, and Salomon's attorney, Donald Feuerstein. Feuerstein thought Mozer's act was criminal, and the group decided that the New York Federal Reserve must be informed of what happened. Curiously, the Federal Reserve wasn't told of "irregularities and rule violations" until four months later in August 1991 and then only when Salomon was faced with a federal investigation.

Buffett later described management's dereliction of duty to inform as "inexplicable and inexcusable."[10] Charlie Munger referred to management's silence and inaction as "thumb sucking."[11] This proverbial thumb sucking was due to management's fear that disclosure could jeopardize Salomon's critical need for funding. Salomon relied on refinancing billions of debt that matured each day, and if the company were deprived of this funding, it would be like unplugging an oxygen tube. The funding depended on trust.

Like a top-heavy inverted pyramid, Salomon's balance sheet leverage at the end of 1990, measured by its total assets to equity, was an unwieldy 31x. By mid-1991, Salomon's assets were $150 billion, or 37x its $4 billion in equity. For perspective, this exceeded Goldman Sachs's leverage ratio, which ballooned to 26x in 2007, just prior to the financial crisis, but by the end of 2016 had been reduced to 10x. Salomon had over $140 billion in debt, not including billions of dollars in off-balance sheet derivatives that entangled global counterparties supported by just $4 billion in equity. Salomon owed more money than any other financial institution in the U.S. except Citicorp. Most of the assets were funded with short-term loans that matured anytime from the next day up to six months later.

Gutfreund was remiss not only in neglecting to inform the Federal Reserve of the U.S. Treasury auction bid violation in a timely manner but also in neglecting to tell the Salomon board in a scheduled meeting about having just received a threatening letter from the Federal Reserve of New York. The letter indicated that the Fed was "deeply troubled" by Salomon's long-delayed disclosure of the bid violation, so much so that the Fed questioned its "continuing business relationship" with Salomon.

Buffett only became aware of the letter more than a month later, when the New York Federal Reserve bank president Gerald Corrigan referred to the letter in his testimony to Congress. Corrigan assumed that Gutfreund forwarded the letter to Salomon's board, especially given its grave implications, and Corrigan concluded that the board's inaction was an arrogant snub to the Federal Reserve. Buffett later reflected, "Understandably, the Fed felt at this point that the directors had joined with management in spitting in its face."[12]

Trust had been broken between Gutfreund and the board, and with the Federal Reserve. Moreover, trust was damaged with Salomon's creditors who wanted out. Solvency and return of capital was more important to them than earning a few extra basis points of interest as a lure to stay. After redeeming about $700 million of debt, Salomon stopped trading in its own securities. If Salomon wasn't confident in its own securities, why wouldn't investors demand their money back and run for the hills, let alone provide funding? Gutfreund and Strauss were desperate to regain trust in Salomon to restore funding, even if it cost their jobs.

Enter the Savior

Gutfreund and Strauss called Buffett and agreed to resign. Since Buffett was the largest equity holder with $700 million in preferred stock, he was the logical person to lead the company as interim-chairman until order was restored. Buffett didn't want the job, but he felt he had no choice. On August 18, 1991, he agreed to work for an annual salary of $1. Buffett said, "I read *Liar's Poker*, and my job is to prevent *Liar's Poker II* from being written."[13] At stake was not just his investment, but the careers of over 8,000 employees; the capital of thousands of shareholders for whom he was responsible as a board member; and the health of the financial system, which would likely have suffered a chaotic financial meltdown with worldwide repercussions if over $100 billion in debt suddenly defaulted. Buffett believed the egregious misconduct was a serious but local and excisable cancer that hadn't metastasized throughout Salomon.

After John Meriwether also resigned, Buffett faced the difficult task of choosing which senior member of Salomon would become the new head of securities. He interviewed a dozen candidates for about ten minutes each and asked each one who they thought was most qualified to become president and chief operating officer. The majority chose Deryck Maughan, as did Gutfreund. Maughan was the forty-three-year-old head of Salomon's Asian division for five years, a former British treasury official, and co-chairman of investment banking. He wasn't a U.S. national and wasn't a trader, but Buffett was sufficiently impressed with his integrity and ethical character to ask him to establish and enforce controls on Salomon's brash traders. As interim chairman, Buffett said he would help Maughan "clean up the sins of the past and capitalize on the assets of the firm."[14] Buffett was also impressed that Maughan never asked how much he would be paid.

Satisfied that Gutfreund, Strauss, Meriwether, Paul Mozer, and Tom Murphy (who led the government securities trading desk) were gone, and reassured by Buffett's reputation and integrity, the Federal Reserve partially reversed its preliminary decision to suspend Salomon from bidding on Treasury auctions, which would have been a dagger in Salomon's heart. Influenced by Buffett's personal appeal to Treasury Secretary, Nicholas Brady, and Buffett's threat to leave if Salmon was forced into bankruptcy, the Fed allowed Salomon to participate in auctions only for its own account and not for clients. Salomon was also allowed to trade in the secondary market for the resale of existing Treasury securities.

Buffett and Maughan instituted new trading rules that included more detailed record-keeping and daily reports, confirmed all customer orders in writing, and restricted advance trading in treasuries before auctions to the government securities desk. Meanwhile, Buffett deleveraged the balance sheet by selling billions in assets and dramatically cut bonuses and paid them in stock. He also had every treasury bid double-checked for accuracy.

Buffett followed his advice to others managers dealing with a business crisis, "Get it right, get it fast, and get it out." A mere eleven days after Buffett volunteered to serve as interim chairman, he published a letter to shareholders that appeared in *The New York Times*, *The Wall Street Journal*, and *The Washington Post*. He candidly and clearly outlined several reforms:

- Appointed Deryck Maughan as chief operating officer at Salomon Brothers Inc. along with a new management team. Buffett said appointing Maughan was his best decision since assuming his post. He later described Maughan as a man of talent, integrity, intelligence, and who was shareholder-oriented and business-wise.[15]

- Installed new rules and procedures.

- Designed new monitoring mechanisms including setting up a compliance committee of the board.

- Appointed himself as chief compliance officer and encouraged exemplary behavior that went beyond just following rules. He said, "I believe we can earn these superior returns playing aggressively in the center of the court, without resorting to close-to-the-line acrobatics. Good profits simply are not inconsistent with good behavior."

- Established a $200 million reserve for legal costs, which, while costly, was entirely manageable compared to Salomon's $4 billion equity base. The reserve was much lower than feared by investors. Management estimated that Salomon earned only about $20 million in profits from improper bidding in eight auctions, but this didn't include an estimate of client losses.

- Reformed an unsound and irrational compensation plan for one that linked pay for performance. Buffett noted that even though Salomon earned just 10 percent on equity, far below the average business, 106 employees were each paid over $1 million. Though earnings before compensation in 1990 was flat compared to 1989, total compensation swelled by more than $120 million. Beginning in 1991, highly paid employees would receive up to 50 percent of their compensation in stock, which they were required to hold for at least five years.

- On August 16, 1991, two days before Buffett became interim chairman, total assets were about $150 billion. By September 30 assets fell to $97 billion, and the asset/equity ratio dropped from 37x to 24x. Buffett explained his aversion to amassing leverage for marginal returns.

"Larger totals can actually lead to smaller profits: Undisciplined decision-making is a frequent consequence of ultra-easy access to funding, as both commercial and investment banks learned in recent years."[16]

- The parent company, Salomon, Inc., had two operating subsidiaries: the financial services division, Salomon Brothers, and the energy trading and oil refiner, Phibro Energy. Buffett said each business would be measured in their own right by the return on the equity capital they each required. Each would be evaluated independently and fairly. Phibro would no longer be an overlooked stepchild.

Salomon eventually agreed to settle its misdeeds for $290 million, and afterward the U.S. Treasury removed its sanctions, thereby allowing Salomon to resume bidding in U.S. Treasury auctions for clients.

Buffett served as interim-chairman for ten months while Paul Mozer, who started the scandal, paid a fine of $30,000 and was sentenced to prison for four months. Buffett rescued Salomon and further cemented his reputation for ethics and integrity by emphasizing compliance, transparency in reporting, and behavior that was well within the lines. He restored Salomon's credibility and reputation enough for Travelers, led by Sanford (Sandy) I. Weill, to buy Salomon in 1997 for $9 billion or $81.43 a share. Travelers issued stock to acquire Salomon and Berkshire received $1.8 billion for its ownership interest in Salomon.

Buffett praised Sandy Weill's accomplishments at Travelers on the day the merger was announced: "Over the decades, Sandy has demonstrated genius in creating huge value for his shareholders by skillfully blending and managing acquisitions in the financial services industry. In my view Salomon will be no exception."

I met Sandy Weill a few years later, and I reminded him of Buffett's high praise in referring to him as a genius. Sandy was still touched by Buffett's compliment. Ironically, Buffett could have easily been referring to his own "genius in creating huge value for his shareholders by skillfully blending and managing acquisitions" at Berkshire.

Buffett concluded the entire Salomon experience prophetically. "We believe that the intense regulatory and investigative focus on Salomon has ended. We can now move forward to show that high ethical standards and meaningful profits are not only compatible objectives, but ones that can reinforce each other."[17]

Buffett's impact on Salomon demonstrates that honesty, putting the interests of clients first, candid reporting, and insisting on firm integrity could beat a culture of measuring your worth solely by how much money you earned, with a sly wink about how you earned it. He embraced regulators with contrition and honesty. "I would like to start by apologizing for the acts that have brought us here. The nation has a right to expect its rules and laws to be obeyed. At Salomon, certain of these were broken."[18] Buffett restored the sacred trust between a public company and its shareholders. The financial "white knight" also wore an ethical white hat—showcasing that good guys do win in the end against arrogant cheats and cover-up distortionists.

David Sokol

When Warren Buffett passes, the role of chief investment officer and chief executive officer at Berkshire Hathaway, both of which are filled by Buffett, will be split between at least two people. Todd Combs and Ted Weschler currently manage billions of Berkshire investments each and are positioned to manage the rest at Buffett's passing. Over the years, speculation about who will succeed Buffett as chief executive officer has included Ajit Jain, Matt Rose, Greg Abel, and until 2011, David Sokol.

Ajit Jain is Vice Chairman of Insurance Operations for Berkshire Hathaway, which is arguably Berkshire's most important business because of its enormous float. Buffett consults with Ajit every day, and Buffett's praise has been effusive:

- "Ajit Jain created out of nothing an immense reinsurance business that produced both a huge 'float' and a large underwriting gain."[19]
- "If you meet Ajit at the annual meeting, bow deeply."[20]
- "Even kryptonite bounces off Ajit."[21]
- "If Charlie, I, and Ajit are ever in a sinking boat—and you can only save one of us—swim to Ajit."[22]

Matt Rose is the CEO of one of Berkshire's most profitable businesses, Burlington Railroad, and Greg Abel is the CEO of Berkshire's large and growing utility business, MidAmerican Energy. Buffett praises both Matt and Greg. "In Matt Rose, at BNSF, and Greg Abel, at MidAmerican, we have two outstanding CEOs. They are extraordinary managers who have developed businesses that serve both their customers and owners well. Each has my gratitude and each deserves yours."[23]

David Sokol was formerly chairman of MidAmerican Energy and a valued, go-to confidant of Buffett's to evaluate prospective acquisitions and repair management issues within Berkshire's businesses. He was referred to as "Warren Buffett's Mr. Fix-It" in a *Fortune Magazine* article of the same name on August 16, 2010. The article said that he was mentioned most often as Buffett's successor. In Berkshire's 2010 annual report, Buffett beamed at Sokol's work:

As you can tell by now, I am proud of what has been accomplished for our society by Matt Rose at BNSF and by David Sokol and Greg Abel at MidAmerican. I am also both proud and grateful for what they have accomplished for Berkshire shareholders.

After two short meetings with Sokol before acquiring a controlling interest in MidAmerican, Buffett described Sokol, then MidAmerican's CEO, as "talented and entrepreneurial."[24] Sokol led MidAmerican's growth from a small $28 million revenue geothermal company into a powerhouse natural gas and electric utility.

A *Barron's* article titled, "Who's On Deck at Berkshire," written by Andrew Bary on March 20, 2006, speculated that his best guess to succeed Buffett was David Sokol. The reasons were that he was relatively young at forty-nine years of age, was the CEO of Berkshire's largest single earnings contributor outside of insurance, had demonstrated deal-making skills, "and appears to possess the ambition and ego needed to fill Buffett's enormous shoes."

In the forward to David Sokol's book, *Pleased but Not Satisfied*, published in 2007, Buffett lauds Sokol:

> He brings the business equivalent of Ted Williams' .406 batting average to the field of business management. I know this because I've had a front-row seat for eight years, watching him manager MidAmerican Energy… I have a small confession to make: by the standards of personal behavior and his value to Berkshire Hathaway, I am more than pleased and fully satisfied by all the experiences I have had with Dave.

Pleased but Not Satisfied is a jewel of wisdom and an excellent primer of management principles. Sokol evaluated over 130 potential acquisitions in twelve years prior to writing the book, of which eighteen were bought and, in almost all cases, he met or exceeded his initial expectation of value. David Sokol's disciplined ten-step process of evaluating acquisition candidates, resonates with Buffett's own criteria and is a valuable resource for an investor to consider when assessing any investment candidate:

1. The future prospects of the business, including such things as its current market participation, its competitive cost structure, its ability to innovate and lead the market as well as its competitive advantages and disadvantages.

2. The past performance of the business and its historic ability to meet challenges, adapt, and innovate.

3. The quality of the management team.

4. Its balance sheet and any gimmickry present, which is often well-hidden in footnotes.

5. The sustainability of its competitive position.

6. The company's historic willingness to invest in its future growth.

7. Legacy costs, which can include but are by no means limited to litigation, environmental, pension or post-retirement liabilities,

8. Cultural issues, which may indicate an overly aggressive set of practices related to accounting, business ethics, or similar areas.

9. An analysis of the company's real cash flow and capital expenditure requirements to actually determine whether the business is creating value, on a treadmill or actually destroying value. Such analysis often is overlooked with grave consequences.

10. Does the business have underutilized or undervalued assets that can be leveraged or utilized more effectively? Or is the business susceptible to a leapfrog technology or regulatory/legislative obsolescence?[25]

Sokol also offered several other key considerations including:

- The past performance of a business and a management team is a very important indicator of future performance. One should be very skeptical that poor historic performance suddenly will transform itself into focused, detailed future success.

- Businesses that consistently report one-time or unusual items deserve genuine skepticism. Are they consistently unlucky or just poorly managed?

- Multiple analyses of a company, such as EBITDA multiples, EBIT multiples, P/E multiples or some of the more exotic recent multiples (such as 'projected pro forma operating income before interest, tax depreciation, amortization and one-time items'), are of no use or, at best, limited use when assessing the genuine value of a business. Each business is so unique that such multiples tell only about 25 percent of the story.[26]

In 2007 Buffett tapped Sokol to boost Johns Manville, which was an under-performing roofing and insulation company. In 2008, Charlie Munger asked Sokol to perform due-diligence on BYD, a Chinese rechargeable battery and electric car manufacturer, which led to a minority investment in the company.

In 2009 Buffett asked Sokol to oversee NetJets, the dominant fractional private jet travel company that Berkshire acquired in 1998 for $725 million. In the eleven years that Berkshire had owned the company, it had a cumulative pretax loss of $157 million including losing $711 million in 2009. Debt soared from $102 million to $1.9 billion, and without Berkshire's guarantee of debt, NetJets would have been bankrupt. Within a week of Sokol's arrival, founder and chief executive officer Rich Santulli resigned. Sokol became chairman and chief executive officer and he lowered costs. He reduced the workforce; ousted half of senior management; sold excess aircraft; paid down debt; eliminated perks such as suites at the Ohio State University football games and free use of airplanes; initiated an integrated business plan with clear goals; and insisted on accountability to the budget. Assessing the turnaround in 2010, Buffett said, "It looks like NetJets will earn $200 million pretax this year. It's as remarkable a managerial achievement as I have ever seen."[27]

Buffett praised Sokol in Berkshire's 2009 annual report:

> Dave Sokol, the enormously talented builder and operator of MidAmerican Energy, became CEO of NetJets in August. His leadership has been transforming: Debt has already been reduced to $1.4 billion, and, after suffering a staggering loss of $711 million in 2009, the company is now solidly profitable.

For a turnaround artist, the world turned upside for David Sokol in early 2011. He bought 96,060 shares or $10 million of Lubrizol, a specialty chemical manufacturer, on January 5, 6, and 7, less than two weeks before proposing to Buffett on January 14th or 15th (Buffett couldn't recall the exact date) that

Berkshire buy the company. Berkshire subsequently announced a definitive agreement to acquire Lubrizol on March 14, 2011, for $9 billion. Initial discussions between Berkshire and Lubrizol began around the start of 2011 according to *The Wall Street Journal*.[28]

Berkshire agreed to pay $135/share which was 13.6x Lubrizol's 2010 adjusted EPS (from continuing operations and excluding restructuring and impairment expenses) of $9.91/share. Lubrizol had a 2013 publicly stated goal of earning $13.50/share in 2013, so the purchase price was, perhaps not coincidentally, exactly 10x Lubrizol's earnings goal to be achieved in just two years. Lubrizol had demonstrated success at passing on higher raw materials to its customers, which resulted in consistent earnings growth.

Sokol disclosed to Buffett in their first discussion that he owned stock in Lubrizol, but importantly, Sokol did not say that he had just recently bought the stock. Buffett thought it was a passing remark and assumed that Sokol had owned the stock for much longer. Later, Buffett admitted with regret that it was a mistake to not press Sokol about when he bought the stock. Neither Buffett nor Sokol believed what he did was illegal, but it did cross the ethical line. Failing to disclose the fact that he'd recently bought the shares was misleading.

On March 28, 2011 David Sokol stunned Buffett and the investment community by submitting a letter of resignation from Berkshire of his own accord. He said that he didn't think he did anything wrong and that his resignation was unrelated to his Lubrizol purchases; he wanted to control more of his time and start his own investment operation. Buffett did not ask for his resignation, and Buffett disclosed that Sokol had attempted to resign twice before, the most recent being in 2009. Buffett talked him out of it both times but didn't discourage his resignation this time.

Berkshire's audit committee later discovered that Sokol had discussions with investment bankers from Citigroup about possible acquisitions and that a Citigroup banker had brought Lubrizol to Sokol's attention. Sokol bought the shares at the time of these discussions. While Sokol had no idea how receptive Lubrizol would be to the idea of Berkshire acquiring it, nor did Sokol have a vote in ultimately deciding whether Berkshire would make an offer, Sokol was the originator of the idea, and he owed a greater duty to disclose his holdings in a timely and fully transparent manner. The audit committee concluded that Sokol's conduct and trading activities violated Berkshire's standards of business ethics and insider-trading policies, which states senior officers "who have access to confidential information are not permitted to use or share that information for stock trading purposes or for any other purpose except the conduct of the company's business."[29] Even the appearance of front-running is a violation of an ethical duty to put clients' or shareholders' interest above that of an insider. Most investment management firms require "access persons"— those who may have knowledge about trading intentions—to submit trades to a compliance officer for pre-approval of trades and then report on their trades monthly or quarterly, in addition to copying the compliance officer on duplicate confirmations of trades. Had Buffett required this of Sokol, perhaps these unfortunate events could have been avoided.

In announcing Sokol's resignation, Buffett said,

> *Dave's contributions have been extraordinary. At MidAmerican, he and Greg Abel have delivered the best performance of any managers in the public utility field. At NetJets, Dave resurrected an operation that was destined for bankruptcy, absent Berkshire's deep pockets. He has been of enormous help in the operation of Johns Manville, where he installed new management some years ago and oversaw major change.*[30]

All of these accomplishments unfortunately were overshadowed by the trading conflict of interest.

Sokol's personal profit of $3 million from his Lubrizol shares that were acquired by Berkshire were minor compared to what he earned in 2009 when he cashed in his options on MidAmerican for $96 million. The amount also pales in comparison to an incident a few years earlier, when Sokol declined $12.5 million in incentive compensation, and suggested the money go to Greg Abel, his second in command at MidAmerican. It is sad that Sokol and Buffett parted ways under these circumstances and that Sokol suffered reputational damage for a trade that wasn't going to materially impact his lifestyle. Buffett thought Sokol's actions were "inexplicable and inexcusable."

David Sokol was interviewed on CNBC on March 31, 2011, two days after he resigned from Berkshire. He praised Warren Buffett as a mentor, advisor, teacher, and said his experience at Berkshire was one of the best of his life. He added that he loved Warren and that there was no individual in business that he respected more in the world. He confirmed that he tried to resign twice before in the previous two years but Buffett talked him out of it to help turnaround NetJets. Sokol explained that he wanted to invest his family's money to build companies and build a mini-Berkshire without the insurance business since that wasn't his expertise. He thought Buffett was "in great shape," "incredibly intelligent and insightful," but not going to leave anytime soon.

The essence of Sokol's belief that his actions did not present a conflict of interest was: 1) he did not have authority to make investments or acquisitions; 2) he didn't think Buffett had any interest when he initially proposed the idea; and 3) "most of the ideas that I've forwarded to Warren over the years just were not companies that he had an interest in." Sokol said he forwarded on average about eight or nine investment ideas a year, and Sokol personally made about three or four decisions a year. He didn't believe he did anything wrong and said that, if he had to do it over again, "I just would never have mentioned it to Warren, and just made my own investment and left it alone. I think that's a disservice to Berkshire, but if that's what people want to do in the future, that's fine."

Unfortunately, Sokol sounded like sour grapes by saying he wanted to take his ball and play at home by himself. The reality was that he was an employee of Berkshire, and his primary responsibility was to act in the best interest of Berkshire shareholders before his own personal interest. Just because he didn't personally make investment decisions for Berkshire, he was a significant influence in working with Buffett, and as such, owed a fiduciary duty to disclose any potential conflict of interest.

While he didn't violate any law, he did violate an ethical code of conduct to put the interest of Berkshire shareholders above his own. Nearly two years later, the SEC concluded that they would not pursue insider trading charges against David Sokol because they couldn't prove that Sokol had sufficient advance knowledge of the Lubrizol deal when he bought the shares. The SEC lacked evidence to prove that Sokol held information that was nonpublic, material, and misappropriated.

I had the privilege of sitting down with David Sokol in his Omaha office on April 30, 2010, to discuss a variety of business topics ranging from long-range capital projects at MidAmerican, government policy as it impacted utility regulation, acquisition criteria, management methods including setting incentive compensation, his role in various turnarounds in Berkshire and in assessing various investments, and his interaction with and admiration for Buffett. He described Buffett as laser-focused and a constant learning machine. Sokol was candid, driven, professional, entrepreneurial, and was an extremely impressive manager. I walked away convinced that he was the leading candidate to succeed Buffett.

Despite David Sokol's valuable contributions for Berkshire, the fact that Buffett was willing to let David Sokol leave was a sad situation but one that reinforced Buffett's desire to preserve Berkshire's culture of integrity and prioritize shareholders' interests above personal gain.

A few years later, Warren Buffett felt so strongly about preserving the reputational advantage of Berkshire that he wrote to his managers that sustaining an unblemished reputation was their first priority:

> *The top priority—trumping everything else, including profits—is that all of us continue to zealously guard Berkshire's reputation. We can't be perfect but we can try to be. As I've said in these memos for more than 25 years: 'We can afford to lose money—even lots of money. But we can't afford to lose reputation—even a shred of reputation.' We must continue to measure every act against not only what is legal but also what we would be happy to have written about on the front page of a national newspaper in an article written by an unfriendly but intelligent reporter.*[31]

Warren Buffett's Mindset

Carol Dweck, a Stanford University psychologist, wrote a jewel of a book called *Mindset*. She discovered that the way people cope with failures and difficulties revealed a great deal about achieving lasting success. She distinguished between people with a fixed mindset and a growth mindset. Someone with a fixed mindset believes that their intelligence and talents are innate and carved in stone at birth. They are concerned with how they are judged by others and are fearful of being wrong, looking bad, and making mistakes. If their reputation is threatened, they will deflect, get defensive, blame, undermine others—or worse, lie or cheat. Someone with a growth mindset believes that their effort, perseverance, and resilience can improve their condition. They also view their mistakes, not as a time to blame, but a time to admit their failures, learn from them, and improve.

Dweck extends the fixed versus growth mindset concept to business leaders. Fixed-mindset CEOs are concerned with their reputation and legacy for personal greatness, have a need to display their superiority by putting their ego before the welfare of the company, manage by intimidation and humiliation, blame others for mistakes, take credit for work the work of others, surround themselves with flatterers, stifle disagreement, and feel entitled to the trapping of wealth.

Growth-mindset business leaders encourage teamwork, mentor others, praise others in public, criticize in private, and believe in working through others. They focus on learning, growing, and moving forward, and have no interest in proving themselves. They are driven to excellence because they have such tremendous drive and enthusiasm for work they love that they don't consider it work, but a passionate mission.

Warren Buffett is so revered not just for building one of the largest and most admired companies in the U.S. from scratch but for the way he conducts himself as a growth-mindset executive of utmost integrity.

Admits His Mistakes

Warren Buffett writes the first draft of his annual letters to Berkshire shareholders as though he is addressing his sisters, who are not that financially literate. He follows the golden rule, which is to explain the company's results to his shareholder partners with the same information he would prefer if the roles were reversed. This means successes and mistakes. When Buffett discusses his mistakes, it endears him to his readers and employees.

Berkshire's 2014 annual report was atypical because it commemorated fifty years of Berkshire Hathaway's history. Buffett wouldn't have been blamed for celebrating the golden anniversary by recalling many of his deserved successes, but he chose to kneel at the confessional to acknowledge his costly mistakes. What was typical was Buffett's honest, transparent, and humble reporting.

He admitted to making capital allocation mistakes in Berkshire's manufacturing, service, and retailing division:

> A few (businesses), however, have very poor returns, the result of some serious mistakes I made in my job of capital allocation. I was not misled: I simply was wrong in my evaluation of the economic dynamics of the company or the industry in which it operates.

More specifically, he cited his initial purchase of Berkshire Hathaway, a dying textile company, where Buffett subsequently spent eighteen years of time and money trying to stitch together a prosperous business plan to no avail. Buffett surrendered the white flag in 1985 by closing the operation. He admitted to compounding this error by buying another New England textile company in 1975, Waumbec Mills, which was also eventually shut down.

He then described an even more egregious blunder when he bought the Omaha-based insurer, National Indemnity Company (NICO), through his 61 percent owned Berkshire Hathaway entity rather than through his 100 percent-owned Buffett Partnership, Ltd. NICO was the foundation for Berkshire's crown jewel insurance business. Buffett estimated that his decision "to marry 100 percent of an excellent business (NICO) to a 61 percent-owned terrible business (Berkshire Hathaway), (was) a decision that eventually diverted $100 billion or so from BPL partners to a collection of strangers." He estimated that this "colossal mistake" cost Berkshire over $100 billion.

The biggest blunder of all was his purchase of Berkshire Hathaway which, as of 2010, cost an estimated $200 billion. As we previously explained, Buffett bought control of Berkshire out of anger when Seabury Stanton's offer for Buffett's shares was one-eighth of a dollar less than the $11.50 than they agreed upon. The textile business was in a decline, and it required major capital commitments. Buffett figured that Berkshire would be worth $200 billion more if he had instead invested directly into the insurance business.

Buffett bought 5 percent of Disney stock in 1966 when the market value of the entire company was less than $90 million and after meeting Walt Disney himself, was impressed with his shared focus, passion for work, and attention to detail. The company earned about $21 million pretax in 1965, which meant that Disney was priced at less than 10x earnings, and it had more cash than debt. He bought Disney at an adjusted price of $0.10 per share and sold it the next year at a 50 percent gain. Buffett confessed in the 1998 annual meeting that "the Disney sale in the '60s was a huge mistake. I should have been buying it. That happened many times."[32]

He also confessed to a loss on a large common stock investment:

Attentive readers will notice that Tesco (a leading food retailer in the U.K.), which last year appeared in the list of our largest common stock investments, is now absent. An attentive investor, I'm embarrassed to report, would have sold Tesco shares earlier. I made a big mistake with this investment by dawdling…. During 2014, Tesco's problems worsened by the month. The company's market share fell, its margins contracted and accounting problems surfaced. In the world of business, bad news often surfaces serially: You see a cockroach in your kitchen; as the days go by, you meet his relatives. We sold Tesco shares throughout the year and are now out of the position… Our after-tax loss from this investment was $444 million, about one-fifth of 1 percent of Berkshire's net worth.

As if this wasn't enough, Buffett said he misjudged the threat of foreign competition when he bought Dexter Shoe in 1993 for $434 million. Shortly after Dexter was acquired, the company was upended by cheaper foreign labor and materials, and its value fell to zero. To make matters worse, Buffett paid for Dexter with Berkshire stock rather than cash. "The story gets worse: I used stock for the purchase, giving the sellers 25,203 shares of Berkshire that at year end 2016 were worth more than $6 billion."[33]

Buffett confessed to making "a very big mistake" in selling McDonald's in 1998 and admitted that other portfolio actions "actually *decreased* our gain for the year." He went so far as to say that "you would have been better off last year if I had regularly snuck off to the movies during market hours."[34]

Buffett admitted that Berkshire Hathaway and Brazilian private equity firm 3G Capital, which partnered 50-50 in a deal to buy H.J. Heinz for $23.6 billion in 2013, overpaid to finance H.J. Heinz's merger with Kraft Foods Group Inc. in 2015. Berkshire Hathaway owns 325.4 million shares or 26.7 percent of Kraft Heinz common stock. Kraft brands include *Oscar Mayer, Philadelphia, Velveeta, Kool-Aid and Jell-O.* In February 2019, the company wrote down the value of its brands by over $15 billion, slashed its dividend by 36 percent, and disclosed an investigation by federal securities regulators. The write-down effectively acknowledged that consumers prefer more natural and healthier foods instead of processed foods, and that packaged food companies have lost bargaining power with powerful retailers such as Walmart, Costco, and Amazon. While many of Kraft's iconic brands thrived in the past, they are less relevant today. Buffett observed that despite a 100-year head start, Kraft-Heinz sales lagged Costco's Kirkland private-label brand by 50 percent. At $32 per share, Kraft-Heinz lost one-third of its value compared to prior to its announcement. While Berkshire's market value of its Kraft-Heinz investment of $10.4 billion is slightly above its cost of $9.8 billion, Kraft soured Berkshire's original investment in H.J. Heinz.

Buffett even admitted that he erred by not selling Coca-Cola and Gillette at their late 1990s peak, when they traded over 50x earnings. "Coke and Gillette weren't the focal point of the bubble, but they achieved bubble prices." He added that as a director of both companies, it would have been difficult to sell Berkshire's stake in the two companies he referred to as *The Inevitables.* Coca-Cola stock reached over $44/share in 1998, and twenty years later, the price was still $44/share. Even great brands can become overpriced.

Does Buffett sound like a CEO who is concerned with his ego and reputation when he added, "We have made plenty of mistakes, and we will make more." Reassuringly, he quickly added, "Our structural advantages, however, are formidable."

Mistakes of omission don't appear on a scorecard, but they can be costly. Buffett once instructed his broker buy Walmart with a limit order rather than a market order. The stock edged above Buffett's limit, so he stopped buying and the stock never gave Buffett another chance. In the same 2014 Berkshire annual report, Munger recalled that not purchasing Walmart stock cost Berkshire shareholders at least $50 billion.

As we discussed in the section on David Sokol, even though Buffett thought Sokol's actions were "inexcusable and inexplicable," Buffett magnanimously took responsibility by acknowledging that it was his mistake for not pressing Sokol on *when* he bought Lubrizol stock. Had he not assumed that Sokol owned the stock for some time, he would have avoided an embarrassing episode for himself and Sokol.

Buffett, as a "constant learning machine," learned from his mistakes. Buffett may quip that his two rules for investing are: "Rule No. 1: Never lose money; Rule No. 2: Never forget Rule No. 1," but he has made mistakes and so will we. As long as they are not made with leverage and the relative amounts are small, we can learn and recover from them with a growth-mindset.

Mistakes of Omission

As successful an investor as Warren Buffett is, he regretted not swinging at pitches that were in his strike zone. One can only imagine what his already incredible record would have been had he had swung at these companies.

Apple, Inc.

For decades Buffett was famously averse to investing in technology companies. Buffett expects to be confident about a company's competitive position and earnings power at least ten years into the future. The rapid changes in technology precluded him from investing in technology companies even though he had insight into the brilliance of management. Buffett had access to many leaders of successful technology companies. Microsoft's founder Bill Gates is a board member of Berkshire. Google's founders visited Buffett in Omaha before the company went public, and did so again years later for his advice on managing a company with disparate operating companies.

Berkshire disclosed a 9.8 million share, or $1.1 billion position in Apple in May 2016 for the period ending March 2016. This was purchased by Ted

Weschler and/or Todd Combs for an average price of $109/share. At the time, Apple had its first quarterly revenue decline in thirteen years due to a slow-down in iPhone sales, and the stock dropped to the mid-$90s from $130/share. Based on Apple's fiscal year ended September 2015, it had free cash flow of $70 billion, or $12/share. This generated a mouthwatering free cash flow yield, based on a stock price of $109/share, of over 11 percent. Apple was actively repurchasing its shares, which were priced 10 percent lower than five years earlier. The company had a fortress balance sheet with over $140 billion in net cash and generated a return on tangible assets of 21 percent, which was even higher excluding cash. Apple also had over one billion loyal active users, and Apple's service business, including iTunes and the App Store, bonded customers even closer to its mainstay iPhone.

In the fourth quarter of 2016, Buffett was convinced of the stock's merit and joined his lieutenants in owning Apple for Berkshire. At the end of 2016, Berkshire owned 61.2 million shares at an average cost of $110.17/share valued at $7.1 billion. By year end 2017, the position grew to 166.7 million shares at an average cost of $125.74/share valued at $28.2 billion.

Apple was Berkshire's largest equity holding at the end of 2018. Based on Berkshire's cost, Apple is by far Berkshire's largest common stock commitment with a cost of $36 billion, more than triple Berkshire's next largest cost allo-cation in Bank of America Corp. This is surprising given Buffett's historical aversion to technology companies. Buffett's conversion to Apple was inspired by how loyal consumers were to Apple's "enormously useful" iPhone. He admired consumer's brand loyalty to Apple. He borrowed from his mental model with branded consumer products such as Coca-Cola, and applied that model to Apple's iPhone. He said,

> I mean, obviously it's very, very, very tech-involved, but it's a consumer product to a great extent too. And I mean, it has consumer aspects to it... people have incredible stickiness with the product...It gets built into their lives...the continuity of the product is huge, and the degree to which their lives center around it is huge.

Buffett observed this firsthand when he took his grandchildren to Dairy Queen and they were glue-eyed to their phones, looking up only when they had to order. Based on his checks with colleagues in the office, Buffett was impressed with how integrated and indispensable the iPhone was in the lives of its loyal consumers. Some old habits die hard, however, since Buffett is still a holdout with a flip phone. He was also impressed that Apple bought back 5 percent of its stock in fiscal year 2016, after repurchasing a similar percent in fiscal year 2015. Share repurchase is a common characteristic of many of Buffett's public company investments. Time will tell if Buffett's purchase was prescient, but he surely regrets waiting until the company had become the largest market-capitalized company in the world—over $700 billion—before finally recognizing the impact of the iPhone. Charlie Munger wryly reflected on Buffett's purchase of Apple at the 2017 Berkshire Annual Meeting, "It's a very good sign. Either you've gone crazy, or you're learning." Munger obviously believed that Buffett, always the learning machine, was still learning.

Amazon

Even though Warren Buffett acknowledged that Jeff Bezos, CEO of Amazon, is probably the best manager he has ever seen—Amazon has delighted customers and their delivery model "is a tough, tough, tough competitive force"—he never bought the stock. When asked why in a 2017 interview on CNBC, Buffett replied,

> Well, that's a good question. …But I don't have a good answer. Obviously, I should have bought it—long ago because I admired it long ago, but I didn't understand the power of the model—as I went along. And the price always seemed to more than reflect the power of the model at that time. So, it's— one I missed big time.[35]

Again in another CNBC interview in February 2018, Buffett confessed,

> I'm amazed at the managerial talent of Jeff Bezos. But I've been a constant fan, really, almost since he started. And the more I see him, the more impressed, you know, I've been with what he's accomplished. But I've blown it in terms of making any money on it.[36]

Google

Buffett acknowledged that he missed Google, since renamed Alphabet, and "that's cost people a lot of money at Berkshire…(we will) miss a lot of things, and we'll keep doing it."[37] Google's founders visited Buffett in Omaha for his advice for the IPO. Buffett also knew that Berkshire's GEICO was paying Google $10–$11 every time someone clicked on an ad. Buffett was impressed that Google bears almost no cost for generating incremental revenue. At Google's 2017 annual meeting, senior management mentioned they had just consulted with Warren Buffett in Omaha a few weeks prior to the meeting. Chairman Eric Schmidt recalled being struck, in his visit over a decade earlier, with Buffett's manner of managing Berkshire's far flung empire from just one floor. Schmidt admired how Buffett established scalability with Berkshire's operating company's strong CEOs, independent operation, and strong branding of those corporations. Alphabet then modeled its own structure after Berkshire. They say the sincerest form of flattery is imitation. Had Buffett been convinced that Google's business model was sustainable, Berkshire's success would have been even more stratospheric.

Costco

"Charlie (Munger) is a director of Costco. Costco's an absolutely fabulous organization. We should have owned a lot of Costco over the years—and I blew it. Charlie was for it, but I blew it…"[38]

Avoids Debt

Buffett believes it is senseless to "risk what you have and need in order to obtain what you don't need." One can argue that Berkshire was built with the huge advantage of a form of leverage: float. Float from the insurance companies is money received up front from premium payments that can be invested immediately, but may or may not need to be repaid for claims depending on its underwriting success. Careful underwriting that produces profits results in a cost of float that is less than zero. In this case Berkshire effectively gets paid to hold float, and with astute investments, produces astounding capital gains. In this case, float is more like equity than debt.

Nonetheless, Buffett urges investors to avoid investing with borrowed funds. His argument is to cite four occasions when Berkshire Hathaway stock sank anywhere from 37 percent to 59 percent in its fifty-four-year history (as of 2018).

Even if your borrowings are small and your positions aren't immediately threatened by the plunging market, your mind may well become rattled by scary headlines and breathless commentary. And an unsettled mind will not make good decisions.[39]

He is living proof, as was Templeton, of the virtues of long-term investing without borrowed funds. This means being content to get rich slowly rather than viewing the stock market as a gaming parlor in a futile attempt to get rich quick.

An Optimist on America

Buffett responded to the pre-election campaign mudslinging about the prevailing fears and worries about our country:

> It's an election year, and candidates can't stop speaking about our country's problems (which, of course, only they can solve). As a result of this negative drumbeat, many Americans now believe that their children will not live as well as they themselves do. That view is dead wrong: The babies being born in America today are the luckiest crop in history... For 240 years it's been a terrible mistake to bet against America, and now is no time to start. America's golden goose of commerce and innovation will continue to lay more and larger eggs. America's Social Security promises will be honored and perhaps made more generous. And, yes, America's kids will live far better than their parents did.[40]

Buffett is optimistic on the future of America for one primary reason: our market system. Although he identified other important factors, including a rule of law, equal opportunity, and immigration from ambitious people looking to improve their life, the overwhelming factor is America's market-based system that unlocks human potential. Buffett's optimism echoed Templeton and Lynch's positive bet on American business:

> You might say that our underlying premise, and I think it's a pretty sound underlying premise, is that this country will do very well. And then particularly, it will do well for business. Business has done very well. The Dow went from 66 to 10,000+ during the 100 years of the 20th century. And we had two world wars, nuclear bombs, flu epidemics, the Cold War—you name it. There will always be problems, and there will always be opportunities in the future. But in this country, the opportunities have won out over the problems over time.[41]

Buffett's optimism is a key to setting a positive culture at Berkshire Hathaway. He wants to promote a culture of innovation and customer service. "That belief that tomorrow is more exciting than today, you just have to have it permeate the organization. The world does not belong to the pessimist. Believe me."[42]

Buffett's reassuring optimism was more evident than ever after the 9/11 attacks on American soil. "There is nothing dumber than betting against America. It hasn't worked since 1776."[43]

Buffett began the May 2018 Berkshire annual meeting with a dramatic example of how it pays to bet on America. He had in hand *The New York Times* newspaper from March 11, 1942, which was the date he bought his first stock. The paper was filled with bad news developments in the Pacific during World War II. Since then, despite wars, financial panics, many recessions, a presidential assassination, a Cuban missile crisis, and terrorist attacks on American soil, Buffett said $10,000 invested in a U.S. index fund that day would be worth $51 million.

CHAPTER 22

Work Habits

Follow what you are passionate about. I think it is crazy to be somewhere where you feel your ethics or whatever is out of sync with your work. You really want to be in a place where you jump out of bed in the morning and you are all fired up to get to work. I have always felt that way.

—WARREN BUFFETT[1]

Well it (tap dancing to work) means that I can hardly wait to get to work in the morning. I mean it's the most exciting part of the day.

—WARREN BUFFETT[2]

Michelangelo said, "Every block of stone has a statue inside it and it is the task of the sculptor to discover it." Part of Warren Buffett's success is that he figured out early how to chip away at the distractions of his workday life to allow the beauty of the "inner statue" to manifest itself in his workplace masterpiece.

Buffett's work habits have allowed him to, in his words, tap dance to work every morning and have allowed Berkshire to flourish. Here are his core work habits:

Do What You Love

The key to tap dancing to work, according to Buffett, is to find your passion:

I was very, very lucky to find it when I was seven or eight years old...You are lucky in life if you can find it. You can't guarantee you are going to find it in your first job, but I always tell college students when they come (to visit in Omaha) to take the job you would take if you were independently wealthy.[3]

When asked to define success personally, Buffett responded by equating success with happiness.

I can certainly define happiness, because happy is what I am. I get to do what I like to do every single day of the year. I get to do it with people I like, and I don't have to associate with anybody who causes my stomach to turn. I tap dance to work, and when I get there I think I'm supposed to lie on my back and paint the ceiling. It's tremendous fun.[4]

Buffett is often asked for advice on living a successful life, and at the top of the list is to develop a first-rate character. He has said that character is a life choice that is best developed at a young age since "the chains of habit are too light to be felt until they are too heavy to be broken." He recommends writing down all of the character traits and habits of those who you like and admire.

Generally, they have an upbeat attitude on life. They are generous people. They are humorous people. They are people that do more than their fair share. They are people that are thinking about something nice they can do for you.[5]

Then he advises writing down all of qualities and habits of those who you dislike.

They take credit for things they didn't do. They don't show up on time. They are a little dishonest about things.

Then commit to emulate the admirable qualities that are all achievable, and eliminate the disagreeable qualities, none of which you need to have. "Why not choose to be the person you admire, rather than the person you can't stand. You choose what kind of human being you are going to be."

He suggests simply practicing the habits of those you admire and avoiding the habits of those your find reprehensible. Practice giving credit to others, being accountable for results, being a team player, being generous, and having a growth mindset until they are an unconscious habit. Then Buffett says you will convert all of your horsepower into output and will find happiness and success.

Be a Learning Machine

Buffett said that by the time he was ten, he'd read every book in the Omaha Public Library with the word *finance* in the title; some of them twice. He repeatedly advises young and old at the Berkshire Annual meeting who ask how they can become a great investor, "Read everything you can."

Charlie Munger described Buffett as a learning machine:

"Without Warren Buffett being a learning machine, a continuous learning machine, the (Berkshire investment) record would have been absolutely impossible."[6]

Buffett was asked by a student at Columbia University School of Business to name the biggest key to his success. He held up a stack of reports and trade magazines that he brought with him and said,

"Read 500 pages like this every day. That's how knowledge works. It builds up like compound interest. All of you can do it, but I guarantee not many of you will do it."

Buffett actually spends about 80 percent of each day reading as many as 1,000 pages, including five newspapers and a journal: *The Wall Street Journal*, *The New York Times*, the *Omaha Herald*, the *Financial Times*, *USA Today*, and the *American Banker*. He said, "I read almost anything I can get my hands on. And I own 100 shares of probably 200 companies just to get their materials. And I read trade periodicals."[7] Buffett found that owning 100 shares of many companies was more reliable than asking to be added to a mailing list. Buffett assesses management on their honest reporting and whether they are stewarding the company with the same mindset as if they owned the entire company. He discerns whether the language is clear, transparent, and fact filled rather than littered with public relations doublespeak and pictures. He spends about forty-five minutes to an hour reading an annual report. His goal is to get his arms around the business—what happened and what is likely to happen; assessing the candor of management; and analyzing the trends in profit margins and market share. He considers reading annual reports of competitors a must.

After the fifty-year anniversary of Berkshire, Charlie Munger in his letter to Berkshire Shareholders, titled "Vice Chairman's Thoughts—Past and Future," added that Buffett's "first priority would be reservation of much time for quiet reading and thinking, particularly that which might advance his determined learning, no matter how old he became."

Buffett enjoys reading and it allows him to think more clearly:

I insist on a lot of time being spent, almost every day, to just sit and think. That is very uncommon in American business. I read and think. So I do more reading and thinking, and make less impulse decisions than most people in business. I do it because I like this kind of life.[8]

Although his usual office hours are 8:30 a.m. to 5:30 p.m., his reading and thinking is non-stop.

He encourages students to have an attitude of discovery. Accounting is the language of business.

If you view a course like accounting as a drudge and a requirement, you are missing the whole game. Any course can be exciting. Mastering accounting is like mastering a new language, it can be so much fun...Accounting is the Rosetta Stone of business.[9]

Buffett plays bridge online ten hours per week under the pseudonym "tbone," which is his favorite food. He believes there is a strong parallel with his approach to investing and playing bridge.

"The approach and strategies are very similar in that you gather all the information you can and then keep adding to that base of information as things develop. You do whatever the probabilities indicate based on the knowledge that you have at the time, but you are always willing to modify your behavior or your approach as you get new information."[10]

Getting new information requires curiosity, an open mind, and a commitment for continuous learning. When asked by a columnist whether his bridge game was similar to how he played the stock market, Buffett responded, "I don't play the market. I buy businesses."[11] Bridge is a game; investing is not.

Focus

According to Buffett and Bill Gates, the most important key to success is focus. Buffett recalled the first evening meeting Bill Gates:

Then at dinner, Bill Gates Sr. posed the question to the table: What factor did people feel was the most important in getting to where they'd gotten in life. And I said, 'Focus.' And Bill said the same thing.[12]

Charlie Munger attributed Buffett's success at Berkshire to his "decision to limit his activities to a few kinds and to maximize his attention to them."[13] In an interview with Alice Schroeder, author of *The Snowball*, a biography of

Buffett, Munger said, "[Buffett] never let his minor obsessions interfere with his major obsession."[14] Buffett once said "intensity is the price of excellence."

Intensity, commitment, discipline, and even obsession with money drove Buffett to bury himself in *The Wall Street Journal* and annual reports when he worked from home while disengaging himself with nuisance distractions. He reportedly would wander off at dinner parties to read the trade journal *American Banker*.[15] At Berkshire, Buffett delegates operating, legal, accounting, and administrative details in order to focus on his value-added responsibilities: allocating capital; choosing CEOs of important subsidiaries based on their trust, skill, energy and passion for the business; and managing investments in securities.

Similar to John Templeton and Peter Lynch, Warren Buffett believes in the value of primary research:

> As you're acquiring knowledge about industries in general and companies specifically, there isn't anything like first doing some reading about them and then getting out and talking to competitors and customers and suppliers and past employees and current employees. If you talk to a bunch of people in an industry and ask them who they fear the most and why, who (in Andy Grove's words) they'd use the silver bullet on and so on, you're going to learn a lot.[16]

Buffett says that he always asks the managers of Berkshire's subsidiaries as well as the managers of any new investment what keeps them awake at night.

At the 2003 Berkshire annual meeting, Buffett said that forty to fifty years ago, he spoke to management frequently.

> I used to go out and take a trip every now and then and drop in on maybe 15–20 companies. I haven't done that in a long, long time. Today everything we do, pretty much, I find through public documents…We do not find it particularly helpful to talk to management…The figures tell us more than the management. Before we buy we look at the record to determine what the management's like.[17]

The advantage of researching companies in the investment field is that knowledge accumulates. This accumulated knowledge from decades of assessing many companies' competitive advantages allows Buffett to lean more heavily on figures.

Buffett doesn't distract himself with macro questions that others like to discuss but will never be able to answer. Some investors are tempted to ponder the short-term direction of the market, the U.S. dollar, interest rates, trade defi-cits, or interest rate moves by the Federal Reserve. Buffett focuses on looking to own pieces of businesses or entire businesses. He says,

> We try to think about things that are both important and knowable. There are important things that are not knowable. And there are things that are knowable, but not important—we don't want to clutter up our minds with those. We ask ourselves, 'What's important and knowable? And what among those things can we translate into some kind of action that's useful for Berkshire?'[18]

When he reads five papers each day, he likely uses the filter of whether a news item is *important, knowable, and relevant* to decide whether to read, scan, or ignore. The rest is just trivia. He eliminates distractions. For a public company, Berkshire unconventionally has no public relations, human rela-tions, investor relations, or legal departments.

Praise in Public

Dale Carnegie advised in his classic bestseller, *How to Win Friends and Influ-ence People*, on how to an effective leader: "Be hearty in your approbation and lavish in your praise." Buffett read Carnegie's book at age eight or nine, and it had a profound influence on him. Carnegie urged others to avoid crit-icism, since it puts people on the defensive, causes resentment, and wounds their pride. Instead, he advocated "giving the other person a fine reputation to live up to by showing sincere appreciation." Buffett heeds the timeless wisdom of praising in public in his daily habits and in Berkshire's widely read annual reports. He said, "There are two things I was told in life many, many years ago that turned out to be terrific advice. One is to praise by name and criticize by category."[19]

As early as 1961 in his partnership letter, Buffett described his secretary, Beth Henley, as "first-class." Buffett's pattern of praise continued unabated each year since as highlighted fifty years later in the 2011 Berkshire Annual report where he praised each operating manager one by one.

Buffett explained his enthusiasm for praising his operating managers in the same letter:

> For good reason, I regularly extol the accomplishments of our operating managers. They are truly All-Stars, who run their businesses as if they

were the only asset owned by their families. I believe their mindset to be as shareholder-oriented as can be found in the universe of large publicly-owned companies. Most have no financial need to work; the joy of hitting business 'home runs' means as much to them as their paycheck. Equally important, however, are the twenty-three men and women who work with me at our corporate office…this home office crew, along with our operating managers, has my deepest thanks and deserves yours as well.

One can imagine the operating managers working that much harder each year to earn the respect and deserved praise in each forthcoming report. The path that Buffett "skips to work on" is paved with praise and credit for those who contribute to his and Berkshire's success. Because Buffett's bias is to never sell a subsidiary, the loyalty extended by Buffett is matched many times over by his operating leaders for their innate desire for excellence and their desire to please Buffett.

Surround Yourself with People You Like, Trust, and Admire

We only want to link up with people whom we like, admire, and trust… We do not wish to join with managers who lack admirable qualities, no matter how attractive the prospects of their business. We've never succeeded in making a good deal with a bad person.

Buffett said that when he bought See's Candy, he only spent an hour on-site with them. When he bought Borsheims Jewelry, he only spent a half hour at Ike Friedman's house, and the sale agreement was less than one page of text. "If I need a team of lawyers and accountants, it isn't going to be a good deal… We've never had an extended negotiation with anybody about anything."[20]

Live Frugally

Buffett relished the competitive game of amassing wealth. Paramount to him was the benefit of independence that wealth offered. Because accumulating wealth was the key to independence that he so desired, letting go of money was difficult. It was an obstacle to his goal of independence. Early in his career, Buffett not only searched for cheap "cigar-butt" stocks, but his early lifestyle was almost as frugal. He operated his partnership out of a tiny study at home that was accessible through a bedroom. He typed his own letters, did his own filing, used his family's single telephone line for business calls, and filed his own tax returns. Buffett bought his first house on Farnam Street in Omaha in 1958 for $31,500, and he still lives in the same house today.

Buffett paid for his three children's college education, although none graduated. When they became adults, he gave them several thousand dollars each at Christmas, but told them that after he died, to expect "enough money so that they would feel they could do anything, but not so much that they could do nothing."[21]

When Buffett's daughter, Susie, became pregnant with her first child, she lived in a cramped house in Washington, D.C. She asked her father for a loan of $30,000 to remodel her kitchen to allow for a table for two. He refused by asking, "Why not go to the bank?"[22] When Katharine Graham, former CEO of *The Washington Post*, asked Buffett for a dime to make a phone call in an airport, Buffett only had a quarter, and he started to walk away to get change before she stopped him.

Philanthropy

Buffett often measured a dollar outlay today as its dollar equivalent if allowed to compound at his expected rate of return in the future. Consequently, most expenditure requests were frowned upon as prohibitively expensive. For many years, Buffett believed that allowing his money to compound over time would result in more money to give away to charities after he passed away, compared to giving along the way. He thought charitable organizations often lacked the discipline for measured outcomes to justify their requests.

An extreme example was an expose by the *Omaha Sun* newspaper of Boys Town, which had strayed from its original mission. Boys Town is an Omaha home for orphaned and at-risk children founded in 1917 by the revered Father Edward Flanagan. In 1971 Buffett tipped the newspaper that the secretive organization had a $162 million investment portfolio, which was more than twice the size of the endowment of the University of Notre Dame. The scandal was that Boys Town was serving fewer boys but was collecting $25 million a year under the guise that it was still operating under Depression-era poverty. Boys Town had operated without a budget, was collecting four times as much as it spent each year, and sent out solicitation letters by long rows of women behind typewriters under the pretense that the letters were written by pleading boys. The revelation, which was publicized in a March 1972 article and won a

Pulitzer Prize, described abdication of fiduciary duty, irresponsible steward-ship, and deception.

In 2006 Buffett announced that he planned to donate the bulk of his fortune to the Bill & Melinda Gates Foundation, which is focused on child mortality, controlling diseases such as malaria and AIDS in Africa, and educa-tion. At the time, Buffett designated ten million shares to the Bill & Melinda Gates Foundation, one million shares to the Susan Thompson Buffett Founda-tion, and 350,000 shares each to his three children's foundations. He planned to gift 5 percent of his designated shares to each foundation annually until his death or until certain conditions are no longer met at the foundations. Buffett's decision to donate his wealth while he was alive was motivated by the tragic death of his wife, Susan, in 2004. Warren expected Susan to outlive him, and he said in a *Fortune Magazine* interview with Carol Loomis that "she really would have stepped on the gas" in terms of giving more money away faster. At the time, Buffett's gift was valued at over $30 billion. This amount was equal to the assets of the Gates Foundation, and the combination of the Gates Foundation and Buffett's contribution dwarfed other foundations. Buffett was impressed with the existing scale of the Gates Foundation and, more impor-tantly, Buffett admired Bill and Melinda Gates' passion, intelligence, focus, and commitment to saving and improving lives of the less fortunate. Buffett was always committed to donating his wealth back to society but he admitted that he didn't have the patience for feedback on philanthropy, and he didn't want to be involved with a lot of folks necessary to convert intention into result. In short, he trusted Bill and Melinda to do the job that he valued but didn't care to do himself. He enjoyed the game of making money too much to bother himself with the details of how it should be given away.

Avoid Market Timing

Forbes Magazine publishes an annual list of the wealthiest 400 people in the U.S., and there are no market timers on the list. On the other hand, there are plenty of investors on the list who participated in America's engine of wealth creation through their time in the market—not from timing the market. Becky Quick of CNBC asked Buffett whether it was prudent to wait for a pullback in the market to buy stocks. Buffett responded,

> *...I don't know anybody that can time markets over the years...the best thing with stocks actually is buy them consistently over time...you are making a*

terrible mistake if you stay out of a game that you think is going to be very good over time because you think you can pick a better time to enter it.[23]

I make no guesses about what the market will do. I don't know what it's going to do tomorrow, I don't know what it's going to do next month, and I don't know what it's going to do next year. I do know that over any period of ten or twenty years, you're going to have some very enthusiastic markets, you're going to have some very depressed markets. And the trick is to take advantage of those markets rather than let them panic you into the wrong kind of action.[24]

In the 2006 Berkshire Annual meeting, Charlie Munger asked Warren Buffett, "When have you done a big asset allocation strategy?" Buffett's response was, "Never." Munger has also noted that, "I know of no really rich sector rotator."[25]

Warren Buffett focuses almost exclusively on analyzing individual business. As much as Warren Buffett disavows market timing he has presciently opined on the market on several opportune occasions in his long career.

November 1974: "Oversexed guy in a harem."

You may recall that Buffett liquidated his investment pool in 1969 after enjoying a twelve-year compound return of 29.5 percent because he could no longer find bargains in a roaring bull market. He was fearful when others were very greedy. The Dow soared another 27 percent from 800 at the end of 1969 to a peak of 1020 at the end of 1972 led by the so-called Nifty Fifty. The Nifty Fifty were a group of fifty blue-chip companies including Coca-Cola, Gillette, Merck, Pfizer, Philip Morris, and Polaroid that reached nosebleed valuations of 42x earnings. They became black-and-blue-chip companies when the Dow sank over 40 percent to 600 in late 1974. At that level, the Dow was just 8x earnings, which made Buffett salivate. Asked how he felt at that time, Buffett responded "Like an oversexed guy in a harem. Now is the time to invest and get rich."[26] Within six months the Dow was back over 1,000 for a gain of 67 percent.

August 1979: "You pay a very high price in the stock market for a cheery consensus."

Warren Buffett admonished corporate pension fund managers who made expensive mistakes by voting for stocks with their emotions in a herd-like mentality. When stocks were high they allocated more pension assets to equities because it felt good. When stocks were cheap, their allocation to stocks slowed to a trickle because they worried things could get worse, and the future was too uncertain.

He noticed that the Dow was selling at a 10 percent discount to aggregate book value in mid-1979 and a long-term investor should expect a normalized 13 percent return on book value. By contrast, ten-year U.S. treasury bonds were yielding 9.0 percent. Despite the evident advantage of owning stocks over the long-term, pension fund managers had recently allocated a record low 9 percent of net new funds toward stocks. In 1972 when the Dow was valued at nearly 150 percent of book value and was 25 percent higher than 1979, pension fund managers allocated 122 percent of net new funds (bonds were sold) toward stocks. This is the trap of rear-view mirror investing—buying high and selling low.

Buffett added his own twist to Ben Graham's maxim to "let the market be your servant and not your master" when he advised, "The future is *never* clear; you pay a very high price in the stock market for a cheery consensus. Uncertainty actually is the friend of the buyer of long-term values."[27] In the next ten years, the Dow outperformed U.S. treasuries 12 percent to 9 percent.

November 1999: "If I had to pick the most probable return (in the next seventeen years)…it would be 6 percent."[28]

On four occasions in the four months ending November 1999, Buffett uncharacteristically offered his views of the general level of stock prices. He noted the symmetry of the previous thirty-five years by comparing the first seventeen years with the second seventeen years. The Dow was essentially flat at 875 for the first seventeen years largely because long-term interest rates on the thirty-year treasury bond climbed from just under 4 percent to over 15 percent and because corporate profits as a percent of GDP fell from 6 percent to 4.5 percent. As Buffett explained, interest rates "act on financial valuations the way gravity acts on matter: the higher the rate, the greater the downward pull."[29]

In the second seventeen-year period ending 1988, the Dow climbed over ten-fold from 875 to 9,181. During this period, the yield on the thirty-year treasury bond fell dramatically from 14 percent to 5 percent, and corporate profits as a percent of GDP reverted back to 6 percent. Essentially interest rates and corporate profits as a percent of GDP made a thirty-four-year-round trip.

Investors were infected by the rear-view virus again. Buffett noted a Paine Webber and Gallup Organization survey, which showed that investors with less than five years of experience expected annual returns for the next ten years of 22.6 percent while investors with more than twenty years of experience expected 12.9 percent. Buffett's best guess was that returns over the next seventeen years ending 2016 would average a more realistic 6 percent, net of commissions and fees, assuming constant interest rates. Even though thirty-year treasury yields fell in half from 6.1 percent to 2.9 percent, the Dow over the next seventeen years averaged 6 percent annual returns—exactly what Buffett predicted—and a far cry from the wildly optimistic consensus view. At the time, Buffett was considered out-of-touch by new age investors swept up with dot-com euphoria when analysts valued internet companies as a multiple of eyeball views instead of "old-school" earnings.

Buffett's warning was prescient. He warned in the Berkshire Hathaway 1999 annual report, which was released just weeks prior to the market top,

"If investor expectations become more realistic—and they almost certainly will—the market adjustment is apt to be severe, particularly in sectors in which speculation has been concentrated."

The aggregate market value of U.S. stocks divided by GDP (which Buffett says is the best measure of overall market valuation) reached 190 percent in late 1999 compared to just 40 percent in 1981 and a long-term average of about 75 percent. The market bubble burst a few months later in March 2000, and in the three years after Buffett's prediction, the Dow fell 23 percent, the S&P 500 dropped 37 percent, and the tech-heavy Nasdaq sank 56 percent.

As remarkable as Buffett's prediction was, Carol Loomis's *Fortune* article included two timeless observations by Buffett worth remembering. The first was that over the long-run, the value of an asset cannot grow faster than its earnings. The second was that investments that reward investors are those that have a durable competitive advantage.[30]

October 2008: "Buy American. I am."

In the wake of the financial crisis that brought many financial institutions to their knees and others to their grave, Buffett was naturally giddy about buying sound stocks when fear was rampant. He wrote an op-ed in *The New York Times* titled "Buy American. I Am" saying,

What is likely, however, is that the market will move higher, perhaps substantially so, well before either sentiment or the economy turns up. So if you wait for the robins, spring will be over…bad news is an investor's best friend…equities will almost certainly outperform cash over the next decade, probably by a substantial degree…

Sure enough, from the date of the article on October 17, 2008, the Dow almost doubled and its total return, including dividends, averaged almost 14 percent per year. "Be greedy when others are fearful" worked again.

Question Conventional Investment Advice

As we discussed earlier, many investment consultants classify investment managers as either growth, value, or blend, and in either small-, mid-, or large-sized companies. They prefer that managers identify themselves in one style and stick to it. This way, the consultants can recommend best of breed managers in each style to their pension fund clients and, in their mind, always be assured that their client will be exposed to whatever style is in vogue. Growth, value, and blend styles are categorized in the same way that Standard & Poor's divides its popular index into growth and value, which is by an arbitrary price/book value.

Buffett cringes at this notion. "Growth is part of the value equation. There is no such thing as growth or value stocks as Wall Street portrays them. Anybody who tells you to put your money in growth or value does not understand investing."[31] Investing is simply the practice of deferring consumption and paying less today than the present value of cash flows a business will generate in the future. It is up to the investor to estimate the amount and likelihood of those cash flows and choose an appropriate discount rate. Growth and value are joined at the hip. Buffett says that he looks at every business as a value proposition. "The potential for growth and the likelihood of good economics being attached to that growth are a part of the equation in a valuation—but they're all value decisions."[32]

Buffett is also dismissive of black-box models that suggest investors should automatically lower their allocation from stocks and increase their allocation to bonds purely because of the investor's age, rather than the more common-sense approach of incorporating valuation. Since there are thousands of individual stocks and bonds—some of which are overvalued and some underpriced—it is foolish to paint them all with the broad brush. It is just as foolish to hear so-called experts speak about the Microsofts or Intels of the world; there is only one Microsoft and only one Intel.

Buffett and Munger don't use a higher discount rate to compensate for a riskier investment. If they don't have conviction about a company's future earnings stream, they don't bother with it. Business schools advocate using a higher discount rate to compensate for more price volatility. They refer to this as a capital-asset-pricing model. The flaw in this approach is that while stock prices may be volatile, the underlying business may not. If a stock price rises or falls more than the market, academics refer to the stock as having a higher *beta* than the market. If a quality company's stock price falls more than the market, all else equal, it doesn't represent more risk—it is a more attractive buying opportunity. Buffett said a great combination is a volatile stock and a stable business, since it presents rational investment opportunities. Buffett dismisses risk-adjusted discount rates: "As for the capital-asset-pricing-model type reasoning with its different rates of risk-adjusted returns and the like, we tend to think of it—well, we don't tend to think of it. We consider it *nonsense*."[33] Buffett doesn't add risk premiums to the risk-free rate to discount cash flows because the company has already passed the predictability filter. To underscore the point, Buffett adds, "We don't pay any attention whatsoever to beta or any of that sort of thing. It just doesn't mean anything to us. We're only interested in price and value."[34]

Volatility of a stock price is not risk. Real risk is the possibility that a business suffers a permanent impairment of intrinsic value. This can arise from a capital structure that has too much debt or from weak competitive advantages. Risk can also occur from an operator in a commodity business that doesn't have a low-cost advantage. It can arise from relying on a dominant customer who changes their mind. Technology can permanently impair businesses, such as network television and retail distribution channels and can even obsolete a business, such as encyclopedias. Investing is deferring gratification today to allow greater consumption in the future. Risk is not achieving this long-term goal; it is not defined as short-term volatility of stock prices.

> For owners of a business—and that's the way we think of shareholders—the academic's definition of risk is far off the mark, so much so that it produces absurdities. For example, under beta-based theory, a stock that has dropped very sharply compared to the market—as had The Washington Post when we bought it in 1973—becomes 'riskier' at the lower price than it was at the higher price. Would that description have then made any sense to someone who was offered the entire company at a vastly reduced price?[35]

While media pundits fill airtime with debates about where the market is headed, Buffett doesn't waste his time on macro-forecasting.

"We do not have, never have had, and never will have an opinion about where the stock market, interest rates or business activity will be a year from now."[36] "Forming macro opinions or listening to the macro or market predictions of others is a waste of time.[37]

Albert Einstein said, "Everything should be made as simple as possible, but not simpler." Investing is not complicated but can be made complex because stock prices are numbers that have histories. Just because something *can* lend itself to mathematical manipulation, doesn't mean it *should*. The quantitative histories of stocks have been correlated with others to produce coincidental but often misguided conclusions. Buffett was more direct, "Correlation coefficients are useless."[38] The more quantitatively abstract and further removed analysis is from understanding the competitive dynamics of the underlying business, the more dangerous the conclusions become. Buffett said,

> *In the academic world, there's been a rejection of actually thinking about stocks as businesses—essentially because there's an enormous amount of data about price, volume, P/E ratios, and dividend yields. Everybody loves to run a million statistical comparisons of this variable versus that variable. They're looking for the answer in a bunch of chicken entrails and ignoring the fact that when you buy a stock, you buy part of a business. It is extraordinary to me.*[39]

A popular belief taught at many universities is Efficient Market Hypothesis. This theory contends that all relevant information about a company is known in the market and already reflected in its price, so there is no advantage to be gained to by active management. In the long-run, stock prices correlate closely with the underlying cash earnings generated by the business. In the short-term, stock prices are governed by emotion—fear and greed based on reactions to a myriad of company specific and general market forces. Buffett capitalizes on these emotional cycles of inefficiency:

> *I think it's fascinating how the ruling orthodoxy can cause a lot of people to think the earth is flat. Investing in a market where people believe in efficiency is like playing bridge with someone who's been told it doesn't do any good to look at the cards.*[40]

John Templeton's analogy was similar when he said that it in the game of tennis, there are as many winners as losers, but it doesn't mean you shouldn't play.

Buffett also abhors the common practice by security analysts to focus on earnings before interest expense, depreciation, and amortization (EBITDA) because it ignores cash capital spending requirements. It is meant to be a short-cut to measure cash flow, but it ignores many of the cash outflow requirements of a business.

Buffett is quick to dismiss overly complex investment theory in favor of the more practical and deceptively simpler approach to investing:

> To invest successfully, you need not understand beta, efficient markets, modern portfolio theory, option pricing or emerging markets. You may, in fact, be better off knowing nothing of these. That, of course, is not the prevailing view of most business schools, whose finance curriculum tends to be dominated by such subjects. In our view, though, investment students need only two well-taught courses—How to Value a Business, and How to Think About Market Prices. Your goal as an investor should simply be to purchase, at a rational price, a part interest in an easily understandable business whose earnings are virtually certain to be materially higher five, ten and twenty years from now. Over time, you will find only a few companies that meet these standards—so when you see one that qualifies, you should buy a meaningful amount of stock. You must also resist the temptation to stray from your guidelines: if you aren't willing to own a stock for ten years, don't even think about owning it for ten minutes.[41]
>
> There is an enormous amount of misspent effort in the investment field—and it's almost proportionate to the IQ of the person doing it—that looks at the past solely on a statistical basis to project the future. If anybody starts giving you long equations with a lot of little Greek letters in them, forget it.[42]

Concentrate Your Portfolio

Buffett believed in concentrating his bets when he believed his facts and reasoning were correct, where the situation had superior qualitative and quantitative qualities, and where there was little risk of permanent loss of capital. Through the first nine years of his partnership, Buffett had five or six situations that exceeded 25 percent weights. He was willing to go to 40 percent in rare situations. "When I ran my partnership, my limit for a single stock was about 40 percent."[43] He was willing to tolerate yearly volatility "with an occasional very sour year" by concentrating heavily in what he believed to be the best investment opportunity if it meant that his long-term margin of outperformance should be superior.

He was especially critical of conventional diversification.

There is one thing I can assure you. If good performance of the fund is even a minor objective, any portfolio encompassing one hundred stocks is not being operated logically...Anyone owning such numbers of securities after presumably studying their investment merit is following what I call the Noah School of Investing—two of everything. Such investors should be piloting arks.[44]

The optimum portfolio depends on the various expectations of choices available and the degree of variance in performance which is tolerable.[45]

The less one can tolerate in annual volatility, the more diversified one should invest, but the expected results will also be lower. Buffett prosaically quoted Billy Rose who said, "You've got a harem of seventy girls; you don't get to know any of them very well."

Buffett said diversification is for the know-nothing investor and concentration of portfolios is for the know-something investor. If you know what you are doing, there is less risk in concentrating the portfolio. He said there is less risk in owning three well-run excellent businesses than fifty mediocre.[46]

Patience

Buffett said that "you don't get paid for *activity*, you get paid for being *right*."[47] He also believes that, unlike competitive diving, you don't get rewarded more for a higher degree of difficulty in investing. "There's no reason to try three and a half somersault dives when you get paid just as well for just diving off the side of the pool and going in clean."[48] He adds that you only have to get one good idea every year or two, so he waits for the fat pitch in the middle of the plate before swinging.

Charlie Munger summarized the keys to their astounding success at Berkshire,

One interesting thing about the extreme outcome is that if you took the top 15 decisions out, you would have a pretty modest record. So success wasn't based on hyperkinetic activity. It was achieved through a combination of non-diversification, a great deal of a lot of patience, and intensely opportunistic behavior on a few occasions.[49]

In Buffett's earlier years, he readily sold an investment if he found a more compelling replacement. As he transitioned to owning first-class companies with first-class managements, he preferred less frenzied trading.

> *It is possible we could earn greater after-tax returns by moving rather frequently from one investment to another. Many years ago, that's exactly what Charlie and I did. Now we would rather stay put, even if that means slightly lower returns. Our reason is simple: We have found splendid business relationships to be so rare and so enjoyable that we want to retain all we develop. This decision is particularly easy for us because we feel that these relationships will produce good, though perhaps not optimal, financial results.*[50]

When asked why more people don't copy his investment philosophy, Buffett responded,

> *Well, it requires patience, which a lot of people don't have and people would much rather be promised that they're going to win a lottery ticket next week than that they're going to get rich slowly—Gus Levy used to say that he was long-term greedy, not short-term greedy. And if you're short-term greedy, you probably won't get a very good long-term result.*[51]

Buffett frequently advises business school students to imagine that they have a punch card with twenty punches on it. Whenever they make an investment decision, they use up a punch. He doubts that we will get twenty great ideas in our lifetime.

Summary

Buffett's 15 Qualities for Investment Success

1. **Temperament and Intellectual Framework.** Buffett said it is all there in Ben Graham's work: the market is your servant, not your master; include a margin of safety; and think of stocks as a part interest in a business. Don't be influence by the crowd.

2. **Understand Accounting.** It is the language of business. Understand it well enough to know when management plays games within the rules of accrual accounting. Focus on cash flow and economic earnings power.

3. **Be Passionate and Open-Minded.** Buffett says to be willing to get rich slowly, don't be in too much of a hurry, and don't let greed take hold of you.

4. **Stay within your Circle of Confidence.** Know what you understand, and be willing to admit you don't know something and pass. You don't have to be an expert on everything; you just have to be right on what you do understand.

5. **Think Independently.** Write down your reasons for owning the stock and monitor the business to make sure it is on track with your thesis. Don't feel pressure to imitate what is trendy. Don't take your cues from price action, focus on the business drivers of value.

6. **Be Patient and Think Long-Term.** Be so comfortable owning stock in a business that you wouldn't care if the stock market were closed for three years. "In the search, we adopt the same attitude one might find appropriate in looking for a spouse: It pays to be active, interested and open-minded, but it does not pay to be in hurry."[52] Don't obsess over short-term earnings or try to predict the stock market.

7. **Develop your conviction from knowledge and facts, not from hunches or feelings.** Conviction will prevent you from selling out of fear at the bottom.

8. **Stay flexible about the types of businesses to buy, but always be price conscious.**

9. **Read Relevant Investment Material.** Annual reports, major newspapers, trade journals, classic investment books written by or about successful investors.

10. **Focus on the Business and not the Scoreboard.** If you are right on the business, the stock will take care of itself over the long-run. Think like a business analyst not as a macroeconomic analyst or a market analyst.

11. **Don't waste time with macro forecasts or market timing.** The wealthiest people focused on their business and didn't waste their time with subjects that may be interesting but are irrelevant or unknowable.

12. **Know how to value your business.** Otherwise you are the patsy of Mr. Market.

13. **Be an optimist about America's future.** John Templeton, Peter Lynch, and Warren Buffett were unabashedly bullish on the future of the U.S. because ingenuity is rewarded in a free market with rules of law.

14. **Relish the challenge and enjoy what you do.** "In a sense, Berkshire Hathaway is a canvas, and I get to paint anything I want on that canvas. And it's the process of painting that I really enjoy, not selling the painting."[53]

15. **Choose the right heroes.** Buffett said if you tell me who your heroes are, he can tell how you will turn out. Choose your heroes carefully.

A Checklist Based on Buffett's Criteria for Investments

The Three Ps: Prospects (for the business), People, and Price

Prospects (for the Business)

- Do you understand the business? Avoid the common mistake of investing in something you don't understand. Is it a simple business?

- Does it have favorable long-term prospects and growing earnings power?

- Does it have demonstrated consistent earning power? Is the business a proven performer (a .300 hitter) already?

- Does the business earn an attractive return on tangible capital; or return on equity with little or no debt? ((Earnings before Interest Expense + Amortization of Goodwill)*(1-Tax Rate)) / Tangible Invested Capital (Short and Long-term Debt + Equity – Intangibles). The most attractive businesses earn more money with fewer assets. Focus on picking wonderful businesses.

- Does the company enjoy a sustainable competitive advantage? "If you want to achieve a great time for swimming the 100 meters, it's a lot smarter to swim with the tide than it is to work on your stroke."[54]

- Are there high barriers to entry?

- Does the business have pricing power? The ultimate advantage over inflation.

- Is the product or service 1) needed or desired; 2) thought by its customers to have no close substitute; and 3) not subject to price regulation?

- Does the company's brand have a loyal following by customers?
- Is the business respected by its competitors?
- Does the business generate free cash flow and use little incremental capital to grow? Free Cash Flow = Cash Flow from Operations less normalized capital spending.
- Are overhead costs low?
- Is the business stable and predictable and not subject to constant change? Is it an economic toll bridge with a high repeat purchase characteristic of its product?
- Do you have a reasonably good idea of where the business will be in ten years?
- Are you happy with the business even if the stock dropped 50 percent? Even the stock price of Berkshire Hathaway fell this much several times.

People

- What is their track record? The best test of competence.
- Is management owner-oriented? Do they treat shareholders as partners? Are their communications candid and transparent?
- Do you like, trust, and admire management? Do they exude integrity?
- Do they demonstrate personal commitment and have general business savvy?
- Is management honest and competent?
- Do they enjoy what they do? Are they enthusiastic?
- Do they control costs?
- Does management repurchase stock when wide discrepancies exist between price and value?
- Does management stick to what they understand—their circle of competence?
- What is their record of allocating capital? Are the rewards of the business channeled for the shareholders or to enriching management?
- Be wary of deceitfulness, arrogance, complacency, recurring write-offs and restructurings, and high management turnover.

Price

- Is the stock price attractive compared to your estimate of intrinsic value which is the present value of future cash flows discounted at the prevailing long-term government bond rate?

- Is there an adequate margin of safety? Is the stock price obviously attractive even if your calculations are off?

- Over time, the company's earnings power will determine value, not stock price action or moving averages. "While market values track business values quite well over long periods, in any given year the relationship can gyrate capriciously."[55]

- "It is far better to buy a wonderful company at a fair price than a fair company at a wonderful price."[56]

- Wait for something obvious. Does it scream at you? Activity is not achievement. Wait for the fat pitch.

- Buy value, but remember that growth is a component of value. "The time to get interested is when no one else is. You can't buy what is popular and do well."[57]

- Is the reason for the stock's decline, a non-structural, fixable, temporary issue; or is it a permanent, structural problem?

- Buy stocks when others are fearful (because it produces good prices), and be fearful when others are greedy. Don't buy a stock just because it is unpopular.

CHAPTER 23

Reflections

There aren't enough superlatives to describe Warren Buffett's accomplishments as an investor, as CEO of Berkshire Hathaway, as a philanthropist, and as a mentor and teacher of rational investment thought. He is a preeminent investor because of his knowledge of underlying businesses, his ability to manage people and assess character, his disciplined investment principles, and ability to allocate capital.

His ability to quickly evaluate character is uncanny. He says he looks for three things in a person: "intelligence, energy, and integrity. And if they don't have the last one, don't even bother with the first two." His ability to size up all three has allowed him to consummate deals with as little as a handshake and a one-page legal agreement.

As we saw in the previous checklist, Buffett looks for three essential ingredients before investing, known as the three Ps: people, prospects (for the business), and price.

You have to really understand the economics of the business and the kind of people you are getting into business with. They (Berkshire operating managers) have to love their business. They have to feel that they have been creative, that it is their painting, I am not going to disturb it, just give them more canvas and more burnishes, but it's their painting, from our standpoint anyway. The whole place will reflect the attitude of the person at the top; if you have someone at the top who doesn't care, the people down below won't care. On the other hand, if you have someone at the top who cares a great deal, that will be evident across the organization...Contracts don't protect you; you have to have confidence in the people.[1]

Buffett often says that he wants to work with executives that he likes, trusts, and admires. The feeling is no doubt mutual with Berkshire executives about Buffett.

Although he is shrewd in what he is willing to pay for a business, Buffett's Midwestern roots are evident in his trust of Berkshire's employees. Berkshire's managers do not even submit budgets to Omaha. Buffett's trust is returned several-fold by Berkshire's operating managers who, out of respect, loyalty, and mutual trust, continue to passionately work as though their business was still wholly owned by them. Buffett has a wonderful way about him where he inspires others to excel even as he downplays his own accomplishments. Berkshire's operating managers don't want to let Buffett down out of respect for him. "We put a lot of trust in people, and I think when you put trust in people, you get more out of them."[2]

Abraham Lincoln said he would rather trust others and be occasionally disappointed, than mistrust and be miserable all the time. Buffett's has a similar philosophy:

We would rather suffer the visible costs of a few bad decisions than incur the many invisible costs that come from decisions made too slowly—or not at all—because of stifling bureaucracy...(so) Charlie and I will limit ourselves to allocating capital, controlling enterprise risk, choosing managers, and setting their compensation.[3]

Buffett never fails to lavish praise on his Berkshire colleagues in his annual letter. Buffett has designed a compensation arrangement that is elegant in its simplicity and is unique for each manager. They are similar in that they motivate the manager for growth drivers under their control and, by charging them a cost of capital, encourages them to keep their capital to a minimum and remit the rest to Buffett to allocate as he sees fit.

Buffett says his job has just two functions: the first is to allocate capital, and the second is to motivate Berkshire's operating managers when they have no financial need to work.

At least three-quarters of the managers that we have are rich beyond any possible financial need, and therefore my job is to help my senior people keep them interested enough to want to jump out of bed at six o'clock in the morning and work with all the enthusiasm they did when they were poor and starting.[4]

The biggest challenges for Buffett's successor will be to allocate capital rationally and to duplicate Buffett's less publicized but equally important management skill.

Because of Buffett's reputation as a brilliant businessman, his sterling integrity, and Berkshire's Fort Knox-like durability, companies seek his stamp of approval when traditional financing sources dry up. Berkshire benefits from lucrative financing terms. Financially stressed and capital-hungry companies impacted by the financial crisis of 1998 such as Bank of America, Goldman Sachs, General Electric, and Dow Chemical benefited not just from Berkshire's financing, but from the halo effect of association with Buffett.

The halo came at a demanding cost. Berkshire earned coupons of 10 percent on preferred stocks from General Electric and Goldman Sachs that also included warrants to buy their common stock. Dow coughed up 8.5 percent coupons to Berkshire to help fund its Rohm and Haas acquisition, which also gave Berkshire the right to convert the preferred into common stock. In the wake of the financial crisis in 2011, Berkshire injected capital into a struggling Bank of America with a $5 billion investment in BofA's 6 percent preferred stock and warrants to buy 700 million common shares. Berkshire tripled its investment in BofA in less than seven years by exercising the warrants in addition to the 6 percent coupons it earned while it waited for the common stock to rebound. Buffett's bet was largely based on his faith that the Federal Reserve would provide enough liquidity in the infusion pump for the economic patient that was on the emergency room operating table:

It was a bet essentially on the fact that the government would not really shirk its responsibility at a time like that, to leverage up when the rest of the world was trying to de-leverage and panicked.[5]

Warren Buffett has an exceptional ability to clearly articulate business principles in a way that is understood by anyone. He liberally sprinkles his annual letters with metaphors and suggestive quotes. For instance, in advising investors to concentrate investments in their highest conviction, he said, "Why not invest your assets in the companies you really like? As Mae West said, 'Too much of a good thing, can be wonderful.'"

Warren Buffett is referred to as the Oracle of Omaha to acknowledge him as one of the greatest investors of all time. Berkshire Hathaway is like a Smithsonian of American businesses, with consistent earnings, strong management, loyal consumers, and a business that is easy to understand. It is a collection of Normal Rockwell-like companies with character and nostalgia. Buffett is a comforting throwback to quality values amid a fast-paced, buyer-beware world of Wall Street promoters. His sage advice for acquisition hungry CEOs and investment advisors is patience. He is a trusted voice of reason who articulates common-sense investing and business principles while debunking arcane theory. His deals are friendly, and his managers are friends for life. His attitude is partnership, and he respects and communicates with his shareholders as partners. His Berkshire salary has remained at $100,000 for over twenty-five years, and he receives no bonus or stock options.

I prefer to think of Warren Buffett as "The Incomparable" to highlight his unmatched long-term record. It is also a deliberate play on words to recall the name of the corporate jet Buffett bought for Berkshire in 1989 for $6.7 million and sheepishly called "The Indefensible." Just as I did with John Templeton and Peter Lynch, I wrote Warren Buffett many years ago (before email) to describe my *Empower Your Investing* project (it was then called *Lessons From the Masters*) and mentioned the nickname I used for him. Three days later, I was amazed to receive a letter in the mailbox from Warren Buffett that said, "Thanks for your letter—it made my day! I like your name for me better than the name Charlie has for our plane."[6]

When I taught an investment seminar years ago on *Empower Your Investing*, I used two symbols to demonstrate the essence of Buffett's investment style. The first was a box of See's candy as an example of what a simple moment of pleasure for consumers, from an inexpensive, high-quality franchise product, can do in the long-run for investors. The repeat-purchase nature of Coca-Cola soda, Gillette razors, American Express card fees, Wells Fargo banking fees, and *Washington Post* subscriptions made billions for Berkshire.

The second symbol was a baseball bat, which was used to demonstrate how important it is to ignore the "Swing, you bum" investment pressure and wait for the fat pitch to hit in the middle of the strike zone. Buffett recalled that Ted Williams explained in his book, *The Science of Hitting*, that he divided the strike zone into seventy-seven cells, each the size of a baseball. Williams said that if he only swung at the balls in his best cell, he would hit .400, but if he swung at balls in his worst cell but still in the strike zone, he would only hit

.230. Waiting for the fat pitch made all the difference. Buffett explained that unlike a baseball hitter, investors have no called strikes. Investors should just sit with their bat on their shoulder and wait for the fat investment pitch. While it may be better to buy a wonderful company at a fair price, it is even better to swing at wonderful companies at wonderful prices. Warren Buffett has been hitting grand slams in business and investing for decades. It is unlikely his record will ever be broken, and as a role model for investing with intelligence, energy, and integrity, he is in a league all by himself.

CHAPTER 24

Similarities and Differences

I constantly see people rise in life who are not the smartest, sometimes not even the most diligent, but they are learning machines. They go to bed every night a little wiser than they were when they got up and boy does that help, particularly when you have a long run ahead of you.

—CHARLIE MUNGER[1]

John Templeton, Peter Lynch, and Warren Buffett were/are brilliant learning machines. Templeton read company reports and research reports while he walked in the ocean. Lynch worked eighty to eight-five hours each week, including Sunday mornings before church, and he even kept a chart book on his bed nightstand for quick reference. Buffett voraciously reads five newspapers and 500 pages each day for about five to six hours, and he is a regular in his office on Saturdays. If there was a Hall of Fame for investors, they would be unanimous first-round selections. Just like athletic Hall of Famers, they each had their unique style that redefined the conventional notion of investing. Templeton pioneered investing in emerging markets before anyone heard of the term. Lynch refused to be defined by growth or value but proved that great investment ideas are there if you work hard enough and are open-minded enough to find them. He also proved that size was no anchor to performance. Buffett validated his mentor's Benjamin Graham truism, "Investing is most intelligent when it is most businesslike." Buffett mastered capital allocation and was indifferent to whether he invested in part of a public company or whether he owned the entire company. This mastery was famously manifested as he transformed a humble investment in a dying textile company to become one of the five most valued companies in the U.S. His genius is also evident in how he is able to communicate his business philosophy in a way that is accessible and understandable for everyone. Buffett is underrated in his ability to inspire and manage Berkshire's division CEOs with minimal interference but with maximum loyalty and positive results.

As you define your own investment style, it may be helpful to review the similarities and differences between the three master investors.

Similarities between Templeton, Lynch, and Buffett

From their earliest childhood, all three master investors demonstrated a passionate mind for business and a strong entrepreneurial streak. They all began with modest means and a burning desire for financial security.

John Templeton, at the ripe age of four, grew beans from seed and sold them to the country store. When he was eight, he bought fireworks from a catalog off-season and sold them for five times his cost just before July 4th. In eighth grade, he bought two broken-down Ford trucks for $10 each and used the spare parts of one truck to restore the other, which he then used for transportation throughout his high school years. In the summer before college, he sold Good Housekeeping magazines door-to-door.

After Peter Lynch's father passed away tragically from brain cancer when Peter was eleven years of age, Peter felt responsible to help support his family financially. He found work caddying part-time, which he continued throughout high school and college.

At age six, Warren Buffett sold Juicy Fruit gum for a profit of $0.02/pack, and he famously bought a six-pack of Coca-Cola for twenty-five cents from his grandfather's grocery store and sold each bottle for five cents, making five cents per pack. When he was seven, he asked Santa Claus to give him the gift of a book called *Bond Salesmanship*. By eleven years old, Buffett marked prices on the slate in the boardroom of his father's office, and he bought his first stock. He also made money retrieving and selling lost golf balls, published a horse racing handicapping sheet, delivered up to 500 newspapers per day, and operated a pinball machine business.

All three were driven by their love for financial independence born from the influence of the Depression era, which they either lived through directly or indirectly through influential relatives. They used their savings and investment prowess to fund their college tuition. Templeton financed his college tuition partially from his poker winnings. Lynch financed his Wharton graduate school tuition with gains from buying Flying Tiger Line. Buffett experimented with various investment methods until he discovered Benjamin Graham's *The Intelligent Investor* during his senior year in college. They relished the individual competitive challenge to achieve excellence in an ultra-competitive industry as much as they felt a duty to their clients. The combination of their relentless work ethic and insatiable desire to learn and discover investment opportunities resulted in astounding performance records.

The three master investors are notable not only for their dazzling investment records but also for their integrity as businessmen. Hollywood tends to dramatize the transgressions and greed of Wall Street, which overshadows the legions of unsung positive business role models. Chief among them are these three master investors who built their careers on a foundation of business integrity. They lived Buffett's directive to Salomon employees "to ask themselves whether they are willing to have any contemplated act appear the next day on the front page of their local paper, to be read by their spouses, children, and friends...." The three masters made their share of investment mistakes. Peter Lynch said that "you are great in this business if you are right six times out of ten."[2] However, their integrity and business reputations are worthy of canonization.

In an industry that often plays its cards close to the vest, all three masters were willing to share their investment philosophy with others. They are all teachers. John Templeton wrote his guide to investment wealth, *Global Investing: The Templeton Way,* but he also wrote more than a dozen books about spiritual wealth. Peter Lynch wrote three books demystifying investment principles and explaining the advantages that common investors have over professionals. He was also a frequent columnist for *Worth* magazine and a regular member of the *Barron's* roundtable. Lynch said he wanted to be remembered for trying to teach people to be careful with their money...to view stocks as owning a piece of a company and not as a lottery ticket. Long after retiring as a fund manager, Peter Lynch continues to mentor analysts and portfolio managers at Fidelity. Both Templeton and Lynch were frequent guests on Louis Rukeyser's *Wall Street Week* and sometimes appeared together on the same episode.

Warren Buffett's letter to shareholders in Berkshire Hathaway's annual reports is his favorite forum for teaching his business and investing principles.

Some say, and I agree, that a careful reading of his fifty-plus annual letters is more valuable than a graduate degree in investing—the only tuition cost is your time reading. At the 2017 Berkshire Hathaway annual meeting Buffett, when asked how he would like to be remembered, said,

> With me, it's pretty simple. I really like teaching. I've been doing it formally and, you could say, somewhat informally all my life, and I certainly had the greatest teachers you could imagine. So, if somebody thought that I did a decent job at teaching, I'd feel very good about that.

Buffett formally taught a night class at the University of Nebraska, "Investment Principles," when he was only twenty-one. Just as Templeton and Lynch were frequent guests on the preeminent television show on investing at the time, Buffett is a frequent special guest on CNBC, where he is candid about answering a wide range of questions about business and investing.

All three were willing to make bold investment bets to back up their logic and reasoning. The only time Templeton borrowed money was to invest $10,000 in every stock in the U.S. stock exchange that was selling for no more than $1.00/share on the eve of the U.S. entering World War II, after the market had fallen 50 percent. Four years later he sold for a four-fold gain. Templeton made his career-defining bet on Japanese stocks before investment restrictions were lifted. When they were lifted in 1971, Japanese stocks were already a sizable percentage of the Templeton Fund and grew to over 60 percent in the early 1970s, and the rest is history. When conventional wisdom feared to wade in to Chrysler, Fannie Mae, and General Public Utilities on concerns about bankruptcy, Lynch dove in with large percentage weights with multi-bagger gains. Buffett invested 40 percent of his net worth in American Express in 1962 and owned over 40 percent of Berkshire Hathaway stock personally for many years. Recall Buffett's advice to Will Danoff, who manages Fidelity's Contrafund with more than $100 billion in assets, "Bet big on your best ideas." Buffett would be quick to add: but only if your facts and reasoning are correct. All three were willing to put their courage behind their convictions.

Templeton, Lynch, and Buffett were unflinching optimists about American business. They shared faith in how capitalism, innovation, and free markets enable the U.S. to accelerate our standard of living, become resilient to economic downturns, and regenerate itself with new wealth generating opportunities. In every guest appearance on *Wall Street Week* with Louis Rukeyser,

John Templeton was optimistic about opportunities in America and grateful for the blessings of America's accomplishments. He often peppered his presentations by reciting a series of under-recognized facts such as "50 percent of all the scientists that ever lived are alive today, 50 percent of all the books published were published in the last sixty years, 50 percent of all scientific discoveries ever made were in this century...."[3] He was always gracious and thankful for a country that allows people to pursue their God-given talents: "We need to recognize that we are living in the most glorious period of world history."

Lynch was an unshaken optimist about the U.S. capitalist economy and was always fully invested. Shortly after the 9/11 attack, Peter Lynch offered consolation and hope, "If you believe in the strength of the American resolve, hard work, and innovation, then take a long-term view and believe in our economic system. I certainly believe."[4]

Buffett is consistently optimistic on the future of American business due to our market-based system that unleashes human potential. "For 240 years it's been a terrible mistake to bet against America, and now is no time to start."[5]

All three master investors gave generously of their time, talent, and treasure. Templeton gave at least 20 percent of his earnings to charities beginning in his 30s and even more in his later years. As we read in Chapter 3, his namesake, the Templeton Foundation program of Prizes for Progress in Religion, had a cash award at its inception that was greater than the Nobel Peace Prize or any other award.

Since 1990 Peter Lynch and his wife Carolyn, until her passing in 2015, managed their family foundation focused on museums, Catholic charities—especially in Boston's inner-city schools—healthcare, and education.

Warren Buffett has pledged to return 99 percent of his wealth back to society. In 2006 he famously announced that he would gradually donate the bulk of his wealth to the Bill & Melinda Gates Foundation. For eighteen consecutive years through 2017, Buffett has auctioned a private lunch with himself to benefit the Glide Foundation, raising $24 million. He has been an advocate for convincing other wealthy Americans to pledge 50 percent of their wealth to charities. He seeks to rectify a somewhat distorted market system that rewards a money manager like himself with billions of dollars for detecting mispriced securities while influential teachers are rewarded with thank-you notes.

They shared the following similarities:

- Displayed quick and decisive action.
- Totally dedicated and professionally competitive.
- Patient.
- Willing to adapt their investment approach within a value-oriented style.
- Didn't use options or short stocks.
- Ignored the obsession of forecasting the general market or interest rates.
- Healthy disrespect for academic perspective on efficient market theory.
- Rational temperament.

Each investor was tested with company developments, either rumored or real, that challenged their assessment of a company's competitive advantage. They rationally discerned the merit of the news, assessed whether the issue was temporary or structural, and whether the issue was material to the company's earnings power.

- Did not use a computer for investing. Peter Lynch said, "A pile of software isn't worth a damn if you haven't done your basic homework on the companies. Trust me, Warren Buffett doesn't use this stuff (Bridge, Shark, Bloomberg, etc.)."[6]

…and differences:

- Templeton and Lynch think more like stock market operators, while Buffett thinks like a businessman.
- Lynch and Templeton were more flexible and eclectic than Buffett.
- Lynch and Templeton acted more like fiduciaries for their shareholders who felt compelled to become an expert in areas outside their immediate competence. Buffett stays within his competence.
- Lynch likes retailers and restaurants for their ability to clone a good concept. Buffett says he doesn't understand retailers for their lack of durability and ease of entry. Buffett has said that it is hard to establish a permanent competitive moat in retail that will keep competitors out.
- Buffett prefers the solitude of Omaha, whereas Templeton sent his analysts to Thailand, Brazil, Korea, and Spain; Lynch worked heavily with other Fidelity managers and analysts.

John Templeton and Warren Buffett

In a 1985 interview with Adam Smith, John Templeton was asked how he distinguished himself from a handful of other investors who have consistently beaten the market, such as Phil Fisher and Warren Buffett. He replied,

> *Probably in the fact that I look worldwide more than the others do and search in a wider variety of areas. Probably because I make earnings estimates more into the future than others are. And certainly, I rely on prayer in everything we do. We open all of our directors meeting with prayer. We pray (for wisdom) about every decision we make.[7]*

In the same interview, Templeton echoed his investment counseling motto of over four decades, "To buy when others are despondently selling, and to sell when others are others are avidly buying requires the greatest fortitude and pays the greatest reward." This is similar to Buffett's version of the same bargain-hunting concept, "to be greedy when others are fearful, and be fearful when others are greedy."

There are many other similarities between Templeton and Buffett. They were both taught by, and admired, Benjamin Graham. But both recognized that Graham's net-net working capital bargain metric was too restrictive and transitioned to more relevant valuation tools, especially measuring current price to future core earnings power.

They both had superior performance results working in isolated surroundings. Buffett preferred the familiarity of his hometown Omaha, Nebraska, while Templeton chose to operate from the serenity of New Providence Island in the Bahamas. Both retained a mental aloofness from the crowd and focused on research based on fact instead of Wall Street stimulation. In Omaha or in the Bahamas, they focused on what a business is worth rather than subjecting themselves to the bias of short-term thinking so prevalent on Wall Street. Buffett's aversion to the hype of Wall Street was similar to Templeton. Buffett said, "I worked on Wall Street for a couple of years, and people came up whispering to me every ten seconds, and I got overstimulated...."[8]

Both made a conscious effort to focus their time on the value-add of researching investment ideas instead of allowing themselves to get sidetracked with trading shares or running an investment company. Neither individual had a committee for making investment decisions. Buffett said his idea of an investment committee is to look in the mirror. Both were consistent, not flashy performers. Both had the courage of their convictions and made decisive bold bets.

Both filled their "dead time"—the waiting time for spent on airlines, buses, trains or waiting for appointments—with reading company SEC filings such as 10-Qs (quarterly reports) and 10-Ks (annual reports), annual reports to shareholders, and other research reports from *Value Line*, Standard & Poor's or Moody's.

Both were flexible in their approaches but at heart emphasized preserving capital by bargain hunting. Templeton said to buy at the point of maximum pessimism to limit downside risk. Buffett said the only real rule of investing is to not lose money. Buffett emphasized that if you buy a group of companies that are far below what they are worth, you basically don't lose money.

Both Templeton and Buffett had an almost surreal detachment from the emotions of the market and sought to exploit the market's folly. They were not swayed by the emotions of the crowd. Instead, they took advantage of the volatility. Buffett said the most important quality of a successful investor is not intellect, but an even temperament. He said, "This is not a business where you take polls, but where you think."[9] Both Templeton and Buffett were patient, calm, and dispassionate, but also bold and confident. Buffett says that price alone doesn't tell you anything about a business. He prefers to not even know the price of a company before he values the company so it doesn't influence his decision. Only afterward does he prefer to compare its value to the price. He invests with the mindset that he wouldn't care if the stock market were closed for five years, the same attitude an investor would have when buying a farm or investment real estate.

Templeton was, and Buffett is, an ardent optimist and positive about the ingenuity, drive, and resourcefulness of societies operating in a free market system. Both thrived on finding overlooked bargains and neither one used a computer to do so. They focused on the long-term. They launched their flagship investment portfolios at almost the same time (1955–1956). They were both dedicated to investing for life.

The inaugural issue of *CFA Magazine* in 2003 featured a cover story called "Living Legends" that had a conference call interview with seven investing legends including Templeton and Buffett. When asked what one piece of advice they would consider most valuable to a twenty-five to thirty-year-old investment professional, Templeton said, "I would recommend being humble. Be open-minded, and do not be conceited." Buffett advised, "I'd say be realistic in defining your circle of competence. Try to figure out what you're capable of knowing, stay within that, and forget about everything else. It means deciding which businesses you know enough to value and which ones you don't know enough to value."

When asked what timeless thought investors would most appreciate, Templeton said, "the great opportunities are the places that have been neglected, where other people are not looking." Buffett said, "Always leave a margin of safety, stick with what you understand, and quantify."[10]

There were differences between Templeton and Buffett; some subtle and some more significant. John Templeton once remarked about Warren Buffett,

> I'm a great admirer of Warren Buffett. But he has been focused primarily on
> U.S. investments. That is strange. To that extent, I think he's short-sighted—
> or small sighted. Small sighted, I think. If he had spent more time in foreign
> nations, he would be better off.[11]

Over time Buffett transitioned to shop beyond American borders for investments when Berkshire acquired the Israel-based metal-cutting firm ISCAR and German motorcycle accessory company Devlet Louis Motorradvertriebs, or invested in the U.K. retailer Tesco, the German insurer Munich Re, and the Chinese battery and car maker BYD.

Templeton viewed himself as a fiduciary of capital for clients, and Buffett views himself as a steward of capital for Berkshire. If Templeton saw an opportunity for an apparent bargain, he believed that he had the responsibility to acquire the expertise to evaluate the situation. Buffett, on the other hand, defines his circle of competence, and if an opportunity lies outside the circle, he ignores it. For decades Buffett didn't invest in technology stocks as he explained in a 1985 interview with Adam Smith: "You know, there are all kinds of things I don't know about, and that may be too bad; but you know, why should I know all about them?" Templeton on the contrary said, "I would part company with Buffett on this. I think you should try to understand companies or you should hire someone who understands any company, any industry, where there appears to be a good buy." Templeton deployed analysts all around the world, while Buffett has an extensive network of contacts, especially within Berkshire, but prefers to work almost entirely on his own.

More recently Buffett appears to have followed Templeton's playbook after he followed his trusted Berkshire investment lieutenants, Todd Combs and Ted Welscher, in their original purchase of Apple. After disdaining technology for years as outside his circle of competence, by mid-2018, Berkshire owned just under 5 percent of Apple shares. Charlie Munger reflected on Buffett's ability to adapt:

> The nice thing about the game we're in is that you can keep learning, and we're still doing it…He's (Buffett) changed…I don't think we've gone crazy, I think the answer is we're adapting reasonably to a business that has gotten very much more difficult.[12]

Templeton's average holding period was six years. While that is long-term compared to the frenzied trading in many hedge funds today, it is relatively short-term compared to many of Buffett's holdings within Berkshire. Buffett absolutely views stocks as owning part of a business that he would like to own forever, whereas Templeton was happy to sell a stock if he found another with enough upside.

Lynch and Templeton

John Templeton and Peter Lynch thought time was precious. Templeton set his watch ten minutes fast to ensure he was prompt for a meeting and made sure he brought reading material if he had to wait. Lynch presided over weekly presentations by Fidelity fund managers where they pitched their best ideas. Lynch timed the presentations initially for three minutes each, and later, shortened them to ninety seconds. Templeton spoke in an easy Tennessee drawl that belied his intense work ethic. Lynch's rapid-fire, roll-up-your-sleeve style of work echoed his speech pattern, which was often peppered with witty barbs targeting out-of-touch investment professionals and ivory-tower academics.

A strong faith in God was important to both Templeton and Lynch. Templeton prayed for wisdom, clarity of thought, and thanksgiving before board meetings and before making important decisions. Lynch is Irish Catholic and dedicated *One Up on Wall Street* to his family, his colleagues at Fidelity, his shareholders at Magellan, and "to Holy God for all the incredible blessings I have been given in my life."

Both Templeton and Lynch were popular guests on *Wall Street Week* with Louis Rukeyser. They appeared together on the show in tuxedos just after the 1987 Crash and were just as classy with their commonsense investment advice and optimism. They advocated doing your homework to understand what you own, were selective and patient, focused on the long-term correlation between earnings and stock prices, ignored macro fears, and took advantage of bargain prices. They were both widely diversified and believed that any company could be a candidate for purchase at the right price. Both liked to ask management, "Who is your toughest competitor? Who else do you admire?"

Lynch and Buffett

The centennial issue of *Forbes* magazine celebrated its birthday by asking one hundred of the top living business minds to share their wisdom. They included Peter Lynch and, on the cover of the magazine, Warren Buffett. Peter Lynch recalled the time when he received a surprise call from Warren Buffett asking Lynch if he could use one of his lines from *One Up on Wall Street* for the Berkshire Hathaway annual letter. Buffett said, "I have to have it. Can I please use it?" Lynch replied, "Sure. What's the line?" Buffett said, "Selling your winners and holding your losers is like cutting the flowers and watering the weeds."

While many other contributors to the magazine touted their advice for success, Lynch humbly admitted to his biggest mistake: "That one line he picked in my whole book has been my greatest mistake." Lynch recalled that he visited the first four Home Depots ever built, bought the stock, and triumphantly sold after it tripled. Afterward, the stock proceeded to climb fifty-fold. The experience taught him, and us, that time is the friend of a great business.

Buffett also loved Lynch's line that "it's better to buy a great business with mediocre management than great management with a mediocre business because the reputation of the business will dominate." Lynch questions how we can really be sure that management is brilliant. Buffett's analogy is similar: "It matters more what current you are in than how hard you row."

Peter Lynch said that you should be able to explain to a ten-year-old in two minutes why you own a stock. He quipped, "Because this sucker's going up" is no answer. Buffett sounded eerily like Lynch:

> You should be able to write down on a yellow sheet of paper, 'I'm buying (for example) General Motors at $22, and GM has 566 million shares for a total market value of $13 billion, and GM is worth a lot more than $13 billion because ____.' And if you can't finish that sentence, then you don't buy the stock.[13]

Both Peter Lynch and Warren Buffett preached the core truth in investing: there is a high correlation between a company's earnings and its stock price over the long-run. Lynch made the observation in 1990 about Merck and Coca-Cola, whose profits and stocks in the previous twenty years both went up fifteen-fold.[14] Similarly, nine years later, Buffett observed, "The inescapable fact is that the value of an asset, whatever its character, cannot over the long term grow faster than its earnings do."[15]

Peter Lynch supported Warren Buffett's strategy in 1999, which was one of Berkshire's worst performing years when Berkshire's stock fell 19.9 percent compared to the S&P 500's rise of 21.0 percent. Technology was the rage amidst a pre-Y2K buying frenzy by companies to avoid a Year 2000 software bug that many feared would cause their computers to fail. Buffett, a self-described "lifetime technophobe" dug in his heels and appeared to be out-of-touch. His favorites, Coca-Cola and Gillette, proved fallible in 1999. Coca-Cola's stock fell 11 percent in 1999 as its reputation went flat for their slow response to a contamination scare in Europe. Gillette's stock was nicked by 30 percent, due to several warnings of disappointing earnings driven by mismanaged inventory and bloated overhead. As Buffett was criticized as losing relevance, Lynch presciently defended Buffett, "His investing method is as true today as it was ten years ago. It's a little harder to find the same opportunities, but his system hasn't gone out of favor."[16] The tech bubble burst eight months later in March 2000—a year when Berkshire's stock price rose 26.6 percent compared to a decline of 9.1 percent in the S&P 500.

Lynch and Buffett had a few significant differences. At one point, Lynch owned over 1,500 companies in the Magellan fund but did make large bets on his strongest convictions. Buffett preferred to concentrate on his best ideas and typically owned less than a dozen stocks. To be fair, Lynch owned very small positions in hundreds of stocks to more closely track their progress and determine whether they should graduate to a larger weight, similar to Buffett, who bought one hundred shares in companies order to receive their financial statements.

Lynch operated out of Fidelity's Boston office, which was a must-stop by management teams touring the country with their strategic updates. There was an endless flow of companies pitching their advantages and availing themselves for questions. Lynch worked with and mentored dozens of Fidelity analysts and portfolio managers. Lynch's favorite method of due diligence was visiting with companies directly on-site at their headquarters or place of business, such as the mall. Visiting management at their place of business allowed Lynch to better assess whether management was frugal or lavish, hungry or complacent, transparent or opaque. Visiting their business on location gave Lynch a sense of how the business resonated with customers. These insights were much more valuable than relying on a research report or betting on macro-economic trends.

Buffett preferred to think from the quiet of his office in Omaha. His network of valued contacts included Berkshire directors Charlie Munger, Walter Scott Jr., Steve Burke, Tom Murphy, and Bill Gates. His network expanded tremendously with each company Berkshire acquired. Buffett relished visiting companies directly early in his career, but in later years, he relied on his cumulative experience and growing network as inputs for making investment decisions.

Warren Buffett was interviewed by phone just days after Peter Lynch announced his retirement. Buffett described Lynch:

> He does what he says he does. Uses common sense. Invests in things he knows and understands which are a lot more things than I do. I'm like a groundhog who comes out of the burrow once a year for a little while and looks at a few things. Where I own only a few things, Lynch owned and followed 1,400 stocks. It just shows that there are a lot of different ways for getting to heaven.[17]

In Conclusion

While there were differences between the three master investors, they were equally passionate and disciplined with their research and valuation of companies. They bet big only when they were convinced their facts and reasoning were right. They took advantage of mispricing, which was typically caused by an overreaction to a news event or unappreciated earnings power. Though their results were heroic, they were quick to admit their mistakes and were generous with their wealth. They are not only master investors, they are terrific role models.

CHAPTER 25

The Pyramid of Growth

No wise pilot, no matter how great his talent and experience, fails to use a checklist.

—CHARLIE MUNGER

In a sense, Berkshire Hathaway is a canvas, and I get to paint anything I want on that canvas. And it's the process of painting that I really enjoy, not selling the painting.

—WARREN BUFFETT[1]

A common assignment in art classes is to ask students to copy a master-piece. By studying the nuances of a master artist, the student develops a closer awareness and appreciation of the techniques of the artist. I once visited the Louvre and saw an artist copying the Mona Lisa with a remarkable likeness. The impressionist Claude Monet studied under Eugene Boudin, who convinced him that drawing caricatures was a waste of time and to focus instead on painting the light of seascapes and landscapes. Monet also drew upon Édouard Manet, whose figure paintings departed from popular realism in favor of an impressionistic, almost unfinished, style. Monet was an avid collector of Japanese art, in particular by Katsushika Hokusai, whom many credit for Monet's inspiration for his water lily paintings. Monet absorbed these influences, as well as those of his contemporaries such as Pierre-Auguste Renoir, Camille Pissarro, and Alfred Sisley to ultimately develop his own authentic style of blending light, color, and atmosphere to become *the* master of impressionist painting.

A colleague once said there are many ways up the investment mountain. John Templeton, Peter Lynch, and Warren Buffett began their climb by learning from their mentors but each blazed his own trail. John Templeton learned to be an opportunistic value hunter from his father and his Depression-era background. His mother influenced his love of knowledge, instilled his enterprising work ethic, and gave him his appreciation for geographic and cultural diversity. He assimilated these values to form his own investment discipline to look for the most attractive bargains worldwide.

Peter Lynch's love of stocks was born from listening to success stories from his golf caddie clients. He was profoundly influenced by one such client, D. George Sullivan, Fidelity's president. The combination of Fidelity's unequaled access, Peter's intense curiosity, his relentless "kick the tire" work ethic, and his flexible, open-minded approach to unconventional companies allowed him to scale record summits.

Warren Buffett borrowed heavily from five investor mentors but clearly forged his own distinct investment path. From his father, a broker and politician, he learned the value of integrity and character above all else. Benjamin Graham branded three timeless investing principles onto Buffett's heart: 1) think of stocks as a fractional ownership of a business, 2) insist on a margin of safety discount between the stock price and its intrinsic value, and 3) the stock market is your servant, not your master, so capitalize on its volatility. From Philip Carret, he appreciated the beauty in owning an enduring quality company with steadily growing earnings and holding them for the long-term. From Phil Fisher, he learned to apply a "scuttlebutt" research approach to invest in a concentrated group of wonderful companies held long-term. From Charlie Munger, he learned to apply common sense filters for his investments, the futility of buying a business to replace poor managers, and that it is much easier and more rewarding to pay a fair price for a wonderful company than to pay a (so-called) wonderful price for a fair company.

The three master investors borrowed from their investing influences and adapted them to create their own masterpieces. They had their differences, as we discovered in the previous chapter, but I wondered if was possible to borrow their best practices to form my own investment process.

"Well, I guess you're it." With that encouraging endorsement from the chief investment officer of a West Coast investment firm, my career in portfolio management was launched more than twenty-five years ago. I was promoted to manage a growth stock mutual fund when the fund was ranked in the cellar of its peer group for performance, and the firm had changed lead portfolio managers for the third time that same year. At that time, I had a BA in Accounting, an MBA in Finance, earned my Chartered Financial Analyst (CFA) designation, taught several years of evening review classes for CFA candidates, and had thirteen years of experience as a financial and securities analyst. Yet I felt unprepared in my new responsibility as a portfolio manager.

Only after digesting the case studies of successful stocks, personal backgrounds, work habits, research methods, and investment disciplines of Templeton, Lynch, and Buffett did I feel fully confident and prepared to invest personally and professionally. The best practices of Templeton, Lynch, and Buffett became investment cornerstones for my investment process called The Pyramid of Growth. After four years of applying The Pyramid of Growth process, the mutual fund I managed was awarded the highest rating of five stars by Morningstar, Inc. Years later, I co-managed a new mutual fund with a small team of portfolio manager partners using the same process, and it also achieved a five-star ranking. This investment process has been consistently applied for over many market cycles with superior performance and less risk. It has worked because it is based on a foundation of enduring business principles backed by the successful execution of master investors. No investment process can guarantee success. The Pyramid of Growth, however, is a synthesis of quality business and investment principles and, well-executed, can improve your investment results.

The Pyramid of Growth concept was borrowed from the Pyramid of Success developed by the beloved former UCLA basketball coach John Wooden, whom ESPN named Coach of the Century. Coach Wooden's Pyramid of Success is a teaching tool whereby he illustrated the qualities necessary for individual and team success. Each block of the pyramid represents a behavior, attitude, or value ingredient for success, including enthusiasm, industriousness, self-control, poise, confidence, and competitive greatness. Ultimately, he defined success as "peace of mind that is a direct result of self-satisfaction in knowing you made the effort to become the best you are capable of becoming." Coach Wooden's pyramid and definition of success inspired me when I first read his book, *They Call Me Coach,* as a freshman in high school. They have guided me ever since, particularly as I had the honor of personally knowing Coach Wooden in the last eight years of his life.

John Wooden Pyramid of Success

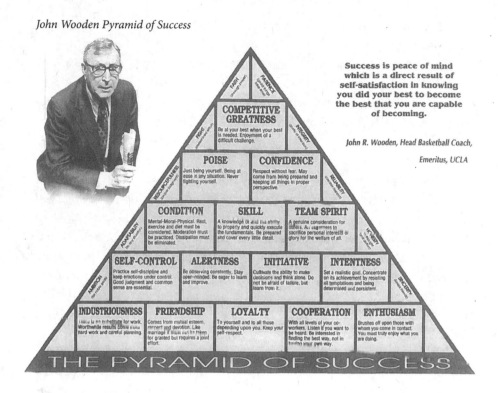

Well executed, The Pyramid of Growth is designed to provide financial peace of mind by participating in the success of companies with enduring quality and compounding growth.

Investment Philosophy

Charlie Munger emphasizes the importance of using a latticework of mental models to investing. These mental models form a framework for gathering, processing, and acting on information. They are holistic guideposts that lead to powerful approaches to investment evaluation. Munger advised,

> You've got to have models in your head. And you've got to array your experience—both vicarious and direct—on this latticework of models. You may have noticed students who just try to remember and pound back what is remembered. Well, they fail in school and in life. You've got to hang experience on a latticework of models in your head.[2]

353

The Pyramid of Growth is grounded in a latticework of seven mental models:

1. Capital Preservation. The first investment priority is to preserve your capital. The first step in making money is to not lose it. In order to break-even after a 50 percent loss, an investor has the daunting task of doubling their return, which could take years. Warren Buffett famously stated his basic rules for investing: "Rule No. 1: Never lose money. Rule No. 2: Never forget Rule No. 1."

Investing is a process of managing two primary risks: business risk and price risk. Business risk is the risk that a company's competitive advantage will erode or be lost altogether, causing a permanent loss of capital and intrinsic value. Recent examples include the loss in pricing power of branded products due to private-label competition, the decline in subscription of newspapers, magazines, and cable due to online content, the substitution of email for postal service, and the threat to physical retailers from cheaper warehouse clubs and online retailers, such as Amazon. A company's competitive landscape demands constant vigilance.

Price risk is the risk that an investor overpays for a sound company. Price risk can be minimized by conservatively estimating a company's intrinsic value and buying stock when the price is at an adequate discount to its value. When each stock is purchased with an adequate a margin of safety, downside risk protection is built into the overall portfolio.

2. Long-Term Perspective. In the short-term, stock prices may react to world political news, currency devaluations, central bank changes in monetary policy, rumors, changes in sell-side analyst recommendations, forced selling by mutual funds experiencing redemptions, trading by momentum-driven speculators, short covering, option expirations, quarter-end window dressing, or computer-driven block trades. These factors may have little to do with a company's intrinsic value but may present opportunities to take advantage of temporary differences between market valuation and inherent value.

Charlie Munger said that he and Buffett

> ...made the money out of high-quality businesses...Over the long-term, it's hard for a stock to earn a much better return than the business which underlies it earns. If the business earns six percent on capital over forty years and you hold it for that forty years, you're not going to make much different than a six percent return—even if you originally buy it at a huge

discount. Conversely, if a business earns eighteen percent on capital over twenty or thirty years, even if you pay an expensive looking price, you'll end up with one hell of a result.[3]

In the long-term, stock prices correlate closely with a company's earnings and cash flow. For instance, in the twenty-five years ending June 2018, Johnson & Johnson's earnings grew 10.4 percent annually on average, and the stock returned 10.4 percent annually (see chart below from Securities Research Company.)

Focus on a company's long-term earnings prospects. The heart of Sir John Templeton's stock picking method was to favor stocks that had the lowest stock price relative to his five-year earnings forecast. Warren Buffett prefers to be measured over a rolling five-year period and has said that he wants to have a reasonably good idea of what a company will earn in ten years. Peter Lynch said that you might as well flip a coin to decide if stocks will be higher or lower

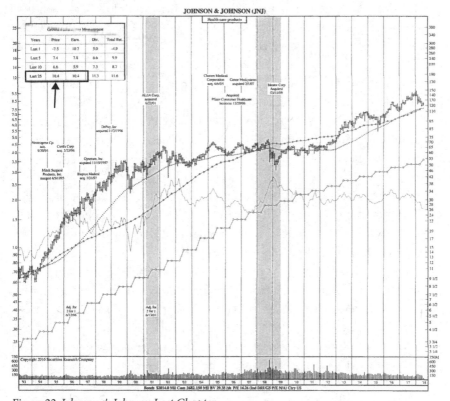

Figure 22. Johnson & Johnson Last Chapter

in two to three years, but that stocks are relatively predictable over twenty years. While one cannot forecast five-year-forward earnings with 100 percent accuracy, the earnings-based analytical process focuses on the right variables, such as the durability of a company's competitive advantage and the predictability of the business.

3. Quality Holdings. Quality can mean different things to different people; some say you know it when you see it. In art, we have Rembrandt and Monet; in jewelry, we have Tiffany and Cartier; in watches, we have Rolex; and in automobiles, we have Rolls Royce. These products and brands have achieved a unique market advantage that has enduring value. Look for similar enduring quality attributes in the businesses in which you invest.

Quality businesses are those having sustainable competitive advantages that are difficult for a competitor to replicate. Warren Buffett refers to these barriers to entry as a company's "economic moat." Competitive advantages include patent protection (pharmaceutical and biotech drugs), trusted brands with great customer goodwill (Disney), regulatory licenses (Moody's), high switching costs (banks), cost advantages (Costco), scale/size advantage (Amazon), and a network effect (Facebook). Companies that have earned a competitive advantage and can sustain that advantage typically generate returns on invested capital (ROIC) far above their cost of capital and generate tremendous cash flow and shareholder value.

The ideal quality business would have a durable competitive advantage, high ROIC and free cash flow with little to no debt, a shareholder-minded management team of high integrity, and a "tollgate/repeat purchase" predictability to its business.

Be skeptical about reported earnings, which can be manipulated with accrual accounting to appear higher than the actual cash generated by the business. In April 2001 I visited Enron management at their Houston headquarters to understand how the company could report years of *positive* income, but have a *negative* cumulative five-year free cash flow and pay almost no taxes. Enron was then a popular energy services company with a $70 billion market valuation. I left without an adequate explanation and thereby avoided a potential loss since the company filed for bankruptcy eight months later.

4. Embrace Stocks as Business Owners. The barriers to owning a stock are low, but the barriers to understanding a business, its competitive advantages, risks, and value, are high. With a few online clicks and adequate funds, one can buy a stock in a fraction of a second. But becoming a long-term investor, as opposed to a short-term market trader, one must know the company and the reasons for owning the company. Without this hard-won knowledge, one cannot withstand the inevitable headwinds that tempt the uninformed to sell with the crowd. Fear-induced selling based on misinformation locks in poor results.

A long-term investor understands the difference between a company's intrinsic value and the market price of the stock. It is not uncommon for a stock price to vary as much as 50 percent from its high and low during a year. These are opportunities to capitalize on the disconnection between the relatively stable intrinsic value and the more volatile stock price. View owning a stock as a partnership with management, and expect management to communicate and behave accordingly. You may monitor stock prices regularly, but focus on the business's fundamentals to ensure that your investment rationale remains valid.

5. Concentrated Portfolio. A selective approach offers the advantage of allowing winners to make a significant contribution to performance. First-class businesses bought at compelling price discounts to intrinsic value can generate superior portfolio returns with less risk. Truly outstanding business gems are not usually on sale, but when they are, act on them. Imagine Babe Ruth's impact to a Yankees game if he had to wait his turn to bat once all the other starters and benchwarmers had their turn at the plate. Focusing on your best ideas will avoid diluting your time following marginal companies that merely occupy space in a portfolio.

6. Low Turnover. Low turnover allows you to be selective and patient enough to wait for Mr. Market to throw the fat pitch in the middle of the strike zone before swinging. This is in contrast to the average mutual fund portfolio that has 100 percent turnover, often with at least one hundred stocks. The "buy and hold" strategy allows you to enjoy the compounding benefits of superior growth companies and minimize the commissions and taxes that are obstacles to growing capital. The majority of the Forbes 400 wealthiest individuals earned their place on the list by owning outstanding businesses held for many years.

7. All-Cap Flexibility. Be flexible in selecting first-tier businesses led by all-star managers at attractive prices, regardless of the size of the company. Many professional money managers have a mandate to stay within their defined style-box of, for instance, large-cap growth, even if large-cap growth stocks are overpriced. Manage your portfolio with the best companies at the best value regardless of size or category.

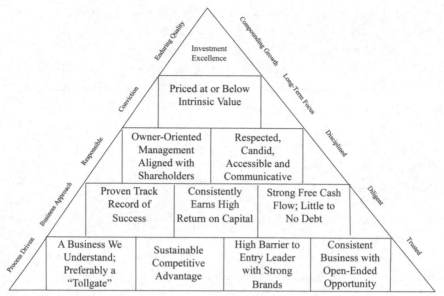

The Pyramid of Growth

Charlie Munger also advised that "No wise pilot, no matter how great his talent and experience, fails to use a checklist." The Pyramid of Growth is an investment process and checklist that is clearly defined and rooted in proven and timeless investment principles. The goal is to build a portfolio of outstanding companies possessing sustainable competitive advantages with high returns on capital and free cash flow, preferably with little to no debt, at a price that is a discount to their intrinsic value.

The cost of convenient access to data in today's Google search society is information overload. The challenge is not accessing information but converting information to timely insights and actionable knowledge that builds wealth. Investment candidates can come from a variety of sources, including discussions with company executives about their respected competitors, customers, suppliers, and distributors. Ideas also come from reading the general business press, trade journals, colleagues in the industry, and data rich sources such as *Value Line.*

Once a viable investment candidate is identified, it is then filtered through The Pyramid of Growth. In its simplest form, the Pyramid of Growth criteria assesses the quality and durability of the business and its risks, the excellence of management, and whether the market price is attractive compared to the company's intrinsic value.

High-Quality Business

These criteria determine if the investment candidate business is high-quality business and has a sustainable competitive advantage:

- A Business You Understand; Preferably a Tollgate. Only swing at pitches in the strike zone—those you understand. Tollgate businesses have recurring revenues with repeat transactions that enhance earnings predictability and allows for more accurate intrinsic value estimates. Companies that have recurring revenues are "all-weather" companies that deliver consistent results despite weak economies. Look for companies with limited competition, produce free cash flow with low capital needs and, ideally, have pricing power. For example, Visa and MasterCard generate revenues from fees paid by its customers based on payment volume. Each swipe of a credit or debit card benefits the payment processors. The higher the dollar transaction, the higher the fee to Visa and MasterCard without either company incurring added costs. Standard & Poor's and Moody's bond rating service enjoy a combined market share over 80 percent split evenly between them. However, since most bonds are dual rated, this means that S&P and Moody's each have over 80 percent of the market. Their ratings enhance liquidity and lower borrowing costs for the issuer. Corporate debt issuance is consistently about 40 percent of gross domestic product. As the economy grows, corporate debt issuance rises in tandem and so does the need for ratings—another tollgate.

- Sustainable Competitive Advantage. Competitive advantages that are long-lasting create enduring value. Examples include patent protection, trusted brands, regulatory licenses, high switching costs, cost advantages, scale/size advantage, and a network effect. Evidence of competitive advantages include a low threat of new entrants, little threat of substitution, strong bargaining power over customers and suppliers, and minimal rivalry among competitors. Visa and Master-Card have strong brands based on their worldwide acceptance, trust in their ability to quickly and safely process transactions, and offer a safe and convenient method of payment to the cardholder. Their scale advantage in processing capability generates nearly 90 percent profit margins on incremental transactions.

- **High Barrier to Entry with Strong Brands.** Trusted brands can be a company's most valuable asset and create customer loyalty. Customer loyalty generates repeat sales which are more profitable than the cost of attracting new customers. Favor one-of-a-kind businesses with no close substitute.

- **Open-Ended Opportunity; Exploits Secular Trend.** Focus on companies that can benefit from an open-ended market opportunity with a tailwind of demand for a product that is needed or desired. When MasterCard became a public company in 2006 and Visa in 2008, they said that their primary competitor was cash, since cash and checks account for 85 percent of world transactions. In 2018, they both still say 85 percent of worldwide transactions are done with cash and check. As e-commerce takes market share from physical retail stores, digital payments create more opportunity for the payment processors.

- **Proven Track Record of Success.** Look for proven performers that have been tested by economic storms and competitive threats. An excellent track record is not a guarantee of future performance, but it beats empty promises. Buffett said the past record of management is the best single guide to assess competence:

    "Records are important. Human qualities are important."[4] *"The best judgement we can make about competence is not what other people thought at the time, but simply the record...If I'm going to bring a fellow up from Triple A baseball to the major leagues, I want one who's been a top batter in Triple A: I don't want someone who's hitting .220 who says, 'I'm saving myself for the majors.'"*[5]

- **Consistently Earns a High Return on Invested Capital (ROIC).** All else equal, the most valuable businesses are those that deliver more cash flow and income with fewer assets. A company that generates $25 of cash income with $100 of invested capital in the form of debt or equity is more valuable, all else equal, than another company that only generates $10 of cash income with the same $100 of invested capital. Generating a ROIC substantially greater than a company's cost of capital is a primary driver of creating shareholder value. A high ROIC is the best indicator of a company's productivity and evidence of a competitive advantage.

- Strong Free Cash Flow; Little to No Debt. Companies that generate free cash flow (cash flow from operations less capital spending) are self-funding businesses that are masters of their own financial destiny. Free cash flow can be used to pay dividends, repurchase shares, retire debt, and make acquisitions. Warren Buffett says Berkshire doesn't "rely on the kindness of strangers" for the lifeblood of its operations, especially when lending and stock financing vanish in a tough economy. A company with no debt is unlikely to go bankrupt.

Management Excellence

- Owner-Oriented Management Aligned with Shareholders. Look for management whose compensation and actions indicate that their interests are aligned with shareholders as equitable partners. Determine whether management is trustworthy, passionate, focused, energetic, cost conscious, and loves the business. A friend and former partner assessed management by asking whether he would be happy with his daughter marrying the CEO. Preferably management will repurchase stock opportunistically when the price is below intrinsic value. This benefits remaining shareholders since future earnings are spread over fewer shares which increases value per share. Buffett emphasized this point:

> At BPL (Buffett Partnership Limited) and Berkshire, we have never invested in companies that are hell-bent on issuing shares. That behavior is one of the surest indicators of a promotion-minded management, weak accounting, a stock that is overpriced and—all too often—outright dishonesty.[6]

The red flags are managements that are afflicted with what Buffett calls the "ABCs of business decay, which are arrogance, bureaucracy, and complacency."[7]

- Respected, Candid, Accessible, and Communicative. Look for management that is admired and respected for their integrity and accomplishments, especially by their peers. Also look for management to be candid and transparent in their communication with shareholders.

Price versus Value

Lastly, the Pyramid of Growth includes a test to determine whether the stock price is "on sale" compared to its intrinsic value.

- Priced at or Below Intrinsic Value. Warren Buffett says, "Be greedy when others are fearful, and fearful when others are greedy." Look for opportunities to benefit from the inevitable decoupling between a business's intrinsic value and its market price. Intrinsic value is the present value of a business's future stream of cash flow discounted by the rate that reflects the risk of future uncertainties and investors' need to be compensated for postponing consumption. Intrinsic value for bonds is easy to calculate because the future cash flows are determined by the coupon rate. The challenge for equity investors is to estimate future "coupons" for stocks. Intrinsic value may be estimated using discounted cash flow, free cash flow yield, enterprise value (debt and equity) to cash earnings, price earnings ratios, and price to book value for financial companies. In the long run, intrinsic value tracks closely with the trends in cash flow generated by a business. In the short run, market volatility triggered by macro-worries or company specific issues that are temporary, fixable, and non-structural, present opportunities to benefit from businesses on sale.

When to Sell

Stocks should be bought with the intent to hold them indefinitely. Change is inevitable, however, and changes in business fundamentals or market prices may warrant a portfolio change. There are five reasons to consider selling a stock.

- *Egregiously overvalued.* Sell a stock if the price is excessively overpriced relative to its intrinsic value. Sell if a stock price is discounting earnings several years forward or if its valuation ratio is well above its historical range. If a stock price is only modestly overvalued, for instance by 10–20 percent, hold the stock if you are confident it will grow into its valuation in the near future. Outstanding companies are not frequently on the bargain counter. Avoid the temptation to sell an exemplary company that is only modestly overvalued with an expectation to buy it back cheaper. All too often the stock does not give the opportunity, and the cost to the investor of foregone profits is enormous.

362

- *Deteriorating fundamentals/eroding competitive advantage.* Companies that enjoy high returns on capital and superior operating profit margins attract competition. Sell if the barriers to competition erode and your original expectations for owning the company are no longer valid. The worst trap is to re-rationalize holding onto a sinking ship.

- *Better idea with more conviction and higher upside return.* Constantly evaluate new investment candidates to become starters in your portfolio lineup. If a starter becomes permanently injured or is too pricey, make the substitution.

- *Key management departure.* Warren Buffett and Peter Lynch said they try to buy stock in businesses that are so wonderful that an idiot can run them, because someday one will. The reality is that management does matter. Companies once moribund have been resurrected to prosperity because of a change in leadership. Other companies have had wealth destruction due to weak, misguided, or greedy management. When key management leaves a company, re-evaluate the new leadership to ensure you still like, trust, and admire the new team, its incentive compensation structure, its communication, and its strategy.

- *Recognizing a mistake.* Despite your best effort to apply The Pyramid of Growth in assessing the sustainability of a company's competitive advantage, the competence of management, and your estimate of intrinsic value, you may occasionally make mistakes. These are mistakes of commission, where you buy a stock that does not meet your expectations, and you sell to limit your losses. Look also to minimize your mistakes of omission where you don't buy a stock that qualifies for purchase, which subsequently creates massive wealth.

In Summary

The Pyramid of Growth is a powerful tool that can help improve your investment results because it borrows from the best practices of successful master investors and is based on timeless business and investment principles. It is a tool that requires discipline, good judgement, relentless curiosity, and patience. Well executed, it can help you achieve the financial independence that motivated Templeton, Lynch, and Buffett. They forged their own path to the top of the investment mountain, and by modeling their best practices, so can you.

Enjoy the journey!

References

Berryessa, Norman and Eric Kirzner. *Global Investing: The Templeton Way*. Homewood: Dow Jones-Irwin, 1988.

Carrett, Philip L. *A Money Mind at Ninety*. Burlington, Vermont. Fraser Publishing Company, 1991.

Ellis, Charles D. and James R. Vertin. *Classics an Investor's Anthology*. Homewood: Dow Jones-Irwin, 1989.

Graham, Benjamin. *The Intelligent Investor: The Definitive Book on Value Investing*. New York: Harper & Row, Fifth Revised Edition, 1973.

Greising, David *I'd Like the World to Buy a Coke: The Life and Leadership of Roberto Goizueta*. New York: John Wiley & Sons, Inc., 1997.

Kilpatrick, Andrew. *Of Permanent Value: The Story of Warren Buffett*. Birmingham: AKPE, 1998.

Lowenstein, Roger. *Buffett: The Making of an American Capitalist*. New York: Random House, 1995.

Lynch, Peter and John Rothchild. *Beating the Street*. New York: Simon & Schuster, 1994.

Lynch, Peter and John Rothchild. *One Up on Wall Street: How to Use What You Already Know to Make Money in the Market*. New York: Penguin Books, 1990.

Morgenson, Gretchen. *Forbes Great Minds of Business*. New York: John Wiley & Sons, Inc., 1997.

Munger, Charles T. *Poor Charlie's Almanack: The Wit and Wisdom of Charles T. Munger*. Virginia Beach, VA: PCA Publications, L.L.C., 2005.

Proctor, William. *The Templeton Touch*. Garden City: Doubleday & Company, Inc., 1983.

Schroeder, Alice. *The Snowball: Warren Buffett and the Business of Life*. New York: Bantam Books, 2008.

Smith, Adam. *Supermoney*. New York: Random House, 1972.

Tanous, Peter J. *Investment Gurus: A Road Map to Wealth from the World's Best Money Managers*. Englewood Cliffs: Prentice-Hall, 1997.

Templeton, John Marks. *Discovering the Laws of Life*. New York: The Continuum Publishing Company, 1994.

Templeton, Lauren C. and Scott Phillips. *Investing the Templeton Way: The Market-Beating Strategies of Value Investing's Legendary Bargain Hunter*. New York: McGraw Hill, 2008.

Templeton, Sir John. *Golden Nuggets from Sir John Templeton*. Philadelphia and London: Templeton Foundation Press, 1997.

Train, John. *The Midas Touch: The Strategies That Have Made Warren Buffett the World's Most Successful Investor*. New York: Harper & Row, 1987.

Train, John. *The Money Masters*. New York: Harper & Row, Publishers, Inc., 1980.

Sokol, David L. *Pleased but not Satisfied*. Sokol, 2007.

Endnotes

INTRODUCTION
1 2006 Berkshire Hathaway Annual Meeting.
2 1982 Berkshire Hathaway Annual Report.

SIR JOHN TEMPLETON
CHAPTER 1
1 John Templeton, *Discovering the Laws of Life* (Continuum, 1994), 4.
2 *Wall Street Week with Louis Rukeyser,* November 27, 1992.
3 The Chartered Financial Analyst (CFA) charter is an investment credential awarded by the CFA Institute, the largest global association of investment professionals, to candidates that pass three sequential six-hour exams, have at least four years of qualified professional investment experience, join the CFA Institute, and adhere to the CFA Institute Code of Ethics and Standards of Professional Conduct.
4 William Proctor, *The Templeton Touch* (Doubleday & Company, Inc., 1983), 17.
5 Bloomberg Business News, "Templeton, 83, Heavily Weighted in Religion," *Investor's Business Daily,* August 30, 1996.
6 Proctor, *Templeton Touch,* 28.
7 Charley Ellis, "Living Legends," *CFA Magazine*; inaugural issue 2003 January/February; interview with John Templeton, 20.
8 The Money Men," *Forbes,* July 1, 1994; 24.
9 Lauren C. Templeton and Scott Phillips, *Investing the Templeton Way* (McGraw Hill, 2008), Foreword by John M. Templeton, x.
10 Proctor, *Templeton Touch,* 47.
11 Sir John Templeton, *Golden Nuggets,* (Templeton Foundation Press, 1987), 58, 62.

CHAPTER 2
1 Norman Berryessa and Eric Kirzner, *Global Investing: The Templeton Way* (Dow Jones-Irwin 1988), 164, © McGraw-Hill Education.
2 The Dow Jones Industrial Average didn't calculate total return, including dividends, until September 1987. The MSCI index didn't begin until 1988.
3 Jonathan Clements, "Templeton Sets Sale of Funds to Franklin," *The Wall Street Journal,* August 3, 1992, C19.
4 Jonathan Clements, "Templeton Sets Sale of Funds to Franklin," *The Wall Street Journal,* August 3, 1992, C19.

5   Wikipedia, "John Templeton," *https://en.wikipedia.org/wiki/John_Templeton.*

CHAPTER 3

1   Proctor, *Templeton Touch,* 97.

2   Proctor, *Templeton Touch,* 64.

3   Lawrence Minard, "The Principle of Maximum Pessimism," *Forbes,* January 16, 1995; 68.

4   Stepane Fitch, "Sir Real," *Forbes,* May 28, 2001; 136.

5   *Outstanding Investor Digest,* February 14, 1992.

6   Proctor, *Templeton Touch,* 72.

7   Proctor, *Templeton Touch,* 79.

8   Berryessa and Kirzner, *Global Investing,* 123, © McGraw-Hill Education.

9   *Wall Street Week with Louis Rukeyser,* November 16, 1990.

10 Proctor, *Templeton Touch,* 81.

11 *Wall Street Week with Louis Rukeyser,* December 8, 1978.

12 *Wall Street Week with Louis Rukeyser,* October 23, 1987.

13 *Outstanding Investor Digest,* February 14, 1992.

14 "Sir John Templeton…on investing in a World in Radical Change," *Bottom Line/ Personal* Franklin/Templeton Distributors, September 15, 1993.

15 Proctor, *Templeton Touch,* 98.

16 Proctor, *Templeton Touch,* 85.

17 Proctor, *Templeton Touch,* 91.

18 *Wall Street Week with Louis Rukeyser,* August 14, 1987.

19 Proctor, *Templeton Touch,* 94.

20 *Wall Street Week with Louis Rukeyser,* October 23, 1987.

21 *Wall Street Week with Louis Rukeyser,* April 8, 1994.

22 The Independent Institute, "Dinner to Honor Sir John Marks Templeton," *http://www. independent.org/events/transcript.asp?id=51*

23 Proctor, *Templeton Touch,* 111.

24 Proctor, *Templeton Touch,* 110.

25 Tim W. Ferguson, "Long View Sees Global Gain, No Surge in Wall Street Graft," *The Wall Street Journal,* September 24, 1991.

26 Proctor, Templeton Touch, 114

27 Sam Zuckerman, "Templeton Sees Opportunities in Global Chaos," *San Francisco Chronicle,* October 2, 1998.

28 Proctor, *Templeton Touch,* 110.

29 AIMR (now CFA Society) newsletter on John Templeton's acceptance speech for receiving the first AIMR Award for Professional Excellence, May 21, 1991.

30 Dean Rothart, "Pioneer in World-Wide Investing Still Believes Emerging Markets Offer Best Opportunities," *The Wall Street Journal,* March 25, 1985.

31 Charles Ellis with James Vertin, *Classics: An Investor's Anthology* (1989) 745-747.

32 Adam Levy, "When John Templeton Speaks, Investors Listen," *Bloomberg,* June 16, 1993.

33 Tim W. Ferguson, "Long View Sees Global Gain, No Surge in Wall Street Graft," *The Wall Street Journal,* September 24, 1991.

34 *Wall Street Week with Louis Rukeyser,* March 30, 1990.

35 *Wall Street Week with Louis Rukeyser,* November 27, 1992.

36 *Outstanding Investor Digest,* February 14, 1992, excerpted from the Templeton Funds annual meeting.

CHAPTER 4

1 Berryessa and Kirzner, *Global Investing*, 142, © McGraw-Hill Education.

2 Berryessa and Kirzner, *Global Investing*, 123, © McGraw-Hill Education.

3 Berryessa and Kirzner, *Global Investing*, 125, © McGraw-Hill Education.

4 *Wall Street Week with Louis Rukeyeser* May 22, 1981.

5 Berryessa and Kirzner, *Global Investing*, 49, © McGraw-Hill Education.

6 Berryessa and Kirzner, *Global Investing*, 124, 126, © McGraw-Hill Education.

7 Berryessa and Kirzner, *Global Investing*, 124, © McGraw-Hill Education.

8 John Train, *The Money Masters* (Harper & Row 1980), 172.

9 Berryessa and Kirzner, *Global Investing*, 191, © McGraw-Hill Education.

10 Berryessa and Kirzner, *Global Investing*, 125, © McGraw-Hill Education.

11 *Wall Street Week with Louis Rukeyser*, December 8, 1978.

12 Train, *Money Masters*, 172.

13 *Wall Street Week with Louis Rukeyser*, November 16, 1990.

14 Berryessa and Kirzner, *Global Investing*, 47, © McGraw-Hill Education.

15 *Wall Street Week with Louis Rukeyser*, May 22, 1981.

16 *Wall Street Week with Louis Rukeyser*, December 8, 1978.

17 *Wall Street Week with Louis Rukeyser*, November 27, 1992.

18 Berryessa and Kirzner, *Global Investing*, 137, © McGraw-Hill Education.

19 *Wall Street Week with Louis Rukeyser*, January 11, 1980.

20 *Wall Street Week with Louis Rukeyser*, May 22, 1981.

21 Berryessa and Kirzner, *Global Investing*, 137, © McGraw-Hill Education.

22 *Outstanding Investors Digest*, February 14, 1992.

23 *Wall Street Week with Louis Rukeyser*, November 16, 1990.

24 *Wall Street Week with Louis Rukeyser*, November 27, 1992.

25 *Wall Street Week with Louis Rukeyser,* November 27, 1992.

26 *Outstanding Investors Digest*, February 14, 1992.

27 *Outstanding Investors Digest*, February 14, 1992.

28 Associated Press, "Profits Belong to Steady Investors, Advises Financial Guru Templeton," *Investors' Business Daily*, 1990.

29 Gene G. Marcial, "I Have Never Seen So Many Stocks…So Undervalued," *Business Week*, November 5, 1990.

30 Lawrence Minard, "The Principle of Maximum Pessimism," *Forbes*, January 16, 1995.

31 *Wall Street Week with Louis Rukeyser*, October 23, 1987.

32 *Outstanding Investors Digest*, February 14, 1992.

CHAPTER 5

1 Berryessa and Kirzner, *Global Investing*, 209, © McGraw-Hill Education.

2 *The Wall Street Journal*, September 9, 1983.

3 Berryessa and Kirzner, *Global Investing*, 176, © McGraw-Hill Education.

4 "Sir John Templeton…on investing in a World in Radical Change," *Bottom Line/Personal* Franklin/Templeton Distributors, September 15, 1993.

5 *Wall Street Week with Louis Rukeyser*, September 9, 1983.

6 *Wall Street Week with Louis Rukeyser*, November 16, 1990.

7 Sir John Templeton, "16 Rules for Investment Success," *World Monitor*, February 1993.

8 John Templeton's Memorandum to Clients, February 15, 1954.

 9   John Templeton's Memorandum to Clients, February 15, 1954.

10   Berryessa and Kirzner, *Global Investing*, 200, © McGraw-Hill Education.

11   *Wall Street Week with Louis Rukeyser*; September 13, 1985.

12   Templeton letter to clients 1959.

13   *Wall Street Week with Louis Rukeyser*, September 9, 1983.

14   *Wall Street Week with Louis Rukeyser*, January 6, 1989.

15   *Wall Street Week with Louis Rukeyser*, December 8, 1978.

16   *Wall Street Week with Louis Rukeyser*, November 27, 1992.

17   *Wall Street Week with Louis Rukeyser*, December 8, 1978.

18   *Wall Street Week with Louis Rukeyser*, December 8, 1978.

19   Proctor, *Templeton Touch*, 66.

CHAPTER 6

 1   Berryessa and Kirzner, *Global Investing*, 137, © McGraw-Hill Education.

 2   *Wall Street Week with Louis Rukeyser*, June 18, 1982.

 3   Berryessa and Kirzner, *Global Investing*, 137-138, © McGraw-Hill Education.

 4   James H. Stewart and David R. Hilder, "Union Carbide Could Face Staggering Gas-Leak Damage Claims, Experts Say," *The Wall Street Journal*, December 6, 1984.

 5   Berryessa and Kirzner, *Global Investing*, 138, © McGraw-Hill Education.

 6   Berryessa and Kirzner, *Global Investing*, 138, © McGraw-Hill Education.

 7   George Anders, "Carbide's Destiny Shaped by Holders," *The Wall Street Journal,* January 7, 1986.

 8   George Anders, "Carbide's Destiny Shaped by Holders," *The Wall Street Journal,* January 7, 1986.

 9   George Anders, "Carbide's Destiny Shaped by Holders," *The Wall Street Journal,* January 7, 1986.

10   George Anders, "Carbide's Destiny Shaped by Holders," *The Wall Street Journal,* January 7, 1986.

11   *Wall Street Week with Louis Rukeyser*, June 18, 1982.

12   By a Staff Reporter, "Alcoa, Reynolds and Alcan Post Quarterly Losses," *The Wall Street Journal*, January 21, 1983.

13   *Wall Street Week with Louis Rukeyser,* May 22, 1981.

14   *Wall Street Week with Louis Rukeyser*, May 22, 1981.

15   Junius Ellis, "Templeton: Buy Stocks in War, Buy Bonds If There's Peace," *Money,* February 1991; 179.

16   Junius Ellis, "Templeton: Buy Stocks in War, Buy Bonds If There's Peace," *Money,* February 1991; 179.

17   *Wall Street Week* with Louis Rukeyser; December 8, 1983.

18   Pamela Sebastian, "The Next Bull Market May Be Strong One, Templeton Believes," *The Wall Street Journal*; November 21, 1985.

CHAPTER 7

 1   John Marks Templeton, *Discovering the Laws of Life* Continuum Publishing Company 1994), 221-222.

 2   Edwin A Finn, Jr., "Some Brave Investors Play the Stock Markets Of the Third World," *The Wall Street Journal*, October 31, 1985.

Endnotes

3 John Marks Templeton, *Discovering the Laws of Life* Continuum Publishing Company 1994), 281-282.

4 Eleanor Laise, "Trailblazing Investor Spotted Market Opportunities Where Others Weren't Looking," *The Wall Street Journal*; July 12-13, 2008; A12.

PETER LYNCH/CHAPTER 8

1 Peter Lynch, *Beating the Street* (Simon & Schuster, 1994), 141.

2 Peter Tanous, *Investment Gurus* (Prentice Hall, 1997), 116.

3 Peter Lynch, *One Up on Wall Street* (Penguin Books 1990).

4 Peter Lynch, *One Up on Wall Street* (Penguin Books 1990), 30.

5 Interview with KQED, "Betting on the Market" May 1996.

6 Tanous, *Investment Gurus*, 123.

7 Lynch, *One Up on Wall Street*, 32.

8 KQED interview, "Betting on the Market" May 1996.

9 Christopher J Chipello, Michael Siconolft and Jonathan Clements, "Both Fidelity Investors and Firm Are at Sea as Magellan Boss Goes," *The Wall Street Journal*, March 29, 1990.

10 Digby Diehl, "Peter Lynch – The sage of the stock market shows how to buy, sell—and retire at age 46," *Modern Maturity*, January-February, 1995.

11 Tanous, *Investment Gurus*, 120.

CHAPTER 10

1 Lynch, *One Up on Wall Street*, 51.

2 National Press Club speech; October 7, 1994

3 Pamela Sebastian and Jan Wong, "Fidelity Is Scrambling to Keep Flying High as Magellan Slows Up," *The Wall Street Journal*, August 15, 1986.

4 Jaye Scholl, "Neff and Lynch: Contrasting Styles, Comparable Success," *Barron's*, August 10, 1987.

5 Jaye Scholl, "Neff and Lynch: Contrasting Styles, Comparable Success," *Barron's*, August 10, 1987.

6 Lynch, *One Up on Wall Street*, 86.

7 "Peter Lynch? Who's Peter Lynch?," *Business Week*, May 20, 1991.

8 Christopher J. Chipello, "Manager Seeks Old-Line Growth Stocks," *The Wall Street Journal*, August 29, 1988.

9 Tanous, *Investment Gurus*, 117.

10 *Wall Street Week with Louis Rukeyser*, October 29, 1982.

11 National Press Club speech; October 7, 1994.

12 Lynch, *One Up on Wall Street*, 93.

13 Lynch, *Beating the Street*, 27.

14 Peter Lynch speech to the National Association of Investors Corporation (NAIC) October 15, 1998.

15 Peter Lynch speech to the National Association of Investors Corporation (NAIC) October 15, 1998.

16 *Wall Street Week*, September 1992.

17 Peter Lynch speech to the National Association of Investors Corporation (NAIC) October 15, 1998.

18 Peter Lynch speech to the National Association of Investors Corporation (NAIC) October 15, 1998.

19 *Barron's*, 7/22/85.

20 Peter Lynch speech to the National Association of Investors Corporation (NAIC) October 15, 1998.

21 *Wall Street Week with Louis Rukeyser*, January 5, 1990.

22 Peter Lynch, "Mind Your P's and E's," *Worth*, February 1996.

23 Peter Lynch, "The Second-Half Effect," *Worth,* June 1994.

24 Peter Lynch, "The Second-Half Effect," *Worth,* June 1994.

25 Peter Lynch, "The Second-Half Effect," *Worth,* June 1994.

26 Peter Lynch speech to the National Association of Investors Corporation (NAIC) October 15, 1998.

27 Lynch, *One Up on Wall Street*, 41.

28 National Press Club speech; October 7, 1994.

29 KQED Interview "Betting on the Market," May 1996.

30 Peter Lynch, "The Stock Market Hit Parade," *Worth,* July/August 1994.

31 Peter Lynch speech to the National Association of Investors Corporation (NAIC) October 15, 1998.

32 Lynch, *Beating the Street,* 45.

33 Lynch, *One Up On Wall Street*, 292.

CHAPTER 11

1 Lynch, *One Up On Wall Street*, 235.

2 *Outstanding Investors Digest,* November 25, 1992.

3 *Wall Street Week with Louis Rukeyser*, November 11, 1990.

4 Tanous, *Investment Gurus,* 114.

5 *Wall Street Week with Louis Rukeyser,* March 1984.

6 Peter Lynch, "The Stock Market Hit Parade," *Worth*, July/August 1994.

7 Constance Mitchell, "Small Firms Fueled Top 1st-Quarter Funds," *The Wall Street Journal*, April 6, 1989.

8 *Wall Street Week with Louis Rukeyser*, February 1985.

9 *Outstanding Investor Digest*, November 25, 1992.

10 Lynch, *Beating the Street,* 161.

11 *Wall Street Week with Louis Rukeyser*, November 16, 1990.

12 Lynch, *One Up on Wall Street*, 214.

13 *Wall Street Week with Louis Rukeyser*, January 10, 1986.

14 Interview with Charlie Rose; December 4, 2013.

15 Tanous, *Investment Gurus,* 121.

CHAPTER 12

1 *Wall Street Week with Louis Rukeyser*, March 1984.

2 Lynch, *Beating the Street,* 157.

3 *Wall Street Week with Louis Rukeyser*, March 1984.

4 Peter Lynch speech to the National Association of Investors Corporation (NAIC) October 15, 1998.

5 *Wall Street Week with Louis Rukeyser*, March 1984.

Endnotes

6 Lynch, *One Up on Wall Street,* 256.
7 Lynch, *One Up on Wall Street,* 258.
8 Digby Diehl, "Peter Lynch–The sage of the stock market shows how to buy, sell—and retire at age 46," *Modern Maturity;* January-February 1995.
9 Lynch, *One Up on Wall Street,* 150.
10 Lynch, *One Up on Wall Street,* 152.
11 Lynch, *One Up on Wall Street,* 153.
12 *Wall Street Week with Louis Rukeyser,* October 29, 1989.
13 Kathryn M. Welling, "Lynch Lore, The Magellan Magician Tells How He Does It," *Barron's,* July 22, 1985.
14 *Wall Street Week with Louis Rukeyser,* November 16, 1990.
15 Alan Abelson, "Our Roundtable: Where Do We Go from Here?" *Barron's,* July 20, 1992.
16 Digby Diehl, "Peter Lynch – The sage of the stock market shows how to buy, sell—and retire at age 46," *Modern Maturity;* January-February 1995.
17 KQED Interview "Betting on the Market," May 1996.
18 Lynch, *Beating the Street, 12.*
19 *Wall Street Week with Louis Rukeyser,* March 1984.
20 *Wall Street Week with Louis Rukeyser,* March 1984.
21 *Wall Street Week with Louis Rukeyser,* September 18, 1992.
22 KQED interview "Betting on the Market," May 1996.
23 Digby Diehl, "Peter Lynch–The sage of the stock market shows how to buy, sell—and retire at age 46," *Modern Maturity;* January-February 1995.
24 *Wall Street Week with Louis Rukeyser,* Jan. 27, 1989.
25 *Forbes Great Minds of Business* (John Wiley & Sons, 1997), 88.
26 "Barron's Roundtable 1988," *Barron's,* January 25, 1988.
27 KQED Interview "Betting on the Market," May 1996.
28 KQED Interview "Betting on the Market," May 1996.
29 Peter Lynch speech to the National Association of Investors Corporation (NAIC) October 15, 1998.
30 Peter Lynch, "What's next?," *The Wall Street Journal,* October 1, 2001.
31 Peter Lynch speech to the National Association of Investors Corporation (NAIC) October 15, 1998.
32 *Forbes,* Centennial issue, September 28, 2017.
33 Tanous, *Investment Gurus,* 115.
34 *Forbes Great Minds of Business,* 108.
35 *Forbes Great Minds of Business,* 115.
36 *Outstanding Investor Digest,* Nov. 25, 1992.
37 *Outstanding Investor Digest,* Nov. 25, 1992.
38 Peter Lynch, "How to Invest a Million," *Worth,* March 1997; 61.
39 Tanous, *Investment Gurus,* 124-125.
40 Tanous, *Investment Gurus,* 125.

CHAPTER 13
1 Lynch, *One Up on Wall Street,* 246.
2 Tanous, *Investment Gurus,* 123.
3 *Wall Street Week with Louis Rukeyser,* October 29, 1982.

4 KQED interview "Betting on the Market," May 1996.
5 *Wall Street Week with Louis Rukeyser*, February 1985.
6 Kathryn M. Welling, "Lynch Lore, The Magellan Magician Tells How He Does It," *Barron's*, July 22, 1985.
7 Lynch, *Beating the Street*, 110.
8 *Barron's*, July 22, 1985.

CHAPTER 14
1 Interview with Charlie Rose, Dec. 4, 2013.
2 Douglas R. Sease & Robert L. Simpson, "Chrysler, Having Cut Muscle as Well as Fat, Is Still in a Weak State," *The Wall Street Journal*, July 15, 1983.
3 Douglas R. Sease & Robert L. Simpson, "Chrysler, Having Cut Muscle as Well as Fat, Is Still in a Weak State," *The Wall Street Journal*, July 15, 1983.
4 Lynch, *Beating the Street*, 111.
5 Lynch, *Beating the Street*, 111.
6 Amanda Bennett, "After Three Bad Years, Many Auto Executives See Permanent Scars," *The Wall Street Journal*, August 16, 1982.
7 KQED interview "Betting on the Market," May 1996.
8 *Wall Street Week with Louis Rukeyser*, October 1982.
9 *Wall Street Week with Louis Rukeyser*, October 1982.
10 Lynch, *One Up on Wall Street*, 203.
11 *Wall Street Week with Louis Rukeyser*, October 1982.
12 Lynch, *One Up on Wall Street*, 203, 244.
13 Lynch, *One Up on Wall Street*, 260.
14 Kathryn M. Welling, "Last but Not Least," *Barron's*, January 13, 1986.
15 Kathryn M. Welling, "Last but Not Least," *Barron's*, January 13, 1986.
16 Staff reporter, "Fannie Mae Sees 'Healthy' Increase in 1986 Earnings," *The Wall Street Journal* April 8, 1986.
17 Lynch, *Beating the Street*, 264.
18 Kathryn M. Welling, "Lynch Lore, The Magellan Magician Tells How He Does It," *Barron's*, July 22, 1985.
19 *Wall Street Week with Louis Rukeyser*, September 18, 1992.
20 Kathryn M. Welling, "Premier Pickers," *Barron's*, January 23, 1995.
21 Peter Lynch, "The Next Oil Boom," *Worth*, February 1995, 43.
22 Peter Lynch, "Self-Service," *Worth*, October 1996, 49.

CHAPTER 15
1 Paul Katzeff, "Fidelity's Will Danoff Outperforms with Focus On 'Best-Of-Breed' Stocks," *Investor's Business Daily*, March 7, 2016.
2 Digby Diehl, "Peter Lynch..." *Modern Maturity;* January-February 1995.
3 *Forbes Great Minds of Business*, John Wiley & Sons, 1997; 109
4 Gerard A. Achstatter, "Fidelity's Peter Lynch: How He Conducted the Research That Made His Fund Best," *Investor's Business Daily*, February 2, 1998.
5 Peter Lynch, "What's next?," *The Wall Street Journal*, October 1, 2001.
6 *Forbes Great Minds of Business*, John Wiley & Sons, 1997; 114.
7 *Forbes Great Minds of Business*, John Wiley & Sons, 1997; 94.

Endnotes

WARREN BUFFETT/CHAPTER 16
1   New York Security Analysts luncheon honoring Benjamin Graham, November 1994.
2   *Outstanding Investor Digest*, September 24, 1998, transcripts of 1998 Berkshire annual meeting.
3   Nicole Friedman, "Buffett Sings the Praises of Israel Bonds," *The Wall Street Journal*, June 23, 2017.
4   Charley Ellis, "Living Legends," *CFA Magazine*; inaugural issue January/February 2003, Interview with Warren Buffett, 21.
5   Adam Smith, *Supermoney* (Random House, 1972), 181.
6   L.J. Davis, "Buffett Takes Stock," *The New York Times Magazine*, April 1, 1990; 17.
7   *The Wall Street Journal*, March 24, 2010.
8   Berkshire Hathaway Annual Report, 1988; 41.
9   Smith, *Supermoney*, 182.
10 *Good Morning America*, transcript of interview by Charles Gibson with Warren Buffett, May 16, 1991.
11 "And Now, A Look at The Old One," *Fortune*, October 16, 1989; 98.
12 Smith, *Supermoney*, 194.
13 L.J. Davis, "Buffett Takes Stock," *The New York Times Magazine*, April 1, 1990; 62.
14 Train, *Money Masters*.
15 Adam Smith's *Money World television show*, interview with Warren Buffett, June 20, 1988; 7-8.
16 Adam Smith's *Money World television show* interview with Warren Buffett, May 22, 1990; 10.

CHAPTER 17
1   Buffett Partnership, Ltd., Letter to Limited Partners 1957.
2   Buffett Partnership, Ltd., Letter October 9, 1967.
3   Buffett Partnership, Ltd., Letter January 1968.
4   Buffett Partnership Ltd., Letter May 29th, 1969.
5   Buffett Partnership Ltd., Letter December 5, 1969.
6   Robert Lenzner, "Warren Buffett's idea of heaven: 'I don't have to work with people I don't like,'" *Forbes*, October 18, 1993; 42.
7   Buffett Partnership Ltd., Letter, January 18, 1965.
8   CNBC Squawk Box Transcript, March 3, 2014.

CHAPTER 18
1   Alice Schroeder, *The Snowball, Warren Buffett and the Business of Life* (Bantam Books 2008), 63.
2   Benjamin Graham, *The Intelligent Investor* (Harper & Row, Publishers Inc., Fourth Revised Edition, 1973), Preface.
3   Warren E. Buffett, "Benjamin Graham 1894-1976," *Financial Analysts Journal*, November/December 1976.
4   Charley Ellis, "Living Legends," *CFA Magazine*; inaugural issue January/February 2003, interview with Warren Buffett, 21.
5   Graham, *Intelligent Investor*, 286.
6   Graham, *Intelligent Investor*, 110.

7 Schroeder *The Snowball*, 130.

8 Schroeder *The Snowball*, 135.

9 Schroeder *The Snowball*, 166.

10 John Dorfman, "Eyewitness to History," *The Wall Street Journal*, May 28, 1996.

11 Karen Richardson, Mr. Maguire Trades One Stock All Day Long," *The Wall Street Journal*, November 12-13, 2005.

12 John Dorfman, "Eyewitness to History," *The Wall Street Journal*, May 28, 1996.

13 Douglas Martin, "Patience? This Man Practically Invented It," *The New York Times*, November 11, 1995.

14 Philip L. Carrett, *A Money Mind at Ninety* (Fraser Publishing Company 1991), 210.

15 *Forbes*, "How Omaha Beats Wall Street," November 1, 1969.

16 Berkshire Hathaway Annual Meeting May 1997.

17 Philip Fisher, *Common Stocks and Uncommon Profits* (Business Classics, 1984 Revised Edition), 11.

18 *Outstanding Investor Digest*, September 24, 1998, transcripts of 1998 Berkshire annual meeting.

19 CNN Interview with Pattie Sellers, Sr. Editor-At-Large *Fortune*, November 7, 2013.

20 Graham, *Intelligent Investor,* Appendix reprinted from the Fall 1984 issue of Hermes, Magazine of the Columbia Business School, 1984.

21 CNN Interview with Pattie Sellers, Sr. Editor-At-Large *Fortune*, November 7, 2013.

22 CNN Interview with Pattie Sellers, Sr. Editor-At-Large *Fortune*, November 7, 2013.

23 *Outstanding Investor Digest*, May 5, 1995, transcript of Charlie Munger's lecture to USC School of Business April 14, 1994.

24 CNBC interview with Becky Quick, May 5, 2014.

25 *Business Week*, "Warren Buffett is breaking his own rules," April 15, 1985.

26 Robert Lenzner, "Warren Buffett's idea of heaven: 'I don't have to work with people I don't like,'" *Forbes*, October 18, 1993; 42.

27 Robert Lenzner and David S. Fondiller, "The not-so-silent partner," *Forbes*, January 22, 1996; 79.

28 Whitney Tilson (lighted edited), "Three Lectures by Warren Buffett to Notre Dame Faculty, MBA Students and Undergraduate Students," Spring 1991.

29 Buffett Partnership Ltd., Letter January 25, 1967.

30 Buffett Partnership Ltd., Letter February 25, 1970.

31 Charlie Munger, "Vice Chairman's Thoughts – Past and Future," from letter commemorating 50 years of Berkshire Hathaway, 1994 Berkshire Hathaway Annual Report.

32 James Grant, "Free advice for Warren Buffett," *Grant's Interest Rate Observer*, September 23, 1994.

33 United States of America Financial Crisis Inquiry Commission Interview of Warren Buffett, May 26, 2010.

34 *Dow Jones News*, "Billionaire Buffett Takes a Swipe at Trust Fund Kids," October 3, 2000.

CHAPTER 19

1 *Daily Journal* Annual Meeting, February 15, 2017.

2 Adam Smith's *Money World* television show, June 20, 1988.

3 CNBC interview October 24, 2012.

4 Stephen Gandel and Katie Fehrenbacher, "Warren Buffett's All-in Clean-Energy Bet," *Fortune*, December 15; 201.

5   Berkshire Hathaway 2009 Annual Report.

6   Buffett Partnership Ltd. Letter, January 25, 1967.

7   Buffett Partnership Ltd. Letter, January 25, 1967.

8   Buffett Partnership Ltd. Letter January 24, 1968.

9   Buffett Partnership Ltd. Letter, January 20, 1966.

10 Buffett Partnership Ltd. Letter October 9, 1967.

11 Buffett Partnership Ltd. Letter January 24, 1968.

12 *See Breeze*, an internal See's Candy, Special Historical Issue 1995.

13 United States of America Financial Crisis Inquiry Commission interview with Warren Buffett May 26, 2010.

14 Whitney Tilson (lighted edited), "Three Lectures by Warren Buffett to Notre Dame Faculty, MBA Students and Undergraduate Students," Spring 1991.

15 2006 Berkshire Annual Meeting.

16 *See Breeze.*

17 *See Breeze.*

18 *See Breeze.*

19 *See Breeze.*

20 Scott Chapman letter of October 21, 1995 to Richard Van Doren, VP Marketing See's.

21 Schroeder, *Snowball*, 345-346.

22 Berkshire Hathaway 1991 Annual Report.

23 Berkshire Hathaway 2015 50th Anniversary Book.

24 *Outstanding Investor Digest*, May 5, 1995, transcript of Charlie Munger's lecture to USC School of Business April 14, 1994.

25 Berkshire Hathaway 1983 Annual report.

26 Berkshire Hathaway 1991 Annual report.

27 *Outstanding Investor Digest*, June 23, 1989, transcripts of 1989 Berkshire Hathaway annual meeting.

28 *Outstanding Investor Digest*, June 30, 1988, transcripts of 1988 Berkshire Hathaway annual meeting.

29 Berkshire 2016 Annual Meeting.

30 Berkshire 2009 Annual Report, 9.

31 Berkshire 2008 Annual Report, 7.

32 Berkshire 2016 Annual Report, 12.

33 The first year that Berkshire presented BHE's summary financial statements when it was first permitted to consolidate the business.

34 BNSF Video News Interview with Warren Buffett by BNSF CEO Matt Rose, December 3, 2009.

35 Berkshire Hathaway 2016 Annual Meeting comments.

36 United States of America Financial Crisis Inquiry Commission interview with Warren Buffett, May 26, 2010.

CHAPTER 20

1   As of March 13, 2017.

2   F. McGuire, "Fidelity's Will Danoff Is the $108 Billion Man Who Has Beaten the Market," *The Wall Street Journal*, October 22, 2016.

3   Jack Otter, "Fidelity's Will Danoff: 7 Stocks He Likes Now," *Barron's*, April 1, 2015.

4 2006 Berkshire annual meeting.

5 Berkshire Hathaway 2009 Annual Report.

6 United States of America Financial Crisis Inquiry Commission Interview with Warren Buffett, May 26, 2010.

7 *Outstanding Investor Digest*, December 18, 2000, transcript of 2000 Berkshire annual meeting.

8 1996 Berkshire Hathaway annual meeting notes.

9 *Outstanding Investor Digest*, December 18, 2000, transcript of 2000 Berkshire annual meeting.

10 Carol Loomis, "Mr. Buffett on the Market," *Fortune,* November 22, 1999.

11 2006 Berkshire Annual Meeting.

12 *Outstanding Investor Digest*, December 18, 2000, transcript of 2000 Berkshire annual meeting.

13 1996 Berkshire Hathaway annual meeting notes.

14 1996 Berkshire Hathaway annual meeting notes.

15 *Outstanding Investor Digest*, June 22, 1992, transcripts of 1992 Berkshire Hathaway annual meeting.

16 *Outstanding Investor Digest*, May 5, 1995, transcript of Charlie Munger's lecture to the USC School of Business in 1994.

17 *Outstanding Investor Digest*, April 18, 1990, transcript of Buffett's lecture to Stanford Business School.

18 Staff Reporter, "American Express Says '63 Net Rose 11% to a Record," *The Wall Street Journal,* January 6, 1964.

19 Staff Reporter, "American Express Says '63 Net Rose 11% to a Record," *The Wall Street Journal,* January 6, 1964.

20 Berkshire Hathaway 2015 Edition 50th Anniversary Book, letter from Warren Buffett to Howard Clark, President American Express dated June 16, 1964.

21 Staff Reporter, "American Express Holders Assail Concern Fort Its Involvement in Salad Oil Scandal," *The Wall Street Journal,* April 29, 1964.

22 Smith, *Supermoney,* 193.

23 Berkshire Hathaway 2015 Edition 50th Anniversary Book, letter from Warren Buffett to Howard Clark, President American Express dated June 16, 1964.

24 L.J. Davis, Buffett Takes Stock," *The New York Times Magazine,* Business World April 1, 1990; 62.

25 L.J. Davis, Buffett Takes Stock," *The New York Times Magazine,* Business World April 1, 1990; 62.

26 Interview on CNBC's "Squawk Box," February 27, 2017.

27 *Outstanding Investor Digest*, December 18, 2000, transcript of 2000 Berkshire annual meeting.

28 Leah Nathans Spiro and David Greising, "Why Amex Wooed Warren Buffett."

29 Berkshire Hathaway 1995 Annual Meeting.

30 Berkshire Hathaway 1997 Annual Report.

31 Berkshire Hathaway 1994 Annual Report.

32 Smith, *Supermoney,* 193.

33 Whitney Tilson (lighted edited), "Three Lectures by Warren Buffett to Notre Dame Faculty, MBA Students and Undergraduate Students," Spring 1991.

Endnotes

34 Michael J. McCarthy, "Coke Stake of 6.3%, 2nd Biggest Held in Soft-Drink Giant, Bought by Buffett," *The Wall Street Journal*, March 16, 1989.

35 David Greising, *I'd Like the World to Buy a Coke* (John Wiley & Sons, Inc., 1997).

36 Coca-Cola 1980 annual report.

37 John Huey, "The World's Best Brand," *Fortune*, May 31, 1993.

38 John Huey, "The World's Best Brand," *Fortune*, May 31, 1993.

39 John Huey, "The World's Best Brand," *Fortune*, May 31, 1993.

40 Berkshire Hathaway 1985 Annual Report.

41 Betsy Morris, "Coke Hopes Old Pro Is Still 'Real Thing," *The Wall Street Journal*, October 12, 1988.

42 Michael J. McCarthy, "Buffett's Thirst for Coke Splits Analysts' Ranks," *The Wall Street Journal*, Heard on the Street, March 17, 1989.

43 Michael J. McCarthy, "Buffett's Thirst for Coke Splits Analysts' Ranks," *The Wall Street Journal*, Heard on the Street, March 17, 1989.

44 Berkshire Hathaway 1989 Annual Report.

45 Berkshire Hathaway 1990 Annual Report.

46 Berkshire Hathaway 1993 Annual Report.

47 Berkshire Hathaway 1993 Annual Report.

48 *Outstanding Investor Digest*, Berkshire Hathaway Annual Meeting notes, June 30, 1993.

49 Berkshire Hathaway 1997 Annual Report.

50 Berkshire Hathaway 1993 Annual Report.

51 Meeting with Muhtar Kent in Atlanta at Coca-Cola's annual meeting April 29, 2015.

52 John Huey, "The World's Best Brand," *Fortune*, May 31, 1993.

53 Berkshire Hathaway Annual Report 1996

54 WSJ Live video, Warren Buffett on Meeting GEICO's Lorimer Davidson, August 24, 2014.

55 Schroeder, *Snowball*, 137.

56 Warren E. Buffett, "The Security I Like Best," The Commercial and Financial Chronicle, December 6, 1951.

57 Berkshire Hathaway 1995 Annual Report.

58 Robert Lenzner, "I don't have to work with people I don't like," *Forbes*, October 18, 1993.

59 Berkshire Hathaway 1995 Annual Report.

60 Graham, *Intelligent Investor*, 288-289.

61 Schroeder, *Snowball*, 430.

62 John Train, *The Midas Touch* (Harper & Row, 1987), 23.

63 Roger Lowenstein, *Buffett: The Making of An American Capitalist* (Random House, 1995), 196.

64 Schroeder, *Snowball*, 430.

65 Lowenstein, *Buffett*, 199.

66 Berkshire Hathaway Annual Report 1980.

67 Berkshire Hathaway Annual Report 1980.

68 Berkshire Hathaway Annual Report 1980.

69 Berkshire Hathaway Annual Report 2016.

70 *Outstanding Investor Digest*, June 30, 1988, transcripts of 1988 Berkshire Hathaway May 23, 1988 annual meeting.

71 Schroeder, *Snowball*, 437.
72 Suzanne Woolley with Joan Caplin, "The Next Buffett," December 2000.
73 Berkshire Hathaway annual report 1985; 10.
74 Timothy D. Schellhardt and Leslie Scism, "Buffett to Buy Rest of Geico for $2.3 Billion," *The Wall Street Journal*, August 28, 1995.
75 Berkshire Hathaway 1995 Annual Report, 10.
76 Schroeder, *Snowball*, 430.
77 Schroeder, *Snowball*, 430-431.
78 Berkshire Hathaway 2002 Annual Report.
79 Robert A. Bennett, *The New York Times*, "The Banker Who Would Be Scrooge," Dec. 3, 1989.
80 Bennet, *The New York Times*, "Banker," Dec. 3, 1989.
81 "Moody's Sees More California Loan Problems Banking," *Los Angeles Times,* July 1990.
82 John R. Dorfman, "Wells Fargo Has Bulls and Bears, So Who's Right?," *The Wall Street Journal,* Nov. 1, 1990.
83 Wells Fargo 1994 Annual Report.
84 Berkshire Hathaway 1990 annual report, 16.
85 Berkshire Hathaway 1990 annual report, 17.
86 Gary Hector, "Warren Buffett's favorite banker," Forbes, October 18, 1993; 46.
87 *Outstanding Investor Digest*, November 25, 1992.
88 *Outstanding Investor Digest*, August 10, 1995; 6.
89 *Outstanding Investor Digest*, August 10, 1995, transcripts of 1995 Berkshire Hathaway annual meeting.
90 *Outstanding Investor Digest*, August 10, 1995, transcripts of 1995 Berkshire Hathaway annual meeting.
91 John R. Dorfman, "Wells Fargo Has Bulls and Bears, So Who's Right?," *The Wall Street Journal*, Nov. 1, 1990.

CHAPTER 21
1 Berkshire Hathaway 2014 Annual Report, 24.
2 Berkshire Hathaway 2014 Annual Report, 25.
3 CNBC Interview with Becky Quick, October 18, 2010.
4 CNBC interview with Becky Quick, October 18, 2010.
5 CNBC Interview with Becky Quick, October 18, 2010.
6 Anthony Bianco, "Salomon and Revlon: What Really Happened," *Business Week*, October 12, 1987.
7 Anthony Bianco, "Salomon and Revlon: What Really Happened," *Business Week*, October 12, 1987.
8 Charlie Munger interview with BBC: Charlie Munger Reveals Secrets to Getting Rich.
9 Berkshire Hathaway Annual Report 1990.
10 Carol J. Loomis, "Warren Buffett's Wild Ride at Salomon," *Fortune*, October 27, 1997.
11 Carol J. Loomis, "Warren Buffett's Wild Ride at Salomon," *Fortune*, October 27, 1997.
12 Carol J. Loomis, "Warren Buffett's Wild Ride at Salomon," *Fortune*, October 27, 1997.
13 Gary Weiss, "Behind the Happy Talk at Salomon," *Business Week*, November 11, 1991.
14 Lawrence Malkin, "5 Top Officers Leave Salomon As Buffett Takes Control of Firm," *The New York Times*, August 19, 1991.

15 Warren E. Buffett, "Salomon, Inc. A Report by the Chairman on the Company's Standing and Outlook," *The Wall Street Journal*, October 29, 1991.

16 Warren E. Buffett, "Salomon, Inc. A Report by the Chairman on the Company's Standing and Outlook," *The Wall Street Journal*, October 29, 1991.

17 Andy Kilpatrick, *Of Permanent Value—The Story of Warren Buffett* (AKPE, 1998 Edition), 422.

18 Warren Buffett's opening statement before the Subcommittee on Telecommunications and Finance of the Energy and Commerce Committee of the U.S. House of Representatives, May 1, 2010.

19 Berkshire Hathaway 2014 Annual Report, 41.

20 Berkshire Hathaway 2012 Annual Report, 8.

21 Berkshire Hathaway 2010 Annual Report, 11.

22 Berkshire Hathaway 2009 Annual Report, 7.

23 Berkshire Hathaway 2012 Annual Report, 11.

24 Berkshire Hathaway 1999 Annual Report, 11.

25 David L. Sokol, *Pleased but not Satisfied* (Sokol, 2007).

26 Sokol, *Pleased but not Satisfied*.

27 Brian Dumain, "Warren Buffett's Mr. Fix-it," *Fortune*, August 16, 2010.

28 Serena Ng and Erik Holm, "Deal 'Itch' Gets Scratched," *The Wall Street Journal*, March 15, 2011.

29 Peter Lattman and Geraldine Fabrikant, "A Conspicuous Absence at Berkshire Meeting," *The New York Times*, April 26, 2011.

30 Warren E. Buffett, "Warren E. Buffett, CEO of Berkshire Hathaway, Announced the Resignation of David L. Sokol," March 30, 2011.

31 Warren E. Buffett, Memo to Berkshire Hathaway Managers, December 19, 2014.

32 *Outstanding Investor Digest*, September 24, 1998, transcript of 1998 Berkshire annual meeting.

33 Berkshire Hathaway 2016 Annual Report.

34 Berkshire Hathaway 1998 Annual Report.

35 CNBC Interview with Becky Quick, May 2017.

36 CNBC Interview with Becky Quick, February 26, 2018.

37 Berkshire Hathaway Annual Meeting May 6, 2017.

38 2000 Berkshire Hathaway Annual Meeting.

39 2017 Berkshire Hathaway Annual Report.

40 Berkshire Hathaway 2015 Annual Report.

41 *Outstanding Investor Digest*, December 31, 2004, transcripts from May 1, 2004 Berkshire Hathaway Annual Meeting.

42 On stage interview at Coca-Cola annual meeting with CEO Muhtar Kent, April 24, 2013.

43 Devon Spurgeion, Shirley Leung, and Patricia Callahan, "When Business Isn't Usual," *The Wall Street Journal*, September 24, 2001.

CHAPTER 22

1 University of Nebraska Business magazine, Fall 2001.

2 YouTube, Charlie Rose interview with Warren Buffett and Carol Loomis on her new book "Tap Dancing to Work," *www.youtube.com/watch?v=9syL5Z53akY*, November 26, 2016.

3 Alex Crippen, "Warren Buffett Shares His Secret: How You Can 'Tap Dance to Work," CNBC, November 21, 2012.

4 Brent Schlender, "Gates & Buffett," *Fortune*, July 20, 1998.

5 YouTube, NDTV India Prannoy Roy interview with Warren Buffett and Ajit Jain, *https://www.youtube.com/watch?v=oZ1fiQmQIsE*

6 USC Commencement Speech May 1, 2007.

7 *Outstanding Investor Digest*, June 23, 1989, transcripts of 1989 Berkshire Hathaway annual meeting.

8 *Bloomberg,* August 27, 2013.

9 Cynthia H. Milligan, "Warren Buffett," *Nebraska Business*, University of Nebraska – Lincoln Alumni Business magazine, Fall 2001.

10 Benny Evangelista, "Playing Bridge with Buffett," *San Francisco Chronicle,* August 27, 1998.

11 Benny Evangelista, "Playing Bridge with Buffett," *San Francisco Chronicle,* August 27, 1998.

12 Schroeder, *Snowball*, 623.

13 Charlie Munger, "Vice Chairman's Thoughts – Past and Future," Berkshire Hathaway 2014 Annual Report.

14 Schroeder, *Snowball*, 417.

15 Schroeder, *Snowball*, 632.

16 *Outstanding Investor Digest*, September 24, 1998, transcripts of 1998 Berkshire annual meeting.

17 *Outstanding Investor Digest*, Year End 2003 Edition, transcripts of 2003 Berkshire annual meeting.

18 Notes from 1988 Berkshire Hathaway annual meeting.

19 CNBC Interview with Becky Quick, May 2017.

20 *Outstanding Investor Digest*, April 18, 1990, Buffett's lecture at Stanford Business School.

21 Carol J. Loomis, "Should You Leave it all to the Children?" *Fortune*, November 21, 2012.

22 Schroeder, *Snowball*, 523.

23 May 2017 interview with CNBC.

24 Adam Smith's *Money World* television show, May 22, 1990.

25 *Outstanding Investor Digest*, May 5, 1995, transcript of Charlie Munger's lecture to USC School of Business April 14, 1994.

26 Warren E. Buffett, "Look at All Those Beautiful Scantily Clad Girls Out There!" *Forbes*, November 1, 1974.

27 Warren E. Buffett, "You Pay a Very High Price in the Stock Market for a Cheery Consensus."

28 Warren E. Buffett, "Mr. Buffett on the Stock Market," *Fortune*, November 22, 1999.

29 Warren E. Buffett, "Mr. Buffett on the Stock Market," *Fortune*, November 22, 1999.

30 Warren E. Buffett, "Mr. Buffett on the Stock Market," *Fortune*, November 22, 1999.

31 Berkshire Hathaway 2001 Annual Meeting.

32 *Outstanding Investor Digest*, transcripts of 2000 Berkshire Annual meeting, December 18, 2000.

33 *Outstanding Investor Digest*, September 24, 1998, transcripts of 1998 Berkshire Annual Meeting,

Endnotes

34 *Outstanding Investor Digest*, September 24, 1998: transcripts of 1998 Berkshire Annual Meeting.

35 *Fortune*, April 4, 1994.

36 "The top 25", *Forbes*, October 13, 1997; 153.

37 Warren E. Buffett, "Why I Like to Think of Stocks Like Farms," *Fortune*, March 17, 2014.

38 1998 Berkshire Hathaway annual meeting notes.

39 *Outstanding Investor Digest*, June 22, 1992, transcripts from 1998 Berkshire Hathaway annual meeting.

40 *The Business World*, April 1, 1990.

41 1996 Berkshire Hathaway Annual Report.

42 *Outstanding Investor Digest*, June 30, 1993, transcripts of 1993 Berkshire Hathaway annual meeting.

43 *Outstanding Investor Digest*, June 23, 1994, transcripts of 1994 Berkshire Hathaway annual meeting.

44 Buffett Partnership Ltd. Letter, January 20, 1966.

45 Buffett Partnership Ltd. Letter, January 20, 1966.

46 1996 Berkshire annual meeting notes.

47 *Outstanding Investor Digest*, September 24, 1998, transcripts of 1998 Berkshire annual meeting.

48 *Outstanding Investor Digest*, September 24, 1998, transcripts of 1998 Berkshire annual meeting.

49 *Outstanding Investor Digest*, December 31, 1994, transcripts from Wesco Financial annual meeting on May 5, 2004.

50 *Outstanding Investor Digest*, April 18, 1990, Buffett's lecture to Stanford School of Business.

51 Adam Smith's *Money World* television show, June 20, 1988.

52 Berkshire Hathaway 1992 Annual Report.

53 D.C., "Simple Pleasures," *Financial World*, April 3, 1985.

54 *Outstanding Investor Digest*, May 24, 1991.

55 Berkshire Hathaway 1981 Annual Report.

56 Berkshire Hathaway 1989 Annual Report.

57 Ann Hughey, "Omaha's Plain Dealer," *Newsweek*, April 1, 1985.

CHAPTER 23

1 Cynthia H. Milligan, "Warren Buffett," *Nebraska Business*, University of Nebraska – Lincoln Alumni Business magazine, Fall 2001.

2 Colleen Leahey, "Buffett's Promise," *Fortune*, October 5, 2014.

3 Berkshire Hathaway 2009 Annual Report.

4 Brent Schlender, "Gates and Buffett," *Fortune*, July 20, 1998.

5 United States Financial Crisis Inquiry Commission Interview with Warren Buffett, May 26, 2010.

6 Letter to author, November 7, 1994.

CHAPTER 24

1 Charlie Munger, USC Law Commencement speech May 2007.

2 Forbes Centennial issue, September 28, 2017.

3 *Wall Street Week with Louis Rukeyser*, April 8, 1994.

4 Peter Lynch, "What's Next?", *The Wall Street Journal*, October 1, 2001.

5 Berkshire Hathaway 2015 Annual Report.

6 Lynch, *Beating the Street*, 141.

7 Interview with Adam Smith, interview with John Templeton and Warren Buffett, *https://www.youtube.com/watch?v=_eLRAhjOwyg*.

8 *Good Morning America* #1284 May 16, 1991, Interview with Charles Gibson

9 Adam Smith interview with John Templeton and Warren Buffett, *https://www.youtube.com/watch?v=_eLRAhjOwyg*.

10 Charley Ellis, "Living Legends," *CFA Magazine*; inaugural issue January/February 2003; interview with Warren Buffett, 21.

11 Financial Intelligence Report, February 2005; 4.

12 Charlie Munger's comments at the 2017 *Daily Journal* annual meeting.

13 Jason Zweig, "Buffett advice: Buy Smart...and Low," *Money*, May 6, 2008, from a two-hour press conference with Warren Buffett and Charlie Munger during the Berkshire Annual Meeting weekend.

14 *Wall Street Week with Louis Rukeyser*, November 16, 1990.

15 Carol Loomis, *Fortune*, "Mr. Buffett on the Stock Market," November 22, 1999.

16 Gregory Zuckerman and James P. Miller, "Berkshire Hathaway Hits Bumps," *The Wall Street Journal*, June 24, 1999.

17 Jonathan R. Laing, *Barron's*, "Is There Life After Babe Ruth?" April 2, 1990.

CHAPTER 25

1 D.C., "Simple Pleasures," *Financial World*, April 3, 1985.

2 Charles Munger, *A Lesson on Elementary Worldly Wisdom as It Relates to Investment Management and Business*, speech given to The University of Southern California Marshall School of Business, April 14, 1994.

3 Charles T. Munger, *Poor Charlie's Almanack – The Wit and Wisdom of Charles T. Munger* (PCA Publications, L.L.C. 2005), 193.

4 Berkshire Hathaway Annual Meeting, May 3, 2008.

5 *Outstanding Investor Digest*, May 24, 1991, transcripts of Berkshire Hathaway 1991 annual meeting.

6 2014 Berkshire Hathaway Annual Report

7 2014 Berkshire Hathaway Annual Report

Acknowledgments

A book generally has one author, but in reality, it is a team effort. The original suggestion to write the book came from Curt Smith after attending one of my seminars called *Lessons from the Masters* that profiled the investment principles of John Templeton, Peter Lynch, and Warren Buffett. The seminars were offered to security analysts in San Francisco who wanted practical tools to improve their investing skills that wasn't available in traditional textbooks steeped in theory.

Thank you to Sir John Templeton, Peter Lynch, and Warren Buffett, who gave so generously in interviews and in written material over the years that their skills as teachers and exemplars of integrity are as inspiring as their record as investors. The same is true of Charlie Munger.

I am grateful to my favorite graduate business school instructor from over 35 years ago, Geoffrey Heathcock, who read the manuscript and provided sound edits and so much encouragement over the years.

I appreciate the engaging discussions and collaborative research about businesses and the stock market with my colleagues Khateeb Lateef, Roland Underhill, Tom Arrington, Craig Braemer, Paul Lountzis, Bryan Anderson, David Shepley, John Brown, Quoc Tran, Sean McGuinn, David Campbell of Thompson Davis, and Elliott Schlang of Great Lakes Review.

I am indebted to Laura Duggan of Nicasio Press for her eagle-eye editing of the original manuscript. I am thankful for the diligence of Frederick Courtright of the Permissions Company for tracking down copyright permissions from many sources of material.

Special thanks to my literary agent, Laurie Harper, whose experience and suggestions were invaluable, especially for the introduction to my publishing editor, Debby Englander. Debby along with managing editor Heather King shepherded the book through the publishing process with vigilance and poise.

Both Laurie and Debby are consummate professionals and expert resources as well as terrific people.

Writing the book was made more enjoyable with the support and interest from clients and friends including Kiha Pimental, Gerald Twomey, Alapaki Kim, Scott Foulk, Jeaney and Rich Garcia, Alice and Tim Pidgeon, and Larry Harrington. I am beyond grateful for the faith in my work and for the inspiring life lessons I've learned from John Wooden, Jerry Lucas, Oliver Bouligny, and Carol Kaufman. They belong in the hall-of-fame for work ethic, generosity, giving credit to others, and integrity.

Lastly, thank you especially to my family. Their love and encouragement made all the difference in helping push this book across the finish line. Thank you in particular to my parents Shirley and Beau who encouraged me to find my own path, and who shared my anticipation at watching *Wall Street Week* with Louis Rukeyser on Friday nights for its witty and pun-filled programs that made investing approachable and entertaining. Thank you to my siblings, George, Clark, and Claire as well as their spouses, Cheryl, Karen, and Kelly; and my son, Bobby, his wife, Tamara, and my daughter, Gina, to whom this book is dedicated, and most of all, thanks to my wife, Celeste. She has always believed in the book and offered endless love, interest, and encouragement. Thank you all.